Explorations in African Systems of Thought

African Systems of Thought

General Editors
Charles S. Bird
Ivan Karp

Contributing Editors
James Fernandez
Luc de Heusch
Victor Turner
Roy Willis

Explorations in African Systems of Thought

Edited by

Ivan Karp

&

Charles S. Bird

INDIANA UNIVERSITY PRESS
Bloomington

Explorations in African systems of thought.

(African systems of thought)
Papers given at a seminar organized for the African
Studies Program at Indiana University in 1977.
Includes index.
1. Philosophy, Primitive—Africa. 2. Cognition
and culture—Africa. 3. Religion, Primitive—Africa.
I. Karp, Ivan. II. Bird, Charles S. III. Indiana
University, Bloomington. African Studies Program.
IV. Series.
GN645.E92   960   80-7492
ISBN 0-253-19523-3   1 2 3 4 5 84 83 82 81 80

Contents

Preface

This volume is the first in a new series, African Systems of Thought. We hope in this series to explore the diversity of approaches to the analysis of systems of thought found in African societies and to provide a forum for the presentation of research documenting such systems. Our emphasis in the series is decidedly cross-disciplinary. The analysis of African systems of thought belongs to no one discipline and the critical evaluation of research has crossed disciplinary boundaries in the past and will continue to do so in the future. In this first volume we have collected a number of essays, all original, which we think will introduce the reader to many of the different problems researchers are currently addressing. The essays reflect debates currently occupying specialists in this field, but they are also analyses of specific systems. Future volumes in this series will include monographs that examine either specific systems, such as a set of myths found in neighboring societies, or the thought systems of single societies. All of these studies will be based on extensive research conducted in African societies and will explore the meaning these systems have for the members of the societies in which they are found.

Charles S. Bird
Ivan Karp

Bloomington
December 1979

Explorations in African Systems of Thought

Introduction

by Ivan Karp

The papers in this volume are the result of a speakers seminar organized for the African Studies Program at Indiana University during the fall of 1977.[1] Speakers at that seminar were given the task of illustrating what they considered to be important issues and approaches to the analysis of African systems of thought, using materials from their own research. We were impressed with the quality of research presented by the speakers and struck by an increasing sense that the differences and similarities among the various contributions were distributed in such a way as to give an overview of both the variety and the directions presently characteristic of studies of African systems of thought.

The editors of an earlier volume on the same subject concluded that disparities among the contributors were complementary rather than contradictory (Fortes and Dieterlen, 1965). We share this view. Our organization of materials, however, is more diverse. In this earlier volume the approaches to African systems of thought were perceived as divided into two categories which are characteristic of national styles. The French, they argued, were concerned with the systemic aspects of ideational systems, while the British chose to examine African systems of thought in relation to social structure and action. This difference resulted from the French emphasis on cosmology and the British concern with ritual. That these two national styles directed attention to different aspects of African systems of thought is not difficult to discover. Cosmology embodies the systemic aspects of belief; its description leads to an understanding of world view and the more speculative aspects of the conceptual systems of a culture. Ritual, on the other hand, is a standarized form of conduct. Conduct by its very nature is more affected than is belief by the social and natural environments in which it is found. It can be viewed as expressive of the social order and in some cases as constitutive of or leading to changes in status and role. The French interest in indigenous philosophy, therefore, leads in one direction, and the British interest in social structure and process leads in another.

This distinction in terms of national styles, as Fortes and Dieterlen have admitted, is a simplification. In the years following the conference from which their book emerged, the scope of interests and the definition of problems characteristic of the scholars who describe African systems of thought has led to a reevaluation of categories based on this national distinction. In addition, researchers now draw upon a variety of disciplines for their clues to analysis rather than remaining within the confines of their initial training. Thus, the division into two types of approaches is made even more unworkable by the diversity that may be exhibited in a single work of scholarship.

Two studies that emanate from one department in a single university may illustrate how diverse the conception of problem and analysis may be. Evans-Pritchard's *Nuer Religion* (1956) and Middleton's *Lugbara Religion* (1960) present diametrically opposed views on where the system is to be found in the analysis of African systems of thought. *Nuer Religion* argues that the religious conceptions of the Nuer are defined in terms of a belief in Spirit and its penetration into the material world. Complexity of belief, Evans-Pritchard asserts, is the result of the association of Nuer religious beliefs with the social order. The bewildering variety of religious representations are "refractions," as he calls them, resulting from the intersection of belief with history, society, and nature. Finally he concludes that Nuer religious action, ritual, can be shown to be logically entailed in the Nuer definition of religious experience.

Evans-Pritchard's student, John Middleton, takes precisely the opposite position in his excellent work, *Lugbara Religion*. He argues that Lugbara religious conceptions have no system at all at the level of belief.

> Lugbara have no set of interconsistent beliefs as to the nature of man and their world. Their beliefs are significant in given situations and their consistency lies in the way in which they are used in ritual action (25).

Middleton then shows that the invocation of different mystical entities by the Lugbara (ancestors, witches, and so on) is related to such factors as the type of conflict, structural positions of the actors, the strategy employed by different persons, and the stage of development of local groups. In Middleton's study we are presented with an analysis of the political uses of belief.

What sense is to be made of these differences? Are readers to believe that the Nuer are proto-structuralists while the Lugbara are

lumpen pragmatists? This question is not easily answered. Differences
in approach, appearing even between a scholar and his student, indicate that the entire problem of description and comparison must be
treated carefully. There is no doubt that African systems of thought
differ in the degree of systematization as well as in the degree to
which this systematization varies for specialist and laity, as Willis has
shown (1972).

The differing impressions of the thought systems of the Nuer and
the Lugbara presented by Evans-Pritchard and Middleton are a case
in point. Middleton's observation about the absence of system at the
level of belief must be regarded with suspicion until he provides an
analysis of the sort found in Evans-Pritchard's book. Until Middleton
brackets the effects of nature, society, and history on Lugbara thought,
we will be unable to assess the truth of his observation that "the Lugbara have no set of interconsistent beliefs. . . ." Similarly the degree to
which religion acts as a mechanism of social control among the Nuer
will not be known until this problem is investigated in their society.
In *Nuer Religion*, Evans-Pritchard does not analyze the belief system
in these terms, although one may discover hints in the material he
presents.[2]

The degree to which the system of thought of an African people
strikes the observer as consistent or not may derive from the manner
in which the thought system is interconnected to the social order. The
Lugbara have a system of ancestor worship which, as Fortes pointed
out for the Tallensi, is intrinsic to the constitution of the lineage system (1959; 1961); the Nuer do not. It would be useful to compare the
belief systems of the two societies in terms of what Nadel called the
"competencies" of religion, "the things religions do for individuals or
societies . . ." (1954:259). As Nadel shows in *Nupe Religion*, African
societies differ in the degree and manner to which their belief systems
are related to aspects of the social order. The question of the relationship of thought to the context in which it is articulated is one that
has not often been explored in the study of African systems of
thought.[3] The papers in this volume, particularly those by Fernandez,
Karp, Burton, and Packard, contribute to this investigation. At the
very least, they illustrate how complex the solutions must be.

We may see then how difficult it is to account for diversity in approaches to the study of African systems of thought. French rational-
ism and British empiricism are no doubt a component of the variation,

but there are other aspects of the context of the research which may affect the image of the system as it is represented in the reports of the investigators. These aspects are derived from a number of sources. There are, for example, problems of an epistemological sort. The nature of the problem to be investigated may affect the image of the system because data elicited within different frames of reference are not wholly the same. On the other hand, there are practical matters over which an investigator may have no control. These may include the language competence of researchers as it affects their ability to understand nuances of meaning, or simply the amount of time available for investigation. This second factor is especially important when investigating rites which may occur over a time period of more than a year. The great rituals of the *gada* age systems of the Oromo-speaking peoples are a case in point. An investigator may never have the opportunity to observe what his informants describe, given the notorious inability of the various Oromo peoples to hold the ceremony within the eight-year period they specify (Baxter and Almagor, 1978). It is well known that informant accounts differ between circumstances when they are asked to recall performances and circumstances in which they are asked to comment on performances observed by both the informant and the researcher. Finally, aspects of the relation of belief to its contexts will affect the representation of the system made by the researcher. I have discussed these above in the contrast I drew between the religious systems of the Nuer and the Lugbara.

In spite of all these problems it appeared to the editors that the contributors to this volume tackled a limited number of issues, although a number of papers dealt with more than one of the issues and could have been included in more than one section. Taken together the essays in this volume stress problems of analysis over questions of content. We believe that the reason for this methodological orientation is that the study of African systems of thought has passed through a phase in which undue emphasis was placed on the content description of various aspects of systems in order to make them (the systems) more comparable to each other. Too many studies are of the "witchcraft and sorcery or spirit possession among the so-and-so" type rather than of the theory and interpretations of misfortune and its relationship to other patterns of belief and experience among the so-and-so. Actually, many of the best studies, such as Evans-Pritchard's *Witchcraft, Oracles and Magic among the Azande* (1937) and Fortes' studies of ancestor worship among the Talensi (1959; 1961), do just what we have suggested, but they have been misunderstood.

We believe that the most important task before us is to provide models for the analysis of thought in relation to experience and not to describe pieces of systems. The essays in this volume have this as their goal. Vaughan's essay illustrates this point. His is not a description of a system of divine kingship found among the Margi of Nigeria. Instead he argues that ritual and political aspects of Margi kingship can only be understood when related to such existential dilemmas as aging and succession. Among the Margi, divine kingship is an attempt to solve real problems that can only be understood within the context of the community's thought system and not in terms of the isolation of a partial system, such as divine kingship in this case, spirit possession or ancestor worship in other cases.

The organization of this volume follows from our conviction that models for the analysis of the existential aspects of African systems of thought currently present the most interesting problems to investigators. The first section, "Modes of Thought," illustrates this approach in two ways. First, it addresses the hoary problem of how to interpret expressions of thought from members of other societies. This problem raises fundamental issues concerning modes of thought in translation. The study of thought systems in other cultures has passed beyond typologizing differences, as MacGaffey reminds us in his essay which concludes the volume. Instead, scholars are now concerned with describing the organizing metaphors in terms of the systems of thought and ritual practice that are articulated. De Heusch's paper provides an example of this description by using the structuralist approach he has pioneered for Africa, the most notable example being *Le Roi Ivre* (1972). In his paper for this volume de Heusch's analysis differs from Lévi-Strauss' structuralism in that he does not limit himself to analyzing myth, but attempts as well to treat ritual as a system of implicit mythology. In so doing he provides a bridge between an emphasis on the ideational found in the structuralism of Lévi-Strauss and a concern with situational aspects of meaning found in Victor Turner's pioneering studies of symbolism (1967; 1968).

The paper by James Fernandez illustrates another facet of the problem of interpreting modes of thought. He asks to what degree both the context and the rules of performance affect the image of systems scholars abstract from their informants' accounts and actions. In studies of the differences in mentality between literate and nonliterate cultures, Fernandez suggests that the differences perceived are not so much results of different structures on either side of the "great divide," as they are results of learning different rules of relevance in the context of performance. Thus while de Heusch analyzes the metaphors that organize ritual performance and symbolic expression in diverse contexts, Fernandez seeks to discover the effect of the definition of the situation on the expression of thought. Not only do the two authors complement each other, they show the importance of taking into account both structure and performance before drawing conclusions about the nature of modes of thought.

The two essays by Bird and Kendall and Ray illustrate the second dimension of analysis of thought that is highlighted in the section "modes of thought." In both essays, the authors utilize diverse types of materials that are not part of the standard body of data collected by social anthropologists. Bird and Kendall's elegant analysis of the theory of social action implicit in the Sunjata epic shows that the epic cannot be understood without knowledge of the cultural background, particularly the indigenous "theory of the person." They also show, however, that the theory of the person is dramatized for the Mande in their oral art. Thus an analysis that neglects the forms in which the system of thought is presented to the people risks misinterpreting the nature of the thought involved, a point made strongly in the Fernandez essay as well. Finally, Ray obliterates conventional anthropological categories in his analysis of the theme of the origin of death. He shows that what anthropologists call "kinship" has to be understood among the Baganda in terms of their implicit ontology and reverses his analysis to illustrate the fact that ontological notions can only be understood in the context of prevalent forms of social relations in a society. Perhaps it is not an accident that Bird and Kendall are linguists and Ray is trained in philosophy and the history of religions. They bring to their analyses sensitivities that are often ignored in the sorts of questions anthropologists are trained to ask.

The second section, "Images of Social Experience," is devoted to what might be called indigenous social theory and moral philosophy. The thrust of the papers here is away from the ideational and towards the experiential. These papers are concerned with what Godfrey Lienhardt has called the "imaging of experience" (1963), the uses to which actors put collective representations in order to make sense out of their

experience of the social and natural worlds. Karp focuses upon inde-
terminacy in social interaction and relates that to the experience of
self, other, and social order. He argues that social forms or events are
used by the Iteso in an attempt to achieve desired states of social experience and to express difficulties in arriving at their socially constituted goals. Thus, the Iteso beer party is a vehicle for the expression
of social and moral ideas as well as the indigenous explanation of why
those ideals prove so difficult to capture in social practice. For the
Iteso, the beer party encapsulates both prescriptive and explanatory
dimensions of their image of self and society.

Vaughan and Beidelman turn to the intersection of social and natural worlds. Both are concerned with the construction of aging in society. Beidelman seeks to discover constraints placed upon the cultural
construction of age in the biological differences among the sexes. He
argues that differences in the experience of sexuality and role of reproduction limit the means by which aging in women may be interpreted
to a far greater degree than those for men in subsistence-based societies. Vaughan sees divine kingship as an image of aging and succession writ large, among other things, and argues that its hold upon the
Margi is based in their own experience. In the process of presenting
his argument, he provides a means of viewing divine kingship from
the "inside," as it were, by interpreting it in terms of universal processes. Finally, Arens returns to the old standby topics of witchcraft
and sorcery to remind us that whatever the cultural definition of misfortune, ongoing social experience will affect the immediate interpretations made by the members of a community as well as the image of
the system seen by the analyst.

Section three addresses the difficult problem of "Dynamics." Intellectual history in societies without written records poses problems
that do not admit of easy solutions. Kopytoff's provocative paper con-
tends with the functionalist dogma that systems of thought have to be
formulated vaguely so as to be able to fit with the social order. Implicit in this conception of culture and society is the notion that systems of thought change in response to social change. In contrast Kopytoff argues that belief systems may have associated with them an internal dynamic. His analysis of revitalization cults indicates that they
rise and fall because they don't work. Furthermore, they do not work
because the Suku view their social world as entropic. They need new
cults in order to revive a failing social and natural world.

Entropy also seems to be at work in the social theory of Ethiopian societies described by Bauer and Hinnant. This may constitute a basic theme in African systems of thought, and further research into revitalization movements may bear upon this insight. In any case, the papers in this section show that scholars in their accounts have not stressed sufficiently the dynamism of African systems of thought. This dynamism may be of a number of varieties. Kopytoff shows that changes may result from the conception of nature. In a splendid piece of historical research, Packard takes the position that because African systems of thought provide frameworks for the interpretation of experience, changing social conditions feed back upon the ideas in terms of which they are interpreted in the first instance. This may result in radical conceptual change or "conversion" as Packard calls it. Bauer and Hinnant show that the function of a conceptual system such as divination is related to conditions of social change. Their comparison of divination in Tigre and Guji societies provides a controlled comparison of the manner in which belief is affected by social change of the sort that is seldom found in analyses of conceptual systems. Finally, Burton shifts our concern with change over time to change over space. His analysis of the social dynamics of Atuot religion suggests that the image of the systems may be affected by the conditions and the places in which the research is done.

In the final section on "Comparisons," MacGaffey undertakes a pioneering analysis of whole systems of thought by focusing on the entire complex of roles in terms of which the system is organized. Thus he shows that such types as "witch" and "diviner" cannot be analyzed except in relation to each other and that comparison among systems may only be made in terms of sets of relationships and not in terms of isolated roles. MacGaffey's comparison on the basis of social roles is not the only sort of comparison that may be done, but the principle of comparing patterns of relationships and not isolated roles or ideas is a valid one, if extremely difficult to achieve. It may explain why comparative studies have so rarely been successful in the analysis of African systems of thought.

Benjamin Ray's recent book *African Religions* may provide a starting point for further comparisons. He elaborates a framework for description based on the elements of myth, symbol, and community. As noted, MacGaffey's comparison focuses upon the role sets found in the community dimension. As Ray has suggested in a comment on

MacGaffey's paper, cosmological and ontological aspects of African systems of thought such as Ray describes in his own contribution may not be encompassed in the sociological dimension to which MacGaffey directs his attention.

The difficulties that beset comparative analysis are similar to those earlier described for the description of single systems. The analysis will depend upon the problem undertaken by the researcher and the conditions of the research, all compounded, of course, by the multiple origins of the data. Problems do not come unbidden to the mind of the researcher, however, nor are they derived solely from theory. The researcher has an obligation to describe the contours of experience as organized by the subjects of his research. The images in terms of which members of a society experience their world, the symbols through which they express that experience, and the forms of their expression are situated at the core of the analysis of African systems of thought. It is towards the description of such phenomena that this volume is dedicated.

NOTES

1. Additional papers were solicited from W. Arens, Dan F. Bauer and John Hinnant, Benjamin Ray, John Burton, and Wyatt MacGaffey. We are grateful for the support given by the staff and students of the African Studies Program at Indiana University.

2. In his description of the Nuer concept of *thek*, "respect," and its relationship to ideas of sin, Evans-Pritchard notes the following:

> The purpose and function of these respect relationships are evident. They are intended to keep people apart from other people or from creatures or things. . . . Some of them have important secondary functions in the regulation of the social order—for example, those which determine behavior between affines and between parties to feuds; but we need not inquire why they concern some persons, things and situations and not others, nor what these persons, things and situations have in common. We are concerned only with the fact that a violation of the prohibition is to a greater or lesser degree a fault which in many cases brings disaster to the transgresser (1956: 180–81).

Thus, he concludes that the intersection of ideas about *thek* with certain aspects about the social order will not provide a better understanding of the problem to which he has set himself; viz. what is the cultural logic of Nuer religious beliefs.

3. Certain types of context are involved in particular studies. Thus Fortes' exemplary work *Oedipus and Job in West African Religions*, for example, examines ancestor worship among the Tallensi "in the context of the situation, the context of personal history, and the context of social relations. . . ." The interrelationships among belief, symbol, and context have rarely been explored in detail.

BIBLIOGRAPHY

Baxter, Paul, and Almagor, U., eds. 1978. *Age, Generation and Time*. London: C. Hurst and Co.
Evans-Pritchard, E. E. 1937. *Witchcraft, Oracles and Magic among the Azande*. Oxford: The Clarendon Press.
————. 1956. *Nuer Religion*. Oxford: The Clarendon Press.
Fortes, Meyer. 1959. *Oedipus and Job in West African Religion*. Cambridge: Cambridge University Press.
————. 1961. "Pietas in Ancestor Worship." *Journal of the Royal Anthropological Institute* 91:166–91.
Fortes, M., and Dieterlen, G., eds. 1965. *African Systems of Thought*. London: Oxford University Press.
de Heusch, Luc. 1972. *Le Roi Ivre*. Paris: Gallimard.
Middleton, John. 1960. *Lugbara Religion*. London: Oxford University Press.
Lienhardt, Godfrey. 1963. *Divinity and Experience*. Oxford: The Clarendon Press.
Nadel, S. F. 1954. *Nupe Religion*. London: Oxford University Press.
Ray, Benjamin. 1976. *African Religions*. Englewod Cliffs: Prentice Hall.
Turner, V. W. 1967. *The Forest of Symbols*. Ithaca: Cornell University Press.
————. 1968. *The Drums of Affliction*. London: Oxford University Press.
Willis, R. G. 1972. "Pollution and Paradigms." *Man* 7:369–78.

SECTION I.
Modes of Thought

The Mande Hero
Text and Context

by Charles S. Bird and Martha B. Kendall

The Mande, center of the great thirteenth-century Mali Empire, is located geographically in that region of West Africa where the Upper Niger River intersects the borders of Mali and Guinea. The modern peoples who trace their ancestry to the Mande, the Mandinka, Maninka, Malinke, Mandingo, Manya, Bambara, Dyula, Kuranko, and Wangara, are dispersed throughout the West African savannah, from the Gambian coast in the west, eastward to Ouagadougou in Upper Volta, and from the Mauritanian border in the north to Abidjan in the south. The present distribution of these groups is largely the result of imperialistic campaigns made during the period of the Mali Empire.

Despite their widespread geographic distribution, the modern descendants of the original people of the Mande speak dialects of Mandekan (Bird, 1970), and all share sociocultural values defining kinship, political organization, and economic activities. That which unifies the Mande peoples culturally, i.e., that which gives coherence to their social structures, is not simply recognition of common ancestry; it is, rather, a system of commonly held beliefs—a philosophy, ideology, or cosmology—which defines appropriate behavior for individual actors and allows in turn the interpretation of the behavior of others.

Our concern in this paper is with a particular aspect of Mande ideology: that which defines heroic behavior and calibrates that against more mundane action. The hero, we will argue, is someone with special powers used to work against the stabilizing and conservative forces of his society; he is someone who, in pursuing his own destiny, affects the destinities of others. He is the agent of disequilibrium.

Because heroic action is defined in contrast to ordinary behavior, the hero cannot be considered in isolation from the social matrix in which he operates. His actions, standing out in relief against the actions of others, point to a system of dynamic tensions holding between groups and individuals, between integrating and disruptive principles, between the ordinary and the extraordinary. To understand the Mande hero is generally to understand Mande theories of social actor and social action.

Our concerns in this study revolve around the issue of translation of texts. Language in all of its forms reverberates against a background of cultural understanding and assumptions without which it remains vague and imprecise. A text without context is like the message in a bottle washed up on the shore. When the context is filled in, the meanings of the texts become clear, illustrating their value as mediators of ideology and behavior. Texts, we contend, serve to render unambiguous actions in situations, particularly in terms of indigenous theories of person, but texts as modes of expression can only be understood in terms of the ideological matrix (the context) in which they serve to interpret behavior.

The Context

The Mande peoples recognize a dialectic tension between the individual and the group. This tension should not be understood as a polar opposition, but rather as the intersection of two axes: the axis of individuality, referred to as *fadenya* "father-childness," and the axis of group affiliation, referred to as *badenya* "mother-childness."[1] On the *fadenya* axis actions are oriented toward individual reputation and renown. On the *badenya* axis they are oriented toward the total set of rights and obligations provided by the social groups to which the actions are affiliated.

A child is born with a reputation, primarily its father's—and by extension, that of its patrilineage. The reputation is both an impetus to and a constraint on action. A child of a given clan will be expected to perform at a given level according to this heritage, but performing at that level will not be noteworthy. Individuals gain reputations by surpassing the collective deeds of their predecessors and placing their own names firmly in their clans' historical records. In doing so, of course, they make the same achievement that much more difficult for those who follow. In the Mande world, a name must be won not only in the arena provided by one's peers, but also in that abstract arena created by one's ancestors. This conception of the patrilineage as competitor is captured in the proverb: *i fa y'i faden folo de ye*, "Your father is your first *faden*."

The weight of the father's reputation is the first barrier to over-come on the *fadenya* axis. *Fadenya* may thus be seen as a temporal axis measuring the worth of individuals against the actual accomplish-ments of their predecessors and the anticipated challenges of their descendants. A person's starting point in the social system, then, auto-matically constrains his chances to make his mark, and simultaneously shapes his assessment of these chances.

The *fadenya*-oriented actor regards obligations to the social group as impediments to his individual quest for reputation—impediments which he must overcome, actually or symbolically, to be recognized as special. In the Mande world *fadenya* is thus associated with centri-fugal forces of social disequilibrium: envy, jealousy, competition, self-promotion—anything tending to spin the actor out of his established social force field.

Badenya, "mother-childness," is associated with centripetal forces of society: submission to authority, stability, cooperation, those quali-ties which pull the individual back into the social mass. Since ideally one cannot refuse the request of a *baden*, an individual's wishes must often be subordinated to the interests of other members of his group. From *badenya* arises social solidarity, security, and assurances that members of a group will act in concert to defend their collective worth. The larger the social collectivity, the greater its social gravity or force.

This characterization of *fadenya* and *badenya* amounts to a social theory of inertia in which bodies of great mass are difficult to dis-equilibrate. Bodies of least mass—individuals in this case—are more easily set in motion, but only insofar as they resist the social drag of their *baden* affiliates. Recognizing this, and recognizing at the same time that the forces of *badenya* inhibit the dynamism necessary for society's survival, Mande peoples focus much socialization activity on the fostering of *fadenya* behavior. They know that they depend upon the individual who resists the pull of the established social order, just as they depend upon the individuals who do not resist; they know that they require the individual who will change things, even if these changes are potentially destructive. Their ambivalence toward the *fadenya* actor, of which the hero is a primary example, is reflected in a second proverb: *ngana ma man di fo kojugulon,* "The hero is but welcome on troubled days."

Because the hero, *ngana*, acts as if impervious to the primary in-

strumentality of the *baden* group, which is *malo*, "shame,"[2] he is a
threat to the social order. However, because he is shameless, he has
the capacity to act when social conventions paralyze others. In times
of trouble, the hero may be the only one with the means to reestablish
the very social equilibrium that is so abhorent to him. His motivations
may be selfish and self-aggrandizing; nevertheless his special powers
or means to act may have beneficial consequences for all his people.

The philosophy of action in the Mande world is keyed to the notion of *nya*,[3] "means," a concept more psychological than material.
One's birthright, as we mentioned, provides an initial set of means to
actions, the ability to perform particular acts and, more importantly,
to be protected from the consequences of those acts. A blacksmith is
born into a caste which enables him to smelt iron ore, to transform the
shapes of iron, earth, and wood, and to survive the forces unleashed
by his transformations. A freeman, *horon*, might, through madness or
accident, perform a blacksmith's act, but his horon's birthright offers
him no protection against its consequences.[4]

The means or powers required to perform an act are referred to
as *dalilu*.[5] The dangerous forces released through the performance of
dalilu are referred to as *nyama*.[6] All acts and their associated instruments have *nyama*. A person's inherited *dalilu* may protect him from
the *nyama* of his actions, or he may acquire protective *dalilu* in other
ways—by acquiring fetishes and talismans, for example. Much of this
protection comes from the *nyama-kala*, "nyama branch," who are
casted smiths, bards, and leatherworkers. The inherent *dalilu* of the
nyama-kala affords protection against the *nyama* they release, and
they, in turn, protect their *nya* by practicing endogamy. Hunters, on
the other hand, are not *nyama-kala*, and consequently devote much of
their early training to the control of *nyama*, manipulating it through
ritual and sacrifice, warding it off with special garments and trophies.
Nyama-laden parts of a hunter's kill—skin, horns, teeth, claws, feathers
—are incorporated into his fetishes, his talismans, and clothing. These
serve to control the *nyama* released by each kill, protecting the hunter
from potential destruction; but they also empower him to perform
greater deeds.

Dalilu and its associated *nyama* are dangerous to *badenya*. Maintaining equilibrium requires that activity be rigidly constrained so
that the *nyama* associated with action can be kept under control. Will-
ful or inadvertent violation of ritual releases *nyama*; this act threatens

not only the transgressor, but his kinspeople and village as well. In the hunters' epic *Fakuru*, a great warrior-hero returns to his village, bringing with him the *nyama* he has accumulated in the course of many bloody victories.[7] Because he has far exceeded his destiny, the *nyama* he brings back is uncontrolled. Not only does it destroy him, but it causes others to treat the members of his family as outcasts for the next two generations. The epic recounting the exploits of Sunjata, founder of the Mali Empire, contains an episode during Sunjata's exile from the Mande in which one of his hosts sacrifices an unborn child over Sunjata's fetishes.[8] The terrible *nyama* this act releases destroys the host at the same time as it empowers the fetishes and gives Sunjata the power to act.

Because *nya* and *nyama* can be controlled, augmented, or diminished by manipulation, it follows that the devices associated with this manipulation, *dalilu*, should be kept secret. For if the instrumentalities guaranteeing one actor's capacities to perform heroic acts were available to everyone, then either all actors would be able to perform the same acts, which would render them ordinary rather than heroic, or all the actors would be able to counter every other actor's *nya*, which would have the same effect. The hero, seeking every means possible to distinguish himself, cloaks himself and his instruments of action in great secrecy. At the same time, he does what he can to weaken or destroy the *nya* of an adversary, which involves "seeking his means" (*k'a nya nyini*), and attacking them with spells and magic.

The Texts

There is an extraordinary rich oral literature in the Mande world. The standard folk literature of such things as fables, proverbs, and riddles, is complemented by an extensive heroic literature which focuses on the valiant deeds of hunters and warriors. There is, as well, a highly elaborated tradition of political epics recounting the rise and fall of the great West African kingdoms and empires and the adventures of their associated heroes. The many exciting characteristics of this literature cannot be discussed here. We limit our concern to the general motifs and themes that describe heroic actors and action, the manner in which conflicts unfold, and the manner in which these conflicts are resolved.

Resolution of all conflicts in both political and heroic epics in-

volves the recourse to spells and magic. Often the heroic figure is attacked and must find an antidote to free himself from the spell. The
Sunjata epic contains myriad examples of curses and countercurses
effected as steps on Sunjata's way to heroic status. The first was the
the result of circumstances attending his birth. Sunjata's father had
two wives who became pregnant at the same time and gave birth on
the same day. Sunjata was born second, but, as his name was an-
nounced first, his father proclaimed him as heir. The father's first wife
became enraged and, "finding Sunjata's means," had a spell cast on
him so that he could not walk for nine full years. Through the inter-
cession of a *jinn* (and in some versions, a pilgrimage to Mecca), Sunjata finds the means to break the spell, makes the appropriate sacrifices, and rises. Striding out to his father's field, he rips a giant baobab
from the earth, swings it atop his head, strides back to his mother's
compound, and drives the tree into the earth before her house.

While he is involved in this heroic display, his mother, Sogolon
Kutuma the hunch-backed sorceress, sings a long series of praise songs
for her newly risen son, and in one of the songs she refers to him as
"stranger":

> *Luntan, luntan, o!*
> *Sunjata kera luntan ye bi.*
>
> Stranger, stranger, Oh!
> Sunjata became a stranger today.

The text of this song equates the hero and the stranger, the powerful and the esoteric, the extraordinary and the unknown. When
Sunjata crawled upon the ground, his actions were predictable, and he
was incapable of surprises. When he broke the curse placed on him,
he did it through means known only to himself. No longer predictable,
Sunjata was no longer safe. His secret knowledge made him like a
stranger, like someone who does not feel the pull of *badenya*.

The quest for strange or esoteric knowledge, for the secrets underlying an adversary's *nya* defines the content of Mande heroic literature. The degree to which this theme dominates the literature constitutes a striking contrast between European and Mande epic traditions.
These differences emanate from very different concepts of action and
heroic activity.

We have argued that in the Mande world, to act is to have *nya*
or "means." Means are initially created by birthright, subsequently

enhanced by sorcery and secret knowledge, and ultimately bounded by destiny. Once one has the means to act, the actual performance of an act is not of any great consequence, for it follows more or less automatically from attaining the *nya*. As a result of this, the unfolding drama of Mande epics, then, centers more on the acquisition of *nya* than on any kind of physical heroic action in the Western sense of the word.

For Westerners familiar with the Homeric tradition or with the medieval epics like *Chanson de Roland*, where so much of the text is devoted to the instruments and operations of battle, Mande epic texts may seem curious. They contain no extensive references to warfare, and few descriptions of physical prowess, yet they show great attention to detail where the particulars of sorcery and its outcome are at issue and where the tokens of power are described.

Physical descriptions of heroes in the texts frequently elaborate their nonheroic qualities. Sunjata, for example, is portrayed as crippled and infirm until he overcomes the curse placed on him. Fakoli, one of his great generals, is characterized as exceptionally short, with an enormous head and a large mouth. The heroic stature of these men is nevertheless indexed in the *nyama*-laden objects they carry with them. In the *Janjon*, the Hero's Dance, these lines describe Fakoli's garb:

> He entered the Mande
> With skulls of birds
> Three hundred three and thirty
> Hanging from his helmet.
> He entered the Mande
> With the skulls of lions
> Three hundred three and thirty[9]

Sunjata's great adversary, Sumanguru, receives the following awesome description in the Hero's Dance as well:

> Sumanguru entered the Mande,
> His helm of human skin.
> Sumanguru entered the Mande,
> His pants of human skin.
> Sumanguru entered the Mande,
> His gown of his human skin.

Where the descriptions of power objects are fulsome, descriptions of confrontations are, as we mentioned before, marvelously laconic. In one version of the Sunjata epic we collected, the bard telling the story sings for three hours about Sunjata's quest to discover his adversary's *nya*, then describes the war ensuing between them in three lines.

> The Mande and the Soso came to battle.
> The laughs went to the Mande.
> The tears to the Soso.

In the twelve other versions of this epic which we examined in detail, none devotes more than fifty lines to describing Sunjata's final battle against Sumanguru, but all devote thousands of words to Sunjata's search for the source of Sumanguru's *nya*. This is not at all atypical, as Mande epics tend to follow the same general pattern:

A. The hero and the adversary confront each other with no resolution.

B. The hero consults seers, wisemen, diviners and/or fetishes to determine a course of action.

C. The hero is informed that his adversary's power emanates from an occult source (fetish, talisman) which the hero must obtain.

D. The hero, usually with the help of a woman, discovers the occult source of power and separates it from the adversary.

E. The hero returns with the source of power to the wisemen who develop an antidote, usually in the form of various sacrifices and/or *dalilu*.

F. The sacrifices are performed, the *dalilu* engaged, and the adversary falls.

Two of the greatest Mande epic poems are astonishing variants of this theme in that they are reflexive: heroes' songs about heroes' songs. The *Janjon* praises the exploits of Fakoli, nephew of Sumanguru, the blacksmith king of the Soso and Sunjata's powerful foe. The *Janjon* tells how Sunjata wages campaign after unsuccessful campaign against Sumanguru to no avail—until Fakoli comes to join him. When Fakoli enters the camp, he finds bards singing the *Janjon* for Sunjata. He offers to help Sunjata defeat Sumanguru in exchange for the song, an offer which sends the entire camp into gales of laughter at the diminutive hunter with the huge head and the great mouth. Nevertheless they decide to put him to a test and, therefore, ask him to kill one of Sumanguru's fiercest generals. Fakoli returns the next day with the general's head, asking for his song. Another test is posed, and Fakoli meets it too. This time when he asks for the song, Sunjata's hesitation angers him and his anger swells in him until he grows so large that the roof of Sunajata's hut sits on his head like a bush hat. Recognizing Fakoli's terrible power, Sunjata's bards sing the *Janjon* for him and the song becomes his forever.

The Duga, "Vulture," tells the story of two enemy heroes who have become kings: Da Monson, King of the Segou Empire, and Duga Koro, great warrior and hunter, King of Kore.[10] At the beginning of the story the Duga is sung only in praise of Duga Koro, who, sure of his power and spoiling for a battle, insults his enemy, Da Monson. Da Monson marshals his forces and besieges Kore, but cannot breach the walls even after many efforts. Duga, Koro's senior wife who is bribed into betraying him, reveals the secret of his magic to Da Monson, who then successfully attacks and seizes his fortress. Duga Koro commits suicide before he can be captured, but Da Monson's warriors sack the town for booty and slaves, and Da Monson claims the Duga song for himself.

That Mande heroes risk so much for praise songs is the whole point of Mande praise songs. A great song guarantees the hero's renown, guarantees his immortality. A great praise song stirs his blood, heats up his heart, spurs him on to heroic accomplishments. A great praise song has *nyama*. It is a paean to *fadenya*.

Interplays of Text and Context

Literature in a literate culture becomes fixed in a given historical period. Jane Austen's style is quintessentially nineteenth-century, and —heretical as it may sound—Homer's concerns are not concerns of our day and age. Reading these authors and gaining access to their insights and sensibilities does not come naturally. It requires training, work, and patience, which many people do not have. Oral literature is constantly reshaped to its contemporary context—at least in its interpretation. The origins of heroic poems that we have been discussing might well date back several millenia, but these songs mark ideologies and behaviors that have current relevance.

Heroic poems are sung continually in the Mande world. Bards sing them for all social ceremonies—births, baptisms, marriages, funerals. You hear them over the radio daily—with their traditional musical phrasing or in Afro-Cuban dance rhythms, with pachanga and charanga beats. In the capital cities and in the remotest villages, Sunjata's praise song is sung, Fakoli's hero's dance is sung, the praise of Tira Magan is sung, Duga Koro's praise song is sung.

The texts and the melodies are not purposefully modified, but the musical arrangement may be. Lyrics may be modified by bad exegesis, but the ideology they celebrate, the very basis of their esthetic tension—the pullings and tuggings of *badenya* against *fadenya*—remains unchanged. These praise songs thus constitute a conservative record of Mande ideology, which, by virtue of its constant exposure and repetition, guarantees an effect in the socialization of Mande youths.

Socialization recapitulates much of what we have discussed here. Raised in large and extremely close-knit families, youths nevertheless learn that their culture lavishes esteem and adulation on its rebels. The figures preserved in history are those who broke with the traditions of their village, severed the bonds of *badenya*, traveled to foreign lands searching for special powers and material rewards, but just as importantly, they are also the ones who returned to the villages and elevated them to higher stations. This image of the rebel hero who breaks with, but ultimately returns to his people is not without relevance to the modern Mande child. It has probably always been this way and will probably always continue to be so. The pull of this great literary tradition is to *fadenya*, and its effect has been to spin the headstrong youth out in to the world of adventure.

The adventures do not have to be as stupendous as Fakoli's, for what counts is the impression the adventurer thinks he is creating among his *baden*. In Mali, for example, less than 30 percent of the children attend school. In many areas of the bush, this figure is less than 10 percent. A child entering school is treated as a hero–rebel, breaking with the traditional behavioral patterns of his village. He presents himself as a young person of destiny, and his villagers respond by suspending many of the obligations required of his agemates. The school child is in many respects held at arm's length away from his village. He often does not undergo the traditional education proffered through various initiation societies after circumcision. He is in essence forced to define his life outside the village. The role models for his extra-village life are nevertheless traditional models, as they abound in the traditional literature. A youth may not be called *ngana*, but he is led to believe that he is on the right road, and that he is a person of destiny.

The Mande migrant workers in the Ivory Coast and France share much the same psychology. They live and work in unspeakable conditions, their hope sustained by the image of themselves they project to the people back home. The brief one or two week periods in which they return home are times of intense joy and congratulation for all concerned. The prodigals are adulated and praised. They distribute their hard-won savings munificently among their friends and kin. They return to their miserable conditions on the streets of Paris or Abidjan, revitalized for several more years of back-breaking, soul-crushing labor. The further out they are flung in their search for adventure and fortune, the more important becomes the group which cast them out.

Bazin's study of the history of Segou (Bazin, 1971) demonstrates that this process has long been the rule in the Mande world. Bazin shows that the Segou region was always labor poor, able to produce the surplus to pay its taxes only with continual infusions of slaves. One contributing factor is that the young men of the local villages all preferred the adventures of war and trade to the *badenya* activities of farming. For them glory lay in returning booty and slaves to the village, not in producing themselves the agricultural surplus necessary for the village's general economic survival.

If a person's *fadenya* activity ceases, as would happen, for example, should adventurer-rebel-hero seek to settle down, the collectivity closes in around him. An ever expanding set of *baden*, all with serious and pressing needs, eat at his meager resources. Hard-won prizes are spread through the group, and the once heroic actor sinks back into the social mass.

The Mande system of *fadenya-badenya* is structured so as to assure the prevalence of *badenya*. The system spins out its potential heroes, but their dynamic energies are dissipated by the inertia of the group. The system remains in relative equilibrium. The societies defined therein are relatively secure, but often the individuals that constitute them are resentful of demands made upon them and suspicious of the activities of their co-citizens and kin. It is not a high risk system in the sense that normal activities will be supported by an extensive collectivity. If in the course of normal activity one should come upon misfortune, the collectivity will uphold the unfortunate, maintaining equilibrium. The risks are taken, not by the collectivity, but by the individual hero-rebel-adventurers, the *nganas* of Mande culture. When they succeed, the group will reap the benefits, and the hero is rewarded with adulation and praise. When they fail, the group forgets them.

The crucial thing to note here is the mutual interdependence of the hero and the group. The *baden* group casts individual members forth, encourages them, supports them, covers them in glory when they return, but they rig the whole system so that the hero *must* return. The hero is not an altruist, he performs his deeds to gain reputation for himself and to insure his own immortality. Still, he cannot sing his own praises in life any more than he could sing them in death. His *baden* group holds the key to the real treasure he seeks.

NOTES

The data upon which this paper is based are drawn primarily from fifteen years of research concerning Mande language and culture. It would be impossible to cite all those to whom we owe appreciation for their assistance. We cannot help but cite Seydou Camara, Bourama Soumaoro, Massa Maghan Diabaté, Mamadou Kanté, and Yamuru Diabaté, his family and friends in Keyla, all of whom have contributed immeasurably to our understanding of the Mande world. To each we owe a different debt, and none is responsible for the particular analysis at which we have arrived.

1. The orthography used is the official orthography of the Republic of Mali. The values of the symbols are in general similar to those of French with the exception that the mid vowels *e* and *o* are always closed and tense, whereas *è* and *ò* are open and lax. Tone is not marked in the orthography. Where tone distinctions are relevant, they will be discussed in the notes. Readers who wish to ascertain the tones of particular items may consult the *Lexique Bambara* (Education de Base, Bamako, 1968). Readers familiar with the literature on Mande ethnography will find far-ranging interpretations of the Mandekan vocabulary items in this paper. These differences in interpretation may result from differences in the level of abstraction of the inquiry, as they may result from inaccuracies in both linguistic and ethnographic analysis.

2. Both *fadenya and badenya* axes exploit the instrumentality of *malo* "shame." The *ngana* is called *malobali*, "shameless," by those with *badenya* orientation because the *ngana* does not respect the supportive rituals of *badenya*, violations of which would be the cause of shame to a *badenya*-oriented actor. The *ngana* is not in the least impervious to *fadenya*-generated shame, related, for example, to notions like courage.

3. It is not unlikely that the word *nya*, translated here as "means" is

the same as the word for "eye, fore, front." This would likely be a metaphorical extension where it is understood that the eye is the primary avenue to intelligence, understanding, and hence to action. To control someone's "eye" would be in this sense a clear domination of means.

This analysis gains support in the complex verb forms:

nya labò	have its eye come out, hence explain, clarify
nya lamini	have its eye twist, hence confound, confuse
ko nya nyini	seek a thing's eye, hence understand completely
mogo nya nyini	seek a person's eye, hence understand a person completely, hence manipulate [cast a spell on, charm] that person

Cissé (1964) seems to treat the two words as homophones, nya "means" being related by Cissé to ni "soul, life force," perhaps by the adjunction of the abstract suffix -ya, whence ni-ya > nya. This analysis is not entirely implausible and it accords with the tonal behavior of the word.

4. This is a jural projection. The nyamakala groups are now and have always been permeable. The major path of accession to nyamakala status is elevation from slavery into occupations such as smithing or bardship.

5. The reader is invited to consult MacNaughton (1978) for a more detailed discussion of dalilu with specific reference to blacksmiths.

6. The literature dealing with nyama is quite extensive. In spite of the many efforts, nyama has no clear etymology relating it to nyagaman "chaff" hence "waste, garbage," or ni "soul, life force, spirit." The tone of nyama is low, whereas ni is high. The reader is invited to consult Dieterlen (1951), Cissé (1964), Tauxier (1942), Monteil (1924), Labouret (1934), and Delafosse (1912) for various treatments of this concept.

7. We recorded this version sung by Seydou Camara in Bamako during the spring of 1974. It is currently being prepared for publication.

8. The version of the Sunjata epic to which we refer in this paper was sung by Fadigi Sisoko in Kita in 1968. It has been transcribed and incorporated in Johnson (1978). It will be revised and expanded for publication in 1979. The recording is available at Indiana University's Archives of Traditional Music. There is an increasingly important body of scholarship on the Sunjata epic and the Mali Empire. The reader is invited to consult, for example, Niane (1965), Pageard (1961), Levtzion (1963), and Monteil (1929).

9. The extracts of the Janjòn come from a performance by Yamuru and Sira Mori Diabaté in Keyla, Mali, 1972. A literary version of the Janjon is presented in Diabaté (1970).

10. The version of the Duga to which we refer was performed by Ba Koné in Segou, 1968. The reader is invited to consult Monteil (1924), Tauxier (1942), and Bazin (1971) for details relating to the reign of Da Monson and the Segou Empire in general.

BIBLIOGRAPHY

Bazin, Jean. 1971. "Recherches sur les formations sociopolitiques anciennes en pays bambara." Etudes Maliennes 1:37–53.

Bird, Charles S. 1970. "The Development of Mandekan: A Study of the

Role of Extralinguistic Factors in Linguistic Change." *Language and History of Africa*, edited by David Dalby. London: Cass, pp. 146–59.

Bird, Charles S. et al. 1976. *The Songs of Seydou Camara*. Vol. 1. *Kambili*. Bloomington, Ind.: African Studies Center.

Cissé, Youssouf. 1964. *Les Manding et leur langue*. Paris: Larose.

Delafosse, Maurice. 1912. *Haut-Sénégal-Niger*. Paris: Larose.

Diabaté, Massa Maghan. 1970. *Janjon et autres chants populaires du Mali*. Paris: Présence Africaine.

Dieterlen, Germaine. 1951. *Essai sur la Religion Bambara*. Paris: Presses Universitaires de France.

Johnson, John W. 1978. "The Epic of Sun-jata: An Attempt to Define the Model for African Epic Poetry." Ph.D. dissertation, Indiana University.

————. 1979. "The Epic of Sunjata According to Magan Sisoko." Bloomington, Ind.: Indiana University Folklore Publications Group.

Labouret, Henri. 1934. *Les Manding et leur langue*. Paris: Larose.

Levtzion, N. 1963. "The Thirteenth-and-Fourteenth-Century Kings of Mali." *Journal of African History* 4, no. 3: 341–53.

McNaughton, Patrick. 1978. "Komo: Bamana Power-Sculpture." Unpublished manuscript in possession of the authors.

Monteil, Charles. 1924. *Les Bambara du Segou et du Kaarta*. Paris: Larose.

————. 1929. "Les Empires du Mali." *Bulletin du Comité d'Etudes Historiques et Scientifiques de l'Afrique Occidentale Française* 14, nos. 3–4.

Niane Djibril Tamsir. 1965. *Sundiata: An Epic of Old Mali*. London: Longmans.

Pageard, Robert. 1961. "Soundiata Keita et la tradition orale." *Presences Africaine* 36:51–70.

Paques, Viviana. 1954. *Les Bambara*. Paris: Presses Universitaires de France.

Tauxier, Louis. 1942. *Histoire des Bambara*. Paris: Guenther.

Heat, Physiology, and Cosmogony
Rites de Passage among the Thonga

by Luc de Heusch

First of all I thank the African Studies Program at Indiana University for giving me the opportunity to discuss with a well-informed American public the method of analysis that I propose to apply to Bantu societies. I hope that reading my former work, consecrated to the analysis of myths of the origin of the state, and placed under the sign of drunken Noah, did not leave the impression that I too worked under the sign of drunkenness (de Heusch, 1972). In that work I tried to convince my historian colleagues and, in a more general way, all those who are not satisfied with functionalist descriptions, that these founding epics belong completely to symbolic thought. This symbolic thought endeavors to express in terms of human history the contradictions of the society and the world. I don't ignore the fact that by adopting this position I have exposed myself to the thunderbolts of Marvin Harris (1968), who accuses French structuralists of being the heirs of Descartes, Hegel, and Durkheim. I'll let the genealogists determine whether or not this filiation, quite honorable although a bit hybrid, is exact.

I shall not discuss the complex theses developed by Lévi-Strauss. I do not believe that any future anthropology can refuse to take seriously his theoretical propositions, as they are the foundations of the analysis of kinship and symbolic thought, just as psychology cannot ignore Freud and Piaget, or sociology, Marx. I hasten to add that the philosophical developments that Lévi-Strauss, Piaget, Freud, and Marx gave their works remain an open problem. What I find more interesting is the heuristic fertility of the structuralist method when used to disengage the principles of coherence of a hidden organization from conventional social attitudes, whatever be the reasons for this symbolic expression.

Too long we have lived under the illusion that man's behavior is transparent—on this point the works of Freud, Marx, and Lévi-Strauss concur. Lévi-Strauss has done his best to reveal something of the profound structures of meaning in apparently senseless narrations told by men when they imagine their relationship with other men and with

the world. We know that this chit-chat, which fills the language of
political men, theologians, scientists, and poets, has been totally neglected by most schools of anthropology. I realize that the quarrel
about meaning is endless. In order to achieve some progress each
time, the debate should be argued in terms of a precise problem. Let
us examine together some rituals of a Bantu society at the beginning
of the twentieth century, before the effects of the massive emigration
of men to the work camps of South Africa's mines was felt with as
much intensity as it is today (a situation which makes this analysis
somewhat absurd). In order to illustrate my approach, I will be satisfied if I bring this work to a successful end, disengaging with maxi-
mum economy and coherence the intellectual principles that govern
these rites and their sequences.

Victor Turner's analysis of the Ndembu of Zambia (1967) already
underlines the fact that Bantu societies have not developed elaborate
cosmogonies or myths of origin. Symbolic thought works essentially
on the level of ritual activity whose function is not to explain the universe of human beings but to operate on them. In order to interpret
this activity among the Ndembu, Turner principally relied on the commentaries of his most qualified informants as well as his analysis of
the position of signs in an "ensemble" and the way they were used.
We know that Lévi-Strauss, discussing Turner's thesis, characterizes
these fragmentary exegeses as implicit mythology (Lévi-Strauss, 1971:
596–603). Lévi-Strauss' position, when faced with ritual, seems to have
changed over time. In the last pages of *L'Homme Nu*, he asserts, cu-
riously enough, that all things considered, the nature of ritual itself
differs radically from that of myth, be it explicit or implicit, because
"the gestures executed, the objects manipulated, are but means by
which ritual avoids speaking" (Lévi-Strauss, 1971:600). If so, the function of ritual is not to reinforce mythic thought but to overthrow
it. Thus, Lévi-Strauss also presents ritual to us a "bastardization of
thought," a desperate attempt to affirm the priority of "living" over
that of "thinking."

I shall try to convince you of the contrary; the approach that
Lévi-Strauss proposes to apply to the analysis of myths is profitable
when applied to ritual, but only when one is confronted with an "ensemble" of rites, described with sufficient precision. My purpose is to
show that the ritual acts, far from abolishing thought, belong to im-

plicit or explicit codes, that action and thought form one and the same system.

I have chosen to discuss the Thonga of southern Africa because they present us with a challenge. They have elaborated very few myths but numerous rites, both individual and collective; these rites are accompanied by seemingly little exegetic commentaries.

This analysis will be limited to *rites de passage* of young children. I shall offer a privileged reading of the semantic web, spun by both the succession of gestures and the manipulation of objects. Obviously the interpretation of this silent language could be considered totally arbitrary if I was unable to link this analysis to fragmentary discourses uttered by the Thonga concerning fire and water, sickness, and menstrual blood.

Naturally I must also take into account the social structure and, in particular, the respective roles of men and women. For doing structural analyses of symbolic thought does not necessarily entail sinking into a sociological void as many anthropologists might think.

The case of the Thonga is remarkable in more than one respect in the history of African ethnography. These people have the quite distinct privilege of being the first in the Bantu world to have been studied in minute detail by a highly talented observer. Nothing predisposed this observer, Henri-Alexandre Junod (1863–1934), a Swiss protestant missionary and author of a doctoral thesis on "The Perfect Holiness of Jesus Christ" (1885), to engage in scientific work at a time, before Malinowski and Radcliffe-Brown, when anthropological research in Africa was virtually nonexistent.

The Thonga belong to the Southeastern Bantu. They form a large nation devoid of any political unity. At the beginning of this century the population was estimated to be between 700,000 and 900,000 men. The Thonga live essentially in southern Mozambique, but as a result of the formidable Zulu invasions from 1835 to 1840, an important contingent of Thonga emigrated to Transvaal.

The population grouped by Junod under the label *Ronga* inhabit the southern region of the cultural area (Junod, 1936:33). Most of his principal informants belong to this important group which constituted a powerful chiefdom during the sixteenth century. This strong political structure explains the important Thonga expansion in southern Mozambique in the middle of the eighteenth century (Smith, 1973:572,

576). The Ronga were able to remain independent of the Zulu chiefs because they placed themselves under the protection of the Portuguese at the time of the Zulu invasions of the nineteenth century. Thus they preserved a relative independence until the consolidation of the European colonization at the end of the same century (Junod, 1936:33).

Once one examines the family network that unites the villages of the Thonga, one is struck by its extreme homogeneity. The residential unit is, in fact, an extended patrilinear family. The village includes a central shelter for cattle. The enclosure for goats is separate. Young boys take care of the goats until they are ten or eleven years old, after which they are entrusted with the care of the oxen from which the women are rigorously kept apart. The majority of the agricultral jobs, however, fall upon the women's shoulders.

Religious life is without a doubt based on ancestor worship. The village is encircled by a small hedge; to the right of the main entrance is the altar of the paternal ancestors, the center of which is a common cooking pot called *gandjelo* (Junod, 1936; vol. 2:343). There, members of the founding lineage normally dispose offerings of all kinds for the ancestors. But many offerings are directed to maternal ancestors; this fact should be seen in the light of the Thonga kinship system which grants a privileged religious and social role to the avuncular relationship (Junod, 1936, vol. 1:299; vol. 2:344). This appears in sacrifices, but not in the *rites de passage* we will now consider.

Fire and Gestation

Junod's article which describes the physiological conceptions of the south African Bantu clearly suggests the close symbolic relationship that exists between fire and birth: "Child is the product of successful firing" since he is "considered to be a clay utensil that has been fired and has not cracked" (Junod, 1910:138). Several indications show that it is a question of moderated firing as opposed to a series of dangerous overheatings. Sickness is the result of excessive heat: the word *hola*, used to designate the recovery of a sick person, is also applied to a "cooking pot, heated by fire, that is put aside to cool." During menstruation a woman suffers from a dangerous "heat" (Junod, 1910:138). The blood of a woman who has suffered a miscarriage is particularly dangerous because it affects rainfall: it causes the blowing of the scorching winds that dry up the countryside (Junod, 1910: 140). Any sexual act is defined to some extent as a release of heat, and this is liable to become dangerous for society in certain circumstances (Junod, 1910:147).

Lévi-Strauss has shown that in a number of very different societies, "the individuals who are 'cooked' are those deeply involved in a physiological process: the newborn child, the woman who has just given birth, or the pubescent girl" (Lévi-Strauss, 1969:336).

> In America, Pueblo women gave birth over a heap of hot sand, which was perhaps intended to transform the child into a "cooked person"—in contrast with natural creatures and natural or manufactured objects, which are "raw persons." It was the habit of various California tribes to put women who had just given birth and pubescent girls into ovens, hollowed out in the ground. After being covered with mats and hot stones, they were conscientiously "cooked"; the Yurok, incidentally, used the same expression "cooking the pains" to refer to all curative rites (Lévi-Strauss, 1969:336).

Lévi-Strauss arrives at the following conclusion: "The conjunction of a member of the social group with *nature* must be mediatized through the intervention of cooking fire" (Lévi-Strauss, 1969:336). But he himself qualifies this definition as "provisional" and adds that these practices "should be methodically described and classed."

I will show that the Thonga complicate this process to a certain extent. The biological development of the embryo is already a natural firing; it will be followed by a ritual cooking. But the child's progressive integration into his paternal lineage inversely calls for a cooling down treatment, as does healing. I hope to demonstrate that this physiological "heat code" reflects a cosmogonic code. The transition from the one code to the other is particularly clear in the ideolgy that surrounds the birth of twins.

The birth of twins is one of the principle threats of drought. The twin's mother is impure and other women must avoid contact with her possessions. Particular precautions are observed with her when she must participate in mourning. "She must lie face down on the ground near the deceased's hut, there where the wall has been perforated in order to take out the corpse. Then the grave digger brings a few burning coals in a *potsherd*, pours a little water on them and dips his finger

in this water; he encircles the woman's waist with his hands so as to
to heal her within" (Junod, 1936, vol. 2:391). The ashes assume the
same functions in the treatment of twins when they participate in a
funeral ceremony: one of the grave diggers welcomes them at the entrance of the village calling them "sons of the sky"; he deposits some
ashes on their fontanel ("the extremity of the tree of life"). Junod in-
terprets this rite as a prophylactic measure: the twins are in a state of
weakness and the impurity of death could affect them more than other
children (Junod, 1936, vol. 2:390). But their quality as "sons of the
sky" calls for a better explanation. Twins are in fact the result of a
dangerous conjunction of the sky and the earth. Their mother "rose in
the sky"; the Thonga also say that she is the sky or that she carries
the sky. They also attribute death to the power of the sky: "[long
ago] it was frequently said that 'the sky had fallen on such and such
a village'" (Junod, 1936, vol. 2:391). Thus these twins are bearers of a
death-carrying power. The latter is associated with heavenly fire.
Among the Ronga, in a case of great drought, the mother of twins
conducts the rain ritual in order to influence the sky "which is busy
killing the earth by the sun's dreadful heat" (Junod, 1936, vol. 2:391).
The rite consists essentially of pouring water on the graves of twins.

So impurity that affects the twins and their mother is an excess of
heat; we can now understand that the evil which menaces man as well
as nature must be fought with the signs of antifire (i.e., water, ashes).
The birth of twins must then be interpreted as an excessive intrauterine firing placed under the sign of heavenly fire. In order to lessen the
danger of twins' births, the Thonga formerly killed the weakest infant.
For reasons we shall explain later on, the infant's corpse underwent
the same funeral rites as those used for all dead babies; it was placed
in a cracked cooking pot, buried at ground level, "its opening half
covered with a layer of ashes, in such a way that there is a passage
for air" (Junod, 1936, vol. 1:158; vol. 2:387). Junod explains the raison
d'etre of this custom concerning twins: the soul of the child (moya,
"breath") must be able to leave, to fly away otherwise the mother
could never again bear children (Junod, 1936, vol. 2:388). The layer of
ashes through which the breath must pass clearly indicates anew the
desire to temper the excess of heat that the cracked pot so strongly
connotes. Do not the Thonga compare a normal child to a "clay
utensil which has been fired and has not cracked" (Junod, 1910:127)?

The instigator of the intrauterine firing of the child is none other than the menstrual blood. The "heat" it gives off is normally a source of great danger for the husband; the wife has not "cooled off" until the ninth day of her cycle (Junod, 1910:138). This same menstrual blood accumulates in the body of the woman when she becomes pregnant: the doctor must make tiny incisions near her breasts and on her legs (Junod, 1936, vol. 1:180). This rite, the function of which is to "take away the blood," assuredly tempers the intrauterine fire. Indeed, a remarkable, peculiar gradation is involved in the fear of feminine blood: it is applied with increasing intensity to menstrual blood, blood of birth (*lochia*) and blood of miscarriage (Junod, 1910:139). The latter is marked by a particularly dangerous release of heat. Throughout Thonga country, miscarriages figure as one of the principal natural causes which impede rainfall. It is not the premature birth as such that is alluded to but the great danger presented by the blood of natural abortion if the mother has not buried the foetus with the proper ritual precautions. An informer specifies: "When a woman has had a miscarriage, when she let the secretion flow out without saying anything, and she buried the premature child in an unknown place, it is enough to cause the blowing of the burning winds, which dry up the countryside." The mother's fault is "to have spoiled the land because she hid blood that was not yet arranged well enough to form a human being" (Junod, 1936, vol. 2:272). The buried foetus is dug up and the hole is sprinkled with medicine. Some earth is set apart, pulverized, and thrown into the river; finally, water from this same river is poured in the grave. With some of the contaminated earth (from the grave) the old women make a ball that the magicians break up in order to make a powerful medicine. This medicine is sprinkled everywhere so that the rain will return.

Along the river Limpopo the ritual is a little different: when the divining bones reveal that the countryside is unclean, the women take off their clothes and exhume the bodies of premature babies that have been buried in the dry sand of the hills. They place the remains in potsherds that they bury in the mud near the river. They then pour water in the now empty graves in order to "extinguish the fire." Among the Ronga the same rite (*mbelele*) is conducted by a mother of twins. She leads the women to the graves of twins and sprinkles them (Junod, 1936, vol. 2:272–74).

The anthropo-cosmogonic code that we have just examined clearly indicates that menstrual blood and blood of birth are linked in a

certain way with solar heat. One will further note that all infants release heat until undergoing the rite of tribal integration, the *boha
puri*, which takes place at the end of the first year, and marks the resumption of sexual intercourse for the parents. Indeed, the child must
be buried in humid ground if he should die before this ceremony and
in dry ground, like adults, if he dies after having undergone this *rite
de passage* (Junod, 1936, vol. 1:59).

All this shows extraordinary coherence in a thought system which
assimilates gestation to a process placed under the sign of fire.

But during this entire procedure the child is symbolically sent
back to a mythical place which is humid and cool: the original reed
marsh from where mankind is issued (Junod, 1936, vol. 2:259, 303).
Little children "are but water" and a small piece of reed, containing
a magic powder, is attached to their carrying-bag in order to protect
them from the dangers of the bush (Junod, 1936, vol. I: 48, 49, 52, 59).
A Thonga infant must pass from an amorphous state to the solid state
of socialized individual.

Birth and Smoking

First let us examine the rite to which the baby is submitted
shortly after it is born. A few days after birth, when the umbilical cord
falls off and before the first coming out of the maternal hut, the male
baby is exposed to a particularly disagreeable fumigation. The medicine man brings pieces of all sorts of wild animals; he places them in
an old potsherd and roasts them, while the child sneezes, coughs, and
cries from the smoke. Then he grinds and pulverizes what is left in
order to make an ointment with which he rubs the child's body so as
to favor his growth. Junod proposes a metaphorical explanation to this
rite: "the child having been exposed [symbolically] to all the exterior
dangers that the wild animals represent, can leave the hut" (Junod,
1936, vol. 1:48). We suggest rather another type of interpretation. We
may wonder whether this rite, which is performed on the threshold of
the house, and allows the child to leave the burning place of his birth,
is not related to the very process of gestation.

One will note that the child, who leaves his mother's womb as a
hot pot, is not literally smoked. Junod stresses the fact that the medicine man exposes the child and its body, face, and mouth to the smoke

for a long time (Junod, 1936, vol. 1:48). He adds that the potsherd rite constitutes notably the great preventive remedy against convulsions. This indication reveals the cosmogonic reach of the operation. Convulsions are caused "by the mysterious power of the sky" (Junod, 1936, vol. 1:49). Although Junod does not establish any relationship between the two facts, it is clear that the convulsion is explained in the same way as are twin births: by a torrid conjunction between the sky and the earth. This danger always menaces infants after birth. It is in turn combated by a cooking ritual, that which transforms the child into smoked meat. The process of smoking is endowed with a specific disjunctive power. The separation, the placing of a distance between the fire and the newborn infant, contrasts with the situation of the embryo which is directly exposed to the intrauterine fire. The potsherd rite authorizes the transition from the interior of the maternal hut to the external social space. It is only after the performance of this rite that the father is allowed to enter the hut; it was previously forbidden because the heat of *lochia*, "blood of birth," would expose him to grave dangers (Junod, 1936, vol. 1:47). Now the child itself can also be taken outside (Junod, 1936, vol. 1:50).

The biological formation of the embryo and the potsherd rite are interconnected. The watery foetus is contained in a cooking pot that must not crack when fired. After the umbilical cord has fallen off, a broken pot is used for the smoking rite. I suggest that this potsherd symbolizes the definitive rupture with the womb. The Pedi confirm this interpretation. Among this neighboring tribe, the ritual of birth consists of washing the newborn with fresh water which is kept in a broken claypot, while "the afterbirth is thrown into a claypot filled with water" (Mönnig, 1967:100–01). Mönnig, author of a monograph on the Pedi, gives the same explanation that I do for the Thonga potsherd rite: "The broken claypot is symbolic of the transitional condition of the child" (1967:100).

The potsherd rite transforms the child into an autonomous object that is separated from the world of its mother and associated with the masculine world of hunting. This is achieved through a radical reversal of the intrauterine process. A passage is made from firing to smoking, cooking through the separation of fire and object.

The general observations of Lévi-Strauss must be adapted to this particular context: the newborn baby is separated from nature, from his mother, by a culinary operation—in this case smoking. But smoking is a transformation of a natural process that is itself conceived of as a cultural production: the fabrication of a pot.

Cooling Down and Growth

The cooling down process begins three months later, with the presentation of the child to the moon, the *yandla* rite. This takes place after the first new moon following the resumption of the mother's menstrual cycle (Junod, 1910:130; 1936, vol. 1:55). When the moon reappears in the sky

> the mother takes a torch, or simply a burning brand and the grandmother follows her behind the hut. On arriving there, the mother hurls the brand at the moon, and the grandmother throws the child in the air saying: 'There is your moon.' Then she lays the baby on the pile of ashes. The little one cries and rolls in the ash dump. Then the mother picks him up abruptly, nurses him, and they go home (Junod, 1936, vol. 1:56).

After the fulfillment of *yandla*, the father is authorized for the first time to take the child in his arms.

It is altogether remarkable that twins are excluded from this rite (Junod, 1936, vol. 1:390). We must keep in mind that the twins have a solar connotation, and it is through the exclusion of objects, such as twins, associated with the sun that the function of *yandla* becomes clear: by the refreshing action of the moon, this rite tempers the feminine fire of gestation which is related to the dehydrating power of the sky. The child is conjoined to the moon, like the blazing brand that the mother hurls at it. Associated with this burned-out torch, the child is then layed in the ashes; he is left to wallow on this cooled-off fire before his mother nurses him. At the same time as the child is thus symbolically disjoined from his mother (maternal fire), he is conjoined to his father who, for the first time, has the right to take him in his arms. The cooling off action of the moon is coupled with that of the ashes. Moon and ashes are opposed to sun and fire. It is remarkable that the grandmother (most probably the father's mother) plays a mediatory role: she throws the child, the mother merely throws the brand.

The moon is feminine among the Thonga, the evening star (Venus) is considered to be her husband (Junod, 1936, vol. 2:264). The association of the cosmogonic code and kinship order is evident in neighboring societies: among the Venda, Pedi, and Lovedu, the moon is presented to the child as its paternal aunt (Roumegure-Eberhardt, 1963: 29). These comparative indications suggest that the moon connotates the preeminent social role of women as instruments of matrimonial alliance by opposition to the purely biological relation of mother and child. A new bond with the mother is set up, a distanced socialized relationship that finally permits more intimate contact between the father and the child.

It is a pity that we do not know very much of the Thonga oral traditions concerning the moon and the sun. The moon's (feminine) action is associated with the child's physical growth in his father's social sphere. The symbolic connection of the child and the moon metaphorically activates physical development. Indeed, the *yandla* rite can be compared with a custom (more like a game than a ritual) that the Thonga call *kulakulisa*, "to make grow." "When a traveller from afar passes through a village, he takes the infant in his hands, raises him, and throws him in the air saying 'grow up, grow up, reach such and such a place' and he gives the name of the locality from whence he comes." Junod perfectly understands the common function of the *yandla* rite and this game: to develop the child's faculties (Junod, 1910:130; 1936, vol. 1:56). He fails, however, to see that they both belong to the same symbolic spatial schema: the *yandla* unites the sky and the earth, the *kulakulisa* unites two very remote places. The second rite substitutes a horizontal axis for the vertical axis of the first rite.

Although the action of the sun in the intrauterine firing is not clear, the treatment reserved for premature but viable infants suggests that the feminine menstrual fire is related to this celestial fire. This unfinished firing and cooking calls for the positive action of the sun; wrapped in the leaves of the castor oil plant, the premature baby is placed in a big cooking pot that is exposed to the sun's heat (Junod, 1936, vol. 1:45). It is not just a question, as Junod supposes, of obtaining a result analogous to that of a modern nursery incubator. The symbolic effectiveness of the sun is at least as important, since this celestial fire corrects an unfinished firing. Let us not forget that the excess action of the sun is responsible for the drought that threatens the earth when a mother gives birth to twins after having herself given up to the sky during her pregnancy.

But over time the sun and the moon are indeed associated at different and complementary moments of the child's development. In the case of the sun, the firing of the embryo is involved, whereas the case of the moon involves the formation of a social personality. The *yandla* rite takes place during the first phase of the moon. It is at this time that the child is given a name corresponding to the month inaugurated by the reappearance of the moon (Junod, 1936, vol. 1:45). This custom, however, is disappearing. Because the rite is supposed to "open the child's chest" and "prevent his ears from dying," the *yandla* signifies the introduction of the child into the social world of communication (Junod, 1936, vol. 1:45). The moon's first crescent is itself compared to a newborn infant; its weak light is still dominated by the sun, says one of Junod's informers (1936, vol. 2:263). This metaphor functions in both ways because, in fact, for a few more months, until the *boha puri*, "tribal integration" rite, the child is marked by an excessive solar heat: we have seen that he cannot be buried in a dry place if he should die before this new *rite de passage*.

The progressive degradation of the birth's heat is very easy to decode in different types of funerals: if the child dies during an overheated stage, the baby is buried in a cracked cooking pot covered with a layer of ashes in which an opening is provided so that the heat can escape. If he dies before the *boha puri*, he must be buried in a humid place. This new rite reinforces the bond between the child and his father already created under the sign of the moon. It also permits without danger the reunion of the parents, who until then had to abstain from sexual relations, a source of heat (Junod, 1910:132). This time the child is put in contact with his father's sperm or penis. This rite takes place when the child starts to crawl (Junod, 1936, vol. 1:59). "When the moment has come to *fuya*, "possess" the child, when he can stand up, the father and mother have sexual intercourse that evening *semine non emisso*" for the father must not impregnate his wife. The mother smears a cotton cord with the father's "impurity" (*usila*), and the two of them attach it around the child's loins, the mother holding the little one and the father tying the cord. But there is an easier way to *fuya* the child. After intercourse the father simply has to touch the child's loins, in front and behind, with his penis (Junod, 1910:131–32). Thus the presentation to the moon, then the contact with the very seed of the father, constitute two stages in the same sequence: the child passes progressively from the hot maternal world to the cool social world of the father. The *boha puri* is the last step in early childhood; it signifies incorporation into the paternal lineage which really "owns" him (Junod, 1910:132).

Until he is about three, however, the child will depend on his mother's breast. The weaning rite is rigorously similar to that performed at the end of an illness (*hondlola*). Now, sickness is also conceived by the Thonga as a state of heating up, just as menstruation. Therefore a symbolic association is created, under the sign of fire, between gestation, early childhood, and illness. To heal is also to cool; the image of the heated cooking pot is a metaphor for both pregnancy and illness. The metaphor for healing (a heated cooking pot put aside to cool down) could be applied just as well to the first three years of childhood which, just as illness, is ended by the *hondlola* rite which cools off the sick person (Junod, 1910:138).

At the *boha puri*, the body's temperature has reached the desired degree of coolness. Later, at puberty, it will be necessary to reheat the boy's sexuality, under the sign of the sun and menstrual fire in the circumcision camps. In contrast to the boys, girls will have the dangerous heat of their first menstruation tempered with daily baths. In short the very conception of the human being among the Thonga and most southeastern Bantu belongs to a sort of perfectly original thermodynamic philosophy.

Finally, we examine the curious periodic steam bath to which the mother and infant are submitted after the *yandla*. After each new moon and when the moon is full, the child undergoes a medical treatment called *biyekata*. The mother and child are shut up in an enclosure, and covered by a cotton cloth. They bend over vapor released from a cooking pot where the medicine man has boiled an infusion, and also over smoke released by a ball of grease with medicinal properties which the medicine man grills on the embers. This rite, which involves complementary magical operations, has the explicit function of expelling impurity from the child's body and facilitating its growth (Junod, 1936, vol. 1:57). It thus prolongs the *yandla's* action, while introducing a new symbolic element into the biological code. Contact is maintained between the child and fire, but this contact is mediated by steam. The growth and purification of the baby are associated with this new burning element, that is both water and fire. Whereas only the child is subjected to a process of smoking in the potsherd ritual, this time he is associated with his mother under the same cloth. Everything happens as if the *yandla* only partially disjoins the mother and child. The intrauterine process continues but is transformed from a firing to a steaming, and steam cooking facilitates the development of the child's still unhardened body. This steam bath, which implies physical intimacy between the mother and the child, again takes over the very process of gestation Biological maturation continues, then, at the same time as social maturation.

Biological birth	*Social birth*
End of the firing of the intrauterine pot.	First coming out. Smoking (with a potsherd).
Biological maturation	*Social maturation*
Steam cooking (*biyekata*).	*Yandla* (presentation to the moon and laying on ashes).

In a way Thonga thought shifts the "locus" of articulation of nature and culture: the cooking fire or potter's fire is at work within the burning uterus; the steaming of the baby prolongs the natural process by a cultural method. On the other hand, smoking appears here as the symbolic mark par excellence of entrance into the cultural world, that of men. That is why masculine signs (hunting signs) intervene: the medicine man roasts pieces of wild animal skins on a potsherd.

Let us summarize our results. If gestation is thought of as a harmonious conjunction of earth and sun, each at a good distance from the other, development in the exterior world implies a new cosmogonic equilibrium that brings the moon into play. The effectiveness of the feminine and lunar *yandla* rite is reinforced by the medical treatment, *biyekata*, which is itself connected with the lunar rhythm. On the other hand, the abusive conjunction of the earth and sky brought about by the mother of twins during pregnancy involves both the social equilibrium of single births and the well-tempered cosmogonic order. All twins births jeopardize the alternation of seasons in so far as they originate in a precipitated displacement of the pregnant woman towards the sky during the firing stage, when the sun's influence is preponderant.

Albinos, for their part, represent the alternative: these monstrous creatures are called "charcoal-lightening" because they were burned by the descent of another celestial fire: a thunderbolt. The fire of the thunderbolt is vigorously opposed to terrestrial fire: it is forbidden to warm oneself by a fire kindled with the wood of a tree struck by lightning or to use his wood as fuel (Junod, 1936, vol. 2:269). Twins and albinos are thus inverse expressions of the burning conjunction of sky and earth.

An anthropo-cosmogonic system stands out with precision:

Premature babies:	Insufficiently fired, they must be exposed to the sun.
Normal babies:	Products of a normal firing, their heat calls for a progressive cooling down, assured by the lunar rite *yandla*. The *biyekata* rite maintains a cooking system at a good distance from the fire.
Twins:	Caused by an excessive firing, by the dangerous ascension of the mother into the sky, they represent a permanent threat of heat (illness) and drought.
Albinos:	The result of an inverted excessive conjunction between the sky and earth (descent of thunder), they are children burned by lightning.

A new incident, threatening the world's order, can arise during growth: the appearance of the first incisors in the upper jaw. All the Thonga interpret it as a bad sign, but the northern groups, like the Pedi, implicitly class it as a danger of drought, saying that at his death, this man must be buried in humid ground (Junod, 1936, vol. 1:54).

Furthermore, this anthropo-cosmogonic code allows an understanding of a peculiarity in the *yandla* rite: not only is the father authorized to take the child in his arms at this time, but he can also sing songs to console the child when he cries, something forbidden before presentation to the moon (Junod, 1936, vol. 1:56). The father's (and apparently also the mother's) obligation to remain silent before the burning newborn infant can be explained if one remembers that the same ritual attitude is necessary when confronted with devastating fire: when a fire destroys the prairie, it must be extinguished in silence. "If one makes noise, if one cries, it will rush straight to you" (Junod, 1936, vol. 2:281). Silence is also enforced in the presence of a child seized by convulsions. The function of the potsherd rite is precisely to avoid this affliction, believed also to be caused by the burning conjunction of sky and earth. The same attitude of reserve is imposed in other circumstances characterized by a release of heat. Silence is expected, for instance, of women during war expeditions or when their husbands hunt hippopotamus (Junod, 1936, vol. 2:281). With this in mind we can understand that the newborn infant, issued burning from his mother's womb, must be welcomed with the same silence.

Another aspect of the potsherd rite also becomes clearer in light of this code. The newborn infant is forced to cry violently because of the acrid smoke (see p. 36). If silence assures the disjunction of earth and celestial fire, the cries of the child provoked during the rite assuredly facilitate the conjunction of two spaces which were previously separate. The function of the potsherd rite is to connect the interior of the hut (extension of the womb) and the exterior world: not only does the child appear in public, but for the first time since the birth, the father can enter the house without danger.

This acoustic code, related to the cosmogony, is completed by a third element which is situated exactly between the cries and the silence: a magic flute allows one to ward off that other burning conjunction between the sky and the earth realized by the thunderbird, who is responsible for the birth of albinos (Junod, 1936, vol. 2:169).

This acoustic code hinges on a sociological and spatial code:

	Consequences of the potsherd rite	Consequences of the *yandla* rite
Sociological code	The son is placed in the presence of his father, who remains silent.	The father takes the child in his arms; he is allowed to sing lullabies.
Spatial code	Creation of a bond between the interior of the hut and the exterior world.	Creation of a bond between the child and the moon.

The *yandla* rite, which implies a moderate vertical cosmogonic conjunction between the earth and the sky, completes the horizontal connection of the interior of the hut with the outside world, realized by means of the potsherd rite. Providing that this data is considered as a symbolic set, we ascertain that the interiority of the house (i.e., the maternal relation) is to the exteriority of the social order (constructed by the exchange of women) as the earth is to the moon. We can better understand that the latter is often assimilated to a paternal aunt in southern Africa. Let us finish by singing an old French song, which seems to be à propos and whose poetic mystery remains intact despite any structuralist attempt to compare it to the *yandla* rite:

> Au clair de la lune, mon ami Pierrot,
> Ma chandelle est morte, je n'ai plus de feu . . .

I wish to thank the two women who toiled with me on this paper: the translator Linda O'Brien and the typist Yvette Noppen. The paper has subsequently been edited by Ivan Karp.

BIBLIOGRAPHY

Harris, Marvin. 1968. *The Rise of Anthropological Theory.* New York: Crowell.

de Heusch, L. 1972. *Le roi ivre ou L'origine de l'Etat.* Paris: Gallimard.

Junod, H. A. 1910. "Les conceptions physiologiques des Bantous sud-africains et leurs tabous." *Revue d'Ethnographie et de Sociologie* 1:126–69.

———. 1936. *Moeurs et coutumes des Bantous.* Paris: Payot. 2 vols.

Lévi-Strauss, C. 1969. *The Raw and the Cooked.* Translated by John and Doreen Weightman. New York: Harper and Row.

———. 1971. *L'Homme nu.* Paris: Plon.

Mönnig, H. O. 1967. *The Pedi.* Pretoria: Van Shaik.

Roumegure-Eberhardt, J. 1963. *Pensée et sociétés africaines. Essais sur une dialectique de complémentarité antagoniste chez les Bantu du Sud-Est.* Paris: Mouton.

Smith, A. K. 1973. "The Peoples of Southern Mozambique: An Historical Survey." *Journal of African History* 14:565–80.

Turner, V. W. 1967. *The Forest of Symbols.* Ithaca: Cornell University Press.

Edification by Puzzlement

by James Fernandez

> By indirections find directions
> out!
> POLONIUS
> He gives me ideas even when I
> don't understand him.
> E. LEACH ON C. LÉVI-STRAUSS

Administered Intellectuality

The colonial mentality is generally associated with a set of racial attitudes produced in a privileged class of administrative, merchant, or sometimes, missionary plenipotentiaries well suited to justify and preserve privileges and exclude the claims of the administered peoples upon those privileges. These attitudes most often were expressed in observations on the moral behavior of native peoples such as their irresponsibility and deviousness or their lack of the more refined feelings. But the colonial mentality was also a set of beliefs about mentality itself. These beliefs were most often expressed in observations on "time sense," childishness, or prelogical reasoning. To the very end of the colonial period, colonialists bewailed the granting of independence to local peoples who wouldn't have the wits to run things, whether it was the Suez Canal—these days it has been the Panama Canal, one of the last outposts of the colonial attitude in its purest form—the Kariba Dam, the Katanga copper mines, or the Ghana Cocoa Marketing Board. Of course, all these constructions are still running, although perhaps not in their former manner. Not all peoples have the gift of the northern European peoples for self-abnegating administration. Most peoples tend to express themselves more by administering and maintaining structures of exchange and control.

The point of this postcolonial preamble is not to deny that there are differences in mentalities or in modes of thought. Indeed, there are, and we should be interested in them. But on the other hand, we should always be wary of the imperial impulse—the possibility that any interest in mentalities is betrayed by a *petitio principi*, a preexistent interest in maintaining and justifying a structure of privileges. It is perfectly natural to seek to maintain privileges, but this is not the purpose of anthropology, which seeks some simple knowledge of the species which surpasses our impressive capacity for self-interested and self-contained activity.

This caution is by no means over drawn. I remember when I administered the Segall, Campbell, Herskovits visual illusions protocol in a Fang village in Gabon.[1] Now I had good rapport in that village. I carried a local name. I came as a bachelor and later captured a wife, a North European wife at that, and brought her to the village—a palpable strengthening of the lineage. But that was a difficult protocol to administer. On the one hand I seemed to be getting a lot of extraneous answers, and on the other hand several of the younger villagers seemed mistrustful. It was during the De Gaulle Referendum, and politics were a strong interest among the young. For whom was I doing the protocol? they wanted to know. And what reason did I have for wanting to know such things? Admittedly those kinds of questions and the "laboratory" type conditions required of the test administration were much different from my customary participant-observer and notes and queries role. That role was more fitted to the reason I had given for being in the village, that is, to do a history of the Fang way of life and to make it known to "esi merika," the land of the Americans. The protocol was a harder-headed social science, to use terms from the hard–soft continuum which is a favorite metaphor in academic life. Some of the villagers sensed it as such, although most admittedly took such things as the Sander parallelogram and the Müller-Lyer illusion as just a peculiar kind of riddling popular to Europeans.

I had to admit, if not to my interlocutors, at least to myself, that the harder-headed social science was more highly regarded in my country than the softer kind I usually practiced. In part this was because the culture of science prefers hard data to soft data, but also in part because that harder data was more useful to those hard-headed people who sought, if not to maintain a world system of privileges, at least to engage in competent tough-minded administration of world order. It is of interest, incidentally, to note that the most fruitful and well-funded psychological testing, that of the Rockefeller ethnographic psychology team, has found a congenial field laboratory in Liberia, a country whose administration is quite interested in maintaining a well-ordered system of inherited privileges. I have no doubt that it is quite coincidental as far as the Rockefeller team is concerned. These days one does social and psychological science where one can.

The difficult questions raised by my young informants must be answered. We have some obligations when, as Geertz (1973) says, we plague subtle peoples with obtuse questions. Why, really, are those who sponsor that research really interested in sponsoring it? Is disinterested inquiry as widespread as we would like it to be? Fang respondents were not so optimistic and trusting as I was about the scientific neutrality of the protocol.

The Rockefeller ethnographic psychology team under Michael Cole and Sylvia Scribner has been conducting studies of the impact of literacy on rural Liberians. These are valuable studies concerning memory, the ability to recall, pattern recognition, and perception.[2] They have also been attempting to get hard data on that perennial bugaboo, logical thought process. This they have been doing by administering a series of protocols which employ that old reasoning device: the syllogism. Here are some examples from West African and Mexican protocols.

> All people who own huts pay hut tax.
> Boima does not pay a hut tax.
> Does Boima own a hut?

> So that Jose can carry corn from his farm to
>   the town he needs a cart and a horse.
> He has the horse but he doesn't have the cart.
> Can Jose carry his corn from his farm?

The results of administering these syllogisms support a number of generalizations: 1) in all cultures populations designated as "traditional" have a just somewhat better than chance solution rate; 2) within each culture there is a large discrepancy in performance between schooled and non-schooled; 3) within schooling there is little between-culture variation in performance—grade in school, rather than society, is most determinate of performance.[3] The results seem to be that schools teach you to solve syllogisms. They are a particular genre, a kind of lore, as it were, typical of that milieu. If you haven't been to school you won't be clued in on the need to suspend disbelief in order to accept the propositions. You have to be schooled to accept Boima's or Jose's hypothetical plight as real. You also have to be schooled to the fact that you don't have to search elsewhere for a solution to such questions. The answer to the question posed in the syllogism is found in the syllogism itself; it is self-contained.

Now what is most interesting, it seems to me, are the ways in which traditional rural peoples go wrong, that is, fall into logical errors in respect to conjunction, disjunction, and implication. When responding to these syllogisms, rural peoples, since they aren't schooled enough in the self-sufficiency of the syllogism itself, most often introduce new personal evidence. This is not surprising. Sylvia Scribner gives many examples of the way informants question the facts: "We don't carry corn in carts." "We don't pay hut taxes here!" In other cases they are stimulated into elaborate personal accounts recalling experiences relevant to the subject matter of the question, though not to the requirements of the syllogism.

What seems to occur is that these rural uneducated subjects tend to ignore the arbitrarily imposed relations among the elements in the problem and the rules of criterion implied. They tend to "go beyond the information given" and give consideration to the context in which the question is posed, such as the colonial context of domination and subordination evoked by my younger Fang visual illusion informants or the cultural context of the question—corn is not carried in carts, and not all huts are taxed. They creatively introduce personal experiences and use these academic riddles as an opportunity for edifying commentary on life in general. Or they simply introduce new evidence. Once you take the premises of the new evidence into account, the reasoning of these people turns out to be quite logical. Scribner calls this kind of reasoning "empiric" explanation as opposed to the theoretic or "schooled" explanation of syllogistic argument. Rather than fulfill a formal task, the respondent seeks concrete examples and particular correlative circumstances. Informants either reject the information given or verify it by imputing new evidence.

Lancy, who has worked with the Cole-Scribner ethnographic psychology team and encountered the same problem (the tendency of rural nonwesterners to ignore the rules involved and to answer in terms of setting and personal involvements) points out that responses to the syllogisms are like a certain kind of riddle solving found among Kpelle. There is no single right answer to these riddles. Rather, as the riddle is posed to a group, the right answer is the one among many offered that seems most illuminating, resourceful, and convincing as determined by consensus and circumstance.[4] This emphasis on edification as a criterion for "rightness" is found in Kpelle jurisprudence as well. The successful litigant is the one who can make the most resourceful and edifying argument. The argument is not simply the application of a set of legal rules, but involves taking a problem situation as a personal opportunity to explore the context of the problem and its relevant precedents. Application of a perceived rule is not nearly so important as is availing oneself of the opportunity of a puzzlement—those latent possibilities for the expression of verbal and intellectual skills found in any riddle. The well-schooled are much more anxious about right answers and develop heuristics, formulas for rule applications, to obtain them.

There are various kinds of riddles, but on balance, I think it is a mistake to see riddles as simply an exercise in the application of academic rules. It is certainly a mistake to say that "a riddle is always closer to an academic test than to creative research" as Köngas Maranda (1971:296) has argued. Indeed it is the main point of this paper that such puzzlements as riddles have creative—or at least constructive—and edifying consequences in the more traditional non-schooled socities.

Images and Answers

Just the same, Köngas Maranda's work on riddles is some of the most interesting we have, and it is important to recall the main points of her analyses. Köngas Maranda's work is important because she shows that the riddle is really an enigmatic metaphor that follows the logical structure of metaphors and metonyms. Like all tropes, a riddle is the statement of a relation between or within sets (or domains of objects). Like lively poetic metaphor in contrast to dead or unprovoking metaphor, a riddle offers a fresh point of view. Köngas Maranda, in fact, contradicts her notion that riddles are not creative: ". . . that is it causes us to see connections between things that we had not previously perceived." In a Durkheimian manner Köngas Maranda suggests that the final referent of riddles is to some basic aspect of human behavior—a kind of language in which a group speaks of its most basic social action—the union of man and woman. This may be why so many riddles, incidentally, deal with sexual innuendo. In any event, riddles perform a union or conjunction of separated entities on the cognitive level that on the physical level is one of the species' primary preoccupations. Riddles therefore necessarily consist of two parts which are to be conjoined—the riddle image and the answer. These must be analyzed together, though a tendency in riddle analysis has been to concentrate on the image itself.

This conjunction of image and answer in the riddle follows the old Aristotelian definition of an analogy. Analogy exists whenever there are four terms such that the relation between the second and the first is similar to that between the fourth and the third.

$$A/B \quad \text{as} \quad C/D$$

Now any kind of reasoning by tropes—by analogy—rests on two kinds of connection between phenomena: similarity (the metaphoric relation) and contiguity (the metonymic relation). In terms of this Aristotelian formula the similarity relationship runs across sets and the contiguity relation within sets:

$$\text{metonym} \quad \begin{bmatrix} A \\ / \\ B \end{bmatrix} \quad \overline{\qquad \text{metaphor} \qquad} \quad \begin{matrix} C \\ / \\ D \end{matrix}$$

This is better written since we are dealing within sets and across sets relations, A/a as C/c, where A is the human body and C is, let us say, the ocean. In metaphor we are given the analogy by being given both sides of the equation. The arm, a, is to the human body as an extended inlet, c, is to the ocean, hence the arm of the ocean. In a riddle, however, we are only given one side of the equation, say the body side, and we have to discover the other side. Perhaps we are given only the body side and have to discover the other natural object or manufactured object side. Let me send the reader on a riddle-provoked ramble of discovery.

> Riddle a diddle, unravel my riddle:
> "Long legs, sharp thighs, no neck, big eyes."

This riddle gives you the body or natural side, but you must busy yourself to discover the cultural side.[5]

Now all analogies—and riddles are analogies par excellence—have the capacity to establish or suggest connections between experiences within domains and between domains. They are cognitively integrating as it were, and in that way they are edifying. This is basically what I mean by edification: the cognitive construction by suggestion of a larger integration of things, a larger whole. Whereas we customarily discriminate and separate between animate and inanimate objects or draw contrasts between nature and culture, these puzzling predications suggest similarities between, in this case, the human body and a pair of scissors.

Now the very act of suggesting these similarities and noting these contiguities is edifying because the equation between the two sets of experience rests on the fact that both can be shown to belong to a set greater than the two original sets in analogous comparison. Köngas Maranda calls this greater set a *superset*; Keith Basso calls it paradigmatic integration; I have been calling this transcendence.[6] In the case of our riddle, the equation between leggy people and scissors suggests the transcendent superset which we may call the set or domain of articulated things. Though part of the pleasure in metaphor rests in its suggestion of a relation between things thought to be separate if not opposite, at the same time the metaphor or the riddle-metaphor builds a bridge across the abyss of separated, discriminated experience. Jakobson (1960) has argued that before there can be a sense of similarity there must be a sense of contiguity. This is true within sets brought into analogous relation—for we must be clear about the relationship of parts within domains before we can suggest similarities between domains. At the same time, out of the sense of similarities is produced a transcendent overarching sense of contiguity. This transformation of contiguities into similarities and similarities into contiguities is fundamentally edifying. And it is what Lévi-Strauss (1966) means when he speaks with (mysterious) edifying puzzlement about the transformation of metaphors into metonyms and vice versa.

In any event, I would argue, in contrast to Köngas Maranda, that it is this edification of a more integrated world view that is the prime and typical function of this puzzlement. It is not primarily the well-situated discovery and application of rules done in order to find the right answers. Köngas Maranda tends to understand riddles too much in terms of the intellectual efforts of Western school days. There are, it is true, riddling situations in which these puzzles would qualify as what she calls "true riddles." They demand a scanning of the riddle images (or image) for the coded message, i.e., the relevant metonymic relation, in order to discover the right answer, i.e., that relation in another domain. My experience in African riddling situations, however, suggests a prevalence of what she calls the "monk's riddles": riddles that either have a rote answer which one repeats like a catechism or riddles in which there are felt to be a plurality of possible answers and in which the object is creative resourcefulness in providing an answer. Or they are riddles in which no answer is expected from the riddler. The edification is implicit. The audience is left to ponder for itself the mysterious connections between things which are established or implied by the riddles. The riddles here constitute an ambiguous stimulus for creative and constructive responses. They are not instruments designed to provoke the detection and application of certain rules.

This kind of reasoning by the puzzle of analogy is a mode of thought congenial to the older and more wholistic societies because it is serviceable to members of these societies returning to "a sense of the whole" of which they are a part and in which they are ideally to be incorporated. Such reasoning recurrently takes place in these societies. Analysis into parts is not really so important in these societies as is the periodic construction or reconstruction of the whole. The whole is what is truly edifying, and its reconstruction is a purpose which puzzlement can subtly serve.

Cosmogony by Puzzlement

I have seen this kind of reasoning in an African religious movement: Bwiti among the Fang of western equatorial Africa. This is a movement that is providentially trying to return the membership to the whole world in which the ancestors lived and from which the colonial situation has separated them. I became aware of that objective because of a recurrent dictum used by one of the leaders of a main branch of Bwiti, Ekang Engono of Kongouleu. He frequently said "the world is one thing but the witches try to isolate men from each other so they can eat them!" By what are called "likenesses" in Fang this leader sought to knit the world together—to cosmogonize. I should like to examine some of the ways by which this edification proceeds by looking at what the people of Bwiti, the Banzi, call Engono's "miraculous words." Various devices are employed in his sermons, these "subtle words."[7] For example, though the sermons or evangiles are neither didactic nor expository— they seem spontaneous and free-associative in the extreme—they can obtain a kind of integrity by "playing on roots." Thus, the root *yen*, "to see," is bound into different morphemes several different times in an evangile. For example, in a sermon of only five minutes in length we find the root, *yen*, "to see," coming up four different times bound into different words. The word play is, basically, between *yena*, "mirror," and *Eyene*, "he who sees." *Eyene* is the word for the savior figure of this religion, but he is also seen as a mirror who reflects the actions of mankind and whose nature mankind ought to reflect. One other key term in this brief sermon plays with the root: *enyenge*, a deep forest pool in which one sees one's reflection. It is Bwiti belief that not only do men and women see their own faces reflected in these pools, but the sky and the sky deities are also reflected in them. There is in the congregation, in any case, an expectancy gratified by the reiteration of these roots. That reiteration is one source of the sermon's integrity.

In order to get the flavor of these puzzling sermons, I will comment upon selected paragraphs from one of them. More than simply providing for its own integrity by playing on roots and recurrent elemental images, these sermons are designed to suggest an integrity in the religious world in which Bwiti seek to dwell:

1. This thing which I recount is no longer. Zame made us first out upon the savannah. And it was he that pierced and prepared our way through the giant adzap tree. And it was he that began to make it possible to make things of the forest. For Fang are of the forest.

2. Humankind shows four miracles. First he leaves the ground and comes to the foot. And he leaves there and comes to the calf. Then he leaves there and comes to the knee. Then he leaves there and is perched upon whence he came. On the shoulders he is put into the balance for the first time.

3. One fans in vain the cadaver in this earth of our birth. The first bird began to fly in the savannah. The night Cain slew Abel the people built the village of Melen. And after that they never turned back. What we Banzie call *Elodi Tsenge*, Fang call rainbow, and Europeans call *arc-en-ciel*. It was raised over the people. Then they passed through the adzap tree. Then they used the forest to construct things. That was the time of the Oban invasion from the north, the Oban of Olu Menyege.

4. The land of humankind was formed and it is a drop of blood. And that drop grew big and round until the white of the egg was complete and prepared, covering two egg sacks within: the white sack and the black sack. That is the ball of birth and of the earth.

5. Now Fang say that "the star is suspended there high up above." The fruit of the adzap tree is suspended up there high in the adzap. What is found suspended there between these things? Why, it is the raindrop. And that raindrop is the congregation—the group of Banzie.

6. The first food of mankind was the sugar cane, therefore the child takes and presses in his mouth the sweet fruit of the breast. It was Ndong Zame of legend who took up the wheedling ways of children. We are children of the rainbow because we are made of clay.

11. Nyingwan Mebege she is the oil palm. Zame ye Mebege he is the otunga tree. And he died and it is the same as the story of the widow of the forest who conceived on the day her husband died. And she conceived on the day her husband died. And she gave birth in the spreading roots of the adzap tree. They were the first stool. And the adzap we know dries up and dies when sorcerers climb into its branches. And we Fang began at the adzap but we set out quickly from under the adzap tree. Then Zame sat upon the stool and gave his child Eyene Zame. That stool is the otunga and it is also a cross. Adzap-mboga is the road of death. And the first stool, the adzap, was the door to death.

17. The ligaments of the small green bird who cries like boiling water they tie together the earth. Woman has the pierced adzap tree below. Man holds the adzap tree up above. And thus is life tied together. Zame makes life with two materials: the drumming stick is the male. The drum is the female.

As will be seen (the sermons themselves are not explained to the congregation), the interpretation of these midnight sermons requires reference to experiences otherwise acquired in Fang culture. As in a riddle, the images of these sermons send us elsewhere to obtain our answers. They are rich in images which must, however, be contextualized by extension into various domains of Fang culture. The interpretive task is, therefore, to move back and forth between text and context. And while this must always be the case with any interpretation of a text, there is here a much greater obligation to contextualize in order to find meaning due to the lack of expository or didactic aids. There is edification—an emergent sense of a larger meaningful whole—in being so obliged to seek for meaning in the cultural context. Such puzzling sermons, by condensing in one unitary presentation many diverse domains of Fang cultural experience, suggest in that experience an integrity, a relatedness, that Fang in recent years have been at risk of losing. At the same time, by forcing contextualization on the auditor, the cultural experience he is obliged to extend his interpretation to and consult is revitalized. This relating of the parts and revitalizing of the whole of a cultural context is cosmogony of an important kind.

These sermons are examples of what Vygotsky (1962) has called "thinking in complex." The sequence of images—the body images, the forest images, the vital liquids images, the suspended things images, the food images—put forth are not dominated by any overall conceived and stated purpose or by any dominant image. The materials presented cluster around a complex—a sequence of organizing images. These recur, but none is prevailingly nuclear. New materials from various domains of Fang experience are introduced on the basis of association by similarity or contiguity, contrast, or complementarity with this sequence. But then again, abruptly, new elements with all their alternatives are allowed to enter the thought process and raise new thematic preoccupations—and to suggest new possible nuclei of attention. By any standard of administered intellectuality, such sermons seem diffuse and spontaneous in the extreme.

And yet as the sermonizer promises, they "tie together" what brotherly enmity and witchcraft has torn asunder. By a sequence of "likenesses" he shows that the world, fallen into devilish particularities, is really one thing. For the sequence of images is in no way directly or explicitly linked, yet it does not seem especially disjointed to the membership. Nor does it seem to be the product of a mad or drugged mind. The sequences are riddles, puzzles, that force the membership to answers that suggest an overarching order and a relatedness in the diverity of the cosmos. Approached with the cultural knowledge the membership possesses they both condense and integrate that knowledge as they revitalize it. And the sequence of images link together various domains and levels of cultural experience. A cosmological integrity is suggested if not made explicit.

For example, taking any image, we can, even in this sermon segment, follow its transformations into various domains, thereby associating them. In the shorter sermon—not quoted here—to which we have referred in regards to playing on roots we find "the bag of waters" (*abum menzim*) of birth associated with the forest pool of creation (*enyenge abiale bot*), associated to the great river crossed in Fang migration (*oswi ye okua*), associated to the cosmic sea of the origin of all things (*mang*). A sense of reverberation and relatedness between levels and domains of Fang interest and experience is obtained. In circling around one image other attributes of that image embedded in other domains of experience are suggested. Out of our own puzzlement we are extended to larger integrities in wider contexts.

Syllogisms of Association

Extension, condensation, and revitalization are all products of this kind of puzzlement. But what is brought together is more a stimulated thought—a stimulated contextualization—in the auditor than explicit reasoning by the sermonizer. These sermons give their auditors cosmologic ideas even when these auditors don't understand them. The sermonizer himself reasons primarily by playing on roots and by playing on elemental images, by making these elements emerge in different domains and at different levels. His use of analogy is not purely random.

There is here, then, a kind of "reasoning together" of things which is important to the integrity of the sermon experience. We should recognize it for what it is, particularly in light of the academic testing by syllogism to which African subjects have been submitted. We may call this a reasoning by syllogisms of association. It is a kind of reckoning with an argument of images, as it were, which suggests a reconciliation of parts. More particularly, it represents a reconciliation of the social subjects of that thought: men and women, the living and the dead, men and the gods. These subjects are both problematic, inchoate, within themselves—What is a man? Who are the gods?—and they are problematic in their relationship to each other.

As far as the inchoate condition of the subjects themselves, Bwiti regularly, fulfilling its role as a religion, predicates a more concrete and manageable identity upon the believers. That is, metaphors and metonyms are brought to bear upon them personally. In the sermon cited, for example, it is said of Fang that "they are forest," and the identification of the members of Bwiti with trees or with the forest is recurrent and basic. It is what we might exect of a religion in the equatorial regions. Another inchoate subject of concern is life itself. What is life? The sermon offers the metaphor: "life is sugar cane," that is, it comes in sections, and if approached section by section it can be consumed with sweet satisfaction.

More interesting, however, are the sequences of "syllogism-like" predications in which two subjects are related to a middle or common image which is lost in the process of the "argument" leaving the two subjects in a situation of identity, equation, or reconciliation. Thus in paragraph 17 of the sermon cited, women are first equated with the adzap tree below and men with the adzap tree above. By eliminating the common term, the prevalent image, men and women are reconciled. This reconciliation of the sexes is one of the main objects of Bwiti.

The same kind of identification or reconciliation of focal religious subjects is accomplished in paragraph 9 where twins are used as the common term. We are told in brief compass that brothers and sisters are twins, and wives and husbands are twins, and mothers and children are twins. By dropping the mediating image, the central term, all three pairs are equated—as, indeed, they are equated in the archetypal stages of creation in Bwiti mythology.

Often these syllogisms involve complementarity of relationship. We have seen this in the equation of men and women to the adzap tree: men above, women below. In paragraph 17, this is seen in the equation of men to the drumstick and woman to the drum. This follows the Aristotelian formula

> man is to drumstick as woman is to drum
> drum is to drumstick as man is to woman.

Here we see the way that a contiguity is transformed into a similarity and is then translated back into a contiguity or a reconciliation between male and female. For it is not enough to note the metaphor. The spiritual intelligence bound up in the metaphor is that men and women can make music together.

> drum : drumstick :: man : woman
> .they make music together.

We see here, incidentally, an important kind of edification bound up in these puzzling analogies. Orderliness, the structure, perceived in one domain of experience, that of music instruments, is used to inform and structure—edify is the term I prefer—an orderliness in another more inchoate domain of experience, in this case, the domain of social and sexual relationships.

Finally we see in the sermon sequences of associations in which the social subjects of Bwiti undergo transformations of identity. They gain in the process a polyvalence and, at the same time, an equation with other social subjects. For example, in paragraph 11 we begin with an association of Zame to the Otunga tree. He is subsequently associated to the stool of birth, the cross, and finally the adzap tree in that sequence. Subsequently, as we have seen, man and woman are associated to the adzap tree and thus to Zame. We have the following syllogism of association.

$$Zame=otunga=stool=cross=adzap$$
$$man=woman=adzap$$
$$Zame=man \ \& \ woman$$

By this sequence Zame is found in every man and woman—a reconciliation which is a major and frequently stated purpose of Bwiti. It is a reconciliation that is not accomplished by direct statement but indirectly by a sequence of metaphoric predictions. In the end all these mediating subordinate images of the transformaion-reconciliation drop away, leaving the desired edifying equation.

Conclusion: Images of Edification to our Eyes

The very title of this presentation with its mellifluous latinate sesquipedalian intimations of mysterious intelligence—and possible revelation—exemplifies in one sense the mode of thought we have been exploring. In another sense—that of the imageless abstract quality of such terms—it is just what this mode of thought is not. For what we have before us is iconic thought primarily producing and working with images more or less visual and concrete in effect. It is not abstract or symbolic thought in Bruner's (1964) sense and the information it communicates is not coded in rules to be abstracted and applied. It is the nature of iconic thought to have much more of a personal component and also to excite contextualization. We may venture that this is because images arise out of personal experience and excite personal experience in their decoding. And images are, we may also venture, a part of larger contexts and lead the mind out to these larger contexts.

Thus, where it might have been expected of this author that he would stick to his last and develop for a modern science-oriented audience the abstract principles by which edification and puzzlement operate, we find him to be also an iconoclast embarking on his discussion by first contextualizing it into the colonial situation. And why? Because this specific problem of edification reminds me of a personal experience I had administering a narrow-context impersonal intellectual test in Africa. I was suddenly assaulted by a group of young men who sought out the ultimate context for those innocent exercises in visual illusion. They were asking me in effect: "These puzzles you are putting to us, they are a part of what larger whole?" I had, frankly, sticking to my last, given very little thought to that larger whole.

In a compartmentalized society like our own we are very able to compartmentalize our intellectual exercises. We are well schooled to heuristics—to looking for rules and applying them in limited and apparently self-contained contexts. That's intelligence for you! But more traditional societies with pretensions to cosmogony, and most traditional societies have that pretension, are more totalistic. Intelligence is a matter of relating to the context, in developing it, revitalizing it. Hence, it is an intelligence that employs images to a high degree in actual or suggested analogic relation. It plays upon similarities in experience, and in that play it suggests or requires answers that suggest overarching contiguities—cosmologies, totalities which encompass, absorb, and defeat particularities. All this is rarely done in a direct and explicit manner. "By indirections find directions out."

As well schooled as we all are in the modern specialized compartmentalized societies, we tend to misread in a schoolmasterish way the masters of iconic thought. We look for a limited set of applicable rules, or we are simply puzzled, and we fail to see how these masters edify by puzzlement. Our inclination is to deprive puzzles of their mystery—that's science for you—and thus we fail to see how the masters mysteriously suggest an overarching order—how they give concrete identity to inchoate subjects, how they reconcile these subjects. It is hard for us to tolerate ambiguities of this kind, let alone understand their function.

In the end, of course, the error is to suggest too great a difference between this very traditional and modern thought. That was long ago discovered by Lévy-Bruhl (1975) when he looked around and discovered towards the end of his life that there were quantities of prelogical thought going on all around him in French life. And so if we look around in academia, we will find quantities of edification by puzzlement. A great lot of it is found among the structuralists themselves who have so creatively put us on to traditional thought. As Edmund Leach said of Lévi-Strauss: "He gives me ideas even when I don't understand him." For many of Lévi-Strauss' readers, that's a lot of the time. But we all recognize that his work is full of delectable images.

NOTES

1. See the section on the Fang in Marshall H. Segall, Donald T. Camp-

bell, and M. J. Herskovits (1976).

2. The team has brought forth a series of publications on this topic. The first findings are summarized in Cole and Scribner (1973). The team has recently dispersed and left Rockefeller.

3. The use of these syllogisms and the results are reported in Scribner (1977).

4. This observation is taken from a xeroxed paper David Lancy circulated at an African Studies convention. The paper was among my many papers lost on a voyage to Europe aboard the S. S. Stefan Batory in October 1977, thrown overboard as it appears. At the time of writing this article Lancy, who worked in Liberia with the Cole-Scribner team, was in New Guinea. I regret the lack of reference.

5. We might argue, with Lévi-Strauss in mind, that the riddle is the primordial culture-nature transformer.

6. Compare Keith Basso (1976) and J. W. Fernandez (1976–77).

7. For a discussion of these devices, see J. W. Fernandez (1966).

BIBLIOGRAPHY

Basso, Keith. 1976. "Wise Words of the Western Apache." In *Meaning in Anthropology*, edited by Keith Basso and Henry Selby, pp. 93–122. Albuquerque: University of New Mexico Press.

Bruner, Jerome S. 1964. "The Course of Cognitive Growth." *American Psychologist* 19:1–15.

Cole, Michael, and Scribner, Sylvia. 1973. *Culture and Thought.* New York: John Wiley.

Fernandez, James W. 1966. "Unbelievably Subtle Words: Representation and Integration in the Sermons of an African Reformative Cult." *Journal of the History of Religions* 6:43–69.

———. 1976–77. "Poetry in Motion—Being Moved by Mockery, Amusement and Mortality in the Asturian Mountains." *New Literary History* 8:459–83.

Geertz, Clifford. 1973. *The Interpretation of Cultures; Select Essays.* New York: Basic Books.

Jakobson, Roman. 1960. "Linguistics and Poetics." In *Style in Language,* edited by Thomas A. Sebeok, pp. 355–73. Cambridge: M. I. T. Press (Technology Press of M. I. T.).

Köngas Maranda, Ellie. 1971. "The Logic of Riddles." In *Structural Analysis of Oral Tradition*, edited by Ellie Köngas Maranda and Pierre Maranda, pp. 189–232. Philadelphia: University of Pennsylvania Press.

Lévi-Strauss, Claude. 1966. *The Savage Mind.* Chicago: University of Chicago Press.

Lévy-Bruhl, Lucien. 1975. *The Notebooks on Primitive Mentality.* Translated by Peter Riviere. New York: Harper and Row.

Scribner, Sylvia, Forthcoming. "Modes of Thinking and Ways of Speaking: Culture and Logic Reconsidered." In *Discourse Production and Comprehension*, edited by R. O. Freedle. Hillsdale, N.J.: Ablex.

Segall, Marshall H., Campbell, Donald T., and Herskovits, M. J. 1966. *The Influence of Culture on Visual Perception.* Indianapolis: Bobbs-Merrill.

Vygotsky, L. 1962. *Thought and Language.* Cambridge: M. I. T. Press.

The Story of Kintu
Myth, Death, and Ontology in Buganda

by Benjamin Ray

> A Fall of some sort or other—the creation, as it were, of the non-absolute—is the fundamental postulate of the moral history of man. Without this hypothesis, man is unintelligible; with it, every phenomenon is explicable. The mystery itself is too profound for human insight.
>
> COLERIDGE
> (as quoted in Burke, 1979: 174)

In this paper I shall examine one of the most common myths in sub-Sahara Africa: the myth of the origins of death. Typically, this myth tells not only of the origins of death but also of the origins of disease and suffering and of the division between the earth and the sky and the separation between mankind and the creator sky-god. This form of the myth links the origins of death to the wider structure of the universe, and hence is cosmogonic in intent. Many African creation myths begin by depicting a divine sky-world against which the human earthly world developed through acts of human opposition to the creator God. The origin of mortality is thus explained in terms of the wider cosmic and moral polarities between sky and earth, divinity and humanity, and life and death, which characterize traditional African cosmology. In this way African myths of the origins of death often express basic ontological insights into the nature of the human condition and the structure of the universe (see Ray, 1976:24–37).

The Baganda[1] of central Uganda tell a myth of this type. It is called "the story of Kintu" (*olugero lwa Kintu*). Like other myths, the story of Kintu contains several different meanings which are associated with different contexts of interpretation. I shall discuss some of the meanings which the Baganda have ascribed to the story, including

Christian interpretations developed during the colonial period, which I have gathered from sources published in Luganda and from discussions with Baganda themselves. My own analysis will concentrate upon the story's ontological significance in relation to traditional Kiganda social structure and cosmology. My purpose will be to show how the myth employs certain fundamental moral, social, ritual, and cosmological ideas, and "projects" them onto the primordial past in order to explain the ultimate origins of the cosmos and of life and death.

The Story and Its Christian Interpreters

Nowadays, the Baganda are acquainted with the story of Kintu in both oral and written form. The myth was first published in Luganda in 1882 by the Catholic White Fathers who were among the first missionaries to reach Buganda (Le Veux, 1914:449–58). Since then, the story has been available in printed vernacular versions, the most recent being a school book used in the second year of primary school, last printed in 1970 (Mulira, 1951; 1965). The summary of the myth presented here is based upon an authoritative account collected and published in Luganda in 1902 by Buganda's first and foremost ethnographer, Sir Apolo Kaggwa (Kaggwa, 1951:1–8). Although current oral tradition agrees substantially with Kaggwa's account, his version is more significantly detailed, and it is the source of all subsequently published accounts in Luganda.

> Kintu wandered alone into the uninhabited country of Buganda accompanied only by his cow. He was met by a woman called Nnambi who came from the sky with her brothers. Nnambi took an immediate liking to Kintu, despite his unknown origins and barbaric ways (he ate only cow dung and drank only cow urine and did not know from whence he came), and Nnambi told Kintu that she wished to marry him. After hearing of Nnambi's intentions, Nnambi's father Ggulu ordered his sons to steal Kintu's cow and to take it to the sky; whereupon, Nnambi invited Kintu to come to the sky to recover his cow and to take her away. When Kintu arrived, Ggulu subjected him to a series of difficult tests to see if he were "really" Kintu. He was told to consume a houseful of food; to cut firewood from solid rock; to collect a pot full of water from dew; and to find his cow in Ggulu's large herd of cattle. Through his own cleverness and with the help of nature Kintu performed each of these difficult tasks, thus proving that he was the heroic Kintu. Ggulu then pre-

sented Kintu with his daughter Nnambi (as his wife) and provided
them with everything they needed to establish their home on earth:
cows, goats, sheep, chickens, plantains, and millet. Ggulu told Kintu
and Nnambi to depart quickly before Nnambi's brother Walumbe
(Death) returned, and he ordered them never to come back, even
if they forgot something, otherwise Walumbe would want to go with
them. Kintu and Nnambi immediately set forth on their journey.
On the way Nnambi remembered that she had forgotten to bring
the millet for her chickens. When she informed Kintu he reminded
her of Ggulu's warning and told her not to go back. But Nnambi
returned for the millet. When Ggulu saw her, he said, "Didn't I tell
you not to come back for anything that you forgot and that if you
met Walumbe he would not allow you to go with Kintu alone?"
Then Walumbe arrived and said that Kintu had taken away his sister and he told Nnambi that he wanted to go with her. "Alright,"
said Ggulu, "you may go with your brother Walumbe," and they
left to rejoin Kintu. When Kintu saw Walumbe, he said, "We are
not going to be able to manage him because he is mad (insane) . . .
how are we going to cope with Walumbe? Alright, we shall finish
the journey with him." After Nnambi had given birth to three chil-
ren, Walumbe visited Kintu and asked him for one of his children
to be a cook and a household servant. Kintu refused, saying that
otherwise he would not have a child to give to Ggulu as his "share"
of Nnambi's children. Walumbe went away and remained silent.
After Nnambi had given birth to more children, Walumbe again
asked Kintu for a child, and again Kintu refused. Walumbe then
told Kintu that he would kill his children, but Kintu was puzzled
and asked how he would kill them (because no one had died before). When Kintu's children began to die, Kintu went to Ggulu
and complained about Walumbe. Ggulu reminded Kintu of his
warning and said that if Nnambi had not returned, Kintu's children
would not have died. Ggulu then told Kintu to take back Nnambi's
other brother, Kayiikuuzi, who would try to catch Walumbe and
bring him back to the sky. Kayiikuuzi's first attempt failed and Walumbe fled into the ground at a place called Ttanda. Then Kayiikuuzi
devised a plan. He told Kintu to order everyone to stay indoors for
two days and to take their provisions with them; no one was to go
out not even to fetch water or to herd goats, and no one was to
raise the alarm if they saw Walumbe so that Kayiikuuzi could catch
him. Everyone did as they were told, except two young children
who went out to herd their goats. When they saw Walumbe, they
cried out, and Walumbe fled back into the ground and went down
beyond Kayiikuuzi's reach. Kayiikuuzi was angry and told the children that they had done wrong. "Alright," said Kintu, "if Walumbe
wants to kill my children, let him. But he will not be able to finish
all of them because I, Kintu, will always continue to beget more."

When Ggulu heard this, he said, "So be it. Let them (Kintu and his children) stay below. You, Kayiikuuzi, will stay with us."

This myth belongs to the kind of narrative which the Baganda call *lugero* (pl. *ngero*), "story" or "fable." Such stories, of which there are many in Luganda, tell about the adventures of men and animals. Some of these are trickster tales, some are hero tales, some are etiological tales, and most are combinations of these forms (Nabasuta, 1974). Almost all are didactic and allegorical in some way and point a moral lesson. Every *lugero* is therefore said to have one or more "meanings" (*makulu*) which may vary according to the context in which the storyteller relates the tale. Some stories have more or less fixed meanings stated in the form of proverbs (also called *ngero*, specifically, *ngero nsonge*) which appear at the end of the story. Unlike historical narratives (*byafaayo*), which are full of royal names, clan names, and place names, *ngero* involve basically timeless contexts and generalized social circumstances. Compared to historical narrative, *lugero* is essentially fictional. It is a popular literary form, whereas history is highly literalistic and is the product of clan and royal institutions. The purpose of *lugero* is not to record historical fact but to provide verbal entertainment, to teach moral truths, and sometimes to explain the origins of things.

In keeping with its *lugero* form, the story of Kintu therefore lacks any specific sociological and geographical references, and its events occur in the timeless period of the beginnings. It is an etiological and a morally didactic popular story open to a variety of interpretations, depending upon the social and ritual contexts to which it, or even parts of it, may be related. Other "historical" narratives about Kintu form part of royal and clan traditions and are subject to official interpretation.

The structure of the story also exhibits the typical lugero dramatic form: adventure—predicament—resolution. In this instance the sequence is: marriage—death—life. Kintu and Nnambi marry and settle on earth and introduce Death into the world. Despite all efforts, Death remains and continues to kill. Nevertheless, Kintu proclaims partial victory over Death and promises that even though Death will continue to kill people, the Baganda will not die out; thus insuring the collective life of the society. Hence the proverb to which Kintu's concluding words may refer: "The descendants of Kintu will never be finished [die out]."

Most Baganda, I am told, tend to regard the story as a simple tale about how the Baganda originated and how death came into the world, and they take this to be its meaning. Indeed, the story is usually told to children to explain just these matters. But Baganda comments on the story also go beyond this etiological dimension and emphasize the story's general lesson about humanity (*obuntubulamu*) and its particular lesson about disobedience (*obutawulira*). Like many *ngero*, the story of Kintu illustrates a moral lesson with a negative example; it makes clear the norm of obedience (*obuwulize*) by showing the disastrous results which followed from the mythical breach of the norm. More specifically, the Baganda sometimes say that it was Nnambi's disobedience which "brought (or caused) death (*yaleeta olumbe*)," and this is often said to be the story's particular meaning.

The story clearly portrays Nnambi as the bringer of Death, and it also suggests that she was ultimately responsible for human mortality. According to Ggulu's admonishing words to Kintu, "If your wife had not returned, your children would not have died." Even though Kintu and his children were significantly involved in the story, Nnambi is sometimes regarded as the primary agent because she was the first to act wrongly and to disobey. As one of the Baganda told me, "the person who strikes the first blow is fined more heavily [according to Kiganda law] than the one who strikes back." Hence the meaning of the story is often said to be about Nnambi's "disobedience" (*obutawulira*) and "rebellion" (*obujeemu*) against authority. For example, Mulira's primary school version of the story has Nnambe lament "[why] did I rebel (*njeema*) and refuse to obey (*okuwulira*)?" (Mulira, 1970, vol. 2:6). As the missionary anthropologist John Roscoe reported in 1911, Nnambi "is said to have been the cause of all evil, sickness, and death" (Roscoe, 1911:136).

In light of Nnambe's role, some Baganda writers have suggested that the story also explains the inferior position of women in traditional Buganda. Writing in 1901, Kaggwa indicated that "Perhaps all the ritual taboos imposed upon women were the result of Nnambi who brought Walumbe who killed Kintu's children" (Kaggwa, 1934:306). In 1955 Mulira added the following conclusion to his school book edition of the story: "Because of the suffering which she [Nnambi] brought, the female in Buganda was treated like a slave and regarded as a mere piece of property, until the coming of Christianity which brightened her honor" (Mulira, 1970, vol. 2:30).

It seems doubtful, however, that the story traditionally contained this meaning. The social position of women in traditional Buganda does not seem to have been greatly inferior to that of women in other traditional societies. It is more likely that Kaggwa and Mulira, as educated Christians who abhored much of the pagan past (as did their missionary teachers), sought in the Kintu story an explanation for the position of women which Christianity and colonialism tried to modify. Kaggwa's and Mulira's interpretations may also reflect Islamic influence which preceded Christianity in Buganda by some fifteen years. According to Islamic teaching as reflected in Swahili tradition, the inferior social position of women is justified by Eve's behavior in the Biblical Genesis story which Islam shares with Judeo-Christian tradition (Knappert, 1970).

In this connection it is also significant that the first recorded version of the story collected by the White Fathers (in 1882) attributes the initial misdeed of returning for the millet to Kintu, not to Nnambi (Le Veux, 1914:455). Although this version was recorded during the first years of missionary activity from purportedly authentic sources (most likely at the royal palace), it is impossible to tell whether it was merely a local variant or whether it was more widely known. A similar version was collected in 1902 from peasant informants who were said to have been untainted by Islamic or Christian teachings (Johnston, 1902:700–05). Today, at any rate, the Nnambi version is the accepted form of the story, perhaps because of its parallels to the Biblical Adam and Eve account.

During the early colonial period, the Biblical story dominated literate Baganda interpretations of the Kintu myth. Both stories explained the origins of death in terms of a woman's act of disobedience against the commandment of a sky-dwelling Father God. Because of these parallels, Baganda Christians who were eager to relate their own myth to their newly adopted religion began to interpret the story of Kintu in Christian terms in order to reveal its "true" meaning. Moreover, the Baganda began to regard the parallels between the two stories as evidence of an original and independent revelation from God.

It was the Catholic White Fathers who first suggested (in 1894) that the story of Kintu might contain the vestiges of an original divine revelation. According to the White Fathers, the Kintu story revealed the following resemblances to Christian doctrine:

Ggulu would be the King of the skies, the source of all being; Kintu the first man, Nnambi the companion given by God to man; Wa-

lumbe would be death, the result of the disobedience of Kintu; Kayiikuuzi, the Son of the Sky, who devoted himself to the abolition
of death on earth (Le Veux, 1914:449).

Encouraged, perhaps, by their missionary teachers the Baganda
began to comment upon these parallels. Writing in 1912, a contributor
to the newly founded Catholic journal *Munno* pointed out that the
Kintu story "tells us that wrong doing (*okusobya*) came first from
woman" as in the Bible (*Munno*, 1912:50). The same writer also saw
a resemblance between "the fruit which came from a tree and the
millet which also came from a 'tree.'" Similarly, the Protestant historian James Miti pointed out that "both Nnambi Nantuluntulu and
Eve yielded to temptation through the question of food and it was
that that caused death to come into the world (Miti, n.d.:9). More generally, in Kaggwa's view, Nnambi and Eve could be said to have
"brought death in the same way," namely, through disobedience to a
divine commandment (Kaggwa, 1951:115).

For some Baganda these parallels proved that the story of Kintu
contained a divine revelation, showing that the Baganda possessed a
genuine knowledge of God long before the advent of the missionaries.
According to one writer in *Munno*, "our religion (*dini*, Christianity)
did not teach us something new[about God], but reminded us of
something we already knew" (*Munno*, 1916:177).

For both Catholic and Protestant Baganda, the figure of Ggulu
had become identical to the Biblical God whom the missionaries and
the Baganda alike called Katonda, or Creator. According to the Protestant clergyman Bartholomayo Zimbe, "the meaning of the name
Kintu is from the expression *Kintu Kya Mukama*, that is, 'the thing of
the Lord' which means *Muntu wa Katonda*, or 'man of God'" (Zimbe,
1939:6). By equating Ggulu with God, the Baganda could not only
interpret the Kintu story in light of Genesis, they could also adapt it
more closely to the Genesis account to show its Christian meaning.

Miti was one of the first to "re-tell" the Kintu story in this way.
In his version the name of Ggulu was replaced by the name Katonda.
Walumbe was no longer portrayed as the brother of Nnambi but as
an independent "enemy" of man, analogous to Satan. Miti's account
focused upon Nnambi's act of disobedience in returning for the millet
and upon Katonda's curse which expels Nnambi and Kintu from the
sky. "Go away from my sight, you rebels, who rebelled against my
orders," says Katonda, "and now you are taking with you your enemy

[Death], he is sure to go on killing you. . . ." In this version mortality is inflicted upon Kintu and Nnambi by a righteous God as the punishment for disobedience, whereas in the traditional account death is seen as an inevitable, though accidental, consequence. Thus, Miti concludes, it was "through [the] disobedience of Muntu Benne (Kintu) and Namuntu Banddi (Nnambi) to the voice of the Lord God that we are subjected to death" (Miti, n.d.:3–11).

A similar version of the story appears in Dr. Ernest Kalibala's Ph.D. dissertation written in 1946. According to Kalibala, Kintu accused Nnambi of disobeying both himself and God, and he asked God to punish her. God responded by expelling Kintu, Nnambi, and Walumbe from Heaven, "All of you have disobeyed me," God said. "You shall go to earth and toil." On their journey, each person blamed the other. "Kintu blamed his wife for her disobedience; [Nnambi] Nantululu blamed the chicken because she could not let it die; Mr. Walumbe blamed them all for plotting to leave him all alone in Heaven" (Kalibala, 1946:9–14). Because of constant quarrels, Kintu asked Walumbe to leave, whereupon Walumbe threatened to harm Kintu and his children, and he left to become lord over the underworld, or Hell. In this version, human life on earth is therefore regarded as a punishment from God, while death is seen as the result of Walumbe's quarrels with Kintu.

Mulira's school book version of the story, first published in 1951, carried the process of adaptation further and introduced the Christian idea of salvation. An illustration in the first edition depicted Ggulu as an enthroned Father God surrounded by rays of light and by winged angels. Kintu and Nnambi appear as diminutive figures kneeling at Ggulu's feet, their hands raised in supplication. Towards the end of the story Nnambi and Kintu confess that they have "sinned" (okwonoona) before Ggulu and that their sins have driven them from him. The Christian promise of salvation is prefigured in the image of Kayiikuuzi who is referred to as the Savior (Mulokozi), the same term by which the Luganda Bible refers to Christ. When Kayiikuuzi arrives, he informs Walumbe that he has been sent "in the place of the Father," and he pursues Walumbe into the Underworld (Magombe), as Christ pursued Satan into Hell. After Kayiikuuzi fails to catch Walumbe because of the "sins" of Nnambi, Kintu, and the children, Ggulu declares that both Good and Evil will reign over the earth and that people will have to choose between them. The story also draws a prophetic contrast between "The first Nnambi who brought Wa-lumbe" and "Another Nnambi who will bring the Savior (*Mulokozi*)." The story ends with Ggulu's promise that "The Word (*Kigambo*) will be born in Buganda, and it will kill Death. It will save the Baganda. The word will build my house on a firm rock against which Hell (*Magombe*) will have no power" (Mulira, 1955, vol. 2:34).

The Theme of Obedience

While the Christian interpretation is still accepted today, Baganda also recognize the story's traditional moral meaning and its broader moral significance. Baganda have emphasized to me that when the story is seen in its traditional social context, the theme of disobedience clearly extends beyond Nnambi's initial act and includes the acts of Kintu and his children. Thus Baganda say that Kintu could be considered responsible for Nnambi's act of disobedience. According to Kiganda marital ethics, it was the husband's duty to make his wife act obediently. Indeed, Ggulu's words of admonishment to Kintu, "If your wife had not returned, your children would not have died," can be interpreted as a direct moral reproach against Kintu. In a shorter version of the story published by Kaggwa, Kintu's fault is emphasized.

Here, Katonda rebukes Kintu and dismisses his complaint against Walumbe saying, "Did I not tell you to depart early in the morning? Be gone! Do not ask me anything. Go away!" (Kaggwa, 1971:1). As the story also points out, Kintu's children "did very wrong" in diso-beying their father and thus spoiling Kayiikuuzi's plan.[2] In Kaggwa's full-length version of the story, Kintu explicitly assumes responsibility for his children's behavior and admits that he "made a mistake." In the text collected by the White Fathers the matter is put more strong-ly. Kayiikuuzi accuses Kintu of permitting his children to disobey, and he asks rhetorically, "Is Kintu mad?" Mulira's version attempts to distribute the blame more equally and has Kintu confess, "I did wrong, and all my people did wrong before Ggulu."

It is not surprising that the theme of disobedience involves all members of the "primal" family. For, among other things, the Kintu story tells about the origins of the fundamental marital, affinal, and parental relationships which define the traditional Kiganda family. Each of these relationships was conceived in an "authoritarian" way and required acts of obedience and respect on the part of the inferior to the superior parties: wives to husbands, husbands to brothers-in-law and to fathers-in-law, and children to fathers. So fundamental were these norms that failure to abide by them was not just a case of disobedience but ultimately of rebellion (*obujeemu*), for it implied the refusal to recognize authority and hence subversion of the social order.

As the story of Kintu shows, the most important norms of obedience and respect are those which constitute the family. In the past a wife was expected to be submissive and obedient to her husband, or else she was beaten. When a woman married, she left home and pledged herself to a new master. Children, too, had to obey and respect their parents, especially their fathers, and they were physically punished if they did not. Children knelt on the floor when speaking and acted instantly when told to do something. One child wrote in answer to a questionnaire (in the 1950s) that "to disobey a father is the worst crime a child can commit" (Richards, 1964:249).

In the same survey children also reported that disobedience and failure to show respect were the two faults for which they were most frequently punished. Children were often given small tasks and sent on minor errands as a means of obedience training. For boys, who were often sent away from home at a minor age to live with relatives, this training was a key to success in the wider world. In Buganda's traditionally competitive society, dutiful and respectful behavior could lead to one of the many clan offices or to one of the coveted royal appointments. As Richards has noted, the attitude of child to father was characteristic of all subordinate relationships in Buganda, of peasant to lord and of subjects to king (Richards, 1964:270). For this reason, perhaps, filial relationships assume central importance in the Kintu story, which begins and ends with acts of filial disobedience.

The story of Kintu thus served as a powerful social charter by showing the disaster which occurred when the norms of family authority were broken. According to the myth, the Baganda became mortal when their ancestors broke the very norms by which every man, woman, and child must now abide.

Although I have never asked Baganda whether the story expresses something like the idea of original sin or the idea of the fall of mankind, it is clear from the story and from its implicit moral assumptions that it proceeds from the premise of the fallibility of human nature. The story does not say, nor do the Baganda believe, that the

Baganda are morally flawed because of the actions of Nnambi and Kintu. Rather, the story reflects the essential "human nature" or the "humaneness" (*obuntubulamu*) of Nnambi and Kintu, in Nnambi's returning for her chickens and in Kintu's permitting her to return and in permitting Walumbe to join them on earth. According to Mulira's version, "Nnambi had the freedom (*eddembe*) of a woman, and Kintu had the humaneness (*obuntubulamu*) of a man."[3] The story is therefore understood allegorically, like other *ngero*, as a portrayal of the human moral condition, not as an explanation of it.

The Ritual Dimension

Although the moral context is the one to which the Baganda usually refer when discussing the significance of the story, it is not the only context in which the story has meaning. Looked at from the point of view of the context of the funeral ceremonies, the question of human responsibility recedes into the background and the question of non-human agency comes into view. According to Kaggwa, the symbolism of the funeral ceremonies suggests that it was not Nnambi but her chickens which were the ultimate cause of death. After the burial of the corpse, the state of mourning or "death" (*olumbe*) was ended by a ceremony called "destroying death" (*okwaabya olumbe*). This ceremony involved the eating of a chicken by the male relatives who gathered in the house of the deceased. In this house, whose temporary "owner" was Walumbe, the men killed and ate a chicken which they roasted over a fire made from the center post of the house. According to Kaggwa, the chicken was regarded in this context as "the sorcerer who brought [or caused] death" (Kaggwa, 1934:202).

As Kaggwa points out, it was for the sake of her chickens that Nnambi returned and fetched the millet, thus bringing death. By killing and eating a chicken while celebrating the "killing of death" (*okutta olumbe*), the male relatives thereby killed and disposed of the ultimate agent of death. Afterwards, the heir to the deceased's household was installed and the normal processes of life were restored. In the case of royal death, the funerary fowl was a human being. The victim was a captive from Bunyoro, Buganda's traditional enemy. He was wounded with a spear by the newly installed king and taken to the borders between Buganda and the Kingdom of Bunyoro where he

was killed and his body burned in a fire made from the center post of
the deceased king's house (Kaggwa, 1934:13). Following this, the new
king entered his palace, established his capital, and the life of the
kingdom returned to normal.

The story of Kintu thus explains the meaning of the funerary
fowl which was the scapegoat of death; and the sacrificial fowl reveals a further dimension in the myth. In this context, the moral significance of the myth is replaced by a ritual meaning which shows the
funerary fowl-scapegoat to be the ultimate culprit.

Another ritual interpretation has been suggested by Mulira in his
second primary school edition (1965). This edition, which is still in
print, concludes with a speech in which Kintu lays down basic ritual
features of the Kiganda marital process. Henceforth, Kintu declares,
men shall give cows as a marriage dowery, as Kintu himself did;
women may no longer eat chicken, as a sign of Nnambi's momentous
indiscretion; husbands must always respect their brothers-in-law by
giving them a cock, thus avoiding Kintu's fatal mistake of insulting
Walumbe; and women must always carry chickens on the tops of their
heads in remembrance of Nnambi's forgetfulness (Mulira, 1970, vol.
2:29–30).

Mulira does not explain why he changed his mind and abandoned
the Christian interpretation of the story found in his first edition, but
he clearly intends the reader of the third edition to understand the
story as a form of ritual charter for the traditional Kiganda marriage.
According to Mulira, all men and women enter into marriage in the
way that Kintu and Nnambi did, and the basic marital procedures
derive from their original example. In fact, the myth coincides more
closely with the traditional marital procedures than even Mulira's text
suggests.

In the past a young man not only had to give cattle to his prospective father-in-law, as Kintu did, he also had to visit his father-in-
law's home and serve him for a time doing domestic chores, such as
brewing beer and cutting fire wood, to show that he would make a
dutiful son-in-law (Kalibala, 1946:243ff.; Kakooza, 1967:119). In the
myth, Kintu is made to perform similar, though more difficult domestic
tasks, to show that he is "really" Kintu, and thus to prove his worthi-
ness to his prospective father-in-law, Ggulu. Traditionally, the bride's
brothers helped to arrange their sister's marriage, as Nnambi's brothers

did, and one of them presented the suitor to the father-in-law. In the
1930s, Mair recorded a betrothal ceremony in which the brother jokingly voiced the same complaint against his sister's suitor that Walumbe spoke against Kintu. According to Mair's account, "The brother
presented the suitor with jesting statements that he was trying to steal
the girl and that his sister was rebelling *(okujeema)* against him and
no longer wanted to cook for him." Speaking on behalf of the bride,
the girl's paternal aunt said, "I am grown up, my time has come to
marry, I have found my master" (Mair, 1934:80). Thereupon the
father called to his wife and said, "This child has rebelled against us;
she has found her master." As this dialogue implies, every marriage
required that the bride give up serving her brothers and leave her
father's household authority for a new master's. When the bride departed from her father's home for the last time, her father provided
her with provisions for the wedding feast, including livestock (a cow,
goats, and sheep, if he were a chief), plaintains, and chickens, as
Nnambi's father did. So, too, the bride's brother visited his sister's
new home soon after marriage to establish his affinal ties and later
asked the husband for one of his children as his "share" *(ndobolo)*, as
Walumbe did.

From a Kiganda point of view, Mulira's interpretation of the
Kintu story as a marriage charter is therefore entirely plausible. Although Kiganda marriage rites contain no references to Nnambi and
Kintu, Mulira's interpretation fits in with the Baganda tendency to justify institutional procedures by reference to historical or legendary
precedent, especially to the founding deeds of Kintu.

Immortality, Mortality, and the Mother's Brother

Nevertheless, the story does not provide the complete scenario for
the marital ceremonies. Although it draws upon certain social and ritual features which serve to explain and justify marriage rites, the
wider purpose of the story is to explain the origins of death and the
structure of the universe. It does this by utilizing certain social and
ritual paradigms associated with marriage, the main one being the
figure of the mother's brother (*kojja*) who is made to represent death.

If we look at the story from this perspective and also recognize
the fact that the actors are made to implicitly "break" fundamental

social rules—which do not exist yet—in order to establish them, we can
see that the problem of immortality and mortality, life and death, is
presented at the very beginning. It appears first in the unconventional
behavior of Nnambi's father who tries to marry off his daughter without the knowledge of her brother. Given the important role of brothers
in arranging their sisters' marriages and in serving as their sisters' legal
guardians, it is surprising that Ggulu should have deliberately given
Nnambi in marriage to Kintu without Walumbe's knowledge and that
he should have tried to prevent Walumbe from joining his sister on
earth. In doing so, Ggulu was implicitly breaking a fundamental marital principle, the establishment of affinal relations. If, however, Ggulu
already knew that Walumbe would kill Kintu's children, as some versions suggest, then his actions are understandable. Ggulu was attempting to save Kintu's children from the threat of mortality, represented
by Walumbe. In effect, Ggulu appears to have violated Kiganda marital practice in order to keep Kintu's children, the Baganda, immortal.
Ggulu's action thus expresses an implicit opposition between immortality and marriage, as the Baganda know it, including the bearing of
children, which is the mark of the human condition.

The same conflict is apparent in the episode of Nnambi's return
for the millet. Although the millet appears to be an insignificant item,
it is the principal feed for chickens in Buganda, and in one version of
the story Kintu points out that without the millet the chickens will die.
While this, too, might appear to be insignificant, especially at the risk
of incurring death, the loss of chickens would be disastrous for the
conventional Kiganda marriage. It would deprive Kintu and Nnambi
of the chief symbols of paternal authority and affinal relations, without
which the Kiganda marriage cannot exist. In the past, when a bride
departed from her father's home for the last time (after the ceremony
of "returning the butter"), she took with her provisions for the marriage feast, including a cock which was tied to the head ring on the
top of her head. Upon arriving at her new home, the husband lifted
off the cock, and the bride presented it to him while kneeling on the
ground in recognition of his superior authority. The cock was then
killed, cooked, and served to the husband. The gift of the cock meant
that the wife was now truly married (Kaggwa, 1934:175; Roscoe,
1911:91; Haydon, 1960: Chapter 6). (A cock was also given by women
to their husbands as a means of reconciling them after they quarreled.)
The day after the marriage feast the new husband was required to

visit his brother-in-law's house and give him a cock in recognition of his new affinal relationship. After that, whenever a male in-law, especially the *kojja*, came to visit it was compulsary for the husband to provide him with a cock to eat. He had to place it alive in his hands, and the visitor returned it saying "Go and kill it."

As traditional signs and symbols of the marital state, chickens were an essential possession for the married couple and still are in Buganda. If Nnambi had not returned for the millet, her chickens would have died and she would have been deprived of the symbols of being married. Nnambi's return for the millet thus poses again the opposition between immortality and conventional Kiganda marriage. By returning for the millet Nnambi secured the necessary symbols for her marriage but at the risk of her children's immortality.

In contrast to the figure of Ggulu who stands for the celestial principles of immortality and divinity, Walumbe represents the earthly principles of marriage and affinity which define the situation of mankind. As we have seen, Walumbe's insistence upon accompanying Nnambi to her new home is entirely justified by Kiganda marital procedures. Indeed, a brother must pay a visit to his sister's home soon after marriage in order to establish the affinal relationship. In tacit recognition of Walumbe's rights in this matter, Ggulu readily grants Walumbe's request and allows him to accompany Nnambi, even though the consequences will be fatal. As the bride's brother, whom Southwold has appropriately defined as an "affine-parent" of his sister's children, Walumbe represents the institution of marriage and the affinal interests of the wife's clan (Southwold, 1973). Thus Walumbe's actions show that marriage, bearing children, and death go together when defining the human condition.

As for Kintu, his refusal to grant Walumbe's request for a child was in effect, a refusal to recognize what came to be the traditional right of the mother's brother (*kojja*) to the temporary possession of one (or more) of his sister's children. Such a child was called *ndobolo*, or share, and represented the clan's token share in the wife's children. After the birth of the third child, the *kojja* (specifically, the brother who had arranged the marriage) had the right to ask the husband for one of his sister's children to serve in his household. After a few years, the father could redeem his child by paying a token fee of two goats, and the child was returned to his father's home (Le Veux, 1917:546; Roscoe, 1921:165; Mair, 1934:61–63; Haydon; 1960:122). Kintu's refusal to recognize Walumbe's claim was thus an implicit infraction of the rules of marriage. Kintu rejected Walumbe's request by saying that he had already promised a "share" (*ndobolo*) of his children to Ggulu and could not spare any for Walumbe. In saying this Kintu was partly right, for the *ndobolo* could go to live at the house of a grandparent. But Kintu was also partly wrong in light of Kiganda practice; indeed, he was caught in a dilemma. For, by promising his children to Ggulu without Walumbe's consent, he was implicitly denying the rights of the *kojja* to his children.[4] In this respect Kintu, like Ggulu (to whom he wished to give his children), shows himself to be aligned with the interests of immortality and patriarchy and op- posed (initially, at any rate) to the affinal conventions of marriage which later defined the human situation.

Yet, it is Kintu who finally resolves the "problem" of the story. Although he is unable to prevent Walumbe from causing individual deaths, he holds out the promise of collective survival in the form of corporate immortality. "Walumbe may kill people, but he will not be able to finish them off. Let him kill! I, Kintu, shall continue to give birth to people." Thus, according to the proverb, "The descendants of Kintu will never be finished."

At the sociological level the story of Kintu may be seen as an ex- egesis of this well-known proverb. In Mulira's second edition, the pro- verb is uttered defiantly by Kintu at the end of the story. The phrase "the descendants of Kintu" (*abazzukulu ba Kintu*) was, and still is, used by the Baganda as an expression of national pride. Traditionally, it meant that the Baganda were the members of a powerful kingdom which made them superior to their neighbors. More specifically, it im- plied that the Baganda were the bearers of a special inheritance as- sociated with the heroic Kintu. The story shows this inheritance to be a prophetic one, the survival of a people despite the ravages of death. Kintu's promise is thus a "redemptive" prophecy; it is the promise of collective immortality.

The meaning of Kintu's prophetic declaration lies in the central metaphor of the story, the portrayal of death as the mother's brother. As the mother's brother, Walumbe represents the interests of the wife's clan in the marital situation, while Kintu represents the interests of the husband's clan and of patrilineality. According to the rules of marriage and descent, patrilineal clans must give away their daughters in mar- riage to men of other patrilineal clans, and they must give up their claims to their daughter's children, reserving the right to retain only a temporary share. In return, the clans gain new members through the marriages of their sons and thus perpetuate themselves. As a symbol of the patrilineal clan principle, Kintu therefore insures that the Baganda, as a society of exogamous patrilineal clans, will always gain new members. Thus the Baganda will collectively survive despite death, which will always claim a "share" of living clan members. In this sense the story of Kintu reflects the collective social life of the Baganda. Women marry men from other patrilineal clans who keep their children in order to perpetuate themselves, while their brothers take back only a token share of the children as symbolic compensation. Within this circuit of exchange of women and children, originally portrayed in the Kintu myth, lies the collective life of the people and the guarantee of their survival.

Cosmology and Ontology

A final feature of the story is its cosmogonic dimension. The story explains why the Baganda live in a three-story universe consisting of sky, earth, and underworld. Each of these realms signifies a different mode of being. As the realm of divinity the sky (*ggulu*) is known as *olubaale*, or abode of gods. The earth (*ensi*) is the realm of the Baganda and is synonymous with "land" and "country." This is the realm of the "descendants of Kintu" who live in the kingdom which Kintu founded. The underworld (*magombe*) is the realm of the dead where the spirits of the dead (*mizimu*, sing. *muzimu*) present themselves to Walumbe before returning to earth where they hover around their graves. As the Kintu myth explains, these three realms stand in a certain kinship relation. The sky is the domain of Ggulu, the Father God, and was the original domain of Nnambi, the primordial mother; the earth is the realm of Kintu, the primordial father; and the underworld is the domain of Walumbe, the primordial mother's brother. The structure of the cosmos thus expresses the origin and nature of man. Through Nnambi, the Baganda are descended from the immortal realm of the sky. Through Kintu, the Baganda came to live on earth and to seek their destiny. Through Walumbe, the Baganda became mortal beings.

Sky	Immortality	Ggulu	Father God
Earth	Human life	Kintu and Nnambi	Father and mother
Underworld	Death	Walumbe	Mother's brother

The myth also links the origin and structure of the universe to the human life cycle. Every child is born of a woman from another clan and lives his life on earth as a member of his father's clan. He marries a person from another clan and gives birth to children who will succeed him. Eventually he joins his ancestors in the underworld below. Thus the story of Kintu is the story of the origins and destiny of every person. The story enables the Baganda to see themselves as the sons and daughters of Kintu and hence to affirm with Kintu the triumph of Life over Death.

Ultimately, the myth is not only a story about the origins of death, it is also an explanation of how the fact of death is to be understood. According to the social context of the myth, the existence of death is to be understood as a necessary corollary to life, as the claims of mother's brother are a necessary corollary to marriage. From the point of view of Kiganda social structure, the story of Kintu is, then, a story about the complementarity of life and death, and hence it is ultimately a story about the acceptance of death.

NOTES

I wish to acknowledge research grants from the American Council of Learned Societies which initially funded my fieldwork in Uganda in 1972, and from the National Endowment for the Humanities which supported additional research and writing during 1977–78. I also wish to express my thanks to John Rose for furnishing me with several Luganda texts and to Helen Nabasuta, Aloysius M. Lugira, and Fred Welbourn for their helpful advice and criticism.

1. *Baganda* (sing. *Muganda*) are the people; *Buganda* is the kingdom; *Luganda* is the language; *Kiganda* is the adjective for the way things are done by the *Baganda*. In accordance with ordinary usage, I retain all these prefixes (*ba, mu, lu, ki*), as well as the initial vowel in all *Kiganda* verbs and substantives.

2. I have been told another story about the origins of death which is based entirely upon this episode. It seems that a figure named Mpobe was sent by Ggulu to capture Walumbe but he failed because children raised the alarm and scared Walumbe into the ground (S. Byekwaso Mayanja, personal communication, April 1978).

3. Aloysius M. Lugira also informs me that "the lesson of this story according to the traditions of the Baganda is not so much about disobedience as it is about *obuntubulamu*," which in this context he translates as "humaneness" (personal communication, December 1978).

4. *Kojja*, though referring specifically to the brother who arranges a woman's marriage, means all her classificatory brothers (*mwanyina*), with their sons and all their male patrilineal descendants. Hence, *kojja* generally means "male of mother's lineage." Although Walumbe is never explicitly referred to as *kojja* in Kaggwa's text, he is described as one of Nnambi's brothers, and he implicitly performs the role of *kojja* by insisting upon accompanying Nnambi. In Mulira's expanded school book version of the story Walumbe's relationship to Kintu's children is made explicit and Walumbe is referred to as *kojjaabwe*, "their mother's brother" (Mulira, 1970:17). Welbourn has also informed me that some Baganda with whom he has discussed the matter assume that Walumbe is *kojja* and point out that Kintu was therefore wrong to refuse Walumbe's request for a child. Kaggwa's incomplete and simplified version of the story at the beginning of *Bassekabaka* (Kaggwa, 1971:1) refers to Walumbe as Kintu's brother (*muganda*). But in this version, blood and clan relationships are not significant, nor is the motive for Walumbe's killing of Kintu's children mentioned. Roscoe recorded the same version, probably from Kaggwa's text, in "Notes on the Manners and Customs of the Baganda," *Journal of the Anthropological Institute (JAI)* 31 (1901):124–25; also in "Further Notes on the Manners and Customs of the Baganda," *JAI* 32 (1902):26.

BIBLIOGRAPHY

Burke, K. 1979. *The Rhetoric of Religion*. Berkeley: University of California Press.

Haydon, E. S. 1960. *Law and Justice in Buganda*. London: Butterworth.

Johnston, H. H. 1902. *Uganda Protectorate*. 2 vols. London: Hutchinson.

Kaggwa, A. 1934. *Empisa za Baganda*. London: The Sheldon Press. 1st ed., 1901. *The Customs of the Baganda*. Translated by E. B. Kalibala. Edited by May M. Edel. New York: Columbia University Press, 1934.

———. 1951. *Engero za Baganda*. 1st ed., 1902. London: The Sheldon Press.

———. 1971. *The Kings of Buganda*. Translated by M. S. M. Kiwanuka. Nairobi: East African Publishing House. Translation of *Basekabaka be Buganda*. 1st ed., 1901.

Kakooza, J. M. N. 1967. "The Evolution of Juridical Control in Buganda." D. Phil thesis, Oxford University.

Kalibala, E. B. 1946. "The Social Structure of the Buganda Tribe of East Africa." Ph. D. dissertation, Harvard University.

Kampala. Makere University Library. "A Short History of Buganda" [by J. Miti].

Knappert, Jan. 1970. *Myths and Legends of the Swahili*. London: Heinemann Educational Books.

Le Veux, R. P. 1914. *Manuel de langue Luganda.* 2d ed. Algers: Maison-Carree.

————. 1917. *Vocabulaire Luganda-Francais.* 2d ed. Algers: Maison-Carree.

Mair, L. 1934. *An African People in the Twentieth Century.* London: Routledge & Kegan Paul, Ltd.

Mulira, E. E. K. 1961. *Olugero lwa Kintu.* 2 vols. 1st ed., 1951. 2d. ed. Nairobi: East African Literature Bureau.

————. 1970. *Olugero lwa Kintu,* vol. 2. Nairobi: Oxford University Press. 1st ed., 1965.

Munno, no. 15, 1912; no. 71, 1916. "The White Fathers in Uganda." Munno Publications. Kisubi, Uganda [in Luganda].

Nabasuta, H. 1974. "Creative Expression in Kiganda Folk Narrative." B. A. thesis, Makcrere University.

Richards, A. I. 1964. "Authority Patterns in Traditional Buganda." In *The King's Men,* edited by L. A. Fallers. London: Oxford University Press.

Ray, B. C. 1976. *African Religions.* Englewood Cliffs: Prentice-Hall.

Roscoe, J. 1901. "Notes on the Manners and Customs of the Baganda." *Journal of the Royal Anthropological Institute* 31:117–30.

————. 1902. "Further Notes on the Manners and Customs of the Baganda," *Journal of the Royal Anthropological Institute* 32:25–30.

————. 1911. *The Baganda.* London: MacMillian & Co. Ltd.

————. 1921. *Twenty-Five Years in East Africa.* Cambridge: Cambridge University Press.

Southwold, M. 1973. "The 'Mother's Brother' and Other Problems of Meaning in Buganda." In *Nkanga,* no. 7, edited by F. J. Bennett, Kampala: Makerere Institute of Social Research.

Zimbe, B. M. 1939. *Buganda ne Kabaka.* Mengo: Gambuze Printing & Publishing.

SECTION II.
Images of Social Experience

Beer Drinking and Social Experience in an African Society
An Essay in Formal Sociology

by Ivan Karp

Introduction

With few exceptions (Beidelman, 1966; Douglas, 1966, 1975) little attention has been devoted to the analysis of social forms in African societies, particularly to the transformations that social forms undergo in situations other than the mundane and practical. Mutual commensality, the sharing of food and drink, is one such form.

The ethnography of forms of mutual commensality is a subject that has rarely been explored in African contexts, although we know that eating and drinking are activities that are redolent with symbolic significance (Lévi-Strauss, 1978).

In this paper I shall demonstrate that commensal beer drinking provides a synthetic image in terms of which Iteso represent to themselves contradictions in their social experience. In the widest sense, I believe that beer drinking is Iteso social theory. In the complex of belief, custom, and attitude surrounding beer drinking, the Iteso express an implicitly held set of ideas about the nature of their social world and their experience of it. I shall argue, moreover, that it is not possible to obtain a full understanding of the Iteso conception of their social world and their experience of it by conceiving of their thought as an abstractly held structure. Their conception of the social world is not only, and perhaps even primarily, "thought." It is both "lived" and "felt" as well. In this sense to speak or write of an African system of thought is to abstract from the stream of events an arbitrarily selected part of an African world.[1]

In the following sections of the paper I shall describe various as-

pects of beer drinking and beer parties in Southern Iteso life and
thought. I shall be concerned to document the manner in which it
pervades Iteso social activities. Following that I examine the relationship of beer drinking to the contexts in which it is found, and the role
that beer drinking plays in defining those contexts and realizing the
goals of the persons in the situations. Then I describe the beer party,
the actual context of beer drinking, in terms of the patterns of social
relations that are exhibited in the party and the way these social relations relate to basic categories of Iteso social life. This leads me to return to the theme of mutual commensality and social experience. I
argue that beer is a symbol of diffuse solidarity and unencumbered
sociability which expresses the ideal form of relations among men that
Iteso would like to achieve. The association of beer drinking with
sorcery and poisoning, however, points to the inability of Iteso to
achieve desired forms of relations among men. They are unable to
know if the external forms of behavior that they observe do in fact
conform to internal states and intentions. Their dilemma is existential,
part of the human condition. The complex of beliefs and attitudes surrounding beer drinking is a reflection of the Iteso response to this
dilemma.

The Pervasiveness of Beer

The Southern Iteso are a para–Nilotic-speaking people who live
across the Kenya-Uganda border in the region between Lake Nyanza
(Victoria) and Mt. Elgon. Their social organization is based on a pattern of dispersed households formed into local groups that are vaguely
bounded and defined idiosyncratically according to the different social
positions of the persons consulted. These groups, which I call neighborhoods, are termed *adukete* by the Iteso, from the verb *akiduk*, "to
build," and refer to a group of people who have built together and
share mutual obligations to aid and defend each other. In addition,
the Iteso are patrilineal and have dispersed lineages which unite primarily for the performance of ritual.[2]

Beer drinking is an activity whose frequency brings it to the daily
attention of every person living among the Iteso. In the afternoons of
almost every day old men gather their beer straws and carriers, hollow
poles in which to store the reed straws, and wander through neigh-

borhoods in search of beer. The informal status of elder, achieved when one has married sons, entitles entry to many sorts of beer parties from which men without this status would be otherwise barred. During the harvesting season, there is a wide choice of parties to attend and the growing year is punctuated by beer parties organized to celebrate different events or to engage neighbors in help on some agricultural task. During the dry season, when stocks of grain are low and beer is scarce, people complain about its absence. A concern for beer drinking is evident even during those times when it is not available. This statement holds true even for the few people who do not drink beer. They attend and are an important part of beer parties. They both give them and attend them. Hence we may see that the unwillingness or inability to drink beer does not lessen to any great degree the importance of beer drinking in any person's social life.

In addition to beer made from finger millet, the Iteso also make beer from maize and, occasionally, bananas. The drinking of the latter two kinds of beer, however, is an individual affair. Maize and banana beer are drunk from glasses or gourds, while finger millet beer is always drunk from a pot with siphons. When they speak of the other kinds, it is *ajono k'ekurididi*, maize beer, or *ajono k'emuzungu*, European beer.

Finger millet beer might more properly be called an alcoholic, nourishing gruel. The beer is made from ground flour which has been wrapped in leaves and buried in the ground for one week. It is then baked in an open pan over a fire. The flour is placed in a pot and germinated finger millet seed is added as a yeast. Water is also added, and the result is allowed to sit for four to seven days. On the day of drinking, boiling water is added to this fermented mixture in the pot to make a drinkable potion. The Iteso take considerable local pride in their beer and often make invidious comparisons with the beer of some other area. Thus, the people of Lukolis who let their beer ferment in the pot for seven days regard the four-day fermented beer of Amukura as weak and tasteless.

The elaboration of beer drinking is a striking feature of Iteso culture. There is a highly developed vocabulary associated with beer drinking activities. A number of separate verbs are used to refer to highly specialized activities such as "pouring hot water into a beer pot" or to refer to the act of "cleaning a beer straw." There are seven special terms to refer to different stages of fermentation of millet beer, the distinctive Iteso beer, as opposed to other forms of beer. Only with regard to cattle is the Iteso vocabulary as well developed. Another aspect of beer drinking that indicates its importance to the Iteso is its association with effective social relations. Relations among persons in Iteso society can be conveniently divided into two categories, potential and actual. Any extensive or long lasting social relations among the Iteso will be found to be with persons who share beer together in some regular fashion. In this regard an anthropologist can make an assertion for the Iteso that is similar to Evans-Pritchard's for the Nuer (1940), that no matter which subject he wished to investigate, he found himself returning to the subject of cattle. For the Iteso no matter what area of their life is being examined—economics, ritual, or kinship— beer drinking will be found to be a part of it.

It is not simply a matter of beer drinking as a frequent but unnoticed aspect of Iteso life and culture. Iteso express an awareness of the significance of beer drinking in their lives. When I was first introduced at the chief's weekly meeting during my research, one of the first questions asked about me was "Emase ajon?" ("Does he drink beer?"). I was to find that a frequent inquiry during the course of two years' research.

One indication of the awareness Iteso have of the presence of beer drinking in their lives can be found in greetings. Iteso greetings may be elaborate and courtly, but follow a standardized pattern. Greetings are exchanged, followed by inquiries about health (generally treated seriously), followed by questions about food and beer. Thus, one typical set of greetings follows the text given below. [Recorded between two adult men meeting on a path in front of my house.]

Yoga.	I greet you.
Yoga-di.	I greet you also.
Ab'akiro?	What news? (lit., "What are the words?")
Mam'akiro.	No news. (lit., "No words.")
Ing'alejo?	How are you feeling?
Ang'aleong.	I am fine [may be answered in elaborate descriptions of illness].
Eng'ale aberu'kon?	How is your wife? [An elaborate series of these questions may be asked about various persons the questioner knows in the family of the person questioned.]
Edeka. Ing'alejo?	She is sick. How are you?
Ang'aleong.	I am fine. Where is the beer?

An'ajon?
Oreka Seferio.   At Seferio's home. It is the beer of the small
Nesi ajon nukitabo. pot. [Implying that there really is not enough
                       for the questioner if he were to attend.]

Ai ilosi'jo?   Where are you going?
Osokoni.   To the market.
Kedara.   Good bye. (lit., "Keep well.")
Kedara noi.   Good bye. (lit., "Keep well very much.")

The questions "Inyo inyamio ore'kon?" ("What are you eating at your home?") and "An'ajon?" ("Where is the beer?") are part of the customary forms of greeting. They may be asked even if the inquirer is not looking to eat and drink. Eating and drinking communally are indices for the Iteso of sociability (see below). Greetings are more than just fillers in conversation. They are means for both signaling and testing the quality of the relations that exist between actors, "supportive exchanges" or "rituals of reassurance" as Goffman (1971) calls them. The questions about mutual commensality in greetings indicate that there is an awareness that expressions of both politeness and solidarity are associated with eating and beer drinking. Thus, references to beer drinking may serve as suitable markers of sociability in casual conversation.

Iteso are aware that their patterns of beer drinking are unusual by the standards of the ethnic groups surrounding them. Among the other societies of Western Kenya, communal forms of beer drinking are on the decline and the traditional millet beer has been replaced by maize beer. Although the Iteso grow considerable maize and make some of it into beer, they assert that it is prohibited on ritual occasions and unsuitable for large parties. In their opinion the decline of communal beer drinking in their neighbors is an indication of their unneighborliness.

Beer Drinking in its Contexts

Beer drinking is a pervasive feature of Iteso social life and culture. The connections between beer drinking and other aspects of Iteso life are not random, however, no matter how ubiquitous. In order to understand the significance of beer drinking among the Iteso and the nature of the interconnections with their society and culture,

I shall examine three aspects of beer drinking more systematically. The first aspect is economic. Beer drinking as an activity has a use value for Iteso, and it may be seen as related to both production and economic exchanges. The second aspect is situational. Beer drinking is an important part of a large variety of contexts. Thirdly, beer and beer drinking are, themselves, symbols whose significance will aid in explicating Iteso ritual. The explication of Iteso ritual will, in its turn, aid in the understanding of beer as a symbol.

Beer drinking is of considerable importance for the conduct of economic activities. The pragmatic aspect is fairly obvious but nonetheless important. The Iteso economy is based on a form of mixed herding and agricultural activities. Iteso are a sedentary people occupying an area of relatively high rainfall. The main subsistence crops are cassava and finger millet (eleusine), while maize and cotton are raised for cash. There are two growing seasons, one long and one short. Rainfall is plentiful in the aggregate but extremely erratic from one year to the next and very localized. Hence, Iteso experience a high degree of uncertainty as to whether rain will be either sufficient or too great during a given year or whether the paths of rain will fall in their area in even a good year. As a result, their main crops, cotton, maize, and finger millet, may be destroyed if not picked immediately upon ripening. Large labor inputs in short periods minimize the dangers of sudden rain and hail.

Iteso use beer parties to organize work groups that will provide a high labor input in a short period of time. Large scale tasks, such as the mudding or thatching of houses, are also performed by groups of persons "working for beer." The economic motive for giving beer parties is particularly apparent during the weeding and harvesting seasons, but these sorts of beer parties are to be found at all times of the year. The work performed may often be greater than the cost of the beer provided. The provision of beer for labor is not direct. It is part of a complex series of reciprocal exchanges. A person who is unwilling to cooperate in work parties himself is unlikely to find anyone coming to his working parties. Beer is not the item exchanged for labor in communal forms of cooperation among the Iteso. The beer party is instead the vehicle through which cooperation is achieved.

I have no doubt that some other social form could serve as a mechanism for facilitating delayed labor exchanges. I am equally certain that beer drinking is such a mechanism among the Iteso. Although I do not have sufficient numerical data to substantiate this impression, beer drinking is a medium for both equal and unequal exchange. There is a tendency for elders to extract labor from their juniors through the medium of the beer party. Senior men who are in the parental generation are not expected to work at the work parties of their "children." On the other hand, labor exchanges among equals may be facilitated by the medium of beer parties. One type of beer party, *Ajono nuk'ekitai*, "beer for a piece of work," occurs when a working party from one neighborhood is invited to another to perform a specific task. Friendly rivalry between neighborhoods predominates on these occasions, and my Iteso informants asserted that this provides an excellent means for young men, without a store of social credit, to obtain labor for onerous tasks.

The important question for this analysis is to discover how participation in beer parties can operate as a "generalized medium of social interaction" (Parsons, 1963; Turner, T., 1968) such that future intentions to interact in a cooperative fashion are indicated in the beer party, in spite of the absence of specific contractual arrangements. The answer lies in the meaning that beer drinking has for Iteso, to be considered at greater length in the next sections. Both participation in beer parties and the giving of parties are tokens of essential sociability, and sociability indicates to Iteso a willingness on the part of other actors to participate in social and economic exchanges. Thus, participation in the beer party and the week that precedes it are taken as a sign that persons are willing to honor nonspecific obligations. The importance of this for long-term calculations is patent (Bloch, 1973). Neighbors, who are defined by Iteso as "people with whom one shares beer," are the primary source of labor supply for large-scale tasks. The very definition of a neigbor, with implications of generalized reciprocity, is associated with the sharing of beer. (See Karp, 1968A for a more elaborate discussion of neighborhood values and beer drinking.) In the context of work and labor exchange the beer party can be used both to provide the means for the completion of tasks and to store up credit for future tasks on the part of the participants. Like money, beer provides a measure of value in terms of which actors establish credit and bank labor. Unlike money, the measure so provided is imprecise and subject to manipulation as well as having a limited sphere of circulation.

If beer drinking is found in contexts where labor exchanges occur, it is not the only situation in which beer drinking plays a part of the occasion. Virtually all important or extraordinary occasions among the Iteso are accompanied by communal forms of beer drinking. Beer drinking is a social mechanism for indicating that situations are special, and Iteso conceptions of festivity are defined in terms of beer drinking. There are no festive circumstances, no instances of celebration among the Iteso that do not call for beer drinking in one form or another. Even major holidays in the Catholic Church are occasionally celebrated with beer parties.[3]

Iteso nomenclature for the various sorts of celebrations reflect the significance of beer as a context marker. One can announce, for example, that *Apunyas*, the mortuary ceremonies, are going to be held at the home of so-and-so next Friday. This is not a frequent means of referring to the event, however, and there are a number of reasons for this. In the first place, it is not sufficiently specific because there are a variety of ceremonies held at different times that make up the complex of mortuary ceremonies. Secondly, it does not stress the aspect of commensal sharing in the way that the reference to beer drinking does. Instead, it is more customary to refer to the ceremony or celebration that is to be held as "ajono nuka _____" ("the beer of the _____").

The example of *Apunyas*, the burial and mortuary ceremonies, is instructive in this regard. In these ceremonies beer is not a central theme. It serves, instead, as a means of expressing the transfer from one stage to another in the ceremonies. In this sense, it is not what Turner has referred to as a "dominant symbol" but is an "instrumental symbol," a symbolic form that is related to the ritual process as a means for achieving the purposes of the rite (1967). At any stage of the various mortuary rituals the members of the beer party constitute a gathering of mourners and the context of beer drinking can be seen as the appropriate vehicle for expressing the customary sentiments.

The complex of mortuary ceremonies can be divided into five stages. Each stage is a step in the progress of the dead person from the world of the living to the world of the dead. A different sector of his or her social personality emerges at each different stage of the ritual complex. Thus, the mortuary ceremonies are a complex *rite de passage* in which the transition from the status of living to the status of dead is achieved.[4] In the first stage, which begins at a person's death, kinsmen and neighbors gather for the funeral. Burial and mourning take place over a period of two days. After the funeral, the people of the household plus those of the minimal lineage who are not normally resident in that home (*ere*) remain secluded there.[5] Ceremonial bathing and head shaving take place. Beer is brewed by the married women of the household to end the initial period of mourning. This beer is called *Ajono Nukilongiet*, "the beer of the bathing."

In stage two, no agricultural work may be done until beer can again be prepared (usually about ten days). When the beer is brewed, the widower or widow goes to the fields and begins to hoe. He or she is then followed by all the other adults of the home. They return to the homestead and drink the beer, which is called *Ajono Nukirumiet Asoma*, "the beer of the return to work."

Stage three takes place six months to a year after the death has occurred. When enough finger millet has been collected, another beer is brewed. This is prepared from grain collected both by the women of the home and the daughters who have married out. All potential mourners are invited to the home, with the exception of affines. The people who participated in the burial drink from one pot. Each lineage of the clan that is represented at the ceremony ideally has its own pot to drink from, and neighbors and other kinsmen also have theirs. Each group drinks in a different house and is consequently separated from the others. This beer is called *Ajono Nuk'amurwoi*, "the beer of the hindlegs," after the parts of the cow given to the clan during sacrifice.

An unspecified number of weeks after this ceremony, stage four begins. Each daughter who has married out of her home will return to her natal home and brew beer for her husband and his agnates and friends who come about two weeks later. The name of this beer, *Ajono Nuk'akewas*, "the beer of the forelegs," refers to the forelegs of an animal, traditionally alloted to affines at a sacrifice.

Stage five takes place some years later when the bones of the dead person are dug up. If the dead person was male, a bull is sacrificed; if female, a cow. As this ceremony occurs only after illnesses that can be attributed to the *Ipara*, spirits of the dead, this may be properly called a sacrifice. The beer brewed on this occasion is called *Ajono Nukepunyas*, "the beer of the funeral sacrifice."[6]

Each stage of the ceremonies is related to different sectors of the dead person's social personality. Stage one emphasizes the household's and lineage's loss of a member. In stage two the return of the mem-

bers of the household to normal activities is symbolized by the resumption of work in the fields. Stage three brings together all the
mourners, except for affines, into a series of groups that are both separated from each other and united in the single ceremony. Stage four
emphasizes the special relations of affines to the household and lineage
of the dead person. Finally, stage five includes a commensal propitia-
tion of the dead by the living persons who made up his immediate
social circle.

In all of these ceremonies it is the beer party that is the vehicle
for the enactment of the ritual and one of the means by which the
purpose of the ritual is achieved. Through the medium of the sharing
of drink a ritual congregation emerges. Moreover, it is not only the
living who participate in the mortuary beer drinking and are, as a
result, members of the congregation. The *Ipara*, the spirits of the dead,
are reputed to have a liking for food and drink. One of the reasons
that Iteso give for performing mortuary rituals at a given time is that
the home of the bereaved person has been attacked by the spirit of the
dead and the spirit has to be propitiated with a sacrifice and beer.
The Iteso believe that spirits of the dead are greedy creatures who
beset homes with illness to signal their desire to be propitiated with
sacrifices of beer and meat (Karp and Karp, 1979). Funeral sacrifices
are held in the morning. Iteso assert that this is done for two reasons.
First it is "cool" and the spirits like coolness and, second, the morning,
like the evening, is a time when the spirits venture forth, a liminal
state "betwixt and between" light and dark. Evenings are periods
when spirits are likely to "catch" persons and possess them, while
mornings are periods when they appear to be more amiable. Thus
many of the funeral rituals are performed at a time when the spirits
of the dead are likely to cooperate in them.

Furthermore, it is only in the mortuary beer parties given at funerals that the pot of beer is put directly on the ground. On all other
occasions the pot must be placed on a ring; otherwise, my Iteso informants said, the person giving the beer party would be indicating a
desire for the death of his or her brothers and sisters. The earth, of
course, is the place in which the dead are interred, and some beer and
a few straws must be left in the pot for the *Ipara* to drink the next
morning. Hence, the conclusion may be drawn that the mutual commensality which establishes a congregation at mortuary beer parties
is not only among the living but between the living and the dead. Beer

parties become a symbolic form, an instrument, through which the living and the dead communicate and cooperate.

At mortuary beer parties some customs differ from other beer parties, such as the placing of the pot directly on the earthen floor. This illustrates an aspect of beer parties that is related to the different situations in which they are found. While a core of customs remains the same in all beer parties, other customs vary according to context and serve to define that particular beer party as a special occasion related to the purpose for which it is held. One such custom found is the *Ajono nuk'akewas*, the beer party held for the affines for the dead person. The invited affines will invariably request that an invited guest, not of their party, be asked to leave. By this means they display their rights vis-à-vis the members of the home. On any other occasion, their request would be considered rude.

In addition to the mortuary ceremonies, there are a wide variety of formal and informal occasions on which it is either required or simply good manners to serve beer. These occasions, range from the intimate *Ajono nuk'itabo*, "beer of the small pot," which is served by a wife to her husband at night to the highly elaborate and prohibitively expensive *Ajono Nuk'imwatok*, the beer parties held to celebrate the birth of twins. A salient feature of the various parties is the association of beer drinking with hospitality. Often when I asked Iteso if I could come to their homes to interview them, they asserted they would be too embarrassed to have me without beer, and I should wait until they could brew some. If I was able to convince them that the visit was "work" and not a visit, then I might be allowed to come. Otherwise, I found them very reluctant to receive me.

In all of these cases the presence of beer marks an occasion as special or extraordinary. By this I mean that beer drinking is associated with what might be called heightened forms of social experience in which a commemorative element is present. This can be seen for the list of different types of beer parties given in the appendix and from the all-purpose appellation *Ajono Nuk' akinumunum*, the beer for special occasions, which translates literally as "the beer for celebration."[7]

The third aspect of the interrelationship of beer drinking with social life is the use of beer as a symbol in ritual. Further examples in which beer is an instrumental symbol will be given in the next section. In this section I wish to discuss the central importance of beer in a crucial domestic ritual, the ceremony of *Akipudun*, "to bring forth," the ritual in which the newborn child is first brought out of the house in which it is born.

In this ritual a child is given its first name. Iteso have a variety of names. There are baptismal names, and many Iteso have taken to using patronymics. They are also known by nicknames and age grade names as well. The first name given the child, called the "sucking name," is given at the ritual of *Akipudun*. The sucking name is the one by which the child will be known to the members of his natal household all his life. It is essentially the name that stands for his individuality, the basic core of the person onto which other capacities are added.[8]

The mother and child remain in seclusion for a period of about three days after the birth. Before they can be taken out of the house beer must be brewed by or, more usually, for the mother, often by her husband's mother, the paternal grandmother of the child. The wives of the male members of the father's minimal patrilineage are invited to the ceremony; others are excluded. At the ceremony the child is held by its paternal grandmother or some other woman who stands in that classificatory relationship to it. The grandmother dips her finger in the beer and places it in the mouth of the child. At that point its mother calls out the name that has been chosen for it. If the child refuses to swallow, other names are chosen until the child finally complies. After the name has been accepted by the child, it can be taken out of the house. This ceremony is one that has been described to me on repeated occasion by Iteso when asked to name one ritual that is characteristic of their culture. Of the many domestic rituals that flourish among them, the naming ceremony is the one which comes most readily to mind in their conversations with me. I suggest that this consciousness may be accounted for by the importance that the ritual of *Akipudun* has for Iteso conceptions of personhood.

Beer plays an important role in the symbolism of the *Akipudun* ritual. There is first of all the association of beer with mother's milk. The term "sucking name" refers to two kinds of "sucking." There is the sucking that a child does at its mother's breast and then the sucking of beer off the finger of the child's maternal grandmother during the name-giving ceremony. Thus an association is drawn between beer and mother's milk. Both of these are associated with highly charged forms of diffuse solidarity characterized by the tie of matrifiliation and expressed in the symbolism of the mother's sleeping hut. The difference between the two kinds of sucking is that the child sucks at its mother's breast before it accepts a name, while the sucking of beer is indicative of accepting a name.[9] What is crucial for an understanding of the symbolic role of beer is its position in relation to other symbolic forms and actions in the ceremony. The ritual asserts that "The child does *not* drink beer because it is a social being," but rather that "It is a social being because it drinks beer," given the priority of drinking over naming. The capacity to drink beer is a prerequisite for the capacity to undertake social life, as is the acceptance of a name. Hence beer drinking becomes an essential aspect of the onset of personhood in Iteso ritual.

Beer Drinking in Itself

In the preceding section I discussed the connections among beer drinking and three aspects of Iteso culture and society: economics, the organization of situations, and ritual symbolism. In this section I shall examine in detail beer drinking, the beer party, and their relationships to Iteso ideas of sociability. The major difference between this discussion and the preceding one is that I earlier described beer drinking from the outside, in terms of its interrelations with the contexts in which it is found. Thus, for example, some customary usages of beer drinking in mortuary ceremonies were interpreted as resulting from the association of beer drinking with ritual mourning. What remains to be interpreted is the "text" of beer drinking rather than its relations to "context."

When Iteso refer to *ajon*, "beer," they almost invariably mean finger millet beer and not other sorts of beer. Finger millet is both a food and a ritual substance. The ritual for first fruits must be performed by preparing a meal with finger millet, which is then made into both a starch and a beer. As I have indicated in the preceding sections, mutual commensality, the sharing of food and drink, is an important activity for defining contexts for social and ritual action in Iteso society.[10] It also provides a means through which Iteso express their evaluations of other persons.

Iteso concepts of mutual commensality are connected to evaluations of social behavior. These evaluations are in turn associated with specific contexts or nexus of social relations. Labels that are appropriate in one context may appear irrelevant or immaterial in another context. In relations with strangers, for example, standards of appropriateness that are relevant for family situations do not apply. Two significant nexus of social relationships are located in the familial domain and in the neighborhood. For the neighborhood Iteso use two terms, one negative and one positive, to evaluate behavior. The first term, *epog*, is translated by English-speaking Iteso as "proud," carrying with it associations that are found in our use of the adjective "haughty." Iteso have a vivid image of behavior that is *epog*-like. Someone who can be called *epog*, they say, is the sort of person who hides in his hut eating his food and drinking his beer. He is someone who does not participate in the daily interaction that is characteristic of neighborly relations. The reason for this, they suggest, is that the "proud" person does not believe that he needs the generosity of other persons. Hence, the image that is associated with the term is a combination of arrogant self-sufficiency and greed.

The opposite of the person who is *epog*, is someone who is *epaparone*. To be *epaparone* is to be congenial. I find it striking that English-speaking Iteso have used the adjectival form "social" to translate *epaparone*, "He is social." It was only after I returned from the field that it occurred to me that to be *epaparone* might indicate, for the Iteso, a correspondence between positive inward intentions and outward behavior. That this may me so is indicated by informants' assertions that a man who is *epaparone* is "happy with himself" and "likes talking to others in a gentle way, drinking with others, without causing trouble."

The evaluative pair, *epog-epaparone*, is laden with images of the denial and the acceptance of mutual commensality. While many informants were too polite to accuse Europeans of being *epog* in my presence, they were quick to apply the word to students who imitated European manners. In addition to the unwillingness of these students to eat and drink in an "African" manner, other features of their behavior were remarked upon. Particularly notable was the insistence of these young men and women in communicating in a language that many of their elders did not understand.

These behavior patterns are interpreted by Iteso as indicating a denial of the rights of others to share in goods, such as foodstuffs, beer, or social relationships. In the case of the use of secret languages, the nonspeaker is refused a share of the ongoing interaction. These denials constitute a violation of what Fortes (1969) has called "an ethic of generosity" that "in many societies may belong to the domain of kinship and familial relations." There are other societies, he adds, in which the "ethic of generosity" is found in groups constituted on the basis of common residence. Such societies as the Iteso and the Nyakyusa (Wilson, 1951) are of this type, where generosity is expected among members of a residential group, such as the Iteso neighborhood. The ungenerous person is not only typified as greedy but sometimes stigmatized as a witch or sorcerer. Thus, among the Nyakyusa, witches are believed to be greedy for meat and unwilling to share their meat with the coresidents of their age villages. Similarly, among the Iteso, hidden greed and envy are said to motivate the sorcerer.

Iteso accounts of the contrast between "pride" and "sociability" suggest that there are two dimensions to the association of generosity with spheres of social relations. The first is the more commonly mentioned refusal to give generously. The second is the complementary refusal to be drawn into networks of interaction, expressed in the refusal to accept proffered generosity. This second aspect of the Iteso "ethic of generosity" can be discovered in the themes of self-sufficiency and self-centeredness found in the concept of *epog*. To be *epog* does not indicate simple greediness. It stands also for the refusal to be sociable. For the Iteso the theme of generosity and its denial is closely associated with essential aspects of interdependence. They often asserted that "pride" was foolish. Proud persons, in their opinion, are eventually forced to recognize that their survival depends upon the interdependence among men. In an uncertain environment and world, sociability is for Iteso the basis of reciprocity. It may not be stretching the implications of Iteso statements too far to suggest that, in their view, reciprocity is the basis of social order.

This ethic of generosity is expressed in Iteso thought in an idiom of beer drinking, and the willingness to participate in reciprocal beer drinking is a fundamental part of the definition of the sociable person. Since this is the case, examining the beer party will show that the theme of sociability is implicit in the activity.

The membership of the beer parties vary according to the contexts in which they are held. A party may be inclusive, as in neighborhood parties, or exclusive, as when the funeral beer for affines is held. Beer drinking often begins in the afternoon. Depending upon the time of day, the occasion, and the amount of beer brewed, the party will last from five hours to three days. The participants sit either on chairs or on the floor around a pot drinking beer. There is rarely more than one pot, but some of the pots fill an entire room and are capable of holding an enormous amount of liquid. Two or three persons often share drinking straws. Music is provided by a radio or phonograph, if one is available, or, if the occasion is sufficiently important, a band may be hired. Sometimes women who have come to drink beer will play drums in what is regarded as a more "traditional" form of music. If the band has a singer, he sings popular Swahili songs, topical songs, and commemorative songs that glorify the persons at the party or the event. There are special songs for the mortuary beers whose function, according to informants, is to "cheer up" the mourners. If the occasion is sufficiently important, special guests may be fed, usually in another house in the compound. Festive food, such as chicken, is served as the relish to accompany the starch.[11]

The following text records some rules of etiquette provided by the people at a large party.

1. Parents must not sit at the side of the door-shutter while in their children's houses.
2. Women must not sit on the chairs. But this is not so to the present young men.
3. Always ask for permission to speak.
4. Do not hold a straw with a left hand.
5. Women should crawl under the straws.
6. Do not walk over the straws.
7. Do not quarrel.
8. Have your straw out of the pot when sneezing.
9. At the door, inside the house, from out, you should always thank the crowd in the house [men only].
10. Turns should be given between the parents with the [married] children to dance.
11. Always sit facing the pot.
12. Don't stand and look into the pot.
13. Introduction of the people by the owner of the home.
14. Women should not sit at the backs of men.
15. Do not wipe the drinking end of the straw [when you are sharing with someone].
16. A woman should not thank the crowd inside the house when she enters the house.
17. Do not drink with a straw without a sieve.

18. Do not force air through the straw to make some bubbling in the pot.
19. Don't drink out of a pot which is placed on the bare floor.
20. When a straw is put out of the pot, remember not to pass between the straw and the pot. Keep the straw next to the pot, then pass.
21. Ask for permission to leave.
22. Say "Good-bye" before taking a step outside.
23. When drinking, always remember to hold the straw with your right hand or both if you wish [not drinking without holding a straw].

This text provides a list of rules that seem complex. They define a simple system of social identities, however. The rules for seating in the beer party produce two concentric circles surrounding the beer pot, an arrangement of considerable significance. The inner circle is composed solely of women, the outer circle solely of men. The only other axis that divides the party is based on a line drawn across the concentric circles from the door to the rear of the house. To the left of the doorjamb, as it is faced from inside the house, sit the men and women who are related to the host as "parents" and "children." To the right of the doorjamb sit the persons who are related to the host as "siblings," "grandparents," and "grandchildren." The effect is to separate all persons who are in adjacent generations into opposite halves of the circles, and to combine all the persons in the same and alternate generations into a single half of the drinking circles.

The kinship system of the Iteso uses a number of components in its makeup, including relative generation, sexual identity, type of genealogical connection, and affinity. Sexual identity and relative generation are relevant on all social occasions in which Iteso interact with other Iteso. In the seating arrangements of the beer party, sex and relative generation combine in such a way as to create three relationships. The first is one of sexual complementarity, expressed in the two concentric circle of men and women. The second is the polar opposition of the successive generations, as Fortes (1966) calls them. In the opposed halves of the circles sit persons who relate to each other as parents and children.[12] In the opposite half to any ego sit his "parents" and his "children." Both predecessors and successors, persons related to ego by ties of filiation, sit opposite him or her. The final relationship is not one of polarity or complementarity, but one of identifica-

THE BEER PARTY

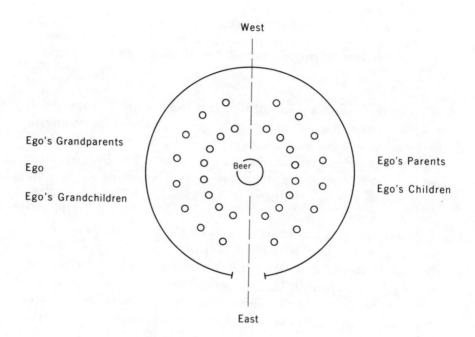

tion. In the same half of the circle as any person sits are to be found his or her siblings, grandparents, and grandchildren, all of whom are identified with each other through the medium of identical placement. For the purposes of the beer party the alternate generation relationship is collapsed into the relationship of siblingship. What puts grandparents and grandchildren together is their filial relationship to the persons in the opposite half of the circles.

This pattern of three relationships, the complementarity of the sexes, the polarity of the successive generations, and the identification of siblings, provides a striking confirmation of Fortes' assertion that social structure "has its roots in the structure of the nuclear field of reproduction" (1966:10). The structure of the nuclear family is reproduced in the beer party and, as a consequence, the primary forms of social relations which Iteso experience, primary in two senses. First, the beer party reproduces the primary social forms through which the Iteso acquire membership in society, the social relationships of the family of origination. Second, it reproduces the forms upon which all other social identities are built, primary components of self-identity onto which other capacities of the social and moral person are grafted.

The social world of the beer party is a compressed mode of social experience in which the distinctions in and roles that are relevant outside of the beer party are denied expression. Two avoidance relationships provide exceptions to this generalization, but they may be modified in ritual practice in a manner in which beer plays a crucial role. Both the avoidance relationships are affinal; they are the relationship between a woman and her husband's father and a man and his wife's mother.

In the first, a wife may lift the avoidance by brewing a special beer for her husband's father. The party is assembled, and before anyone can drink, the wife pours boiling water into the pot and prepares a straw for her father-in-law. He draws on the straw, then hands it to his daughter-in-law, and she drinks. After the drinking is initiated in this formal manner, other members of the party may drink. The wife is rewarded by her father-in-law and other members of his generation with small gifts of money. This ritual, usually performed within a year after a marriage, provides the easing of avoidance through the formal and ceremonious sharing of beer through the same beer straw.

The ritual through which the avoidance between a man and his wife's mother is lifted shows, in an even more remarkable manner, the capacity of beer to act as a symbol of incorporation in Iteso ritual. In this ritual the man and his mother-in-law stand facing each other in the shade of the overhanging thatch roof of the wife's sleeping hut, a space treated as a liminal place in other Iteso domestic rituals.[13] Each person takes a mouthful of beer and asperses the other person with it. Having sprayed each other, they are free to interact with each other and share the same beer straw at beer parties.

In both these rituals the beer is an instrumental symbol that serves as a medium for the achievement of the assimilation of separate and antagonistic social persons. One reason for this ritual power of beer may be its physical properties as a liquid. It both takes the shape of the container in which it is put and encompasses or encloses objects which are put in it. It is thus both incorporatable and incorporating at the same time. As such, it is a suitable vehicle for expressing the themes of incorporation and the negation of separation. In another ritual context the liquid properties of water assume the same role. An accused sorcerer may be asked to spray water from his mouth over the person he has been accused of attacking. If the man who sprays the water is, in fact, a sorcerer, his medicine will turn against him and attack him. This boomerang effect is the result of the incorporation of victim to sorcerer produced by the ritual aspersing of water.

A discussion of the incorporating powers of beer returns us to the theme of mutual commensality. Beer is invariably consumed by more than one person at a time. Fortes has discussed the features of eating and drinking that make them appropriate symbols of incorporation. These activities are, he argues, both individual and social, and in contradistinction to other organic activities,

> can only be accomplished by incorporating permitted items from the external—ultimately non-human—environment. Thus eating is the locus of the indivisible interdependence of the individual, society and environment; and food and drink. . . . are exceptionally adapted to serve as the material vehicles of transactions and relationships of binding moral and ritual force. Nothing so concretely dramatizes acceptance—that is, incorporation in the self—be it of a proffered relationship, or of a personal condition, or of a conferred role and status, as taking into one's body the item of food or drink chosen to objectify the occasion. . . . The intangible is thus made tangible—word is made flesh—and therefore assimilable and manageable (1966:16).

The theme of incorporation is manifest in the act of beer drinking and its use in nullifying avoidance in relationships. The husband/mother-in-law relationship is characterized by a much greater degree of avoidance than the wife/father-in-law relationship. When the husband and his mother-in-law negate the separation between them, they do so by standing in a liminal space and aspersing each other with beer. Beer is mixed with saliva and sprayed over the other person. Through the combination of internal and external aspects of the person, the space between the two persons is closed.

Another ceremony, in which beer is aspersed on an object, confirms this interpretation. This is the ritual whereby a new plow is brought into a home. A newly purchased plow may not be brought into a home until the "beer for a new plow" is brewed. As the plow reaches the gate of the courtyard, all the persons of the home asperse the plow with beer as it is rolled into the household. It is then wound with vines that symbolize fertility, and the women of the house make ululations of joy. Any passerby may join the beer party. In this ritual of incorporation, beer is once again the instrumental symbol of incorporation.

These examples indicate that incorporation through the use of beer as a material symbol takes two forms: a strong form in which beer is aspersed and a weak form in which beer is shared through a siphon. In the beer party, it is usually persons who are in the same half of the concentric circles who share straws. Thus, members of adjacent generations such as a father and his daughter-in-law would be unlikely to share a straw together at a party after they have performed the ritual of lifting the avoidance relationship. Although they are separated by the seating arrangements in the beer party, they are joined in the act of drinking simultaneously from the same pot. Large pots allow the majority of persons participating in the beer party to have their straws in the pot at the same time. The act of drinking obliterates the social distinctions established by the rules of the party.

Evidence for this interpretation and the importance of joint consumption can be found in the persistence of this form of drinking among the Iteso. Both communal forms of beer drinking and the consumption of finger millet beer have declined among the peoples neighboring the Iteso. They make beer from maize and consume it out of calabashes, glasses, or empty tins. The finger millet that is grown is sold at great profit in nearby towns. Among the Iteso the pot and straw remain the primary means for the consumption of beer and are absolutely required in ritual contexts. The pot and straw method of drinking beer is the only practical manner in which beer can be simultaneously consumed by more than one person from the same container. I suggest that the simultaneous consumption of beer may be an important aspect of the communal symbolism of beer drinking, and that sequential consumption is not a satisfactory substitute.

The evidence presented above leads to the conclusion that beer drinking among the Iteso is a form of social communion, a commensal sharing in which persons who participate are stripped of the capacities in terms of which they interact in non–beer drinking contexts. This exclusion is reinforced by the formal pattern of etiquette expected at the beer party. Thus in the beer party and in the act of beer drinking Iteso relate to each other directly and not in terms of the cross-cutting welter of identities and interests that ordinarily divides them.

The following text illustrates the theme of communion through commensality from an Iteso point of view. It was recorded by a friend shortly after he had given the beer party he describes.

A Beer Party in my House

On one of the Saturdays in the month of October of the year 1967, I had *AJONO NUK'EMUSIGO* in my house.

To start drinking, at about one o'clock p.m., I had the five boys who had helped me with the mudding of my present house that I still live in.

In the house, they sat on the chairs at the side of the door-shutter next to my bed. A few minutes later, the parents of the five helpers with my parents came in one by one taking the chairs I had placed on the opposite side of my bed.

Just because I knew each group would come with wives, I had some empty sacks spread on the floor for the women to sit. Whenever every woman came in, she crawled under the straws, sitting in front of the husband on the sacks that I had spread on the floor.

To allow people speak, the five helpers chose one of their friends Mr. Augustine to do the job. Whoever spoke without permission was punished by taking out his straw for a while without drinking. All the time a straw was out of the pot and somebody wanted to go out, she or he made sure that did not pass between the straw and pot. All the time a straw was kept next to the pot.

For music in the house, there were two guitars and vocal being played by Mr. Okumu and Oramis. All the time a song was played, either group had a chance to dance. So that they danced in turns as parents do not dance with children at the same time.

All the time a man went out, and when came in at the door inside, he thanked the people before he sat on his chair.

At about seven p.m., I took the five boys with their wives to the other house for a meal. To keep peace in the house one of the parents acted.

When the boys returned, the parents asked for permission to leave. One by one thanked the house and walked out.

When one of the parents pulled his straw out of the pot, he noticed that he was using a straw without a sieve. And that it had remained in the pot. There was a noise in the house, "take out straws and the sieve be taken out." Straws were taken out of the pot, and one boy washed his hands and pushed into the pot to look for the sieve. It was found and then thrown outside at the door. The remaining people pushed in their straws again and continued drinking.

At about eleven o'clock p.m., the two musicians played their guitars and sang a nice song which pleased the house so that nearly all people stood to dance. Mr. Otwane one of the helpers danced wonderfully well. My wife "Willy" was pleased with Mr. Otwane's style of dancing; she got a full basket of beer-flour and put on the head of Mr. Otwane as a reward.

For the whole night, people kept on drinking and dancing with much understanding in the house among all the drinkers.

At dawn, I went to the kitchen and brought one hen for my visitors to slaughter. This hen was slaughtered just in the house by one of the five boys, and fire was lit next to the pot for roasting the chicken. They cut it into pieces so that each one of them got a piece after the chicken was ready roasted.

At eight o'clock a.m., I gave them breakfast which they took and at about 9:00 a.m., they asked for permission to leave. I did not mind their leaving. I released them. They said "good-bye" to me and off they went.

The enumeration of customs in the text is to be expected in a document recorded for an anthropologist. Of greater interest is the description of the progress of the party. The text records a history of increasing engrossment among the persons attending the party. This involvement is punctuated by expressions that serve to mark it, such as the gift of a basket of beer flour to Mr. Otwane. This type of gift is always accompanied by the women at the party emitting ululations of joy.

Because my wife and I attended and participated in beer parties, we were frequently the subjects of the ritual marking the engrossment of members of the party and their contribution to other people's pleasure, as Iteso described it. Relative strangers were more frequently honored with presents and ululations than neighbors, although this was by no means solely the case. There appears to be a relationship between social distance and the honoring of unusual involvement. The practical logic of awarding engrossment would appear to be that the closer the member of the party, the greater the display of engrossment that is expected, and the further the social or geographical distance the less that may be expected. Hence, as Europeans, who are believed by Iteso to be standoffish and wary of participating in "African" food and drink, our participation was enough to merit an award.

The description of the party given by my friend is characterized by evidence of engrossment, and the party was punctuated by rituals that both highlighted and served to frame the engrossment. In our experience beer parties that were interpreted by Iteso as successful were characterized by the formalization of the evidence of engrossment. This engrossment not only had its own signs but was taken by Iteso in its turn as evidence of "much understanding." The statement "There was much understanding in the house among the drinkers" is revealing. At the time that this text was recorded I had not formulated the hypothesis that for Iteso beer drinking represented intense forms of sociability. I was struck by the "much understanding" phrase and led to pay greater attention to commentary on beer drinking. "Much understanding" is the indication of a successful beer party and its absence the sign that the party has been a failure. Iteso devote a great deal of concern and effort to trying to discover and achieve the communion that they describe as "much understanding." They regard "much understanding" as difficult to achieve and the exclusion of the welter of identities, interests, and antagonisms that are characteristic of interaction outside the beer party as not easy to obtain.

The intoxicating quality of beer is a means for accomplishing both the goal of sociability that is the essence of the beer party and the exclusion of other concerns that are necessary for the achievement of those goals. Iteso maintain a lively interest in the inebriating qualities of beer. The proper length of time for fermentation is hotly debated and different locations are known for the different strengths of their beverages (see above). It is expected that beer as a substance will induce a pleasurable euphoric state and good beer is appreciated both for its flavor and its ability to produce inebriation. The inebriating quality of beer does not produce beer parties that are orgiastic in the vulgar sense of the word. The very organization of the party is designed to guard against this possibility. One duty of the sergeant-at-arms is to call attention to drunken comportment and eject persons who become unruly and obstreperous. The Iteso express considerable concern about such behavior. In their view drunkenness among men leads to fighting and among women to promiscuity. Frequent warnings are given at the chief and sub-chief's weekly meetings about the danger of fighting at beer parties. The very notion of "much understanding" implies for them the absence of antagonism.[14]

The word that Iteso use to describe drunken comportment is instructive in this matter. *Amerit* indicates a loss of control and can describe an outburst of anger, the intoxication characteristic of marijuana, the irrational qualities of madness, or drunken behavior. Inebriation is not drunkenness so long as the person remains in control of himself or herself. It becomes drunkenness when control is lost. Much of the etiquette of beer parties signals, in my view, continued control and something of the Iteso view of human nature may be glimpsed in their attitude towards drunkenness. By glossing a variety of forms of behavior under the same term they indicate the high value they place on controlled behavior. I believe that the same attitude is expressed in their views of nature. They are not romantics. Their image of nature presents a picture of disorder, chaos, and disease. Nature is either to be avoided at all costs or to be turned into culture. Their ritual embodies the idea that the degeneration of culture into nature is a danger that is continually to be avoided (Karp and Karp, 1979).

The Iteso seek a middle ground between sobriety on the one hand and drunkenness on the other. An interesting contrast may be found with some Latin American patterns of drinking. In the Andes public drunkenness is a ritual obligation during feasts (Harris, 1978). For the valley Zapotec, Selby has described a strikingly different attitude towards extreme drunkenness. Becoming drunk in front of another person opens one to vulnerability and shows that a person is a man of "confidence," one who is both trusting and can be trusted, as opposed to a "political man," a person who places interests above people (1974:27). Here extremely drunken comportment is a form of social relationship, whereas among the Iteso it would prevent all such relationships. Both the Zapotec and the Iteso assert that individuals can behave in a deviant manner when drunk, and Selby describes instances in which actions that are otherwise unacceptable are tolerated from drunks. We have observed similar situations among the Iteso, and think that drunken comportment may be used as an excuse for actions that would not be tolerated under other circumstances. The fact still remains, however, that the Zapotec regard drunken comportment as a means of establishing social relationships, and that the Iteso believe that it makes social relationships impossible.

The complex arrangement of social forms, music and dance, inebriation, the compression of social roles, the celebration of engrossment, the accomplishment of "much understanding," that is found in the beer party indicates what Iteso desire to achieve in that context. Participation in these social forms may add up to an intensification of the experience of self and other in the absence of aspects of the mundane world that could interfere with such experience. This may be akin to what Turner has termed the experience of "communitas" in ritual (1969). A critical feature of this intensification of social experience is that it is esthetically motivated, by which I mean to indicate that its qualities are subject to judgment and comment, much as art forms are evaluated in terms of esthetic criteria. "Much understanding" and engrossment are two such criteria.

There are two conclusions that may be drawn from the positive side of the Iteso attitudes to the beer party. The first is related to the esthetic dimension of the beer party. The experience of beer drinking and the beer party can be an enhancement of the positive side of the experience of self, society, and other that is found in the mundane world of everyday activities.[15] This enhancement is the result of the intensification of social experience that they seek in beer parties.

The second conclusion derives from the first. The intensification of social experience that is sought in the beer party requires that the space that normally separates the interior self and its exterior manifestation be closed. The distanced self, which observes and calculates from outside, is incompatible with inebriation and engrossment.

These observations are in accord with George Simmel's perceptive essay on sociability (1974).[16] Sociability, he tell us, is the "play form of sociation," characterized in its relationship to the everyday world as art is to reality. This relationship is one of both the separation or detachment of sociability from mundane social forms and the transformation of seemingly uninportant or peripheral aspects of the mundane world into the very meaning of sociable situations. Unlike ordinary interaction, sociability exists in and for itself. It depends on the exclusion of interests, drives, and individualizing emotions that are characteristic of other forms of interaction. Simmel recognizes that this exclusion is difficult to sustain. It depends, he tells us, on such aspects of sociability as tact and good form. Ordinary social roles are emphasized to the point of caricature, as in the relationship of coquetry to erotic action, and this causes no embarrassment because it is recognized as play, and not as indicating serious intent.

Simmel emphasizes that the play element does not mean that all constraints on behavior fall away. Instead, the emphasis on "good form" requires that behavior be maintained within definite limits. Otherwise it would not be possible to sustain sociability as such.

> . . . the instant the intentions and events of practical reality enter into the speech and behavior of sociability, it does become a lie— just as painting does when it attempts, panorama fashion, to be taken for reality. That which is right and proper within the self-contained life of sociability, concerned only with the immediate play of its forms, becomes a lie when this is mere pretense, which in reality is guided by purposes of quite another sort than the sociable or is used to conceal such purposes—*and indeed sociability may easily get entangled with real life* (1974:134, emphasis mine).

The Iteso data confirm Simmel's brilliant insights. Sociability does, in the Iteso view, "easily get entangled with real life" in the beer party. The exclusion of the welter of identities, passions, and interests that is necessary to sustain the definition of the beer party as a context of pure sociability is not readily achieved. These difficulties are indicative of the darker side of Iteso forms of sociability, to which I turn in the next section.

The "Underlife" of the Beer Party

Violence and sorcery are a dimension of beer drinking that the observer discovers at the same time that he learns about the sociability of drinkers. Iteso believe that the beer party is a place where violence often happens and where sorcery is practiced. A common warning at the weekly chief's meeting was given against drunkenness and fight-

ing at beer parties. Stories are told of obstreperous persons whose behavior becomes intolerable at parties. While I never saw a fight during
the more than two years that I attended Iteso beer parties, Iteso assert
that men become drunk and violent at beer parties and that women
become drunk and sexually loose on the same occasions.

Many of the rules of etiquette given in the list on pages 98–99
are related to suspicions of sorcery. Beer straws may not be held with
the hand around the top. Bubbles are not to be blown in the water.
No one should sneeze when his straw is in the pot. All of these regulations are designed to ensure that a sorcerer does not put poison
in the straw and blow it into the pot or let it be drawn out of the
straw by the person with whom he is sharing.

I was unable to discover any evidence that poisoning was practiced at all and only minimal evidence for the practice of magical
techniques. Nevertheless, I know of no Iteso who do not believe that
sorcery is endemic among them and that most deaths are due to poisoning. This does not result from any failure of inductive reasoning
on their part. They are presented with evidence that confirms the beliefs that they hold. They believe that a sure sign of poisoning, the
primary weapon of the sorcerer, is swelling of the stomach. As chronic
amoebic dysentery, along with other intestinal parasites, is common
among Iteso, all Iteso experience the symptoms that they interpret as
evidence of poisoning at some point in their lives, and in all likelihood, at several points in their lives. As they do not believe that poisoning is necessarily fatal, their medical histories provide them with
continual personal confirmation of their beliefs in sorcery.

Some parts of the Iteso locations are associated with poisoners. I
was once invited to drink beer in an area which is famous for its sorcery and where I was not well known. I was told not to drink from
the mouth of the well in the marketplace because it was probably
smeared with poison and that I should not take a blade of grass to
chew on because the sorcerers often used this as means of poisoning
victims. During the beer party I asked for permission to go outside.
I gave my straw to the man next to me and left. I was followed by
an old woman who accosted me. "You're very stupid," she said. I
asked why. She replied that I should know that this place was full of
sorcerers. Did I wish to be poisoned? I had given my straw to a complete stranger. I replied that I "knew" no one there. (I suggested by
my choice of verb that I had no significant social relations with per-

sons in the area.) Why, I asked, would anyone want to kill me. "You're a European," came the reply. "Here, they would kill you out of curiosity!"

Although sorcerers are thought to kill because of jealousy or malice, they are also believed to kill for the indiscriminate pleasure of it. According to Iteso, killing becomes an addiction for them, and in beer parties, one is visibly reminded of the ever present Iteso fear of sorcery. It is customary for hosts to place the straw they give their guest into the beer pot and start the beer flowing. Keeping beer in the straw is a skill and it is not easy to get it started. It is also, however, a sign that the host is willing to drink his own beer and has not poisoned the pot. One of the reasons given for carrying a personal straw is the prevention of sorcery. Sometimes, a small pot will be placed beside the large one and a person will drink maize beer from it by himself. The explanation given for this special treatment is that that man has been poisoned and is unable to drink finger millet beer any longer. I am not sure why being poisoned prevents a person from enjoying finger millet beer.

In one beer party I attended, I was warned not to share straws with the members of the opposite branch of the lineage that was accompanying our group. When I aked why, I was told that they were notorious sorcerers and that as soon as the surviving senior member of the lineage had died it would surely split, as they did not care to risk their lives every time they attended lineage rituals.

When beliefs about sorcery are added to the earlier descriptions, the beer party begins to appear as a phenomenon about which the Iteso have ambivalent attitudes. It is not only a ceremony of human solidarity. It is also an event laden with risk. Iteso often find themselves drinking with persons they suspect of sorcery. The Iteso problem is that sorcery is, by definition, hidden. It is a form of covert conflict disguised under the outward sign of sociability (compare Lienhardt, 1951). The theme of the discovery of hidden intentions exposed during beer drinking comes up often in accounts of disputes. Many of the cases of conflict I collected contained an almost stereotypic scene in which a person discovers that a former friend or close kinsman has harbored antagonistic feelings toward him. As he passes by a house where the "friend" was drinking beer, the friend is heard to say that the person listening is "proud" or selfish. The man takes this to be a sign of jealousy on the part of the friend. Jealousy is an emotion of the sorcerer and it is discovered, paradoxically, through the medium of the beer party, a context in which antagonistic emotions are supposed to play no part. Yet in this frequently related story beer drinking has brought secretly held feelings to overt expression. The sociability of the beer party leads to antagonism outside of it, and the separation of beer party from everyday life is negated.

Suspicions of sorcery are not only confirmed in the Iteso experience of their illnesses and their disputes. They are also, I suspect, confirmed in the Iteso experience of their own emotions. The emotion ascribed to sorcerers and enemies contains an element of projection. The beer party demands a highly predictable and formalized set of social relations among persons. These social relations express the theme of sociability. The sociable person engages in mutual commensality "happily" with other persons. I suggested earlier that the element of willingness in sociability indicates a congruence between the inner and the outer person; participation in the external social form is supposed to be a sign of an identical interior state.

Iteso, in common with other people, do not experience harmony between their interior states and the outward signs of these states. In addition to providing accounts of the strategic value of hiding their own feelings and intentions, they often interpret the actions of persons close to them as masking antagonistic feelings. This is a prevalent theme in their accounts of antagonisms within lineages, and is related to accusations of sorcery. An important locus of poisoning, they believe, is among lineage mates who compete for scarce resources. Here, as in other social spheres, the contradition of outward sign and inward state is presented to them. Lineage members are among the persons with whom they must drink beer and display the forms of solidarity and sociability. Rituals necessary for the ongoing quality of life, such as mortuary rituals, are impossible to complete without the cooperation of agnates. There are many circumstances in which Iteso believe that the cooperation of their agnates is grudgingly given and dangerous in its consequences. The warning I received about sharing straws with the other members of a lineage who were attending one of the funeral beers is a case in point.

These hidden antagonisms do not result from the act of beer drinking or the beer party. They are brought to the beer party by the persons involved. The same "friend" who is heard to accuse someone of "pride" has been drinking with the person he has denigrated only

shortly before. Thus, the Iteso experience of beer drinking has its ambivalent features. On the one hand, the formal definition of the situation reduces the social personalities of the actors to the basic components of the social order. The beer that is drunk is a material symbol
of incorporation. The act of beer drinking, as well, may even negate
the fundamental constituents out of which the social self is composed.
The ideology of beer drinking associates it with sociability and con-
geniality. It is the index of the valued social personality. Ultimately,
Iteso hope that the beer party will show evidence of the self-involve-
ment that is the indication of its success. On the other hand, beer
drinking has an "underlife," as Erving Goffman might call it (1961).
Iteso are suspicious of the genuine quality of the required displays of
sentiment and fearful of the consequences of taking the outward sign
as true indicators of inward states. Beer drinking expresses both hopes
and goals of Iteso relations among men and the fears they have of the
consequences of taking men for what they seem to be.

This ambivalence may provide a clue to the fascination that beer
drinking holds for the Iteso. In an important essay, Clifford Geertz
has drawn the attention of anthropologists to social forms that are
cultural obsessions for the people of the societies involved. He analyzes a Balinese cock fight as a form of "deep play" in which status
competition among this intensely status conscious people is dramatized (1973). Geertz argues that the cock fight does not really effect
any changes of status but that its hold over the Balinese is that the
cock fight presents their experience to themselves. The affinities with
my analysis of the Iteso beer party should be apparent. There exists
an important difference, however. For Geertz "deep play" appears to
arise naturally out of participation in social forms that appeal to the
social experience of actors at a preconscious level. In the cock fight
the primary factors affecting the degree of "deep play" are high stakes
betting and high status competitors (441). The Iteso attitude is rather
different. For them engrossment is a critical feature of the beer party,
but it is not a preconscious experience; nor is it inevitable. Instead
much of their action is directed towards achieving it and celebrating
that achievement. The beer party is "a managed accomplishment"
(Garfinkel, 1967) that is the primary goal of their interaction. In the
beer party they recapitulate their experience of the social order of
which they are a part. This recapitulation, like their experience, has
both a private and a public aspect, which they must manage as well.

They present themselves with the dilemma of the discrepancy between what is displayed and what is felt, both by themselves and others. This is not a particularly Iteso problem. It is, as Geertz stresses, an existential dilemma; that is, a universal human problem cast in a culturally specific idiom (1973:363). The beer party is the Iteso means of imagining the antinomies of their experience of self, society, and other.

NOTES

I am grateful to a number of people for their comments and suggestions. Ernest Aura guided me throughout my research among the Iteso from 1969 to 1971 and again in 1975 and 1977. I have benefitted from discussions with Peter Rigby, Adam Kuper, Dan F. Bauer, Randall Packard, Nobuhiro Nagashima, John Okelele, and Boneventure Omuse. This paper took its final form in a presentation to John Hinnant's and Robert McKinley's seminar on ritual festivals at Michigan State University. Finally, I owe a debt to my severest critics, T.O. Beidelman, Patricia Karp, and Martha Kendall, for not sparing me the full force of their criticism.

1. Some day an enterprising intellectual historian may write the history of anthropological analyses of cultural forms in African societies. If he or she does, then beer drinking may have its place alongside the more standard forms of exotica such as witchcraft and sorcery, spirit possession, and divine kingship. Three features of beer drinking studies might come to the attention of our intellectual historian. First, anthropologists have been concerned to assert that extensive African involvement in beer drinking activities is not pathological. (See especially the articles by Simmons, Sangree, and Netting.) This is a necessary first step in which an activity, such as beer drinking, is shown to differ from similar phenomena in Western societies. In this case beer drinking is distinguished from the seemingly similar forms of alcohol consumption in Western societies, which many scholars regard as an index of social pathology.

While scholarship has distinguished African beer drinking from its Western counterparts, this approach tells us little about the organization of the phenomena. The second feature of African beer drinking studies is that they reflect changes in anthropological fashion. There are, first of all, what might be called the functional studies. Both Walter Sangree (1962) and Robert Netting (1964) have shown that the public nature of beer drinking in two widely separated societies, the Tiriki of Kenya and the Kofyar of Nigeria, is related to the absence of alcohol abuse. They also note that beer is a "locus of value" and that social relations in beer parties mirror the social structure of the two societies. As a result, they argue that beer drinking is a means of the control of juniors by elders. Other examples of anthropological fashion include an exchange analysis by H.K. Schneider that concludes that beer selling among the Wahi Wanyaturu is a "levelling mechanism" (1970) and a contradictory assertion by Richard Ott that beer selling in Lake Baringo District of Kenya is a means for the appropriation of surplus value by a class of wealthy peasants (1979). In the ecological vein, Netting notes that beer drinking is a mechanism for the achievement of balanced nutrition in the protein poor diet of the Kofyar. More adequate descriptions of beer drinking patterns in various societies are needed to test the general validity of these various conclusions. Finally, T.O. Beidelman (1961) deals with beer drinking in the complexities of ethnic interaction.

The third and most intriguing feature of studies of beer drinking has been the suggestion that beer drinking occupies a prominent part of the topography of the consciousness of many African societies. I cannot prove this assertion without extensive data of the sort not often found in the ethnographic literature. I can tentatively conclude that this might be so from hints found in various sources. Three studies, in addition to those already mentioned, must suffice. In V.W. Turner's study of the Ndembu of Zambia, he describes their work parties as beginning with the display of the pot of beer to be consumed after the tasks have been finished (1957). The form of display may have more to do with the meaning of beer as a symbol than as a material reward, since the labor involved is probably worth far more than the beer consumed. In the absence of further evidence the symbolic gesture is interesting but inconclusive. Peter Rigby's fascinating study of cattle symbolism and sacrifice among the Gogo provides another clue (1971). In sacrificial ritual the Gogo may substitute beer for cattle as sacrificial objects. Symbolic equations are made among the means by which cattle share water, humans share beer, and humans and ancestors share cattle in sacrifice. Thus, beer sharing is, for the Gogo, an appropriate symbol for the creation of a ritual community.

The final example is to be found in Jack Stauder's study of the social organization of the Majangir, an Ethiopian people (1971). The Majangir describe the various levels of their social organization in terms of the goods shared by the members of the different local groups. Thus the neighborhood is described by the Manjangir as a group of people who share "the same coffee," the settlement as persons who share "the same fields," and the community as persons who share "the same beer."

In spite of the symbolic importance that beer drinking appears to have for many African peoples, the studies I have described treat beer drinking either in terms of its functions or as an aspect of some other phenomenon. It is a peculiarity of the anthropological lens that it often enlarges the peripheral features of a phenomenon while at the same time blurring the center. None the less, we may discover in these studies the suggestion that beer drinking is a form of mutual commensality, the sharing of food and drink.

2. See Karp, 1978A and B, for accounts of social organization and social change among the Iteso.

3. The Southern Iteso are predominantly Catholic in religious affiliation.

4. Note, however, the paper by Kopytoff in this volume in which he argues that exclusive concentration on the jural dimension has obscured the fact that not all *rites de passage* create or mark status changes.

5. If it is a married woman who has died, her husband's lineage is secluded in the home.

6. An optional ceremony may be added to stage four. The woman who is the mother of a married male who has died or the mother-in-law of a married female who has died invites her opposite number, the other mother-in-law, to her home to drink beer. The beer party for this occasion is called *Ajono nuk'egura*. *Egura* is the backbone of a cow, the part given to mothers-in-law at funeral sacrifice. Beer for money is sometimes called "Beer of the hip" as a joke, after the manner of funeral beers.

7. I am grateful to John Okelele for pointing this type of beer party out to me. Okelele is a university graduate, and he informs me that one of his first papers for his sociology course was on Iteso beer drinking, which struck him as a remarkable feature of Iteso life as well. Unfortunately, I have not had the privilege of reading Okelele's paper. Incidentally, his name, *Okelele*, means "a circle of old men drinking beer in the evening."

8. See Fortes, 1973, for similar conclusions about Tallensi names.

9. In Iteso naming rituals an opposition is drawn between mother's milk and beer on the one hand, and the privacy of the sleeping house and the openness of the courtyard on the other hand. This association is consistent with other rituals of the life course and is a variant of the inside-outside distinction fundamental to Iteso symbolism and social thought. One possibility suggested to me by Randall Packard is that beer may have a "cooling" effect in the naming ceremony. It certainly does in other contexts, and a closer examination of the beer-milk opposition may reveal indications of a fascinating parallel between the structure of Iteso symbolism in birth rituals and that discussed by Luc de Heusch in this volume for the Sotho-speaking peoples.

10. Iteso culinary symbolism is discussed in Karp and Karp, 1977. A more formal analysis of symbolism than I intend in this article would discuss beer in terms of the structure of Iteso symbolism. Thus I might relate the techniques of beer drinking (which combine all forms of Iteso cookery, rotting, boiling, and roasting) to the role of beer as a mediating symbol. See Lévi-Strauss, 1978, for a formal analysis related to culinary symbolism.

11. Women may also host parties. Except for *Ajono Nuk'aelo* (see the appendix) these are smaller affairs. They are brewers of beer rather than organizers of parties. Women can be hosts of beer parties. They often have *ajono nuk'ekitai*, "beer for work," for example. Even in those contexts they still assume the less prominent roles, and men still assume the coordinating roles in the party. We may say that it is womens' labor that realizes the possibility of beer drinking through the brewing of beer. In contrast it is men's activities in the beer parties that allow the activity to come to a successful conclusion. It is interesting to note in this regard that it is believed that if women play the men's leisure game of *elee* (known as *mweso* in Luganda) they will be unable to brew beer successfully.

12. In ordinary social contexts relatives who are members of adjacent generations practice a mild form of avoidance. In beer parties they may not dance at the same time except for women and their husbands' mothers. This exception appears to violate the rule prohibiting the mixing of adjacent generations. The exception is apparent rather than real. Iteso women call their husbands' mother *tata*, "grandmother." The relationship is placed into one of alternate generations rather than adjacent generations. The common status of the women as wives of male lineage members overrides the distinc-

tion made between them as members of adjacent generations (Karp 1978A, chapter 5).

13. I thank Nobuhiro Nagashima for drawing this fact to my attention.

14. In the course of more than two years fieldwork we observed little drunken behavior. When it did occur it was regarded as more reprehensible in men than in women. Both male and female Iteso told us that men are better able to control themselves than women. Drunken behavior may be more frequent than we were able to observe. Beer parties often outlasted our staying power, and we may not have been invited to many of the parties in which drunken behavior is more frequent. In this regard a remark made to me about my research on the Iteso by a colleague who had worked among a similar people in Uganda is revealing. "You seem to know very well how to be a good Etesot; I'm not sure that you know how to be a bad Etesot."

15. The Iteso attitude to the beer party recalls Herskovits' famous definition of art as "any embellishment of ordinary living that is achieved with competence. . . ." The embellishment dimension of enhancement, as I have called it, seems to me to lead to an esthetic attitude, although Merriam (1964) would argue that esthetics strictly defined is not a cultural universal. One feature of beer parties that they share with art is that they are a "managed accomplishment," to use Garfinkel's term (1967:32). It may have been this aspect of sociability, among others, that led Simmel to compare it with art.

16. I thank T. O. Beidelman for pointing out to me the relevance of Simmel for this analysis.

Appendix

A list of some occasions on which beer is required:

Ajono Nuk'emusigo—Beer of Work
> Beer given as a reward to friends and neighbors who have helped a man with a piece of work.

Ajono Nuk'aelo—Beer of Friendship
> Beer shared by two husbands and wives who have become ritual friends.

Ajono Nuk'apejo—Beer of the Visit
> Beer brewed for people who have come to visit.

Ajono K'aber—Beer of Women
> Beer brewed by women (usually not neighbors) who are friends and who cooperate in work.

Ajono Nuk'akituk—Beer of the Cows
> Beer brewed by the parents of a girl for the parents of a boy on the day that bridewealth is to be decided.

Ajono Nuk'akiteng—Beer of the Cow
> When a father has many cows, he will give one to his son after his marriage. The son then brews for his father and his father's brothers.

Ajono Nuitolomarie—Beer of the Plow
> Beer brewed by a man upon the purchase of a plow.

Ajono Nuk'imwatok—Beer of Twins
 Beer brewed upon the birth of twins.
Ajono Nuk'arusi—Beer of the Wedding
 Beer brewed when a wedding takes place in a church.
Ajono Nuk'atabo—Beer of the Small Pot
 A small amount of beer brewed by a wife for her husband only. Usually consumed late at night.
Ajono Nupudoriet Aiyare—Beer of the First Sowing
 Beer brewed when the finger millet is first sown.
Ajono Nuk'akidweny—Beer of the First Finger Millet Harvest
 First-fruits beer brewed for neighbors and friends at the harvest of the finger millet.
Ajono Nuk'alikodiele—Beer for a person who has been believed to be "lost" and found again. (For example, a labor migrant who has not been heard of for many years returns home.)

BIBLIOGRAPHY

Beidelman, T. O. 1961. "Beer Drinking and Cattle Theft in Ukaguru." *American Anthropologist* 63:534–649.
——. 1966. "Swazi Royal Ritual." *Africa* 36:373–405.
Bloch, Maurice. 1973. "The Long Term and the Short Term: the Economic and Political Significance of the Morality of Kinship." In *The Character of Kinship*, edited by Jack Goody. Cambridge: Cambridge University Press.
Douglas, Mary. 1966. *Purity and Danger*. London: Routledge and Kegan Paul.
——. 1975. *Implicit Meanings*. London: Routledge and Kegan Paul.
Evans-Pritchard, E. E. 1940. *The Nuer*. London: Oxford University Press.
Fortes, M. 1966. "Totem and Taboo." Presidential Address, *Proc. Royal Anthropological Institute*, pp. 5–22.
——. 1969. *Kinship and the Social Order*. Chicago: Aldine.
——. 1973. "On the Concept of the Person among the Tallensi." In *La Notion de Personne en Afrique Noir*, edited by G. Dieterlen. Paris: C.N.R.S.
Garfinkel, Harold. 1967. *Studies in Ethnomethodology*. Englewood Cliffs, New Jersey: Prentice-Hall.
Geertz, Clifford. 1973. *The Interpretation of Cultures*. New York: Basic Books.
Goffman, Erving. 1961. *Asylums*. New York: Anchor Books, Inc.
——. 1971. *Relations in Public*. New York: Basic Books.
Harris, Olivia. 1978. "Complementarity and Conflict: An Andean View of Women and Men." In *Sex and Age as Principles of Social Differentiation*, edited by J. LaFontaine. London: Academic Press.
Herskovitz, Melville. 1948. *Man and His Works*. New York: Knopf.
Karp, Ivan. 1978A. *Fields of Change among the Iteso of Kenya*. London: Routledge and Kegan Paul.

————. 1978B. "New Guinea Models in the African Savannah." *Africa* 48, no. 1:1–17.

Karp, Ivan, and Karp, Patricia. 1977. "Social and Symbolic Aspects of Iteso Cookery." In *The Anthropologist's Cookbook*, edited by J. Kuper. London: Routledge and Kegan Paul.

————. 1979. "Living with the Spirits of the Dead." In *African Therapeutic Systems*, edited by D. M. Warren et al. Boston: Cross Roads Press for the African Studies Association.

Lienhardt, Godfrey. 1951. "Some Notions of Witchcraft among the Dinka." *Africa* 21, no. 4:303–18.

Lévi-Strauss, Claude. 1978. *The Origins of Table Manners*. New York: Harper and Row.

Merriam, Alan P. 1964. *The Anthropology of Music*. Evanston: Northwestern University Press.

Netting, Robert McC. 1964. "Beer as Locus of Value among the West African Kofyar." *American Anthropologist* 66:375–85.

Ott, Richard. 1979. "Economic Change in Lake Baringo District, Kenya." Ph.D. dissertation, State University of New York, Stonybrook.

Parsons, Talcott. 1963. "On the Concept of Political Power." *Proceedings of the American Philosophical Society* 107:232–62.

Rigby, Peter. 1971. "The Symbolic Role of Cattle in Gogo Ritual." In *The Translation of Culture*, edited by T. O. Beidelman. London: Tavistock.

Sangree, Walter H. 1962. "The Social Functions of Beer Drinking in Bantu Tiriki." In *Society, Culture and Drinking Patterns*, edited by David J. Pittman and Charles R. Snyder. New York: Wiley and Sons.

Schneider, Harold K. 1970. *The Wahi Wanyaturu*. Viking Fund Publication in Anthropology no. 48. New York: Werner-Gren Foundation for Anthropological Research.

Selby, Henry A. 1974. *Zapotec Deviance*. Austin: The University of Texas Press.

Simmel, George. 1974. *On Individuality and Social Forms*. Edited by Donald N. Levine. Chicago: The University of Chicago Press.

Simmons, Ozzie G. 1962. "Ambivalence and the Learning of Drinking Behavior in a Peruvian Community." In *Society, Culture and Drinking Patterns*, edited by David J. Pittman and Charles R. Snyder. New York: Wiley and Sons.

Stauder, Jack. 1971. *The Majangir*. Cambridge: Cambridge University Press.

Turner, Terrence. 1968. "Parsons' Concept of Generalized Media of Social Interaction and its Relevance for Social Anthropology." *Sociological Inquiry* 38:121–34.

Turner, V. W. 1957. *Schism and Continuity in an African Society*. Manchester: Manchester University Press.

————. 1967. *The Forest of Symbols*. Ithaca: Cornell University Press.

————. 1969. *The Ritual Process*. London: Routledge and Kegan Paul.

Wilson, Monica. 1951. *Good Company: A Study of Nyakyusa Age-Villages*. London: Oxford University Press.

A Reconsideration of Divine Kingship

by James H. Vaughan

In 1962, Jan Vansina published an article entitled "A Comparison of African Kingdoms," in which he characterized African kingdoms by writing, "First they all have a single leader, regarded as a 'divine king' in the Frazerian sense" (1962:325). In contrast to this, Lucy Mair in 1974 wrote, "not . . . that all African monarchs have been 'divine kings' in the sense that the Pharoahs were, still less that they were what Frazer meant by the term . . ." (1974:150). Clearly, there is either some disagreement as to what Frazer meant or as to the data on traditional African kingdoms, or probably both. This paper will summarize the Frazerian concept, modifications and criticisms of it, and examine in detail data concerning a traditional Margi kingdom, from which I will attempt to reach a conclusion concerning the applicability of the "divine king" concept to Africa. Finally, I will attempt to speak to the broader issue of the concept in human thought and mythology which was the scope of Frazer's formulation.

Review of the Concept

The name of Sir James Frazer has been an important one in anthropology and other comparative studies. His is still a name with unusually broad appeal, and his most famous work, *The Golden Bough*, is considered to be one of the greatest examples of scholarship in the English language. Frazer, although he did not die until 1941, represents the culmination of nineteenth-century anthropological theory. His most famous and enduring work is consistent with the theories of Sir Edward Tylor, Lewis Henry Morgan, Sir Henry Maine, and other nineteenth-century cultural evolutionists. In some ways Frazer's work represented a substantial advance on their theories, for where they presented theories illustrated by examples, he was a true comparativist, literally collecting volumes of data which he applied to the theories of his day.

Yet today, Frazer is virtually ignored in anthropology as anything other than an historical figure. This is in contrast to Tylor, Morgan, Maine, and others whose works, often with less documentation, are still regarded as seminal. Fortes discussed Frazer's neglected role in anthropology this way:

> Why . . . has his influence among his professional successors declined in recent years? Chiefly, I think, because he was not only a great anthropologist and a man of letters, but also a moralist whose zeal in spreading enlightenment too often got the better of his scholarly judgement. That glittering prose hides too many rash conjectures. The hypotheses paraded with so much learning turn out to be little more than descriptive labels for customs and institutions; and the historical and psychological speculations used to eke them out seem naïve today. The smug contempt for the exotic beliefs and customs paraded with such gusto, and contrasted disparagingly with the 'civilized mind,' repels us. Modern anthropology has largely grown away from Frazer; or rather it has outgrown him (1959:7–8).

But as we have seen in the quotations from Vansina and Mair, one cannot ignore Frazer on the topic of divine kingship (nor as we shall subsequently see, was it Fortes' intention to so suggest).

The classic version of *The Golden Bough* is the twelve-volume third edition published between 1911 and 1915. The work's central theme is anticipated in the epigraph before chapter one, lines taken from Macaulay's "The Battle of the Lake Regillus" (verse 10):

> The still glassy lake that sleeps
> Beneath Aricia's trees—
> Those trees in whose dim shadow
> The ghastly priest doth reign,
> The priest who slew the slayer,
> And shall himself be slain.

In that first chapter, Frazier amplifies the scene. He writes, "A candidate for the priesthood could only succeed to office by slaying the priest, and having slain him, he retained office till he was himself slain by a stronger or a craftier. The post he held by this precarious tenure carried with it the title of king; but surely no crowned head ever lay uneasier, or was visited by more evil dreams, than his" (1911–15, vol. 1:9).

Although *The Golden Bough* is unusually complex with digressions and tangents ranging across an array of topics, it is this theme of the priest-king, the divine king, which is its focus, and moreover, by the third and subsequent editions, it is the custom of institutional regicide which seemed particularly to puzzle and fascinate Frazer, as may be noted by reading the preface to the abridged edition (1922:v–vi; see also Seligman, 1934:4). Interestingly the evidence for the existence of divine kings—the source of today's dispute—was never an issue to Frazer; he was confident of their existence (compare Seligman, 1934:2). His concern was primarily with the meaning of the institution and its place in the evolution of culture and religion. By the time of the third edition, the evidence seemed irrefutable, for then he no longer had to rely upon tales from antiquity or the reports of travelers; there were field reports from anthropologists which described the custom in some detail. From C. G. Seligman's description of divine kingship as it existed among the Shilluk of the Nilotic Sudan, Frazer concluded, "On the whole the theory and practice of the divine kings of the Shilluk correspond very nearly to the theory and practice of the priests of Nemi, the Kings of the Wood . . ." (1911–15, vol. 4:28).

It is fair to note, however, that by this date Seligman was very likely influenced by Frazier's earlier work. So assured were anthropologists of the existence of divine kings that interest soon passed from documentation to a search for the institution's origins, particularly as related to Egypt (Moret, 1932; Perry, 1923: chapter 10; Seligman, 1934).

There are a myriad of customs attached to the institution of the divine king as propounded in *The Golden Bough*, and Frazer never concisely defined the concept (Seligman, 1934:4). However, Seligman in two passages has provided what might be considered the classic definition.

> [Divine kings are ones] upon whose correct behavior depends the fertility of the soil, the abundance of the crops, as well as the vigorous reproduction of mankind (1934:48). . . . [and] being held responsible for the right ordering and especially the fertility of the earth and domestic animals, end their lives by being killed or killing themselves with greater or lesser ceremony often at a fixed period (as the oncoming of senescence), or ceremonially expose themselves to the chance of death or else feign to die (1934:5–6).

The concept of a divine king is the consequence of a world view which holds that the king and his kingdom are one; therefore, prosperity and failings in either must be present in both. Consequently, a king can be held responsible for all conditions in the kingdom. Should he be weak or ill, the kingdom will be in danger; or should the kingdom be in failing circumstances, there must be something wrong with the king. Finally, a change in the person of the king will change the conditions in the kingdom. This ideology is manifest in numerous customs in which the king is symbolically identified with his kingdom, but its most striking and puzzling manifestation is in the custom of regicide.

That regicide might become an acceptable institution in societies has proven to be a controversial assertion, and indeed there has been more than enough justification for debate. In the first instance, it is important to note that Frazier's sources, even the more reliable ones such as Seligman, were not based upon undisputed contemporary observations but largely upon reconstructions of precolonial events. Consequently, the more skeptical critics could doubt the authenticity or accuracy of the tales. Secondly, the idealized form of regicide in which the king was regularly and ritually killed, apparently with his own accedence, strained the credulity of social scientists. Seligman's statement, "the Divine King goes cheerfully to his death" (1934:6), epitomizes a view many of us find difficult to believe, though our reactions be based primarily upon introspection.

At this point it would be well to make a distinction between institutional regicide and ritual regicide. Institutional regicide refers to regicide which is accepted by the members of the society as a legitimate way of replacing a king. Ritual regicide refers to regicide in which the king accepts his fate and which might even occur at regular intervals. Frazer never made such a distinction, but it is implicit in his work. Seligman recognized the difference by referring to priest-kings and divine kings respectively. It is important to understand that Frazer's best cases were not of ritual regicide nor did he claim that ritual regicide was necessary to the institution. Apparently he did not believe that even the priest-king of Nemi acceded to his own death. And, for the Shilluk, he noted, "even while he was in the prime of health and strength, he might be attacked at any time by a rival and *have to defend his crown in a combat to the death*" (1911–15, vol. 4:22, emphasis added).

It should be borne in mind that we are discussing an ideology and a custom which can only be manifest in a system of government —a much larger institution. It will follow that exigencies, accidents, and unforeseen events may vary the custom's implementation. One ruler might accept his fate and the next dispute his without invalidating the concept. It is wrong, I believe, to construe the concept as narrowly as Krige, for example, who writes, "Until 1959, when Modjadji III died a natural death, the political system of the Lovedu met the requirements of Seligman's definition" (1975:55).

The Shilluk were to be a classic test of Frazer's case for the role of regicide in the divine king complex. In the Frazer Lecture of 1948, E. E. Evans-Pritchard reexamined the Shilluk materials with the result that if he did not refute Frazer, he radically reinterpreted him.

Evans-Pritchard did not attempt to reject the symbolic nature of the king and kingship, for he stated:

> In my view kingship everywhere and at all times has been in some degree a sacred office. *Rex est mixta persona cum sacerdote.* This is because a king symbolizes a whole society and must not be identified with any part of it. He must be in the society and yet stand outside it, and this is only possible if his office is raised to a mystical plane. It is the kingship and not the king who is divine (1948:36).

However, on the matter of regicide he offered a new interpretation. He made a distinction between kings being put to death ceremonially and kings being killed in power struggles. Of the former he wrote, "In the absence of other than traditional evidence of royal executions in Shilluk history and in view of the contradictory accounts cited I conclude that the ceremonial putting to death of kings is probably a fiction" (21). But he continued, "On the other hand there seems little doubt that Shilluk kings generally met a violent death. My own opinion is that we must interpret Shilluk statements about the matter as indicating not that any prince may slay the king on his own initiative, as has been suggested, but that any prince may lead a rebellion as the candidate of discontent, particularly of the part of the kingdom to which the prince belongs . . ." (34–35). In short, Evans-Pritchard took the mystery out of regicide and made it simply a violent political act.

A modest demur to Evans-Pritchard's interpretation was made in an article by Michael W. Young in 1966 which reexamined kingship among the Jukun of Nigeria. He concluded, "In trying to answer the

implicit question of whether regicide—assuming that it sometimes occurred—was primarily political action with ritual or ideological justification [his interpretation of Evans-Pritchard's position], or a ritual
imperative with political consequences, I conclude—perhaps unfash-
ionably—in favour of the latter alternative" (1966:151). But this interesting and carefully constructed argument has had little effect, undoubtedly because it was a secondary study based upon materials
published in 1931 by C. K. Meek, a government anthropologist—a
study based upon just five months of investigation.

There was considerable merit in Evans-Pritchard's approach. Too
long had we thought of nonliterate societies as encumbered with ritual
and lacking in rationality. (Nor can it be denied that a custom so
bizarre as regicide is something of an embarrassment to anthropologists steeped in cultural relativism). Evans-Pritchard was, in effect,
arguing for a political interpretation of a political office. It is perhaps
relevant that earlier a similar perspective with regard to the study of
witchcraft had led to his breakthrough in the study of that emotion
laden topic (1937). All that Evans-Pritchard left of divine kingship
was a vague symbolism which he said characterized "kingship everywhere," while regicide became merely a technique of political transition and succession. It might be added that the reinterpretation of
divine kingship was coincident with the emergence of what came to
be called "political anthropology"—the study of political behavior in
traditional societies.

Divine Kingship among the Margi

As noted earlier, the data on African divine kingship have often
been hampered by the necessity of relying upon historical reconstructions, and regicide has always lacked authoritative description. In
light of this, data from the Margi Dzirngu are illuminating, for Margi
kingdoms were not greatly affected until very recently either by their
Fulani overlords of the nineteenth century or by the later colonial
regimes. The last attempted regicide on record was 1939. Most aspects
of their governmental system were still in effect when I first began my
studies of them in 1959. I had many informants who had lived through
those times and several who had directly participated in regicides or
attempted regicides.

The Margi Dzirngu are very largely contained within the present district of Madagali in Gongola State, Nigeria. Unlike all the other societies of the area, save for one very small one which is historically related to the Margi, the Margi have dynastic traditions and were divided into small mutually autonomous kingdoms. After about 1825 they existed within the suzerainty of Fulani conquerers. There are, in fact, two dynastic traditions which we might loosely refer to as Eastern and Western. We shall be concerned herein with the Eastern tradition which is characteristic of virtually all of the Margi Dzirngu, as opposed to other regions of the Margi. Futhermore, we shall concentrate upon the single kingdom of Gulagu, though it seems not to differ essentially from the other kingdoms of the Dzirngu area.

The duties of the Margi king were—and in 1959 remained—generally unformulated and imprecise. He was both chief political officer and chief priest of the kingdom. The dual role was not conceived as such, however, and discussion of one to the exclusion of the other lacks cogency and distorts the office. His ritual obligation included presiding over and implementing all public feasts; in addition to specific lesser rituals, offerings, and sacrifices to promote the well-being of the populace and peace within the kingdom. The king was also responsible for adjudicating public disputes and crimes (some on appeal); he provided leadership in contacts with "foreign" authorities; and finally, he was responsible for other things that would promote public order such as insuring peaceful trade and travel within his kingdom.

His authority in former times was based upon the support of his subjects, including the power to levy taxes in money and kind, a power which continued into the 1960s. Conversely, he was expected to be a generous and kind leader who did not use his power for personal gain. It is important to realize that the ritual and secular responsibilities mentioned above were dependent one upon the other. For example, the king's authority to settle a dispute was based upon his priestly sanctity, while at the same time his priestly authority was supported by his skill in settling disputes.

It is undeniable that no king ever had sufficient force at his command to subjugate all of the hamlets of his kingdom had they been opposed to his rule. Furthermore, the disparate traditions and histories of the clans of a kingdom constituted an insubstantial basis for a unified political organization. The unifying force of these kingdoms still found its expression in the 1960s in terms of the mystical powers and person of the king. The mystical powers of a king were the raison d'etre of the political union of the kingdom. The powers ascribed to him became the basis of awe, respect, and loyalty. Underlying all his political skill was his presumed sanctity. Thus the king was a true sacerdotal leader, associated with the sacred which sanctioned his secular power, not only in legend but in fact. The subjects were united in their belief in the ritual powers of a particular king and in their conviction of the religious relevance which he had for them and their lands. In fact, that was precisely how subjects were defined, i.e., those who believed in the ritual relevance of a particular king.

The symbolic identification of a king to his kingdom was revealed, in part, in the public rituals over which he presided (Vaughan, 1964B:391–93). In these ceremonies the king was symbolically identified with the kingdom. At the first, *Yawal*, he was responsible for growth, in the second, *Anngarawai*, his wife was the symbolic fruit of the fields, and in the third, *Digu Digal*, he was the harvest. Two nonritual behaviors might be mentioned in additional support of this symbolism. The king and only the king was permitted to marry into the caste of craft specialists, and when he was buried he would be buried in the manner of that caste. He was the king of all the people, and thus, might and should marry into the caste. Finally, when King Yarkur was once discussing the skills of kingship and the king's relationship with the people, he concluded by saying that a king must always remember, "talaka jangu ptil" ("it is the people who are the king").

The dynasty at Gulagu, which is known by its clan name, Gidum, has shown remarkable dynamism over the three to four hundred years of its tenure (see diagram). Although the kings in the early days of the dynasty seemed to have followed a simple father-to-son succession, this may be an artifact of memory, for if we are to judge by the events of the last six generations, father-to-son succession was rare, and succession was frequently complicated by dramatic events and struggles. This first appears in traditional history with the offspring of the fifth king. There were at least two defections from his royal village. One of his sons established a family line in a nearby village, but the split was not permanent, as he eventually succeeded his father, though many of his descendants are still in the village as a branch of the Gidum dynasty. Three other sons moved farther away altogether and established an independent Gidum dynasty which today is the important kingdom of Dluku.

The Margi rule of succession, while seemingly simple, actually promotes internal stresses. Their rule states that only the eldest living son of a deceased king may succeed to the kingship. However, when a reigning king dies, both his eldest son and his next brother are the eldest living sons of deceased kings, and therefore there is more than one possible claimant to the office. Furthermore, each time that the office moves collaterally, more heirs are created. In 1960, for example, there were at least six heirs to the office. The situation thus created is one in which competition for power is probable. This is particularly notable with the sons of the ninth king of Gulagu, Bulama. Five of them served as kings with the last two serving in the office twice each, for in some instances attempts on the life of a reigning king might have been thwarted, and he escaped only to lead his own coup at a later time. For example, Yeratsada and Wampana, on behalf of their elder brother Digwabu, overthrew Nyamdu, the eleventh king. Then after Digwabu's death they quarreled among themselves. Yeratsada succeeded, was ousted by Wampana, escaped and returned to dislodge his successor, who, nonetheless escaped only to return and kill Yeratsada.

Wampana, the survivor, ushered the Margi of Galagu into the historic period. He is remembered as their greatest king. He was the father of my oldest male informants, the husband of my oldest female informant, and the grandfather of Yarkur, the king throughout all of my research at Gulagu. No one is able to say when Wampana was born or how long he reigned, though it is always said that he reigned for more than fifty years. This is not improbable since everyone agrees that he was very old when he died around 1905. His widow, whom I knew in 1960, was very likely ninety or more, and she and three of his sons all agreed that he had been at least as old as she when he died.

When Wampana died, because of his advanced age, he had at least thirty-two sons, and many of them sought power. He was initially succeeded by his eldest son, Wagla, who chose his next brother, Apagu, to be his "Prime Minister." However, Apagu had higher aspirations, and although stories about him are undoubtedly colored, subsequent events revealed him to be something of a Margi Macbeth.

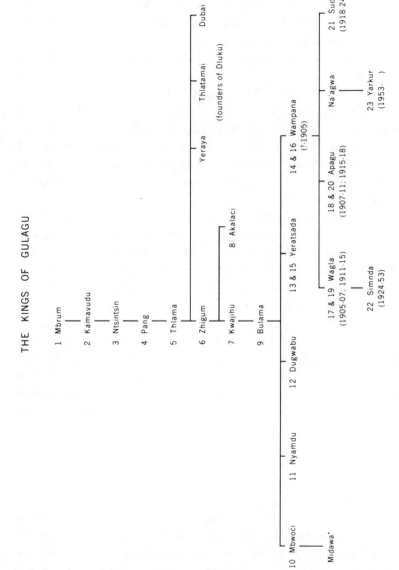

THE KINGS OF GULAGU

1 Mbrum
2 Kamavudu
3 Ntsintsin
4 Pang
5 Thlama
6 Zhigum — Yeraya — Thlatamai — Dubai
        (founders of Dluku)
7 Kwajihu — 8 Akalaci
9 Bulama
10 Mbwoci
11 Nyamdu
12 Dugwabu
13 & 15 Yeratsada
14 & 16 Wampana (?-1905)
17 & 19 Wagla (1905-07; 1911-15)
18 & 20 Apagu (1907-11; 1915-18)
21 Sudi (1918-24)
22 Simnda (1924-53)
23 Yarkur (1953-)
Na'agwa
Midawa*

*Late in Wampana's reign, the Fulani District Head designated Midawa to replace Wampana. However, he was overthrown before he could be installed, and is generally never considered to have been king.

In 1907, Apagu informed the District Head of alleged offenses committed by Wagla, and a raid on the royal village followed. Wagla escaped, but several women from his compound were taken captive. Wagla met with the District Head in an attempt to free the women, but was imprisoned, and Apagu succeeded him as King of Gulagu.

A third brother, Na'agawa, went to the German Administration (a rarely felt force in the area) and with the help of an administrator remembered only as "Baiza," succeeded in freeing Wagla, who went away to collect his forces and plan his strategy. He was able to oust Apagu in 1911 and reign until 1915. Apagu had, however, escaped with his life, and with some of his brothers (one of whom was one of my informants) he attacked the royal village and succeeded in killing both Wagla and Na'agwa. The latter died a heroic death defending Wagla and is particularly revered for it.

Apagu held power until 1918, at which time he was ousted by the combined forces of Simnda, the eldest son of Wagla, and Yarkur, the eldest son of Na'agwa. Yarkur told me that Apagu's life was spared only because their forces had been intercepted by the Fulani District Head, and he had warned them against bloodshed. The succession now passed to Sudi, a much younger son of Wampana, because all of the intervening ones had either been killed in the battles or were allied in exile with Apagu. In 1924, a younger brother of Sudi stole a cow, and Sudi refused to punish him. Shortly thereafter, Sudi was invited to the Provincial Headquarters, and when he arrived he was imprisoned, soon to die therein. The next two eligible sons of Wampana refused the office. One explained to me in the frankest way that the job was too dangerous.

The office finally passed to the next generation. Simnda, the son of Wagla, initially refused the office, and the option then passed to Yarkur, who was considered eligible because of the heroic manner of his father's death and the fact that his father would have succeeded had he not died. (This is highly suspicious reasoning, but Margi have never been ones to let mere rules stand in the way of a good choice. Though I should add that this is the only case I knew of in which the rule of royal succession was deliberately altered.) Yarkur agreed, but Simnda then said if Yarkur became king they would undoubtedly fight, so he finally agreed to accept the office and made Yarkur his "Prime Minister." Simnda turned out to be a man very much in the mold of Wampana and became a respected and beloved ruler. He ruled one month short of twenty-nine years. It was a long and crucial reign, marred only by an attempt on his life in 1939 led by the aged Apagu, who never had given up his obsession with power. This, however, proved to be his last attempt, for he died in prison a few months later. In 1953, the kingship passed to Yarkur when Simnda committed suicide.

Throughout Simnda's long reign, Yarkur had remained his steadfast and able assistant. He had learned a great deal under Simnda's tutelage. Thus, Yarkur was the choice of the Council of Electors, even though in these more peaceful times one of the sons of Wampana sought the office as did the eldest son of Simnda. By this time we are in a period in which colonial rule was more apparent, and the choice had to be approved by the British District Officer. His unpublished diary indicates that there was a very large village turnout with "surprising unanimity" for Yarkur. More than twenty years later Yarkur's wisdom is widely recognized, and he is the most respected of all Margi Dzirngu kings.

Initially, I interpreted these struggles for power as nothing more than examples of a particularly competitive and violent tradition of succession—as history and politics. It was not only my Evans-Pritchardian inclination which led me in this direction, but my royal informants, many of whom had been involved in these contests, viewed them in political terms. Yarkur, for example, explained them as the consequences of rivalry between brothers and jealousy over the status and advantages associated with the kingship.

I began to revise my views, however, when in the western region of the Margi, I asked a group of local men how their dynastic tradition differed from that of the Margi Dzirngu with whom I was more familiar. Their first answer which, I must admit, seemed to come with a certain glee, was: "The Dzirngu kill their kings." Later, in private, I expressed my astonishment at this characterization to a Dzirngu commoner who was traveling with me, for I felt the statement to be outrageous. However, to my surprise, the Dzirngu commoner agreed with the Westerners. Subsequently I discovered that his view was shared by many Dzirngu commoners who saw the struggle for power as an acceptable and traditional way of removing a king. Further, they were able to express the dangers of having a weak king, and they were able to tell me that there was a traditional time of the year at which kings might be killed—during the annual Yawal festival, the festival of growth and virility. Finally, I discovered that the word, *thlida*, which had been used in discussions of the struggles for succession, and which I had understood to be a general term meaning a violent fight or rebellion, refers exclusively to the overthrowing and presumed killing of a king. In short, the Margi have a linguistic category for regicide. When an attempt was made in 1960 to make the office elective and thereby supersede the incumbent, this was somewhat jokingly referred to as a *thlida* because the leader of the movement was the eldest son of the last king and the very person who in former times would have attempted to overthrow the reigning king (Vaughan, 1964A).

It should be noted that the two views of Margi regicide—both the Evans-Pritchardian and the Frazerian—are appropriate, but more importantly, it should be noted that both of these views are held by Margi themselves. On the one hand, there is the political, Evans-Pritchardian view held by the competitors and their supporters (and the political anthropologist), while on the other hand, there is the more detached, Frazerian view of the commoners, a view which discerns a pattern of behavior and views *thlida* as an institution for the removal of failing kings. One might argue for either one or the other as being more realistic. That is basically what the argument in anthropology has been about, but I am convinced that it is not a question of one or the other, rather it is necessary to see that they should never be separated; they are the same. In support of this position I will return to the history of Gulagu.

In 1953 during the reign of Simnda, there were several significant events. In general, there had been pressure for several years from the British administration to get the royal village relocated from atop Mount Gulak to the plains below. This was a matter of convenience in part, but largely an attempt to bring the king of the most prestigious Margi kingdom to a place where he would be more accessible to the forces of modernization. The fact that the mountain was also the abode of many of the kingdom's shrines was doubtlessly not fully comprehended by the administration. Simnda resisted these efforts, and although there is nothing in the government records to indicate that the administration was unduly upset, he was worried about the consequences of his refusal. There was also, in that year, a change in the district head of Madagali District. This was an office traditionally held by a Fulani, the nineteenth-century conquerors of the area; however, at this time there was a split in the Fulani ranks concerning the new headship.

Simnda publicly supported a local Fulani, the son of a much hated man who had ruled in the first quarter of this century. The opposing candidate was the son of an important official from Yola, the provincial capital. The British Administration, who supported the Yola man, was both surprised and angered at Simnda's position, and the District Officer, it is remembered, publicly "lectured" Simnda on the history of Margi relations with the local Fulani. The irony of this situation was not lost on Simnda whose logic was simply "better a known devil than an unknown one." The Fulani from Yola was eventually appointed, much to the embarrassment of Simnda. Slightly later there was a murder in the kingdom, and when the kinsmen of the victim tried to kill the murderer, he was protected by Simnda who preferred to let the law take its course; he was not in any way trying to absolve the murderer. The relatives felt aggrieved and took their case to the provincial headquarters in Yola. Simnda's actions were, of course, upheld, but as it happened they were supported by the father of the newly appointed District Head. Simnda was mortified to have received the backing of the father of a man he had himself failed to support. Shortly thereafter in July, the month of *Yawal*, he committed suicide by falling on his sword.

An inquest into the matter was held, but no resolution was found. Some said he killed himself because he feared being called to Yola over the murder and that he might there, like his immediate predecessor, be imprisoned and die; others believed he was embarrassed at having supported the losing candidate for district head; while others felt he was humiliated by the support of the new District Head's father. Now, none of these explanations seems by itself sufficient for a man in his prime to take his life.

I can only suggest that all the circumstances were such that in a former time there would have been a *thlida*; he had been publicly embarrassed, there was worry that the administration might force them to relocate, and it was the month of *Yawal*. Today, many can remember that the traditional omens had boded ill that *Yawal*. I do not believe that Simnda committed ritual suicide; undoubtedly he killed himself in response to very human passions. But I feel confident that his actions were influenced, perhaps guided, by a larger pattern; it was, in short, time for Simnda to die, and I believe he sensed it.

I am drawn to the conclusion that the Margi Dzirngu did have divine kingship in the Frazerian sense and, further, that they had institutional, though not ritual, regicide as a means of removing kings. Certainly that interpretation seems clear from the viewpoint of commoners. Regicide was sanctioned by their ideology of the peculiar relationship of king to kingdom. That each individual *thlida* had political overtones because it involved competition between leaders, I do not wish to deny. But the political perspective explains the particular and not the general. Both Yarkur's intuitive understanding that he was identified with his subjects and the suicide of Simnda strongly suggest that the ideology of divine kingship was real—if subliminal. Further, the circumstances surrounding Simnda's death suggest that circumstances might well inhibit a king's ability to react to a challenge and perhaps even prompt him to acquiesce his own demise.

My conclusion is not that Evans-Pritchard was wrong and Frazer right; rather that neither, perhaps because of insufficient data, took into consideration the full scope of the institution. In brief, Frazer never seems to have asked "how?"; Evans-Pritchard never asked, "why?"

Interpretation

To this point, I hope that the Margi data have permitted me to make a contribution to our understanding of African kingship and the concept of divine kingship. However, to stop at this point is barely to go beyond history. For too long anthropologists have stopped short of the Frazerian argument. He saw divine kingship as somehow embedded in mankind, not Africa, let alone Shilluk or Margi culture. In this concluding section I wish to return to the Frazerian scope, for as Fortes continued the earlier quotation:

> . . . Sooner or later, every serious anthropologist returns to the great Frazerian *corpus*. For beneath the encrustations of theory, speculation, and prejudice due to the climate of thought in which Frazer lived, there is a vision of mankind which still offers inspiration. It is a vision that takes in the whole of mankind. There lies its greatness. . . . Fallacious though his theories now prove to be, in principle he was right. There are uniformities and common patterns in

the customs and institutions of mankind; and if we want to understand them, we must take into account the common intellectual and emotional dispositions of mankind (1959:8).

The following discussion is concerned neither with documentation of occurrences of divine kingship nor with further elucidation of its operation. Rather, I wish to discuss the themes of the divine king myth and the roles they play in human culture. There are two closely related motifs in the story which I believe have universal appeal. They are the subjects of succession and death, both of which are imbedded in regicide, a topic which has had and continues to have a fascination for us all. The perspective I seek was suggested by Stanley Hyman, who wrote:

> The *Golden Bough* is not primarily anthropology, if it ever was, but a great imaginative vision of the human condition. . . . The key image of *The Golden Bough*, the king who slays the slayer and must himself be slain, corresponds to some universal principle we recognize in life. It caught the imagination not only of Freud and Bergson, Spengler and Toynbee, but of T. S. Eliot, and produced *The Waste Land* . . . (1962:439).

It is self-evident that the divine king myth is concerned with problems of succession, a central topic in political analysis. But our concern here is broader than a conventional political analysis. We are so accustomed to thinking of succession in terms of acceding to high office that we fail to realize that it is a universal social principle virtually applicable to all continuous social institutions.

For example, succession is a major dynamic factor in domestic life. The Oedipal theme is as much concerned with succession as it is with sex. This is not only literally true of the story of Laius, Jocasta, and Oedipus, but it is also true of the Freudian metaphoric usage as well. For if a son hates his father and loves his mother, it follows that the father must fend off his ambitious son and cleave to his wife. Furthermore, the latter is undoubtedly easier to demonstrate than the former.

The father's perspective is clearly demonstrated in the levirate as it is practiced among the Margi. In that system not only may a deceased male's brothers (and classificatory brothers) marry his widows, so may his sons, though a son may not marry his own mother. The complexities of this institution are beyond the scope of this paper, but let it be noted that I have known many Margi men who married their fathers' young widows. From the point of view of an aging father, his young—perhaps sexually demanding—wives are the potential mates of his aspiring sons. Furthermore, whereas the relationship between his wives and his brothers—also their potential husbands—is guarded by institutional joking, there is no such safeguard in the relationship between his wives and sons. In one famous instance, anticipation apparently precipitated the event; the kingdom of Dluku was founded by an outcast from Gulagu who had had a love affair with his father's wife.

In addition to the struggle for succession inherent in the levirate, the aging must anticipate their eventual dependence upon their children since traditional Margi society is almost completely lacking in a general welfare system. As men become weak, and particularly as they become impotent, their former prestige becomes pro forma, they lose their wives, and their farms shrink accordingly. Though I never knew of an instance in which a father literally went to live with his son, I knew many who relied upon their sons in a way which would have been humiliating had anyone dared to discuss it. Thus it is safe to say that among the Margi the struggle between fathers and sons for succession is a social reality at least as much as it is a psychological reality. If sons suffer from Oedipal complexes, fathers suffer no less from Laial anxieties.

The situation for female Margi is more complex and more subtle, nor can it be denied that it might be substantially different in a patrilineal patripotestal society. Certainly overt competition between Margi mothers and daughters is less than that between fathers and sons, and role differentiation by sex is so strong that a discussion of cross-sex succession lacks cogency. Furthermore, the rule of patrilocality assures that daughters customarily marry and reside away from their natal villages, thus reducing the opportunity for competition and reducing succession to a more metaphoric transition. There is, however, one struggle for succession which all women must anticipate: the succession of wives.

For Margi women, marriage is normally terminated when they reach menopause. At that time they leave their husbands' compounds and assume a new status (*malabjagu*). As noted earlier, when men become impotent or sterile they also lose their wives, but the two situations are not analogous. In the first place, sterility in females is inevitable, while for males it is not. Perhaps as a consequence of these circumstances, sterility in males is humiliating and leads to a loss of prestige and position, whereas in females it is recognized as normal and results in a sanctioned change of behavior and a new status with its attendant rights and privileges.

A cursory examination of Margi society and culture might lead one to conclude that women actually look forward to the new status; young women and males of all ages seem to believe this to be so. However, closer examination reveals that in some instances the approach of menopause is not viewed with equanimity, and some postmenopausal women so miss sexual intercourse that they enter into irregular relationships with other men. Consequently, women often try to hide their condition by faking menstruation, and some stay on with their husbands until they are literally forced to leave. The plight of such women is not helped by the fact that their virile husbands are not normally sympathetic and may be actually in the process of trying to please or even acquire one or more younger wives. The older wife can see herself being succeeded by a woman perhaps twenty years younger than she. We have long attributed the competition among wives in polygamous households to jealousy of one kind or another, but the struggle for wifely succession cannot be dimissed. I suggest that among more mature wives who have usually long ago come to terms with problems of jealousy this may be the more important issue.

The problems of domestic succession are not unknown in other societies, though it is often blandly masked by normative descriptions. "The developmental cycle in domestic groups" is a benign discussion of familial succession. Nor should we ignore the possibility that the drama of succession is unrecognized by ethnographers too young to have felt the breath of the next generation on their own necks. In our society any parent who has been bested by his or her offspring in sports, games, domesticity, or professional achievement knows something of the feeling. And in no society is it a totally joyous event, even though it may be marked by festivity and a new status. Succession within a family represents a loss of dominance and a significant change in the power relationships inherent in all families. The problem of succession is the fear of losing dominance, and that is an anxiety we all know. Even as we achieve dominance, our introspective nature tells us we will inevitably lose it. We may suppress the awareness, we may refuse to compete, or we may use other techniques to make the situation tolerable, but in the end we recognize the Priest of Nemi in our mirrors.

The theme of death, while more basic to the divine king myth, is more difficult to interpret than the theme of succession. This may stem from some tendency to avoid the topic, but it seems more complex than this. A king who would more or less go willingly to his death puzzles, fascinates, and repels us; we do not believe it, yet we cannot forget it. Writers have often been inspired by this theme in *The Golden Bough*, and I find that the most penetrating insights into regicide have come from works of literature.

In 1958 Mary Renault wrote a popular book about classical Greece on this topic called *The King Must Die*. It is deficient in many ways—particularly as a history of early Greece—but it does have flashes of insight into the institution of regicide. When the young Theseus asks his grandfather why anyone would want to be king knowing he would die, his grandfather explains:

> Horses go blindly to the sacrifice; but the gods give knowledge to men. When the King was dedicated, he knew his moira. In three years, or seven, or nine, or whatever the custom was, his term would end and the god would call him. And he went consenting, or else he was no king, and power would not fall on him to lead the people. When they came to choose among the Royal Kin, this was his sign: that he chose short life with glory, and to walk with god, rather than live long, unknown like the stall-fed fox (1958:16–17).

This goes very much to the heart of both the political and institutional realities of divine kingship, for in addition to everything else that has been said about regicide, it is an effective check on the excessive use of power by a king. Once a man agrees to give up his life—however remote the time might be—his credibility is entirely different, and we might well expect that his interest in the office changes. In fact, I would suggest that a certain vulnerability is a very necessary thing to have in an official who has unusual power, because I have learned from my many talks with Yarkur that a vulnerable leader is a less aggrandizing one.

But the real insight into divine kingship, as far as I am concerned, comes from Eugene Ionesco's play *Exit the King* (1963). The theme is quite simple: a king and his kingdom are in mutual decay; to save the kingdom he must die. But unlike the Frazerian theme there is no discussion of a successor, no slayer to slay the failed king. The drama concerns the king accepting the state of affairs, his responsibility for them, and finally accepting his death.

The play, of course, is not about kings, but about men, as the divine king myth is about men as well as kings. It is about accepting our responsibilities, but more importantly, about accepting our deaths. Ionesco called writing the play "an apprenticeship in dying." He has said, "*Exit the King* was written in twenty days. I wrote first of all for ten days. I had just been ill and I'd been very scared. Then, after those ten days, I had a relapse and was ill for another fortnight. And at the end of the fortnight, I started writing again. I finished the play in the next ten days" (Bonnefoy, 1966:78). It is well known that Ionesco is a writer obsessed with death. Within the first minutes of his conversation with Claude Bonnefoy he said:

> I've already written about what I felt whenever I saw a funeral— those long processions filing past right under the window of the house where I lived; and how I'd ask my mother what it meant. 'Someone is dead.' 'Why? Why is he dead?' 'He is dead because he was ill.' And I finally understood it, people died because they'd been ill, because they'd had an accident—whatever happened, death was an accident—and if you took great care not to be ill, if you were very good, if you always wore your muffler and took your medicine, if you looked both ways before you crossed the street, then you wouldn't ever have to die. . . . One day I asked my mother, 'We're all going to die, aren't we? Tell me the truth.' She said, 'Yes.' I must have been four years old, maybe five; I was sitting on the ground and she was standing over me. I can still see her. . . . I was very frightened (1966:11–12).

The play explores the childhood myth that death is avoidable. At one point when the king seems ready to die, he says, "I could decide not to die" (72), and the whole argument begins anew. Some audiences have found this disconcerting and the ensuing discussion dramatically repetitive, but Ionesco has deliberately contrived the incident to establish the viability of the childhood illusion and the king's control over events.

For me, the divine king myth has never been more succinctly caught than in a simple exchange between the tormented King and Queen Marguerite (36):

He: Kings ought to be immortal.
She: They are. Provisionally.

In sum, the divine king is a "provisional immortal." The concept represents idealism tempered with realism. Of course, in the end Ionesco's king—and we—must accept the human condition; he finally wills his own death, and through his death his society is saved.

But our deaths will not save our society, so what, to use Fortes' expression, "common intellectual and emotional disposition of mankind" is struck by this myth? Wherein lies the catholic appeal of this great theme? Even Seligman seems to have known that establishing historical origins failed to explain the institution's persistence, for he wrote "the complex of beliefs centering around the Divine Kingship must have appealed to some deep-seated need of early West African man, of which he may not have been fully conscious" (1934:18). I do not think it necessary to suggest an archetype which is a part of the psychic unity of mankind upon which Frazer seemed to base his theory, nor need we inquire into the "deep structures" of the human mind as some moderns might.

At the heart of the divine king myth lies a fundamental paradox known to children and adults in societies all over the world. Like all living organisms humans are programmed to live—often at the expense of other lives. Yet unlike all other organisms, humans are aware that they must die. As Marlow put it: "To die . . . therefore live we all;/ . . . all live to die, and rise to fall" (*Edward II*, Iv. vi. 110–11). Our awareness, however, goes beyond mere thanatopsis and thus beyond Ionesco, for not only do we die, we are succeeded. Sons succeed fathers and watch their sons prepare to succeed them. "The priest who slew the slayer, and shall himself be slain" is the personification of the life cycle with a particular emphasis upon the inevitability of death.

Every society has some way of alleviating the tensions—both personal and social—which are engendered by this knowledge. Beliefs and tales concerning eternal youth, reincarnation, life after death, ancestor worship are all to this point. So too is the myth of the divine king— but in a strikingly different way. The beliefs just mentioned all deny the finality of death and thus teach that the paradox is false or at least avoidable. In contrast, the divine king myth admits that death is inevitable, but it makes death, if not a voluntary act, at least an occasion which one faces with the awareness that it can have purpose.

It is a time of renewal through succession. The myth appeals to us because it does not deny the obvious—we will die—but it says that death need not be pointless. We know succession is constructive because we in our times have succeeded.

The divine king is myth; a myth illuminated by the vision of Frazer, the political insight of Evans-Pritchard, and the artistry of Ionesco. But perhaps it is more than myth, for beyond the scholars I can hear Yarkur saying, "It is the people who are king," and I can imagine Simnda with his terrible sword on that rainy night atop Mount Gulak playing out a drama no playwright ever wrote, validating a custom so obscure that it took fully fifteen years to appreciate it. For too long we have not been able to see the Bough for the leaves.

BIBLIOGRAPHY

Bonnefoy, Claude. 1970. *Conversations with Eugene Ionesco*. London: Faber and Faber. Translation of *Intretiens avec Eugène Ionesco,* 1966.

Evans-Pritchard, E. E. 1937. *Witchcraft, Oracles and Magic Among the Azande*. Oxford: The Clarendon Press.

———. 1948. *The Divine Kingship of the Shilluk of the Nilotic Sudan*. Cambridge: Cambridge University Press.

Fortes, Meyer. 1959. *Oedipus and Job in West African Religion*. Cambridge: Cambridge University Press.

Frazer, James George. 1911–15. *The Golden Bough*. 3rd ed. London: Macmillan and Company.

———. 1922. *The Golden Bough*. Abridged ed. New York: The Macmillan Company.

Hyman, Stanley Edgar. 1962. *The Tangled Bank: Darwin, Frazer and Freud as Imaginative Writers*. New York: Atheneum.

Ionesco, Eugene. 1963. *Exit the King*. New York: Grove Press. Translation of *Le Roi se meurt*.

———. 1971. *Present Past, Past Present; A Personal Memoir*. New York: Grove Press. Translation of *Présent passé, passé présent,* 1968.

Krige, Eileen Jensen. 1975. "Divine Kingship, Change and Development." In *Studies in African Social Anthropology*, edited by Meyer Fortes and Sheila Patterson. London: Academic Press.

Mair, Lucy Philip. 1974. *African Societies*. London: Cambridge University Press.

Marlow, Christopher. 1970 (1594). *Edward II; Text and Major Criticism*. Edited by Irving Ribner. New York: Odyssey Press.

Meek, Charles Kingsley. 1931. *A Sudanese Kingdom*. London: Kegan Paul, Trench, Trubner and Company.

Moret, Alexandre. 1932. "Le mise à mort du Dieu en Égypte." In *The Frazer Lectures, 1922–1932*, edited by William R. Dawson. London: Macmillan and Company.

Perry, William James. 1923. *The Children of the Sun*. London: Methuen and Company.

Renault, Mary. 1958. *The King Must Die*. New York: Pantheon.

Seligman, Charles Gabriel. 1934. *Egypt and Negro Africa*. London: G. Routledge and Sons.

Vansina, Jan. 1962. "A Comparison of African Kingdoms." *Africa* 32:324–35.

Vaughan, James H. 1964A. "Culture, History, and Grass-Roots Politics in a Northern Cameroons Kingdom." *American Anthropologist* 66:1078–95.

———. 1964B. "The Religion and World View of the Marghi." *Ethnology* 3:389–97.

Young, Michael W. 1966. "The Divine Kingship of the Jukun: A Re-evaluation of Some Theories." *Africa* 36:135–52.

Women and Men in
Two East African Societies

by T. O. Beidelman

The woman's cause is man's:
they rise or sink Together.
Tennyson,
The Princess

In 1893, Emile Durkheim contrasted the natural or internal differences between the sexes with those that are cultural or external (1949: 182). He asserted that natural differences are insufficient to support an institution as pervasive and enduring as marriage and concluded that the complementary differences between the sexes, upon which marriage is founded, derive essentially from society or culture rather than nature. Seventy years later, Lévi-Strauss reformulated the problem, though taking us little further than to reveal in a masterly survey how little systematic work has been undertaken to examine the intricacies of this complex problem (1960:261–85; compare 1966:109–34). This is all the more surprising if one accepts the idea that marriage and sexual differences provide the central mechanisms by which social life is ordered in preliterate societies. The family is the institution through which individuals are formed into social persons; it is also the arena in which basic concepts of space (house and settlement) and time (offspring, succession, fertility, veneration of the dead) are conceived of and change as its members age and consequently depart or displace one another. In these respects, sexuality and age are inextricably connected and both in turn convey order and flux in time and the pathos of their effects upon the social person.[1]

The interplay between sexuality and age is the first and least dismissible aspect of social roles and statuses in preliterate societies. It accounts for both assonance and dissonance between natural and cultural qualities of the actors within such societies. By assonance I mean the recognition and use of inherent biological features for social ends, for example, that knowledge is more or less related to age, that the gain and loss of sexuality is related to age, and that women rather than men bear children. By dissonance I mean the failure or rejection by any society to account fully for some of these inherent features. This may involve a failure to incorporate individuals who do not neatly fit into particular stereotypes, such as a barren woman, or the difficulties due to varying sex ratios or numbers of offspring by different co-wives or different siblings. Some of these difficulties are partly smoothed over by such practices as woman-woman marriage, adoption, the doctoring of genealogies, and allocation of unusual types to such roles as those of shaman and curers, or explained away as due to the action of an evil fate (See Fortes, 1959).

The interplay between the biologically and personally inherent and the culturally external is neither smooth nor simple. At times, it even seems difficult to justify such dichotomization. In all cases the relation is both obscured and, more importantly, enhanced by the cultural symbols which raise sex and age to new dignity and force both by the attachment of moral tone and by the extension of these through association with other symbols to cosmic proportions over the entire matrix of a society. Yet despite the fact that particular sexual roles are greatly determined by culture rather than by nature, important differences occur which suggest that at certain levels women are more deeply beings of their biology than are men. To put it another way, the roles of men are more subject to cultural elaborations than are those of women. Of course, I am not suggesting that this is necessarily the case today or that it need be in the future; it does seem the general state of things in most preliterate and preindustrial societies.

In this essay I illustrate a few of these points by contrasting two geographically adjacent African societies with sharp cultural differences: the Bantu language–speaking, matrilineal, sedentary Kaguru, and the para-Nilotic, patrilineal, semipastoral Baraguyu of east central Tanzania.[2]

The Kaguru

Both Kaguru and Baraguyu subordinate women to men, consider women morally weaker, and consequently exclude them from jural authority and related ritual activities. Both Kaguru and Baraguyu women are absorbed in domestic chores which vary little from day to day and show little modification through seasonal changes. While Kaguru women cultivate and therefore have some changes of pace between the dry and wet seasons, their daily tasks of cooking, tending children, and fetching firewood and water recur daily and consume many hours regardless of what else must be done. Females commence such domestic chores while still children and continue them into old age, at first helping their mothers, then running their own households, and finally often helping run the affairs of their married children. In contrast, the activities of Kaguru men vary more with age and extend far beyond the household. Men justify the monotony and regularity in women's tasks in two ways. Women are weak and unstable, and therefore cannot be entrusted with momentous affairs such as litigation, ritual, or making decisions about the allocation of resources. Furthermore, a regular routine enforces orderliness in beings who might otherwise fluctuate dangerously in their moods and actions.

The Kaguru are particularly resourceful in rationalizing such differential treatment. To them the very world of nature reflects such judgments. Kaguru observe that domestic animals and plants have their wild counterparts: chickens and guinea fowl, goats and antelopes, cattle and wildebeests, plaintains and wild bananas, sorghum and grass, vegetables and wild herbs. They maintain that God gave domestic animals and plants to both men and women, but while men, being stable, maintained theirs unto this day, women, being unstable, let theirs degenerate to their present wild and useless condition.[3] Baraguyu women are even more poorly characterized, being blamed for bringing death to humanity through petty jealousy between cowives (Beidelman, 1968:87).

Kaguru notions about physiology and kinship reinforce a wide range of beliefs which go far to explain sexual differences in personality, social statuses, and the ways in which men and women may define and realize their goals in social relations. Children are formed from the blood of their mothers, identical and continuous with the others in a matriclan, and from their father's semen which provides the bone. Here Kaguru are speaking not merely about physiology and descent but about moral character as well. The maternal side is like blood; it is hot and fluid and thus requires containment for physical and moral control and direction. The paternal side is cool and solid, providing the form, order, and measured judgment embodied in male jural authority. Women make matrikin alike through common blood; the members of a matrilineage define their differences and individuality by reference to different fathers. Women provide a passive and unifying essence which may be manipulated and divided by men.[4] Indeed, Kaguru insist that women can be described as being married, whereas men always marry, just as women are considered passive sexually, whereas men perform. The metaphor is repeated by the quintessential accoutrements of Kaguru masculine and feminine roles, the bow of a man which enhances his aggressive, active nature and enables him to subdue the wilderness, and the woman's oil jar which artifically transforms her natural attractions into even more cosmetically alluring ones, thereby facilitating her sexual receptivity.

Such themes pervade Kaguru culture, presumably reinforcing such sexual stereotypes at every turn. Thus, the house is considered a metaphor for a marriage, with the upright and supporting center pole associated with the phallus, and the low hearth, where hot and nourishing foods are prepared, considered woman's domain. Each is a byword for an aspect of the home. So too a proper meal reflects such dichotomies, for it should combine a staple derived from the gardens tended by the domestic couple and pulverized by the wife and a garnish, preferably meat, associated with livestock or game controlled by men or, as a substitute, some vegetable often associated with the bush and the outside. In rituals, women also tend to be contained, as they retire into the depths of houses for such ceremonies. Women mourn with prolonged wailing indoors, while men sit outside providing a stoic and measured account of the morbid events. Men bring gifts of cash and meat and other goods wrested from an alien, outside world, whereas women bring staples from the household store. Men are aggressive dancers, calling signals on whistles and moving energetically and often idiosyncratically to attract and amuse a female audience who drum and move more restrainedly within undifferentiated circles or lines. In expressions related to grain grinding or pounding, to eating, to hunting, and to firemaking, men's and women's active and passive contrasting natures are reiterated in metaphor. Even names display similar contrasts between the covert and explicit: names associated with one's matriclan are rarely used, being considered vulnerable and too intimately involved in one's sexual nature. Instead, people prefer names associated with the father. In the case of women, teknonyms are preferred even over paternal names, reflecting the fact that a woman's jural position is invariably dependent upon some man, a father or husband, and indicating that her esteem and security depend upon the birth of children.[5]

Considering the attributes and practices mentioned above, it should be obvious that Kaguru see male and female sexuality as both complementary and opposed. Male sexuality is readily subject to guidance and order, whereas female sexuality can never be properly controlled. Women are initiated immediately after the first menses and therefore usually singly. Such rituals are described merely as "taking women in hand," "softening," or "cooling" them, but not essentially changing them permanently; in contrast, the "lower" or feminine portion of a man's genitals is removed, consequently making him physically and morally clean in a way different from women.

Since there is no dramatic sign of male maturation comparable to menses, boys are invariably initiated at a set time, in the dry season, and usually in groups. There is thus far more of a sense of age grouping among pubescent youths than among girls. A number of boys enter into courting and adulthood at about the same time and share the same ceremonies, whereas girls, while supported by the other women of the neighborhood, usually go through initiation alone.

Kaguru have complex and contradictory notions about the sexual dispositions of men and women. There is a divergence of standards whereby women are not supposed to sleep with men other than their husbands, whereas men often boast openly of their extramarital conquests. Yet both men and women speak of women being difficult to satisfy and being receptive to any overtures. A Kaguru proverb says: "What woman would refuse a man?" Kaguru men often express concern about their abilities to satisfy their wives and speculate whether their women need many lovers to meet their needs. Certainly it is a fact that men world-wide face the challenge of achieving and maintaining an erection; women need have no interest to engage in sex. In short, a woman's emotions need not be aroused for her to copulate and conceive. Kaguru men are often worried about being able to perform properly and make allusions to *vagina dentata* and other threatening female qualities.

A by-product of the Kaguru male's concern over performance is found in the Kaguru belief that adultery provides more uninhibited sex than does marriage. A Kaguru asks of a sexually uninhibited and knowledgeable wife, "Where did she learn so much?" "How can I alone please such a one?" With another's wife he takes his chances and leaves the problem of faithfulness and total satisfaction to her husband.

I am convinced, however, that some of these sexual tensions derive not only from the universal and perpetual challenge of male performance but from the structure of Kaguru society. Kaguru women have moral claims on offspring regardless of whether they are born in or out of wedlock, whereas men have claims only as fathers or mother's brothers, the latter also not depending upon any marital bond. I asked one Kaguru why it was important that a man's children be biologically his own since they would be jurally his so long as he had paid bridewealth for his wife. The man queried, "How can I curse them if they disobey if they are not mine?" One could argue that the structure of Kaguru society not only prompts considerable concern by husbands about their wives' sexual needs and conduct, but also inordinate and sometimes even what appears to be incestuous concern by brothers regarding their sisters' sexuality. Indeed, a brother-sister-sister's husband triangle is one of the prominent themes in Kaguru oral literature and involves the only situation where Kaguru themselves repeatedly express concern about the possibility of incest.[6]

Women's moral frailty and their problematic sexuality are further expressed in dress, etiquette, and in retrictions observed during menstruation and after giving birth. While boys often go about naked, and men are buried nude, even very young girls wear pubic aprons, and adult women must never be buried unclothed. Menstruating women are periodically excluded from many areas including gardens, places of brewing, and scenes of religious ceremonies and divination, whereas men never face such restrictions. Menstruating women are described as "sick" and should wear dark clothing which will discourage the notice of sexually interested men. Women who have given birth should refrain from sexual relations until after they wean their children, whereas men face no restrictions related to their offspring. Women should follow men when traveling, bathe downstream from men, thereby being excluded from the supposedly weightier matters discussed by men. Men and women do not sit together at church, at court, or at other formal gatherings. What few divisions of labor that exist between men and women are often rationalized as due either to women's polluting nature (such as exclusion from ritual activities and roof building) or to their supposedly undependable nature (exclusion from herding, litigation, and other challenging activities). To some extent such divisions reinforce women's images of themselves. While these aspects are accepted as true by many women, women do not necessarily judge themselves negatively in all contexts. Women derive considerable amusement from describing themselves as sexually voracious, deceitful, and, in general, as posing problems for some men. Old women, in particular, can be quite formidable by flaunting their supposedly disorderly nature with considerable impunity, since they rarely have elder males who exert firm jural control over them.

These rules are culturally arbitrary, but they reflect profound inherent differences between women and men. Male sexuality appears gradually during puberty and persists, apparently with continued fertility, into late age. Even when a male is impotent or homosexual, a blind eye may be turned, allowing a surrogate genitor to produce a child and save a fellow's face. Female sexuality is different. It is, at least in the eyes of Kaguru, clearly marked by menstruation, and it ceases with menopause. Kaguru recognize the fact that elder women may well be enjoyed sexually, but they are far less concerned about accessibility. Legitimatized female sexuality exists within a narrower span of time than does men's, and it is clearly demarcated at both ends of the time scale. Furthermore, with menopause old women assume many attributes of men, being free to enter areas ordinarily restricted from women and to exert influence over other women and even men via their married sons and daughters. For these reasons, old women take on a liminal, ambiguous status for Kaguru, figuring as sometimes benign, sometimes malevolent, but usually powerful figures. They are often so described in oral literature. No such transformation marks aging men. Indeed, Kaguru men do not age sexually in this manner (though men often seem to do so in our society).

While growing up, boys and girls associate separately at an early age. Girls share domestic chores with their mothers and elder sisters, while boys tend herds or gardens, often in association with older youths or even their uncles and fathers. By nine or ten, and certainly always before puberty, children of both sexes will be separated from their parents' dwelling since "knowing" children should rigorously avoid association with the space where their parents have sexual relations. Girls will reside in a nearby house erected for the unmarried girls of a hamlet; boys reside in another. Of course, if a girl has a mother who is widowed or divorced and continent, she may reside with

her. Kaguru traditionally separated both males and females in most
activities, from play and work to eating and sleeping, long before
puberty. I knew of many Kaguru women, widowed or divorced, who
lived alone, but I knew of only one man living alone, and he was
judged odd and perhaps mad. Kaguru men need women more than
women need men.

Kaguru women's sexuality is limited in yet another sense. A woman's social fate rests on her fertility. No one can bear heirs and followers for her. Of course, men too depend on women for heirs, but
while this may make them dependent on variations in female fertility,
no man is necessarily, as is a woman, limited to the fertility of a single
womb. A man may have many sisters and many wives, but only a
woman's own womb is the key to her security and esteem.

I have so far described these sexual differences mainly in terms of
beliefs and customs or inherent biological differences while underem-
phasizing the broader features of Kaguru social structure. Yet certain
principles of Kaguru matriliny underlying many aspects of Kaguru
life determine motives and strategies so as to create different psychological as well as social beings. Men monopolize authority but rely on
their sisters' children to be their heirs and followers. This assumes considerable strength in affectual bonds, especially between siblings as
encouraged through a mother over her adult children. A man, as
mother's brother, is dominant over his sisters, nieces, and nephews in
so far as they submit to the overriding strength of their bonds to their
mother. Furthermore, such men's dominance of these persons endures
only so long as their brothers-in-law and nieces' husbands have somewhat weakened domestic ties. Herein lies a deep ambiguity in Kaguru
society. Men's authority rests on two ultimately contradictory principles: a man's rights as a head of a matrilineage and a man's rights
as head of a domestic group. A woman has no such contradictory commitments. While she may or may not seek to pit her husband against
her matrikin, her own welfare is primarily and inextricably tied to
her children, whether born in or out of wedlock. A woman's moral
hold is expressed in terms of affect and a mystical tie of blood, a power unassailable in mere jural terms. In contrast, men are faced with
competing commitments, trying to be good husbands and fathers yet
also good uncles and brothers, both difficult demands in a world of
limited social resources. Failure to meet such jural obligations may
risk forfeiting allegiance of potential followers. Mothers have no such

divided authority, and that accounts partly for their pervasive informal influence.

Male and female sexuality are further viewed differently by a couple's children. A woman's fertility in no way decreases the influence of her children; indeed, her sons gain with the birth of sisters, though less in the case of added brothers who may eventually compete for authority and control within a lineage segment. In contrast, a father's sexuality may also be expressed through cowives. In such cases, the greater fertility of one wife as contrasted with another may set cowives and their respective children against one another in competing for the allocation of resources from the father. Furthermore, a man's fertility as a father is invariably at odds with his value as a mother's brother since his own children are rivals to his nieces and nephews in terms of assistance and inheritance. Women face no ambivalent choices such as men do, since their interests and those of their children should be the same in all situations.

For Kaguru, women's sexuality, or more exactly, their fertility, is more centrally and blatantly tied to their security and esteem than is that of men. Unlike men, also, Kaguru women are bound closely to social controls during a shorter period of time, coterminous with their actual child-bearing years. While this leads Kaguru women to have intense concern over their own fertility, it also instills in them a set of attitudes and motives regarding their offspring which are clearer, less problematic, and less vulnerable to assault than are those held by men.

The Baraguyu

The Baraguyu construction of sexuality resembles the Kaguru in many respects. Certainly a Baraguyu women's fate is also tied to her fertility. For her, too, barrenness is a calamity. Baraguyu women also are judged to be less stable and sensible than men and, consequently, are excluded from most important ritual, from adjudication, and from formal decisions about the allocation of most livestock. Like the Kaguru, Baraguyu women provide the key points for divisions and allegiances for men within a lineage, even though they are patrilineal rather than matrilineal. Like Kaguru, Baraguyu also speak of descent through blood. Other important parallels may be found, but there are

also important differences, both in regard to how women serve as foci
for divisions between men and in regard to how Baraguyu culture defines masculinity and its relation to age and sexuality. In this, because
age is perhaps as important as sexuality for Baraguyu, men's sexuality
is complexly and ambiguously defined. Since relative age is here closely
associated with authority which in turn is the exclusive domain of
elder men, we find that Baraguyu males undergo a series of modifications of their inherent sexual natures, whereas Baraguyu women, denied formal access to authority, are subject to far less graduated cultural interference. The following data suggest that Baraguyu and
Kaguru conceptions of the person differ from one another as they relate to men, especially in terms of their sexuality, far more than they
do for women. This is because men are less subject to age in terms
of their sexuality than are women, who must be utilized within the
limited period in which they may conceive and bear children. The
very nature of male sexuality or, rather, the illusions which it may
sustain, allows for prolongation of paternity (as contrasted to genitorship), whereas women's biological reality as bearers of children is
clearly less malleable.[7]

I begin with Baraguyu women since formally they present the
less complex aspect of my account. Girls commence a life of activities
which change little through old age. At an early age they begin to
do women's chores of fetching water and firewood, milking, preparing food, making ornaments and clothing, and building dwellings.
They soon tend children as well, so that even many duties of mother-
hood are known before marriage. Long before puberty, girls commence sexual play with men, usually unmarried warriors. In all of
this, female lives do not undergo profound changes in terms of daily
routine. The relations of females with males change, however, from
child, to Lolita-like lover, to wife, to mother, to mother-in-law, and
grandmother. In the first and last three statuses, sensuality is denied,
but in the other phases it is not only recognized but encouraged, often
with a wide variety of partners and considerable freedom for women.
Yet outside the area of sensuality, females' relations with males undergo complex and highly important changes subject to clear rules
and harsh penalties. For example, girls who have undergone clitoridectomy (removal of the male aspect of their genitals) may have
free access to unmarried youths, but may not conceive; married wom-
en make clearly recognized demands upon their husbands to see that

they conceive and also covertly hold expectations to cheat with unmarried youths. They are also expected to sleep with their husbands' age-mates and to perform all of the regular household chores including providing for visitors. Mothers of married men are expected not to be overtly sexual and should probably not bear children.

In sharp contrast to women, the career of each Baraguyu male goes through sharply defined and contrasting phases of development. As a boy he will spend nearly all of his time herding livestock, almost exclusively in the company of other boys or even alone with the herd. Back in camp, as a socially sexless person, he will be free to speak and associate with everyone, although as a minor he will be expected to know his place in deference to those older than himself. As he reaches puberty he will be teased, sometimes harshly, by those who have already been initiated. It is through circumcision that Baraguyu men become proper moral and jural beings. This is done singly or in groups but is invariably considered a group experience since all males circumcised during a four-year period remain for life members of a named age-set. All Baraguyu men may be divided into four age-sets: junior and senior warriors, and junior and senior elders. After the four-year circumcision period has elapsed, circumcision is closed and a new age-set is not initiated for approximately ten years. The four age-sets therefore encompass nearly all adult males, spanning a period of over fifty years. At the junior end of this cycle are a mass of boys clamoring to be initiated into the system, while at the senior end are an ever-dwindling number of elders who will eventually be superannuated by the initiation of a new age-set. At this point, boys will become junior warriors, junior warriors senior warriors, senior warriors junior elders, junior elders senior elders, and the few old senior elders remaining will pass into a respected but ineffectual limbo outside the formal four-part system.

There is intense rivalry between adjacent age-sets, with elders viewing youngsters as displacing them and competing with them in terms of the sexual favors of women. These rivalries are expressed through adultery as well as through verbal abuse, especially at dances where cuckolds are often taunted through allusive songs. In contrast, members of the same age-set are expected to show intense solidarity, pursuing women together while warriors and later, as elders, drinking together and even showing hospitality with wives. Alternate age-sets are considered allied: my rivals' rivals are my friends. The newest

age-set (junior warriors) is sponsored in their initiation by junior elders. Alternate age-sets somewhat resemble fathers and sons in their
relations whereas adjacent age-sets resemble competing elder and junior brothers.

When Baraguyu boys become warriors, they may continue to tend
livestock, especially if there are dangers from cattle rustlers or lions,
but they also now take off a great deal of time to travel in groups
courting girls, attending dances, and generally seeing the country.
This is their first opportunity to travel and visit their peers. It will
continue the rest of their lives, first as amatory and adventurous es-
capades, then later to attend beer clubs, to take part in rituals, to
attend marriages and initiations, to negotiate the loan and purchase
of livestock, and to plan with others about strategies in grazing and
settlement. Unlike their women, Baraguyu men are remarkable travelers and may often be found hundreds of miles from their camps. As a
senior warrior, a young man will continue to pursue a life of herding,
play, and wandering, but by now will have accumulated some livestock, usually as gifts from his parents. He will now hold mixed feelings about the warrior life, relishing its glamor and adventure, yet
also looking forward to becoming a junior elder and thereby being
allowed to marry and establish his own household. With the initiation
of a new set of junior warriors, a senior warrior passes into elderhood.
He will marry and have jurally recognized children, set up his own
home, albeit probably near that of his father and elder brothers. He
will no longer attend dances or openly flirt with women, and he will
be allowed to drink beer. He will now spend the greater part of his
time in the company of other elders, often drinking, and no longer be
required to undertake any chores whatsover, these being the responsibility of women, boys, and, to a limited extent, warriors.[8]

These changes from boyhood to warriorhood to elderhood are
marked by extremely sharp changes in grooming, dress etiquette, and
sexuality. While the statuses and roles of males cannot be understood
except in relation to the roles of women, it is striking that Baraguyu
males are subject to profound modification of their sexuality sharply
in contrast to the lesser modifications to which women are subjected.

Let us first examine this sexual dimorphism in terms of grooming
and dress. For Baraguyu, hair is profoundly expressive. Its excess conveys a sense of disorder, abandon, and yet also force. Body hair is
periodically removed, and the hair of females, from infancy to old

age, is shaved. The only exception involves some relaxation of these rules during certain *post partem* observations which are connected with a woman's heightened fertility. Throughout her life, a Baraguyu female wears much the same type of garb, a leather dress, blackened to indicate density or opacity, an interpretative assumption which I support with the observation that men don blackened garments and female ornaments at certain liminal occasions.[9] A woman is decorated with beads, necklaces, bracelets, earrings, and heavy metal wires wrapped around her arms and legs. Women rarely wear sandals, even though they may walk many miles each day collecting firewood and water. There are, however, some significant changes. After initiation (clitoridectomy) a girl will wear a wide beaded belt which signals that she is now a sexually available person. Girls are initiated while quite young, usually before menstruation, and in any case are forbidden to conceive before marriage. This does not, however, preclude a wide variety of sexual play with warriors, often much older than these girls. The only other important change in dress marking a woman's career is her acquisition of round metal coils, worn in the ears, and a wide leather belt worn underneath the dress, both signs of a married woman. By these signs one may immediately spot the sexual availability and status of females, yet otherwise the garb and grooming of females alter little throughout their lives. It is true that very young and very old women may not wear quite as much jewelry as women in their prime, but there is no rule about this. Girls who are unmarried take part in frequent dances with warriors and on those occasions cover themselves with red ochre, just as warriors do. I argue that in this situation they are indeed vicarious warriors partaking in many of the young men's unruly qualities of sexual allurement and abandon but prescribed sterility.

Dress and grooming of Baraguyu males is more varied and complex than is that for women. Uninitiated boys wear drab single cloths and only the most modest item or two of jewelry. They rarely wear sandals, despite the fact that they spend most of their time trekking about rough country with livestock. Like all Baraguyu males, their cloth togas expose the left sides of their bodies so that as they move about, their genitals and buttocks are often exposed. Baraguyu males of all ages will often strip completely in public in order to groom themselves, rearrange their clothing and gear, or to accomplish a messy task that might soil their garments. No such comparable nudity, however fleeting, is ever countenanced for Baraguyu women. As boys approach puberty they will begin to pierce and distend their ears, but will wear only modest wooden pegs in these apertures, wearing the metal weights for their lobes only after circumcision. Although a herd-boy spends long hours in the bush, he may carry no weapon other than a stick. Boys' hair is cut short exactly like that of women. In many respects, uncircumcised boys are like women, subject to any and all duties, and denied all of the aggressive, arrogant, and narcissistic traits developed by proper warriors.

After circumcision a Baraguyu male assumes a highly stylized image which is a kind of caricature of masculinity. He will now wear a brightly colored toga, usually red but perhaps maroon or blue or rich brown. He will wear handsome jewelry (earrings, rings, armlets, anklets, bracelets, and necklaces). These will be made by women and girls, and therefore all are seen as proof of a youth's sexual charm. He will now wear copper earweights and will always wear sandals. He will carry a snuffbox on a chain for he is now allowed this luxury of adult men and women. He will allow his hair to grow, at times faking the length by weaving in long strands of sisal. This hair will be plaited into elaborate queues and braids which require many hours to create by his fellow warriors and unmarried girls. He will cover himself with red ochre and fat and spend a great deal of time preening, grooming, whitening his teeth, oiling his body, plucking body hair, and making himself beautiful. One of his favorite possessions will be a handmirror. At this time he will carry an array of weapons, a veritable armory: a walking stick, a razor-sharp sword, a knobkerry, and a long spear.

The weapons, grooming, jewelry, and his arrogant but attractive bearing will all signal the warrior's masculinity, his epitomization of what Baraguyu themselves say they value most. Baraguyu men often nostalgically recall their warriorhood as the most glamorous and important phase of their lives. Yet by senior warriorhood, many youths are keen to lose warrior status. This is indeed a time of few responsibities, of dances, adventurous exploits, and flirtation and seduction. Yet ironically these warriors, imbued with a fierce and sexy manliness, are forbidden to marry and, while they may sire children, they may not acknowledge them for these will be the offspring of adulterous unions with the wives of their elders. Baraguyu warriorhood expresses an ambiguous sexuality, a sexuality which is denied the recognized social weight that would lend it power and authority through recognized procreation.

Upon attaining elderhood a warrior will cut his hair, wear little jewelry, and soon acquire a European-style blanket in which he may enfold himself in a dignified manner. He will still wear sandals and carry a snuffbox, but he will no longer carry any weapons except for a walking stick and perhaps a small knife, the latter more for use in cutting meat than for attack, and perhaps a speakingstick. Warriors fight with other warriors and outsiders; no warrior would raise a hand against an elder, and elders consider it demeaning to their dignity to brawl with others. Of course, this is only an ideal, and brawls and beating sometimes occur, but the rule is remarkable in being so generally heeded. This is reflected in the freedom with which elders move about in a highly armed society. The elders wear muted colors, wear no red ochre, and seek to convey a sense of restraint and deliberation. There is no sexual flamboyance and little concern for grooming among them. Indeed, since many elders drink a great deal, their bodies often present a dejecting contrast to the excellent physiques of warriors. Yet it is these old men who are the heads of households, the dispensers of livestock, and the exclusive paters to all children. In this latter sense, their sexuality involves posterity and thus eventually will be envied by maturing warriors who have been encouraged in their self-centered but personally unconstructive play and sensuality.

For Baraguyu, sexual roles are complexly linked to notions of etiquette, food, and space. The staple for Baraguyu is milk, usually fermented into a kind of yogurt. Only women may milk livestock and only women may prepare and store milk. Indeed, most livestock are allocated to the household of a particular woman. In contrast, butchering is the prerogative of men, who tend to monopolize the consumption of meat. The rules associated with these foods manipulate sexual relations. This is nicely illustrated by the rules of hospitality for traveling warriors. They must travel in pairs, never singly, and so properly grouped they must be given hospitality at any camp they visit. This means provision of milk from one of the married women in whose custody all milk lies. Supposedly the pairings of warriors mitigates the opportunities of seduction by such youths. In any case, when warriors visit, they must place their spears outside the doors of the houses they enter. No one is allowed to enter such a house without first asking permission from those inside. What we see then are a set of rules which contradict one another, posing hurdles but not preventing sexual relations between warriors and the women under the elders' control. Baraguyu see such ambiguity as the very spice of social life. I see this as allowing great freedom of choice for women in refusing or accepting lovers.

Baraguyu also forbid warriors to eat any meat which has been seen by a married woman. For their meat feasts warriors retire into the bush to butcher and eat, sometimes alone, sometimes with unmarried girls. No such restrictions apply to elders or, for that matter, to uncircumcised boys.

A Baraguyu camp itself manifests the categories of the Baraguyu moral universe and in so doing conveys several sexual nuances. During the day, men sit in the bush outside of the camp in the area that adjoins the social space; women, however, invariably sit together within the camp in the area vacated by the herd which is out grazing for the day, women being equated with livestock and entering and leaving the camp like livestock received or paid with bridewealth. Similarly, each camp is oriented toward one or more gates out of which cattle must pass. Ideally there should be one gate for each major male in the camp. For example, if a camp is composed of a man, his wives, and several married sons there will be only one gate, for there is only one head, the father. If, however, the camp were composed of two brothers whose father was dead, there would be two gates. Similarly, if two age-mates set up a camp together there would probably be two gates, but if a third person joined them who was poor in cattle and actually more a client than an equal, no third gate would be constructed. Each gate therefore expresses a male authority within a camp and orients livestock and persons within.

Each married woman has her own house. No food is stored or prepared outside the aegis of some married (presently so or widowed) woman, and consequently no person dwells outside some such woman's home. This contrasts sharply with the Kaguru, where unmarried boys and girls dwell in bachelor or spinster houses. Kaguru are shocked that Baraguyu youths and girls sleep under the same roof with their parents and, worse still, that girls and warriors might have sexual relations in such situations or that the parents may have sexual relations when their children might overhear or see.

The houses within a camp are, at least ideally, associated around the gates with the house of the first wife to the right (as one enters) of her husband's gate, the second wife to the left, the third wife to the right, the fourth to the left, and so on. This reveals an important feature of Baraguyu social organization. A man sorts his wives into two groups, with his first wife as head of one group and his second wife as head of the other. In this, a senior wife serves as a surrogate for her husband in controlling cowives. Furthermore, the son of the first wife is assumed to hold perpetual seniority over the sons of the third and fifth wife, and the same of the second wife similarly over the fourth and sixth.

This is only one of many ways in which women serve as the focal points by which men and resources are allocated. Every married man must allocate livestock to each wife with set increases according to the number of her children. He may, however, also retain some stock as exclusively his own to do with as he wishes. While a man retains ultimate control over how all such livestock is utilized, he cannot take livestock from one household complex and use it for another. What this means is that as the years pass resources are in large part allocated in terms of women and their offspring, especially their sons. Cowives are in competition, through their relative fertility, in securing livestock, producing daughters who will marry and bring in livestock as bridewealth, and producing sons who will utilize such stock to take wives in turn. Thus, a woman's ultimate aim will be to exert influence on a set of daughters-in-law and their offspring attached to her sons. Unlike Kaguru society, Baraguyu are not absorbed in their sisters' fertility but are profoundly concerned with that of their mothers.[10] In turn, women are, of course, fond of all their children but have only short-term interest in the lives and fertility of their daughters as compared to immense concern and dependence upon their sons and their sons' wives.

Baraguyu society emphasizes several forms of vicarious sexuality. Men's sexuality is divided into two phases. As warriors men exhibit all the external qualities of masculine attraction and encouraged openly in their flirtations and promiscuous activities. They are even covertly encouraged, if somewhat ambiguously, in their adulterous activities which, however, gain them only prestige in boasts but nothing in actual authority. In some cases, where elders are old and perhaps even impotent or sterile, the service of a hearty warrior may even be welcome. In turn, Baraguyu elders foresake the outer trappings of sexuality but in their muted manner hold the more lasting rewards of sexual life, final control over women and their offspring. Sexual display is the reward for lack of sexual control. Subdued sexual style is the price paid for that control. Warriors are encouraged to remain immature, vain, and flighty, and to think of their current, frivolous life as their salad days. In a gerontocracy, this is sensible. In old age, elders sometimes look back nostalgically on their jaunty and adventurous youth, yet at a crucial period the senior warrior himself, despite his conventional praise of warriorhood, presses to shed that warriorhood and take up the realities of power by becoming an elder.

For Baraguyu, age is profoundly important for both men's and women's sexuality, yet since men buy a womb and need not even be the actual genitors of the children they control, their sexuality may be ideologically manipulated to a considerable extent. Warriorhood serves a necessary function in distracting attention and providing vicarious, transitory rewards for those at their sexual peak who are denied formal realization of their energies.

Baraguyu women, too, in many respects, realize themselves only vicariously. As with Kaguru, barrenness is perhaps the worst misfortune possible. No woman remains unmarried and none has a happy future without sons. If women are to transcend their roles as the primary laborers in Baraguyu society and as the mere bearers of men's children, this is possible only in old age when they may assume in some respects a vicarious authority through their sons. As is the case for Kaguru, much then depends on what degree of affect these women exert over their adult children.

So far I have only briefly mentioned polygyny in discussing both Baraguyu and Kaguru. Given the late age at which Baraguyu men marry (usually after thirty, although this age is becoming lower with successive generations) and the fact that Baraguyu girls leave home and marry soon after puberty, if not before, Baraguyu may exhibit a far greater degree of polygyny than Kaguru. What is more, there is an inverse relation between male vigor and the capacity to secure wives; an elder in his sixties or seventies often possesses the numbers of cattle sufficient to secure young and desirable wives. Besides the problems of sexual adjustment and satisfaction which these arrangements obviously pose (and which have been discussed in terms of adultery and wife hospitality), this also means that there can be a vast gap in age not only between the oldest and youngest cowives but between the oldest and youngest children of one man. In the case of cowives this fosters the dominance of elder over junior women along with the right/left groupings mentioned already. In the case of siblings it confounds some aspects of fraternal bonding with notions of paternalism. Thus, a forty-five-year-old man may have a younger half-brother of a few weeks. In such a case, the elder brother will soon succeed to his father's position and as successor act as a surrogate father to his brother. He may even succeed to some of his father's younger wives, a custom which appalls Kaguru. In such a society where age runs roughshod over the usual expectations associated with generations, the relations of members within a family are sometimes ambiguous or contradictory, indeed, sometimes even before the death of the household head.[11]

Conclusions

The most persisting aspects of sexuality derive from the fact that women alone may give birth and that this capacity is of limited and sharply defined scope in time. In this, women's sexual capacities have serious limitations in terms of just what kind of cultural modifications they may endure. Men, on the other hand, have no such manifest sexual nature. The Baraguyu, in particular, make this clear. Sensuality and fertility may be separated in various ways and masculinity may be divided into discrete sets of attributes to be awarded and enjoyed at different points in men's careers. Paternity and genitorship may be separated, albeit covertly. In short, men's sexuality seems more amenable to cultural manipulation than is women's, and in a large part, this is as much due to men being less bound to time, sexually speaking, than women. Conversely, affectual and personal aspects of sexuality seem to favor women rather than men; the challenge of sexual performance besets Kaguru and Baraguyu males, and in both societies women are quick to abuse men about their manhood, and such vituperation, public and scathing, is keenly feared. Whatever their jural strength, men's actual sensuality is precarious as compared to women's whose concerns center far more on their actual feeling, however perverse; women require no such feelings in order to conceive.[12] Sensuality and fertility confront men and women differently.

It is the way with opposites to attract even as they repel: in

Western culture we find Black/White, Jew/Gentile, old/young, naive/ sophisticated, rich/poor, and even male/female so linked. In none of these relations does any inherent or natural quality survive without profound embroidery by culture. It can surely then be claimed of sexual differences, as Hertz said of the disparities between the right and left, and if they did not exist already they would have had to be invented. Yet the message of my present observations is a bit different from this. Although the profound impact of culture on determining thought and conduct cannot be overestimated, I here suggest that social commentators and analysts have zealously underscored the obvious social fact of the importance of symbols and beliefs at the expense of neglecting the important limitations and directions imposed by inherent attributes such as sex and age. In this Durkheim's emphasis on the importance of culture over nature may have obscured certain significant factors. Furthermore, recent work, especially that by feminists, has so emphasized sexual differences (or lack thereof), whether biological or cultural, as to have lost sight of the significance of age not only as a key to sexual roles but as a factor perhaps even more primary. In this sense, at least in preliterate societies, but probably in our own as well, the inventions and conventions of culture remain subject in part to the constraints of nature.

NOTES

Subsequent to the Indiana University series, this paper was given in more polished form at a formal series of lectures given in memory of the late John Honigman at the University of North Carolina, Chapel Hill. I should like to thank Sandra Cohn, Dale Eickelman, Ivan Karp, and Rodney Needham for reading various drafts.

1. Feminist anthropological literature has sometimes supported this point though, of course, noting that this involves a great many complex cultural values. Yet such work has rarely related sex to age in any methodical manner nor has there been any clear anthropological discussion of a actual differences regarding sexual performance as these may involve different cultural practices for men and women. For example, it must be of some significance that men must be sexually aroused to father children, whereas women may conceive frigidly. For a representative selection of feminist anthropological writing see Rosaldo and Lamphere, 1974.

2. Most of my interpretation derives from exegesis by Kaguru and Baraguyu themselves. Where I have made my own interpretations relying on my observations of what appear to be structural features of these societies, I have tried to make this clear in my discussion.

I spent nearly three years with the Kaguru and only intermittently took days off to interview the neighboring Baraguyu. As a result, the data are not comparable in scope and detail. I hope that this defect will be mitigated by the inherent interest of considering two such different yet neighboring peoples.

3. A more detailed account of such beliefs is available elsewhere, Beidelman, 1973.

4. Such notions are also found in many East African patrilineal societies. The Kaguru and other cases make it clear that this is not merely "a classic patrilineal ideology" (Karp, 1978:6) but more likely represents "virtual universal symbols of descent" (*ibid.*:14).

5. I discuss naming in detail elsewhere, 1974.

6. Kaguru polygyny may also be a factor. Men's interest in their children and households is divided if they have several wives, whereas a woman's is solely focused on her own home and children.

7. Of course, I am aware of such institutions as Nuer woman-woman marriage and Dahomean woman-woman marriage as well as even more unusual practices such as Nuer ghostly woman-woman marriage. Still I think that my argument has considerable weight in that these practices are recognized in some sense as not being the norm even within the societies where they are practiced. Furthermore, these practices still involve the activities of male genitors who often appear to exercise at least some informal controls, see also Barnes, 1973.

8. In the 1950s and 1960s when I did fieldwork, the age-set system was breaking down in that some senior warriors were marrying. This may have happened in the past, but informants all insisted that this was a new thing signifying the decline of the system due to the cessation of raiding and warfare.

9. Similarly, while Baraguyu males either bear no proper weapons (boys and elders) or bear spears (warriors), newly circumcised, liminally defined youths carry no Baraguyu weapons but do carry bows and blunted arrows associated with their enemies.

10. A mother's brother is a warm, sympathetic figure. Obviously men desire juniors who will view them in this way, yet the mother's brother is not usually a person who reaps any striking advantage from his role.

11. Needham remains one of the few writers to examine this issue systematically (1966).

12. Because women's fertility lies outside their emotional life, beyond sensual arousal, men may view women's sensuality with anxiety and hostility. In many societies, women's sensuality is both feared and sought by men, a challenge and an enigma.

BIBLIOGRAPHY

Barnes, J. A. 1973. "Genetrix: Gender: Nature: Culture." In *The Character of Kinship*, edited by Jack Goody, pp. 61–73. Cambridge: Cambridge University Press.

Beidelman, T. O. 1968. "Some Hypotheses Regarding Nilo-Hamitic Symbolism: Baraguyu Folklore." *Anthropological Quarterly* 41:78–89.

————. 1973. "Dual Symbolic Classification among the Kaguru." In *Right and Left*, edited by Rodney Needham, pp. 128–66. Chicago: University of Chicago Press.

————. 1974. "Kaguru Names and Naming." *Journal of Anthropological Research* 30:281–92.

Durkheim, Emile. 1949. *The Division of Labor (De la division du travail social*, 1893). Glencoe, Free Press.

Fortes, Meyer. 1959. *Oedipus and Job in West African Religion*. Cambridge: Cambridge University Press.

Karp, Ivan. 1978. "New Guinea Models in the African Savannah." *Africa* 48:1–16.

Lévi-Strauss, Claude. 1960. "The Family." In *Man, Culture and Society*, edited by Harry Shapiro, pp. 261–85. New York: Oxford University Press.

————. 1966. *The Savage Mind (La pensée sauvage*, 1962). London: Weidenfeld and Nicolson.

Needham, Rodney. 1966. "Age, Category and Descent." *Bijdragen tot de Taal-, Landen Volkenkinde* 122:1–33.

Rosaldo, Michelle Zimbalist, and Lamphere, Louise, eds. 1974. *Woman, Culture and Society*. Stanford: Stanford University Press.

Taxonomy versus Dynamics Revisited

The Interpretation of Misfortune in a Polyethnic Commutity

by W. Arens

Looking back over the history of anthropological thought, it is not overly difficult to recognize the appearance of truly pioneering efforts. By their nature they are few and far between, and hindsight need not be particularly acute, since these contributions still influence our thinking on contemporary issues. Evans-Pritchard's *Witchcraft, Oracles and Magic among the Azande*, first published in 1937, clearly belongs in this restricted category for all the proper reasons.

First, at the time of its appearance it resolved a perplexing issue of the day by laying to rest the then lingering suspicion about the possible existence of a "primitive mentality." Evans-Pritchard achieved this by convincingly demonstrating the inherent logic and rationality of Zande thought about the nature of the natural and supernatural world which had its parallels in Western reasoning and cosmology. It is easy today to dismiss this facet of Evans-Pritchard's achievement, unless we recognize that without such a demonstration, supported by a lucid argument and, more importantly, abundant supportive ethnography, there could have been no anthropology in the form we know it today. I refer here to the prevailing assumption in social anthropology that exotic systems of thought can be penetrated and understood by outside observers and subsequently amenable to cultural translation.[1] Second, the book is characterized by a scholarly modesty deriving from the deep reflection which attends on charting a new intellectual course. As one contemporary admirer has put it metaphorically: "Precisely because these ideas lie a little buried, and have not been put into a balloon, puffed up with a lot of air, and floated into the academic skies with a long label attached, they have received nothing like the attention they deserve" (Horton and Finnegan, 1973:40). Finally, as indicated above, the study was varied enough in terms of ethnographic content and ideas to stimulate a host of replicatory ventures drawing on different strands contained in the original. However, the history of this work's subsequent influence is a complicated affair, deserving special comment, since it bears upon a central concern of this paper.

Structural-Functionalism

As others have pointed out, *Witchcraft, Oracles and Magic* was primarily a study of Azande thought patterns (see Douglas, 1970:xiv). As Evans-Pritchard put it, he was primarily concerned with "the relations of these practices and beliefs to one another, to show how they form an ideational system, and to inquire how this system is expressed in social behavior" (1937:2). Nevertheless, in this massive tome, which in the unabridged version runs to almost five hundred and fifty pages, the author devotes one brief chapter to what he refers to as "the psychology of witchcraft" (Evans-Pritchard, 1937:99). In the process, he examines the social context between the victim of misfortune and the person identified as the culprit during the oracular sessions. He concludes the section with the simple proposal that: "People are most likely to quarrel with those with whom they come into closest contact when the contact is not softened by sentiments of kinship or is not buffeted by distinctions of age, sex, and class" (Evans-Pritchard, 1937:106). In other words, Zande accusations are "a function of personal relations" (Evans-Pritchard, 1937:106).

Despite this modest interest in this aspect of the overall topic, when anthropology revived again after the war most fieldworkers in Africa fixated almost totally on the relational and functional characteristics of witchcraft and sorcery beliefs and the subsequent social action. Nevertheless they claimed Evans-Pritchard's pioneering study as their inspirational fount. However, in retrospect it is clear that, although they shared Evans-Pritchard's interests to some degree, their theoretical orientation was quite different. In the intervening years, this generation of social anthropologists had come under the influence of Radcliffe-Brown and then Gluckman, following their primary concern for the ultimately functional aspects of social behavior. This concern also included action motivated and legitimized by witchcraft and sorcery beliefs. As Douglas has put it, these essentially "micro-political studies dotted the i's and crossed the t's" in confirming the social action element of these belief systems (Douglas, 1970:xviii). Although there are many to choose from, Marwick's contributions (1952, 1964, 1965A, and 1965B) most explicitly exemplified and were the culmination of this rudimentary functional approach. In his full-length study of the Cewa of Zambia (Marwick, 1965), he demonstrates how such accusations of evil-doing adhere to close kinship ties, allow for the expression of the inherent tension in these relations, and legitimize their dissolution and the creation of new ones. His discussion is punctuated by statistical tables identifying the relationship between the accused and accuser and sprinkled with such phrases as "tension points in the social structure," "conflict and stress," and "social strain gauge" (Marwick, 1965: passim), indcating a rather mechanistic structural-functional approach to the subject, even though Marwick claims his study confirms Evans-Pritchard's pioneering insight (1965:281). Needless to say, I am not suggesting there is anything inherently misguided about Marwick's interests and method, but rather that when the investigation is eventually reduced to a psuedomathematical formula (Marwick, 1965B:173), it is then only tangentially related to the source he harkens back to as his inspiration.[2]

Although published two years earlier, Middleton and Winter's edited collection, *Witchcraft and Sorcery in East Africa*, signaled a change in direction by reviving some of Evans-Pritchard's themes and interest in these phenomena. Being somewhat far from the mark, Douglas (1970) suggests that this volume marked the demise of the "structural approach" with the interment presided over by Turner (1970), as the appropriate ritual expert, who intoned his extremely negative evaluation of the essays. However, Douglas is mistaken in her claim, since the editors' introduction, and at least some of the selections, serves as a bridge back to the past, in light of the problems they raise for consideration. In particular, Winter's (1963) essay on Amba belief systems contains a successful frontal assault on some of the basic contentions of the functional school which had dominated anthropological thinking in the years since the appearance of Evans-Pritchard's monograph. In addition, he avoids a discussion of the analysis of Amba beliefs about witchcraft against the backdrop of their social and moral systems. For those not familiar with this essay, the author argues that in a sense the Amba are forced to conclude that witches are members of their own community, and thus attack their own kinsmen, because such evildoers are thought to invert the moral order. This moral system proposes that kinsmen support and aid each other, and see themselves in opposition to other communities which stand as potential enemies. In direct contradiction to these propositions, the Amba logically propose that witches will attack their kin and act in consort with their colleagues who inhabit other villages. Thus, Winter's analysis provides a close contemporary parallel to Evans-Pritchard's line of reasoning which Douglas correctly character-ized as a study of "the social constraints upon perception" (1970:xviii). Indeed, Douglas herself seems to follow the basic outline of Winter's argument in one section of her editor's introduction to *Witchcraft, Accusations and Confessions*, where she identifies and discusses what she considers to be the two main patterns of witch belief, which are (1) where the witch is thought to be an outsider, as opposed to (2) where the witch is believed to be the internal enemy of the commu-nity. Although not referred to in her remarks, the Amba and Winter's analysis of them provide a clear-cut instance of the latter category of belief which, if included by Douglas, would have served further to elucidate and enrich her discussion.[3]

Processual Analysis

Turner's review essay of Middleton and Winter's volume is an-other matter entirely, since he takes the editors and contributors to task on almost every conceivable issue. His basic contention, though, is that the volume is seriously deficient because the authors opted for what he characterizes as a "taxonomic," rather than a "dynamic," ap-proach to the problem. For Turner, the dynamic "process theory" in-volves, in addition to obvious features such as "a 'becoming' as well as a 'being' vocabulary," a stress "on human biology, on the individual life cycle, and on public health and pathology. It takes into theoretic account ecological and economic processes, both repetitive and chang-ing. It has to estimate the effects on local subsystems of large-scale political processes in wider systems" (Turner, 1970:113). All in all, this is rather a grand charge from someone (Turner, 1964) we have to as-sume voluntarily contributed to a volume entitled *Closed Systems and Open Minds*, in which the editor argues that the social anthropologist has "to isolate his field out of the complex reality he observes" and leave to others for analyses most of the items mentioned by Turner above (Gluckman, 1964:14). However, this is only the beginning, for in addition to condemning the contributors for their sins of omission, Turner also finds fault with their commissions.

There are many, but for the reviewer the crux of his critique centers on the editor's decision to follow Evans-Pritchard's lead and make a sociological distinction between witchcraft and sorcery (1970:118) and apply these concepts to the ethnographic data. This involved the definition of witchcraft as a mystical and innate power used by individuals with extraordinary abilities to harm others, while sorcery is conceived of as a learned art involving the manipulation of physical objects for evil intent (Evans-Pritchard, 1937:21; Middleton and Winter, 1963:3). With this dichotomy in mind, the editors raise a number of questions about how and why these notions are employed in various societies in terms of their "fit" with structural principles, e.g., "witchcraft beliefs tend to be utilized in societies in which unilineal kinship principles are employed in the formation of local residential groups larger than the domestic household, while sorcery beliefs tend to be similarly utilized when unilineal principles are not so used" (Middleton and Winter, 1963:12). In response, Turner claims that this conceptual distinction makes sense only for the Azande case. In due course, he points out that many of the contributors to the symposium either do not abide by this distinction or define witchcraft and sorcery in different ways. Thus, he argues, the entire approach to the phenomena with what he calls "an obsession with the proper pigeonholing of beliefs and practices" (Turner, 1970:126) sidetracks the investigation.

In some ways, Turner's uncharacteristic remarks have the flavor of an advertisement lauding the quality of one manufacturer's sparkling, dynamic product over that of the competitors' dull, static wares. Turner's own passion for classification, albeit in a different manner, in rendering his Ndembu material, leads one to wonder why he finds the similar efforts of Middleton and Winter so objectionable. As Turner's own analysis so laudably attests, there is nothing mutually exclusive about processual analysis and classification of ethnographic data. In light of these matters and other relevant though unmentioned side issues, it is clear that the review's counterarguments could be reasonably attacked, or, if so inclined, also defended, by any interested third party. However, for the purposes of this discussion, I would prefer to pursue this single issue of the validity and usefulness of distinguishing between witchcraft and sorcery against the backdrop of different ethnographic material collected during fieldwork in Mto wa Mbu, a rural polyethnic community in Northern Tanzania.[4]

Mto wa Mbu, A Polyethnic Setting

The community in question was founded in the early 1920s by a handful of migrants from various parts of the then Tanganyika Mandate with the encouragement of the British administration. Over the years, the community grew substantially, with the constant entry of new settlers who were drawn by the agricultural potential of this formerly uninhabited by well-watered wooded corner of Masailand in the Rift Valley. By 1969, the population had reached 3,500, represented by seventy different ethnic groups. However, the potential cultural melange was mitigated by the fact that a good portion of the residents were from the central and eastern Tanzanian Bantu clusters who share broadly defined, similar social, cultural, and economic patterns (Arens and Arens, 1978), and spoke Kiswahili either as a first or second language. In addition, due to a variety of shared historical experiences, the community slowly took on a distinct cultural character of its own which set it off in significant ways from the surrounding groups (Arens, 1975). Thus one can reasonably speak of a community culture shared with other such settlements of this type in Tanzania. With this ethnographic context in mind, we can now re-address the question of witchcraft and sorcery.

Although it may not be as possible, in contrast to a single ethnic group, to speak of a well-defined and internally coherent system of thought on this matter, there are enough shared notions among the residents in terms of both their traditional and contemporary community-oriented ideas to sketch a broad outline of beliefs on this aspect of the supernatural. For example, as far as I could determine from discussions with informants or from the literature, almost all the residents maintained a traditional conceptual distinction between witchcraft and sorcery which subsequently had implications for ordering their present views while in Mto wa Mbu. Since some consider linguistic distinctions to be of some importance in discussing this matter, it should be noted that in Kiswahili there is only a single term (*uchawi*) for both witchcraft and sorcery. A practitioner of either sort of mischief is referred to as a *mchawi* (pl. *wachawi*). The existence of this single basic term, however, does not imply the absence of a further conceptual dichotomy involving the belief in different types of evildoers.

As a further evidence of shared perception in the years just prior to independence, as with other areas of the country, Mto wa Mbu experienced an "anti-witchcraft" movement involving the entire population with the aim of ridding evildoers from the community (Willis, 1968). As to be expected, this event had political overtones indicative of changing political fortunes at both the national and community levels (Parkin, 1968). In Mto wa Mbu, the invitation to the witchfinders was opposed by the British-appointed officials and their associates, who were subsequently found by the diviners' tests to have been practicing sorcery. However, those individuals allied with the independence movement who supported the idea of calling in the witchfinders were found to be free of such evil influence. The outcome of the incident lends support to the idea that, prior to independence, the community was bedeviled by sorcerers to a greater extent than it is at present. Finally, in terms of a shared viewpoint, it is possible to cite instances of individuals being driven from the community by public opinion, since they were assumed to have been resorting to supernatural deeds harmful to their neighbors.

However, this is not the total picture, for there is also cosmological agreement on more specific issues. As indicated, there is a public consensus of opinion about the existence of sorcerers who, in the classic sense of the term, indulge in antisocial acts resulting from their knowledge of the art of manipulating physical objects to concoct harmful medicines. One of the commonest fears is that some will resort to this practice to affect the crops of another, or cause the illness of a household member. In more concrete terms, this involves the belief that some individuals have the knowledge of certain plants growing in the forest which can be used to destroy crops or poison others.

Although informants would obliquely allude to this sort of potential, names were rarely mentioned, due to the nature of adjudication in the community. An individual who publicly referred to another as a *mchawi* ran the risk of being cited in the local court for slander-

ing the reputation of another. Thus the self-assumed victim of another's malevolence would find himself the center of a civil action.
Consequently, when accusations did surface, such as in the instances
cited above and in the context of the antiwitchcraft movement, it was
a community supported response with broad appeal against isolated
individuals, rather than the outcome of a particular dyadic relationship. At this point in the process, legitimate political figures would
step in and advise the accused that it would be in the interest of all
concerned if he or she left the community. Two points should be
noted here. First, the intervention of political leaders did not necessarily imply their concurrence with the opinion that the accused were
actually supernatural agents of evil. According to their statements,
they were motivated by the attempt to reduce community conflict and
responded in a political rather than moral sense. Second, by the nature of the process, which involved a fair degree of community agreement on the issue, instances of named sorcerers were rare.

Agreement on the issue of the existence of sorcery was unanimous,
but as to be expected, the matter of who might resort to these acts
was debatable. Many would flatly deny that they or other members
of the ethnic group would ever think of acting in this fashion. Nevertheless, upon questioning, informants would reluctantly admit to the
existence of this knowledge and practice in the traditions of their people. The origin of such lore is also a matter of historical dispute, since
informants often claim that their own people once knew nothing of
these matters until it was introduced among them by a neighboring
group. As to be expected, representatives of the group identified
would claim the exact opposite was the case. Thus, general discussions
on this subject with a group of residents would usually produce as a
by-product some good-natured bantering about the respective reputation of each other's ethnic group on this score. The conversation could
become especially lively if the situation involved individuals whose
ethnic groups recognized a joking relationship (utani) based upon in-
terrelated historical traditions, which is quite common in Tanzania.

In addition to these disputed claims, there are some more pervasive and strongly held opinions about certain ethnic groups whose
representatives are considered to be potential specialists of this art,
since it is widely held that their group, in particular, traditionally
produced and suffered from the existence of numerous sorcerers. This
attitude is so prevalent that those residents from these areas will not

bother to debate the contention and instead contend that this was an aspect of their past. They would argue that since independence, which is seen as the dawn of a new and more perfect era, this is no longer a problem. This is a commonplace ideological assertion since, as just indicated, the established settlers claim that, prior to the contemporary golden age of political freedom, Mto wa Mbu was beset by the constant evildoings of numerous sorcerers in their midst. On the other hand, the day of the specialist in and of malevolent knowledge has not yet drawn to a complete close. Today there are still a number of widely recognized diviners and traditional healers (*waganga*) in the community, who are members of those ethnic groups renowned for their knowledge of these matters. Their continued existence also reconfirms existing opinions alluded to earlier since, as it has been widely reported in the literature and subscribed to in Mto wa Mbu, this knowledge once gained implies the potential for either social or antisocial purposes.

The general point about the above is that the belief in the existence of sorcerers and their ability to effectively function in this culturally heterogeneous, polyethnic setting is a contemporary aspect of community cosmology. However, the same cannot be said about witchcraft.

As indicated earlier, a belief in witchcraft is a feature of many traditional thought systems of the residents, but nonetheless is currently not viable in Mto wa Mbu. Individuals with innate mystical abilities are not thought to be able to use their powers, so that in terms of community cosmology, effectively, the category does not exist. This suggestion can be clarified by pointing out that many of the residents of Mto wa Mbu are cognizant of cultural features of the surrounding groups which, in the most immediate area, include the Maasai, Wambugwe, and Iraqw. They will point out that witches are not a problem among the Maasai, do exist among the Iraqw, and abound among the Wambugwe. This knowledge accords with the anthropological literature, so the residents, or the anthropologists who have worked among these groups, are fairly reliable ethnographers. Among the residents of Mto wa Mbu, the Wambugwe often come in for special commentary because of their belief in the ability of their witches to harm others by merely staring at the food their intended victim is about to eat. Thus, Wambugwe make special efforts during mealtimes to ensure their privacy, in order to protect themselves against the "evil eye." In public, unrelated individuals will eat separately behind some physical shelter or cover themselves and their food with their cloaks (Gray, 1963:163). Upon hearing this ethnographic tidbit for the first time from a Mbugwe or another resident with this information, the listeners most often react with stunned amusement.

To this point little of ethnographic significance or novelty has emerged in the course of this discussion. Anyone conversant with the literature on witchcraft and sorcery will be more than familiar with the outline of the beliefs and practices so far considered here. I would argue that the only compelling issue is concerned with the question of the vitality of the beliefs. The important point is that, despite knowledge on the part of the residents which posits the existence of witches in their own particular traditional milieu as well as in that of other groups, such creatures are not believed to be operative in Mto wa Mbu, while sorcerers are still thought to be effective.

In considering this situation, we are facing a typological question similar to the one raised and discussed by Middleton and Winter, and subsequently defined as irrelevant by Turner's review. However, I do not think that such questions should be so easily dismissed by those interested in systems of thought and action in order to immediately move on to other social arenas for analysis. In addition to being an eminently reasonable concern, the residents' assumption that sorcery is extant while witchcraft is extinct does not present a particularly perplexing issue.

Briefly, I would suggest, as with others, that the belief in the power of witchcraft is related to particular structural features, both organizational and ideational, of the traditional societies involved. For example, if it is assumed that only kinsmen, affines, age-mates, or co-wives can bewitch each other, it would be difficult to maintain this belief in Mto wa Mbu for a resident who might have few or no co-residents who fall into this category. Furthermore, in addition to particular organizational features, such traditional belief systems imply a fairly wide range of esoteric notions about the abilities and characteristics of these creatures which vary from society to society. This would include the evil eye, control over animal familiars, an unnatural lust for human or animal flesh, the power to transform themselves into animals or become invisible. As indicated above in the Wambugwe example, many of the residents consider such beliefs as amusing but childish and dismiss them as beyond credibility. (I suspect that, as with the early Lévy-Bruhl, some residents of Mto wa Mbu subscribe to the existence of a primitive mentality on the part of some of their contemporary neighbors for being able to propound and accept such ideas.) In short, the traditional belief in witchcraft, and the power of such individuals, are aspects of a bounded social and moral universe, making their transference and continuation in a foreign cultural environment untenable.

This can be contrasted to the common belief in sorcery, which involves the idea that, regardless of the social context, any individual can learn and resort to common techniques to harm another. Indeed, as mentioned above, much of this knowledge is seen as already having crossed ethnic boundaries in the past without losing its effectiveness. Transferred to the context of Mto wa Bbu, this continues to mean that anyone could be a potential sorcerer with the knowledge of shared techniques, and thus effective even among those from different ethnic groups. Thus the answer to the question posed demands an examination of the organizational and cultural characteristics of both the traditional and contemporary setting for the residents of Mto wa Mbu. This in turn involves, initially at least, a concern for taxonomic and definitional issues so easily dismissed by Turner.

I would not be so confident in taking this general position in contradiction to Turner if it were not for the fact that the line of reasoning espoused here has demonstrated its utility over the years in the consideration of various types of social and cultural phenomena. This situation is also buttressed by this orientation's applicability to an understanding of the particular issue at hand. Any number of examples could be chosen to support this contention, but I will limit myself to only a few of the most relevant.

Mitchell's (1965) analysis of the interpretation of misfortune among Africans in a polyethnic urban setting is one such instance. In his essay, he demonstrates that in the urban environment migrants must choose from among the possible mystical explanations the one most appropriate. This response may be at some variance with a typical reaction in the traditional rural homeland. Specifically, this involves a greater concern for explaining troubles in terms of the wrath of the ancestors rather than witches. Second, I would refer to Marwick's interpretations (1965A), which in Turner's review receives some laudable mention, despite the fact that this ethnographic data and analysis indicate a Cewa distinction between witchcraft and sorcery, and the applicability of these concepts in differing social contexts. Indeed, Turner's own material contained in his social dramas and situational analyses support the assumption about differing mystical concepts among the Ndembu, who distinguish between the type of supernatural powers available to males and females. For example, there is a category of evildoer, most likely to be a female, who inherits her powers matrilineally and uses them against her husband or junior matrilineal kin (Turner, 1957:144, 150). In addition, males are referred to as resorting to sorcerers for hire in their struggles with political rivals (Turner, 1957:112–13). Clearly we are dealing with two different types of individuals operating in contrasting situations. Third, I would draw attention to Harwood's (1970) full-length study of this very problem in his monograph on the Safwa of Tanzania, which concludes with the proposition that Middleton and Winter's distinction makes much sense in analyzing the expression of these beliefs in terms of the native interpretation of misfortune. Finally, I would draw attention to the fact that, in one of the most recent collections of essays on this topic (Douglas, 1970), the contributors have also found it profitable to discuss their material in terms of the classic distinction. What is important here is that the ethnographic instances go beyond the confines of Africa, since the case studies reflect worldwide distribution, including European historical instances of witchcraft and sorcery.

Further evidence could be marshaled to support the value of this position, but the above should suffice. In retrospect, it becomes clear enough that Turner "won" his debate with Middleton and Winter at the time by default, since the editors failed to file a public response to his critique. However, subsequent developments in the study of systematic explanations for personal misfortunes have shown that Middleton and Winter were on the right track, and that Turner was overly fixated on a particular, though equally valuable, approach to the topic.

I would even hazard the suggestion that Turner's latest major publication supports this contention. In this coauthored study of Christian pilgrimage (Turner and Turner, 1978), the authors write in the preface that they have focused on "institutional structures and implicit meanings" rather than having analyzed, as Turner has done in other works, "the relations and processes in a single circumscribed social field." As they admit, this means putting aside the extended-case method and social drama as analytical devices, for they consider their stance to be a necessary prelude to more detailed studies (Turner and Turner, 1978:xiv). This disclaimer is especially significant in light of the general parallels between the social and cultural context of pilgrimages in world religions and that of witchcraft and sorcery beliefs in small-scale societies. Despite other differences, in both instances, adherents to the faith seek cause and meaning in their reflections on misfortune and seek personal remedy by mystical means.[5] The Turners' present perspective is undoubtedly related to their decision to initially classify the data from various parts of the world on this phenomenon which is not derived from extensive first-hand field research. Thus they find themselves in a position analogous to that of Middleton and Winter, who resorted to the same procedure in ordering the ethnographic data supplied by other anthropologists reporting on different societies. It would be unfair in either instance to diminish these efforts by characterizing them as an obsession for pigeonholing.

Conclusion

The lessons to be learned from a review of this problem are obvious. First, as is so often the case in social anthropology, the perplexing issues of the day do not derive from a lack of ethnographic data, but from an overabundance of such material which in the second stage then generates contemporary controversies when one practitioner demands that a single orientation is the only proper way to order and interpret the material. It is not too difficult to agree with Beidelman (1970:355) when he moderately suggests that: "Analytical dichotomies are useful but, when overemphasized, they may lead to insensitivity at other levels of research and analysis . . ." However, he goes on to argue for more open theoretical approaches and contrasting topical interests in reviewing this problem. This open mind is crucial in dealing with the topics of witchcraft and sorcery, for together they form one of the sustained interests of social anthropology, and such types of explanations for misfortune find a broad temporal and spatial expression, allowing for the continual possibility of general propositions about the nature of human thought and action. Suggesting that we close our minds to certain approaches and adopt instead a particular orthodoxy will not serve the discipline well.

This present reconsideration of the problem and review of the literature demonstrates the value of a multi-faceted approach to the study of witchcraft and sorcery in Africa. Evans-Pritchard's initial interest in this typology allowed Middleton and Winter to speculate on further ramifications of the dichotomy, which was then substantiated by Harwood's more meticulous analysis of a single case. This body of ethnographic literature then provided the key to understanding a particular supernatural viewpoint in a hetereogeneous community in contemporary Africa. Thus, the process has been one of the continued accumulation of ethnographic data in relation to a particular topical interest, permitting continued comparative generalizations about the character and relationship between ideology and social organization. Therefore, we have been dealing with something more than mere pigeonholing or butterfly collecting. Instances of such a progression in social anthropology, as opposed to simultaneous narrowing of interests and conclusions, have been all too rare to be discouraged.

NOTES

1. Needham (1972) has provided the most recent discussion of this issue in his commentary on Lévy-Bruhl's systematic recantation of his prior notion of a primitive mentality and eventual conclusion that all people are governed by an informal logic. As Needham writes: "These conclusions are crucial to the study of mankind . . ." (1972:168).

2. Some years later, a volume of collected essays edited by Gluckman (1972) on the subject of witchcraft and sorcery in honor of Evans-Pritchard ironically returned to the analysis of this phenomenon in terms of a classic structural-functional framework. Not surprisingly the essays tend to honor the theoretical notions and interests of Gluckman, rather than those of Evans-Pritchard.

3. Under the heading of the witch as an internal enemy, Douglas identifies the subtype where the witch is an internal enemy with outside liaisons (1970:xxvii). She includes only one ethnographic example in this category, although this situation also clearly typifies the Amba views on the matter.

4. Fieldwork was conducted over a sixteen-month period during 1968–1969 as a research associate of the Department of Sociology, University of Dar es Salaam. The research was supported by an NIMH Predoctoral Fellowship and Research Award (Grant No. MH 11414–01). A return visit to the community was made possible by a State University of New York Faculty Research Award during the summer of 1973. The assistance of these agencies is gratefully acknowledged.

5. The Turners reflect on some of these parallels, as well as major differences, in their discussion of the meaning of misfortune in European and African "tribal" societies. However, their point of analysis focuses on "rituals

of affliction" in African societies resulting from the belief in the intervention of ancestral shades in response to breaches of the moral order (Turner and Turner, 1978:11–14).

BIBLIOGRAPHY

Arens, W. 1975. "The Waswahili: The Social History of an Ethnic Group." *Africa* 45:426–38.

Arens, W., and Arens, Diana Antos. 1978. "Kinship and Marriage in a Poly-ethnic Community." *Africa* 48:149–60.

Beidelman, T. O. 1970. "Towards More Open Theoretical Interpretations." In *Witchcraft Accusations and Confessions*, edited by Mary Douglas. London: Tavistock Publications.

Douglas, Mary. 1970A. "Introduction: Thirty Years after *Witchcraft, Oracles and Magic*." In *Witchcraft Accusations and Confessions*, edited by Mary Douglas. London: Tavistock Publications.

———. 1970B. *Witchcraft Accusations and Confessions*. London: Tavistock Publications.

Evans-Pritchard, E. E. 1937. *Witchcraft, Oracles and Magic among the Azande*. Oxford: Clarendon Press.

Gluckman Max, ed. 1972. *The Allocation of Responsibility*. Manchester: University of Manchester Press.

Gluckman, Max, and Devons, Ely, eds., 1964. *Closed Systems and Open Minds*. Chicago: Aldine.

Gray, Robert. 1963. "Some Structural Aspects of Mbugwe Witchcraft." In *Witchcraft and Sorcery in East Africa*, edited by John Middleton and E. H. Winter. London: Routledge and Kegan Paul.

Harwood, Alan. 1970. *Witchcraft, Sorcery, and Social Categories among the Safura*. London: Oxford University Press.

Horton, R., and Finnegan, R., eds. 1973. *Modes of Thought*. London: Farber and Farber.

Marwick, M. G. 1952. "The Social Context of Cewa Witch Beliefs." *Africa* 22:120–35; 22:215–33.

———. 1964. "Witchcraft as a Social Strain Gauge." *Australian Journal of Science* 26:263–68.

———. 1965A. *Sorcery in its Social Setting*. Manchester: University of Manchester Press.

———. 1965B. "The Sociology of Sorcery and Witchcraft." In *African Systems of Thought*, edited by M. Fortes and G. Dieterlen. London: Oxford University Press.

Middleton, John, and Winter, E. H., eds. 1963. *Witchcraft and Sorcery in East Africa*. London: Routledge and Kegan Paul.

Mitchell, J. Clyde. 1965. "The Meaning in Misfortune for Urban Africans." In *African Systems of Thought*, edited by M. Fortes and G. Dieterlen. London: Oxford University Press.

Needham, Rodney. 1972. *Belief, Language and Experience*. Chicago: University of Chicago Press.

Parkin, David. 1968. "Medicines and Men of Influence." *Man* 3:424–39.

Turner, V. W. 1957. *Schism and Continuity in an African Society.* Manchester: Manchester University Press.

————. 1964. "Symbols in Ndembu Ritual." In *Closed Systems and Open Minds,* edited by Max Gluckman. Chicago: Aldine Publishing Co.

————. 1970. *The Forest of Symbols.* Ithaca: Cornell University Press.

Turner, V. W., and Turner, Edith. 1978. *Images and Pilgrimages in Christian Culture.* New York: Columbia University Press.

Willis, R. G. 1968. "Kamcape: An Anti-Sorcery Movement in South-West Tanzania." *Africa* 38:1–15.

Winter, E. H. 1963. "The Enemy Within: Amba Witchcraft." In *Witchcraft and Sorcery in East Africa,* edited by John Middleton and E. H. Winter. London: Routledge and Kegan Paul.

SECTION III.
Cultural Dynamics

Revitalization and the Genesis of Cults in Pragmatic Religion
The Kita Rite of Passage among the Suku

by Igor Kopytoff

Religious cults loom large in the ethnographic landscape of sub-Saharan Africa. The ease with which new cults arise is well documented, although we are less well acquainted with the ways in which new and old cults vanish. There is, in all this, a striking religious dynamism that cries out for theories that are no less dynamic. Yet, the anthropological understanding of African religion has, to a large extent, been shaped within a structural-functionalist paradigm that was notoriously unconcerned with dynamics beyond the confines of a single society and a short period of time.

In this essay, I shall try to account for a particular cult among the Suku of southwestern Zaïre: the *Kita*, which has the structure of a *rite de passage*. I shall begin with Arnold Van Gennep's classic formulation of rites of passage and examine some reinterpretations of Van Gennep in the structural-functionalist tradition. I shall then try to account for the *Kita* by drawing upon the other major explicative tradition in anthropology—the one stemming from the Boasian paradigm, with its emphasis on cultural dynamics and process and on the historicity provided by a regional perspective. Finally, I shall trace the implications of my analysis for some theories of religious process and for the Durkheimian view of religion.

Van Gennep and Reinterpretations of Van Gennep

In *Les Rites de Passage* (1909/1960:26), Van Gennep resorts to an arresting metaphor. He likens society—with its many social positions, offices, and roles—to a house with many rooms. Each room shelters people whose publicly recognized state of being is specifically appropriate to it. Hence, to pass from one room to another and from one state of being to another is a serious matter, and the passage is marked by rituals and ceremonies—that is, by "rites of passage."

Some of these transitions involve natural states of being, as in rituals marking birth, adolescence, or death. Most of the states, however, are cultural creations, as in adoption, adulthood, and marriage, or in initiations into priestly or political offices. But though cultural creations, these states of being are also "structural," in that they have to do with social statuses that are part of the structure of social relations. And it is from this perspective that Van Gennep's theory was adapted with great success to the social-structural analysis of ritual.

One result of this success, however, has been to confine the theory to changes in social status (as opposed to other states of being that a society may recognize) and, going further, to perceive changes in status as the raison d'être of the ritual itself. The change in emphasis is a subtle one. Instead of seeing the human mind as being prone to ritualize a change in the state of being—as Van Gennep saw it—the reintepretation sees the change in status as generating the ritual and, taking a step further in the same direction, gives causal primacy to the social structure. This reinterpretation is, to be sure, consonant with classic Radcliffe-Brownian structural-functionalism. Here, culture —including the symbolism of ritual—is treated as epiphenomenal to the social structure, whose "needs" it subserves. The structure of social relations is seen as determining cultural expression and as being, therefore, logically antecedent to it.

Fortes and Gluckman exemplify very well this exclusively social-structural interpretation of Van Gennep. In an illuminating analysis of rituals of office, Fortes takes it for granted that Van Gennep's *rites de passage* involve transitions between statuses, roles, and offices: "If we ask, incorporation into what, the answer is clear: into a new field of social structure, of conjuncture of social relations" (Fortes, 1962:56). And what Fortes takes for granted, Gluckman forcefully asserts—with paradoxical results. On the one hand, Gluckman insists on characterizing Van Gennep's theory as being "about the sequences of rites used to alter people's social relationships" (1962:1). On the other hand, he deplores the fact that Van Gennep addressed his ideas to a range of rituals far wider than those dealing with social relations (1962:10ff.) —which Van Gennep indeed does.

Van Gennep himself held to what may be called a mentalistic view—a cognitive view, to use fancy modern terminology. If we continue with Van Gennep's metaphor of the mansion for society, we can say that Gluckman and Fortes see all the rooms in it as representing only social positions. Were it a manor house, there would be in it the lord's room, and the lady's, and the captain's, the guards', and the servants' . . . and the chaplain's. But is there a room for a chapel in it?—for a room, that is, whose function is other than to accommodate persons in their varied statuses and roles. Van Gennep's own view of the house seems to be more complicated. He sees not only the building but also the mind that builds it. Behind the wide range of rituals he considers—a range that Gluckman deplores—Van Gennep discerns a "logical idea" based on the human perception of "transitions from one state to another" (1909/1960:183). These states of being, however, are not confined to the social realm: "I have tried to assemble here all the ceremonial patterns which accompany a passage from one situation to another and from one cosmic [sic] or social world to another" (1909/1960:10). And indeed, Van Gennep devotes several pages to the ritualization of such transitions as seasonal and calendrical changes (1909/1960:178–83).

As long as the anthropologist confines his attention to those rites of passage that entail changes only in social status, the question of analytical antecedence remains moot. It is, after all, merely a matter of theoretical preference whether one sees the change in social status as, functionally speaking, "giving rise" to the ritual, or whether one prefers to say that it is the human ritualizing mind that insists on marking with ritual the transitions between the statuses. So phrased, it remains a chicken-and-egg kind of problem. Nevertheless, logically speaking, the question of antecedence remains and implies a possible test case. This would be a rite of passage that does not involve any existing social statuses, a rite of passage between states of being that cannot be logically antecedent to the ritual itself. The ideal test case would be one in which it is the ritual itself that defines the transition and the states of being. To return to the metaphor of the mansion, we need a ritual that creates and defines a room—a ritual, say, that consecrates a chapel whose occupants exhibit not a social status but a state of grace. I shall describe here such a ritual: the initiation into *Kita* among the Suku.

The Suku

The Suku are a people of the Central African "matrilineal belt" (see Kopytoff, 1965 for a general ethnographic profile). In precolonial times, they lived in small villages scattered over the rolling savanna— a sparse population in an area of sparse resources. The women cultivated the land while the men hunted, engaged in crafts and professions, and administered the society.

The Suku kingdom encompassed some 80,000 people and was divided into a dozen major chieftaincies. But effective political power was diffuse and its exercise sporadic, and the dominant social and political unit was the autonomous corporate matrilineage, consisting on the average of some thirty or forty persons. Such a lineage was centered upon a particular village that served as its administrative headquarters; the lineage members themselves were, however, widely dispersed among several villages of a given area, residence at marriage being virilocal and patrilocal. This scatter did not preclude constant communication on matters of collective lineage concern: births, funerals, marriages, sickness, inheritance, legal cases, and rituals. Nor did the scatter undermine the very strongly corporate nature of the lineage (see Kopytoff, 1977): every lineage was a strongly corporate jural and ritual unit, poised in a strictly balanced relationship of debits and credits with the other lineages of the area. (I dwell on these points because Suku rituals are overwhelmingly lineage based; however, *Kita* is not).

The relative power of a lineage hinged on the number of people in it. Producers of wealth, people were also a principal form of wealth. But the desire to expand one's lineage was constantly frustrated by the workings of the descent system and by the high maternal and infant mortality.

To reproduce itself, a matrilineage depends on its women members, the sisters of its men. Hence, the reproductive capacity of a matrilineage is limited and relatively fixed over long periods of time. (A matrilineage cannot, as can a patrilineage, acquire many wives in a period of prosperity and expand dramatically within a generation.) The average, relatively small Suku matrilineage was thus quite sensitive about the problems of maintaining itself as a viable social group.

Before the introduction of intensive medical services by the colonial authorities in the 1940s, the Suku population was relatively stable overall, its very high birth rate being matched by its death rate (see Lamal, 1949). But this statistical stability held for the population as a whole; within it, an individual lineage usually saw itself, realistically enough, to be in constant danger of shrinking—and many lineages around it were indeed visibly shrinking. The result was a pervasive anxiety about sickness, death, and birth pathology. Infant and child mortality was extremely high, as was the mortality of mothers in childbirth; and to this should be added the familiar range of tropical diseases and the debilitating effects of a diet woefully deficient in protein. Not surprisingly, then, disease, death, child mortality, and birth deformities were all matters of great ritual concern.

Misfortunes were believed to come from several sources: from the dissatisfaction of dead and living elders of the lineage; from the deeds of lineage witches; and from the intricate action of various magical "medicines" possessed by the lineage. The Suku coped with these threats in various ways, with the lineage as the corporate actor. The lineage elders were cajoled and appeased. The lineage witches were cajoled, threatened, and sometimes killed. And the medicines were handled through a veritable panoply of supernatural technology. Protective medicines were forever sought and endlessly manipulated. Some of the medicines were specifically concerned with birth pathologies and were resorted to either by individuals or, more commonly, corporately by the afflicted lineage.

But beyond such routine handling of particular cases of miscarriages or birth deformities, the Suku also had at hand a periodic ritual, a communal one rather than lineage based. This was the *Kita*, and it addressed itself to a deeper problem—that of preserving and restoring the vitality of the society as a whole, of society as a corporate collectivity.

The Meaning of *Kita*

The Suku consider that *Kita*, with its associated *Tsanga* medicines, arose out of the *Bweni* medicines, a complex of medicines associated with the kingship, the chieftainships, and the headships of lineages. Like most Suku medicines, *Tsanga* is said to have been discovered through divination. The ritual of royal and chiefly installation always includes the renovation of the *Bweni* medicines—an obligatory renovation, for without it there would be disease and death in the country (if the ritual were for a new king), or in the chiefdom, or in the lineage. In the distant past, the Suku say, a great chief's succession was followed by much disease and death. A diviner discovered that this was because the ritual renovation of the chief's *Bweni* complex did not include a hitherto unknown medicine, *Tsanga*, which had accidentally "attached" itself to the *Bweni* without anyone realizing it and which was now acting up. The remedy was the standard one in such cases: a new *Tsanga* medicine bundle was to be put together and made a permanent part of the chief's *Bweni* complex. In addition, a new renovative ceremony—*Kita*—was instituted, and the new chief, the members of his lineage, and the people of the chiefdom had to pass through it. This ceremony was to be periodically repeated in order to induct into *Kita* new people who had not been initiated.

Thus appeared *Kita KiNyengani* (also called *Tsanga Kita*). Later —and, according to the story, in the same way—another *Kita* ceremony, that of *Kita Biketa*, was discovered and added to the *Tsanga* medicine complex. In recent times—and *Kita* was still a vigorous institution in parts of the Suku area in the 1930s—most of the important chiefs' *Bweni* medicines "contained" both *Kita*, and both versions of the ceremony were performed simultaneously but separately. Minor chiefs had only one of the *Kita*. An initiate—male or female—followed the version of his or her father.

The *Tsanga* medicine complex and *Kita* of the king and those of the great regional chiefs were known as the Great *Tsanga* and the Great *Kita*. In time, the *Tsanga* medicine spread to other lineages, as most Suku medicines do. A diviner would attribute a disease in the lineage to its infection by *Tsanga*; thereupon, *Tsanga* had to be added to the inventory of lineage medicines. Thus, "little" *Tsanga* medicine bundles gradually diffused among some of the ordinary nonchiefly lineages. Within a lineage, the *Tsanga* bundle was kept by a specially appointed and initiated woman guardian, called *Kimbanda*.

The renovative *Kita* ceremony was directed by a *Ngaanga Tsanga* —the *Tsanga* "expert"—who was almost always a male. He was also an expert in the *Tsanga* medicine and could initiate the woman guardian of a lineage *Tsanga*, or renovate the *Tsanga* medicines, or make new ones for a lineage taking in the *Tsanga* for the first time. On such occasions, the *Ngaanga Tsanga* would often organize a little *Kita* ceremony as well, to induct into *Kita* those in the area who had not yet entered it.

The woman guardian of a lineage *Tsanga*—the *Kimbanda*—operated routinely on her own as a dispenser of medicines for gynecological problems. Women who came to her were those who had miscarried, or were infertile, or had given birth to twins, albinos, the blind, dwarfs, and the deformed. If her medicines seemed ineffective or if these misfortunes continued to be visited upon the lineage, a diviner might discover that *Tsanga* had infected the lineage permanently. The lineage would then call the male *Ngaanga Tsanga* to make a *Tsanga* medicine bundle for it and to initiate its guardian. When a guardian died, a *Ngaanga Tsanga* was called to initiate the new *Kimbanda*. A *Ngaanga Tsanga* also trained and initiated others into his expertise. This was usually done within the lineage, or the knowledge was passed on by the expert to his son. The expertise was, of course, valuable—it brought fees and one did not want to multiply competitors in one's region.

Initiation into *Kita* was open to all those men, women, and children who had not yet entered *Kita*. The Great *Kita* of a great regional chief (which revitalized his region) or of the king (which revitalized the area around the capital) occurred every fifteen or so years, upon the chief's installation and also in response to periodically felt public malaise. Little *Kita* ceremonies, revitalizing a neighborhood of five to ten villages with a population of several hundred people, were held locally at intervals of a few years. This frequency might logically suggest that the new initiates were all children born since the last *Kita*. In fact, the novices ranged from infants to the middle-aged. There are several reasons for this. Since there were two kinds of *Kita*, and one entered the *Kita* of one's father, only some of the uninitiated were eligible for a given local ceremony. Also, in a given locality, the *Kita* was held in one village; some of those eligible in the neighborhood sometimes feared to travel and stay among strangers while in the ritually vulnerable state of initiation. Finally, some of those eligible were quite simply afraid and used various excuses to postpone their going through a ritual in which, it was proclaimed, they were to be killed and then resurrected.

The notion underlying *Kita* is analogous to the Western concept of entropy. In a given area, or a chiefdom, it came periodically to be widely felt that things were not going as they should, that social life was losing its "force," this is, its vitality. The clues were many, general, and vague. Hunting was not as successful as it had been, or quarrels appeared to be increasing, or the harvests had become more meager. The entropy showed itself most clearly, however, in the realm in which the Suku saw vitality express itself most directly, the realm of human and, therefore, social reproduction. The symbol and the substance of this loss of vitality was the increase of children who—as the standard ritual metaphor phrased it—were not born "with hair and nails." This meant a growing number of twins, albinos, and dwarfs, of deformities and miscarriages. The signs of entropy were cumulative rather than dramatic: as the clues multiplied, general malaise took shape gradually. Moreover, since the entropy was considered to be an inevitable and normal process, the very expectation of it no doubt fed into the perception of its gradual unfolding. In the meantime, one continued to cope with specific misfortunes in ordinary ways: elders were still propitiated, witches controlled as best one could, and the various medicines manipulated. But the entropy grew above and beyond all that, unchecked by particular successful cures or by minor victories over witches.

The entropy as it is conceived here is a slowed-down version of a kindred and more dramatic notion that appears in the Suku interregnum and underlies similar interregna in innumerable African societies where it forms one of the elements of the "divine kingship" complex. This is the conceptual identity between kingship and society. After the death of the Suku king or a regional chief, the respective polity was also said to "die." For a few days, until a successor was installed, "the land was dead" and "the law was dead"; an institutionalized general anarchy prevailed and everyone's possessions and animals were fair game. The enthronement of the successor restored the land and the law, that is, regulated social life. The enthronement was almost always accompanied by a Great *Kita* ceremony, which gave additional vigor to the restored society.

The Setting of *Kita*

The ceremony was called and sponsored by a lineage head or a regional chief, who became known for the occasion as **Phumu Kita**, "master of *Kita.*" He invited the necessary experts and assured the cooperation of the village population but had no ritual role. The ceremony itself was administered by the *Ngaanga Tsanga,* the *Tsanga* expert, whose title in the ceremony was *Ngaanga Kita.* He was usually helped by a woman, the guardian of the *Tsanga* medicine of a local lineage, who happened to be knowledgeable in *Kita* matters; this woman carried, for the occasion, the title of *Ngwa Kita* (an elision of *Ngudi a Kita,* "mother of *Kita*"). Finally, there was *Kahyomba,* the male sentry who remained all the time with the novices and saw to it that no rules were broken by them.

On the outskirts of the village, a larger than usual one-room house, *Kongu Kita,* was built under the sponsor's direction. One door of the house, on the right side of the wall as seen from the village, faced the village; another door, a double one, was placed on the left side of the back wall. Inside, sleeping platforms were installed on both sides of the house, four to five feet high. In the center of the house, just before the ceremony began, the *Ngaanga Kita* planted the *Kunji*—a freshly-cut liana-bound branch of the *muyombu* tree (a tree that is planted when a new village is built or a new chief is installed). Midway on the path from the village to the house stood *Panzu a Kaanga,* the arch that "bars the way," some five feet high, made of branches and fringed with palm leaves.

The initiation into *Kita* conforms to—and may be described in terms of—the classic stages of Van Gennep's *rites de passage.* The separation of the novices from the social world and from their identity as *kaba* (outsiders to *Kita*) was accomplished by "killing" them. They then became marginal *bibindi* (sing. *kibindi*), gradually reshaped into their new identity during the transitional period of their seclusion in the *Kita* house. Finally, they were "reborn" out of the house and rejoined the social world in their new identity of *kita.* The entire ritual was suffused with the symbolism of death, infancy, rebirth, and sexuality. In the following description, I shall consistently refer to those being initiated as "novices" and to those participants who had previously entered *Kita* as "the initiated."

Separation: The "Killing" of the Novices

The day before the ceremony, the father, mother, and mother's brother of a novice each gave him or her a small coin as a sign of their goodwill during the coming period of ritual danger. The father also provided a chicken to be eaten by the novice to acquire strength for the coming ordeal of being "killed."

There was some variation in the pattern of induction. In some areas, all the novices were inducted on the same night; in others, the first male novice was inducted on the first night, the first female the second night, two more the third night, and then small groups of three or four on each subsequent night. In a chiefly Great *Kita*, there could be as many as forty or fifty novices; a little *Kita* could involve as few as a half dozen. When there were a great many novices, the initiation took place in relays: three or four new novices came in every night, while three or four initiates who had stayed in the *Kita* house for several days were returned to society. The stay in the house was normally six days, but it could be shorter. Here, I shall describe a nonserial form of initiation, involving a single group of novices being initiated together.

At dusk, the novices arrived and prostrated themselves in front of the palm leaf arch (the *Panzu a Kanga*), their heads toward the *Kita* house. They remained in this position, with eyes closed, for several hours, while the assembly of the initiated sang, drummed, and danced around them, proclaiming that the novices would soon be killed. Toward midnight, the master of the ceremony, the *Ngaanga Kita*, arrived, carrying a special large stick, *kindi*. He (or a knowledgeable helper) took the role of *Kihonda Kita*, "the killer of *Kita*." The *Kihonda* approached the first novice, murmuring: "It is cold, it is cold, the cold has seized this one." The novice was held down and the *Kihonda* slowly passed the stick over the back of his neck, chanting: "Shall I kill? Shall I kill?"—to which the assembly replied: "Kill!" This was repeated three times, after which the *Kihonda* lifted the stick and struck hard and loud on the ground beside the novice's head. The dull sound of the blow was punctuated by outbursts of shouting from the initiated for the benefit of the other novices and the uninitiated back in the village. Some Suku have told me that they were convinced, until the very moment of the blow, that they would be killed and then somehow resurrected. Others have said that they were told in a whisper at the last moment about the coming deception.

After the blow, the novice was told to remain inert. Picked up and held like a child, he (or she) was carried to the *Kita* house. The novice faced the carrier, legs wrapped around hips, his inert body held up, his head thrown back and bobbing—"like a child," or "a corpse," or "a sexual partner" according to the views of different informants. Dancing, the carrier went around the house three times; then, entering through the front door, he laid the novice on the sleeping platform. A knife and some burning straw were then held over the novice's head and he was asked: "Which way do you wish to die, by the knife or by the fire?" As the novice mumbled about his inability to choose, the knife and the straw were crossed over his head and water and poured over them, and he was told to remember that one could also die by water.

One by one, the other novices were similarly dispatched and brought in. As they were all being stripped of their clothes, the assembly made a loud noise—"Brrrrr"—to let the village know that the novices had all been killed; the clothes were taken to the village as proof of it.

That night, as the assembly sang and danced, the novices weakly joined in or remained inert on the sleeping platforms, the males on the right side and the females on the left. Subsequently, they would be reborn inside the *Kita* house into men and women and would eventually begin to use the double door in the back, each sex using its own half of it. The double door was placed on the left—that is, the female— side of the wall: it was through this opening that the novices were reborn into the world. On the other hand, they would never again use the single front door through which they had been brought in as socially genderless corpses.

The Seclusion in the *Kita* House

Throughout the period of seclusion, the initiated who had previously entered *Kita* (and were known as the "mothers" of the novices) came dancing around the house, while the novices danced inside it. The novices' existence was supervised by *Kahyomba*, the sentry, who joined the *Ngaanga Kita* and the other initiated in instructing the novices.

The Suku believe that the dead shun daylight. So did the *bibindi*, the novices, who did not venture out of the house during the day. They did not even lift their eyes to the roof, for fear of catching a glimmer of light through the straw and contracting leprosy. During the first few days in particular, they lay much of the time inert on sleeping platforms, their bodies gray—like corpses—from the dust and their faces streaked white with *Tsanga* medicine. At night, they joined in the *Kita* dancing, swaying slowly inside the house around the planted *Kunji* branch.

In the days that followed, the marks of death became attenuated; the novices ventured outside the house at night and even went into the bush. As death gave way to rebirth, so the inertness of death faded into the helplessness of infancy. On the morning after the "killing," the first food was brought in through the back door—the one that henceforth served as the novices' link with the world. The food was that ordinarily given to infants being weaned—bananas and peanuts. The sponsor of the *Kita* or the *Ngaanga Kita* masticated the food and dropped the mash into the open mouth of each novice, as a mother would with an infant. After this first feeding, the novices ate on their own, with *Ngwa Tsanga* (the woman guardian of *Tsanga*) tasting the food beforehand. During their seclusion, the novices defecated in one spot inside the house. Normally, defecation is a very private act, to be done in the bush and especially to be hidden from the opposite sex. Only small children defecate openly and inside the house.

The novices were taught secret *Kita* songs and sayings and how to prepare *Kita*-related medicines. As the *Ngaanga Kita* held up each ingredient, he called out: "What is it?" and the novices answered in a chorus. When visitors came into the house, they struck the *Kunji* branch three times before speaking; the novices had to strike the *Kunji* in response and repeat exactly the words that had been said. When *Kahyombe*, the sentry, left the house, he always put a stick between the teeth of every novice so that they would not talk loudly and risk being overheard by noninitiates.

The novices were threatened with dire consequences if they talked later to the noninitiated about *Kita*. *Kahyombo* emphasized this by striking the ground with the *kindi* stick as he exhorted them to keep *Kita* secrets. If a noninitiate glimpsed by accident any of the proceedings or overheard the novices, *Kahyombo* immediately and forcibly took the interloper through the initiation. And if one of a married couple had been initiated, the other was pressured into entering *Kita* in order to forestall secrets being revealed between the couple. The mystification of *Kita* for the benefit of outsiders was quite deliberate. Small crosslike incisions were often cut on a novices' chest; outsiders were told that these were the scars left after the heart had been cut out and replaced. Outsiders were also told that, after being killed, the novices were toughened by being dried by the fire.

The novices wore only a small piece of cloth to cover the genitals. Whenever a male saw an exposed vulva or a female an exposed penis, he or she shouted: "Utembongi!" ("I have had illicit sex with you!"). In some of the dancing, the novices stood in front of the *Kunji* branch, held it with both hands, and imitated the motions of sexual congress. *Kita* songs referred to "sex with *Kunji*" as one of the secrets to be kept.

The concentrated and arousing sexuality and its symbolic enactment in the *Kita* house was, however, accompanied by a prohibition of its consummation. Sexual intercourse was forbidden to the novices. If a married novice or a novice couple had intercourse at night in the bush, the woman was required to announce this on the day of leaving *Kita* and the man paid a fine of a goat and some money to the *Ngaanga Kita* and the *Ngwa Kita*. Without this, the *Tsanga* medicine would sicken children in the woman's lineage. Here, the married couple was, in effect, treated as unmarried for the duration, the threatened punishment and the fine being like those for adultery. Sex was initially forbidden to all those staying in the village. But toward the middle of the seclusion period, the *Ngwa Tsanga* commonly had sex with her husband and paid a fine of a chicken and a token coin to the novices. This lifted the prohibition on the villagers.

Through the seclusion period, a *Tsanga* medicine bundle was gradually put together or, if one had been borrowed, it was reinforced with fresh ingredients and the blood of a chicken. Selected leaves and roots from the forest were used, and, on the last day, all the leaves and litter from the floor of the *Kita* house were added to the medicine. The liana that was tied around the *Kunji* branch was handed over to the *Ngwa Tsanga* together with the prepared medicine.

By the second or third day, the novices took a new name. The first four novices took special names representing the order of their initiation; others took names out a fund of special *Kita* names. It was not obligatory to retain these names after the ceremony was over, but they were sometimes adopted by the initiate—until, as the Suku were wont to do, he or she decided to take on yet some other name.

Reincorporation

The seclusion period varied in length, usually lasting six days. But if many novices had to be processed in a series, each novice might stay as few as three days. On the day before *Kita* was to end, two small uninitiated children, male and female, were quickly taken through the initiation "to close the *Kita*."

On the last day of *Kita*, two women novices went to the river to catch a white fish called *Ngola* and, for *Kita* purposes, *mundele*, "dead man/albino/white man/European." The fish was brought in, the novices were carried to the *Panzu a Kanga* arch, pieces of fish were put into their mouths, and they were returned to the house. The *Tsanga* medicine bundle was then completed.

In the *Kita Kinyengani* version of the ceremony, when the novices came out of the house for the last time, they began a slow dance— eyes closed, arms loosely outstretched, body swaying—and sang repetitively: "Novices of *Kinyengani*, dance to [be able to] look, dance to [be able to] see!" Then, suddenly, they opened their eyes and the assembly began the kind of improvised singing and dancing that is done "for joy."

In the *Kita Biketa* version, the novices sat around the *Ngaanga Kita*, while he completed the *Tsanga* bundle. Each of the novices was completely covered by a piece of cloth, with his or her relatives standing by (for burial, a corpse is wrapped in cloth). At dusk, with the *Tsanga* bundle completed, the *Ngaanga Kita* called out three times: "Kibangu-a-a-a!" (the title of the first female novice). *Kibangu* replied: "Aye-e-e!" and the cloths were jerked off the novices. Without rising, eyes closed and arms outstretched, the novices began a shiverlike movement that started at the fingertips and gradually crept up the arms and into the body. Opening their eyes, they slowly rose, accelerating the movement until it merged into the rhythm of normal dance. They were not *bibindi* anymore, but *batu*, "people," again, and also *Kita batu*.

Kita as a Rite of Passage

I need not dwell on the obvious—that the ritual of initiation into *Kita* conforms very closely indeed to the classic pattern of a *rite de passage*, the symbolism of death-and-resurrection being particularly salient. If *Kita*, then, is clearly a ritual of transition, what kind of transition does it mark? If the ritual form is clear, what is the ritual substance?

The transition here is not connected with any life crisis, nor is it one between social statuses, as in rituals of adolescence, marriage, death, or initiation into an office. The *Kita* ritual does not mark a movement between positions in a social structure, between different social states of being. Rather, the *Kita* ritual itself is what defines the states of being before and after it. The states of being—those of being non-*kita* and *kita*—are wholly independent of sex and age, and they are in no way tied to any social statuses that can be defined by anything except the ritual itself. *Kita* does not lead to incorporation into— to quote Fortes again—"a new field of social structure, of conjuncture of social relations." Rather than arising from the need to mark some logically preexisting transition, *Kita* defines itself, so to speak; it is a self-sustaining *rite de passage*, a ritual that celebrates a grand tautology—the transition that it marks is the one that it has itself created. One goes through the *Kita* ritual in order to make the transition from the state of being non-*kita* to that of being *kita*. The meaning of the ritual does not stop there, to be sure. But this meaning links into ideas about the nature of society and its revitalization—and not into those about social statuses and social structure.

In discussing the *Kita* ritual, the Suku make analogies with the circumcision ceremony in which (to use Turner's summing up of Ndembu circumcision, which is similar to the Suku one) "the novice dies to be transformed or transmuted and attain a higher quality of existence" (Turner, 1962:173). Nevertheless, in circumcision, the male novice is (again in Turner's words) "reborn into masculinity and personality"—features that exist independently of the ritual itself and may be logically seen as preceding it. By contrast, in *Kita*, all one is reborn into is kitahood!

A closer analogy for *Kita* that comes to mind is with some form of sacrament, such as baptism, whose primary significance is religious rather than social—a sacrament or initiation that brings the initiate into a special state of "grace." In my discussions with the Suku, they found the analogy with baptism appealing—one's sex was irrelevant there too, and so, in their experience, was age. Where *Kita* differs from baptism of adults (but not of infants) is that it required no preceding inner conversion and it accomplished the new state of healthy grace rather mechanically. This mechanical aspect brings in another analogy the Suku found not inappropriate—the analogy with vaccination which upgrades the health of each person and, thereby, of the community as a whole. For this is the purpose and perceived accomplishment of *Kita*: to upgrade each novice in order to upgrade, through them, the community's vitality and reverse temporarily its entropy. The point must be stressed: *Kita* does not work directly upon the community as a corporate body—the way lineage medicines, for example, work upon the corporate lineage as a unit. With *Kita*, it is as if, in a list of discrete items, each previously unmarked item were to be marked with a plus sign, with the result that the whole set is upgraded; but meanwhile, the overall structure of the set and the relationship among the items have not been changed in any way.

In such a *rite de passage*, the passage is not from one position to another inside the given structure. Rather, the passage is from one state of being to another, whose essence is not structural but existential—one is or is not *kita*, as one is or is not immune to smallpox or as one is or is not a baptized Christian. This does not mean that the state of being *kita* carries with it no social consequences whatsoever. For example, only initiated elders and councilors can attend to a dying chief and be involved in his burial; only initiated men, women, and children can come to the house where twins have been born. All these events are inherently dangerous, and *Kita* initiates have been immunized against some of the danger. But these are immunities, not social statuses—in the same way that immunity from a typhoid vaccination allows one to sit with the sick or eat certain foods but does not represent a social status.

What *Kita* accomplishes, then, is a transition between purely "invented" states of being, in the sense that they are unrelated to any antecedent social statuses. The statuses involved are ritual and not social-structural. This should surprise no one except those theologically committed to the extreme Radcliffe-Brownian position that all ritual thinking must be epiphenomenal to problems of social structure. The position taken here, by contrast, is one expounded by Boas and some of his students—such as Benedict, Sapir, and Herskovits—that the cultural process is a creative process and not merely a reponsive one; that, moreover, to the extent that it is responsive, human creativity responds to existential problems no less than to problems of social

structure (or economy or ecology); and, furthermore, that human existential problems are, to a considerable degree, sui generis. Symboliza-
tion in the broadest sense is a generative activity of the human mind;
the mind is an active agent that can create its own "behavioral environment," as Hallowell (1955) has called it; and the mind can generate within it new states of being, perceive transitions between them,
and compose rituals to deal with these transitions. In brief, the mind
can create its own cognitive problems and proceed to solve them—
and some of these problems tend to be solved, as Van Gennep said,
in certain patterned ways. Those who see these propositions as mystical may be reminded of Suzanne Langer's memorable discussion of
the mind/brain as an organ; as such, it is as spontaneously active as
the kidneys or the stomach, but rather than juices it happens to generate symbols (Langer, 1942:41). As an efficient cause of ritual activity, the brain is scarcely an entity more mystical than social structure
or social solidarity.

I am not arguing here for mental determinism but rather for a
dialectical relationship between culture and its environment, in which
culture, qua system of meanings, consists of socially standardized mental products and environment consists of physical, social, and mental
events with which the standardized system of meanings must cope. In
this dialectical relationship, either side may be the "independent vari-
able" generating change to which the other side may respond. In the
interaction between culture and social structure, we need not assume
the antecedence of social structure even in those more usual rites of
passage that, unlike Kita, do deal with social statuses. Some social
statuses may indeed grow out of antecedent ritual statuses, rather
than the reverse. Thus, membership in a ritual fraternity may in time
provide the basis for political status—as kitahood, for example, might
have acquired sociostructurally significant attributes.

Returning to Kita specifically, we may now ask the question: if
social structural facts do not account for Kita, what does? The answer
requires that we first differentiate among different aspects of Kita: its
ritual idiom, its ritual pattern, its meaning, and its functions. To account for one of these is not to account for another. Thus, the cultural
idiom of the Kita ritual—its medicines, the initiation hut, the palm-
fringed entrance arch, the patterning of the songs and formulas, and
so on—all this is typically Suku and, beyond that, regional, occurring
in other rituals in the Kongo-Kwango cultural cluster of peoples. In

this, the *Kita* ritual clearly draws upon a regional ritual idiom, putting it to its own ends in a process that Fernandez (1974) has called "metaphoric conversion." Moreover, as we shall see, rituals very similar to *Kita* in pattern and sometimes even in name are to be found among neighboring peoples.

On the other hand, the metaphor of death and resurrection is a world-wide one in rites of passage—though it is not universal—and the metaphor must, therefore, be accounted for in terms of some pan-human psychology of metaphoric symbolism. This is indeed what Van Gennep implies by treating the death-and-resurrection metaphor as peculiarly appropriate to rites of passage. But we must not, in principle, assume the metaphor to be inevitable. The meaning and the idiom must be kept separate in our theory. Rituals of transition may, after all, resort to other symbolic idioms to convey their meanings, and, conversely, the death-and-resurrection symbolism may be used in rituals other than those of transition—especially those of social status transition. Unfortunately, the anthropological view simultaneously encompasses both meaning and metaphor as diagnostic of a rite of passage. It is this conceptual fusion, it seems to me, that has led Gluckman and Fortes to theorize in terms of a particular sociological meaning but take the metaphoric idiom for granted. But what makes *Kita* a rite of passage is its meaning and not the details of its ritual. It is the meaning and function of *Kita*, then, that I shall now try to account for. Given the failure of the kind of explanation advanced by Gluckman and Fortes, my explanation will take the argument in a quite different direction.

Kita as a Cult of Revitalization

We may see *Kita* as a revitalizing cult—one whose declared goal is a periodic though irregular revitalization of the society, which is assumed to be subject to an inexorable process of entropy. In this, *Kita* contrasts with other known kinds of ritual concerned with revitalization. Thus, on the one hand, anthropology is familiar with regular institutionalized rituals that Chapple and Coon (1942:507) have called "rites of intensification"; repetitive, cyclical, often calendrical, they are consciously performed in order to maintain the vital rhythm of life, society, nature, crops, and so on. On the other hand, we are familiar with what Wallace (1956) has named "revitalization movements." The very opposite of institutionalized, they are eruptive, irregular, institutionally innovative, revolutionary. Instead of maintaining and reinforcing existing conceptions, they sweep them aside as inadequate and introduce new ones.

Kita conforms to neither of these two types, yet it shares some features with both. Like rites of intensification, it is institutionalized; but unlike them, it occurs sporadically rather than regularly. Like revitalization movements, *Kita* claims to deal with society globally and when its malfunctioning becomes evident; but unlike revitalization movements, *Kita* does not propose a revolutionary sweep of existing central institutions. Institutionally speaking, *Kita* is "tame" and conservative, unlike revitalization movements that are supposed to be—or claim to be—innovative.

The innovative claims of revitalization movements bear, of course, some scrutiny. The claims are most dramatically convincing at close range and with a minimum of historical perspective. In the longer view, we know that the revolutionary claims of these movements are often naive. Their apparent eruptiveness may, in fact, respond to the regular rhythm of a long-term cycle. For example, Bohannan (1958) has suggested that among the Tiv of Nigeria antiwitchcraft movements may look to the participants and the short-term observer to be irregular, eruptive, and "extra-processual," but turn out to be, in the longer perspective, cyclical and even institutionally conservative. These movements attacked those in authority as witchcraft ridden and corrupt and toppled them from power; yet, by seemingly cleansing Tiv society in such a radical fashion, they drew attention away from some of the inherent contradictions of their system of authority and thus contributed to the long-term continuity of that system. In short, they were rebellions rather than revolutions—"institutionalized," in a sense, but not in the eyes of the participants.

This perception of what might be called a higher-level and longer-term institutionalization of an irregular "repairing" of the ravages of social entropy is usually a theoretical perception made by anthropologists. Yet, this perception also closely parallels the Suku folk sociology that underlies *Kita*. *Kita* is thus an institutionalized representation of what Wallace sees as the unconscious mainsprings of religion —namely, that "men universally observe the increase in entropy (disorganization) in familiar systems" and, consequently, that the "dialectic, the 'struggle' (to use an easy metaphor) beween entropy and organization, is what religion is all about" (Wallace, 1966:38). The Suku, for their part, have not only observed the results of entropy but have generalized them and perceived entropy itself as an ever-active process; the Suku have also made this perception part of their social theory and have acted upon that theory by institutionalizing *Kita*.

By postulating entropy as a general principle, the Suku made subject to it those ordinary religious institutions which were meant to cope with the everyday instances of entropy; that is, the effectiveness of the ordinary medicines and of the relationship with the ancestors was subject to periodic deterioration. And by providing a higher-level institution, *Kita*, to reverse the general entropy, the Suku made culturally manifest the revitalizing process (with its conservative functions) which it is usually the preserve of the anthropologist to understand. Like the Tiv—but unlike them, consciously—the Suku channeled the blame for social malfunctioning to a higher-level social process, which they then proceeded to tame ritually. This meant that the ordinary institutions of everyday coping with entropy—medicines, ancestors, and witchcraft—could be retained instead of being swept away, as they usually are in revitalization movements.

So much for a functional, institutional, and synchronically framed explication of *Kita*. I should like to return now to the question of why, as a cult of institutionalized revitalization, *Kita* should have adopted the idiom and symbolism of rites of passage. Part of the answer may lie in the Suku conception of entropy, not as an organic, but as an aggregate problem. Thus, while the Suku see the society as running down, they see the society as a collection of individuals each one of whom, one by one, is to be immunized from the effects of entropy. The society here is not an organic corporate entity but a mechanical aggregate. Hence, individual transition, which rites of passage exemplify, is an appropriate ritual here.

Further possibilities for explanation are suggested by Turner's (1969:97–99) perception of the many similarities between "millenarian" (that is, revitalization) movements and rites of passage. Turner attributes these similarities to the fact that both deal with transition and liminality—a "betwixt-and-between" marginality. Millenarian movements arise in historical periods when the society as a whole, or major groups in it, are in a transitional, liminal state. "That is perhaps why in so many of these movements much of their mythology and symbolism is borrowed from those of traditional *rites de passage* . . ."

(Turner, 1969:99). As a revitalization cult—a kind of institutionally tamed revitalization movement—*Kita* also deals with transition, be it only a transition to a restored *status quo ante*.

The link between *Kita* and revitalization raises further questions. Granted that *Kita* is institutionalized revitalization, does this have a historical meaning? Is *Kita* historically the institutionalized residue of an actual revitalization movement? We have, alas, no direct historical evidence to help us answer this question, save some bits of oral traditon. Hence, we must turn to the time-honored method of obtaining historical clues from the distributional evidence.

The Processual Function of Revitalization Cults

In most of its ritual details and terminology, the *Kita* ceremony closely resembles certain ceremonies among neighboring and culturally related peoples, such as the Ngongi and Khita among the Yaka (Plancquaert, 1930; Beir, 1975:84ff.) and, among numerous Kongo groups, the Kimba, Khimba, Kimpasi, and Kiphasi (Van Wing, 1920 and 1935; Bittremieux, 1936; Laman, 1962:244ff.). At the same time, however, many of the specific meanings of the details in *Kita* are its own, as is also the case with the other ceremonies. *Kita* is thus a complex that belongs to a cultural area and a diffusional area, like the Guardian Spirit or the Sun Dance complexes in aboriginal North America (see Benedict, 1923; Spier, 1921).

As mentioned before, the Suku say that *Kita* was first adopted when a king's installation was followed by widespread disease instead of a renewed period of vitality. In brief, it was adopted when existing supernatural institutions of coping were seen to have failed—and failed not at the level of a single lineage but at the level of the collectivity. In this respect, the coming of *Kita* is akin to the coming of later, historically documented movements which, coming in from outside, periodically swept through the Suku area and brought with them a ritual of initiation that the Suku endowed with a specifically Suku meaning. Like *Kita*, these later movements claimed to compensate for the inadequacies of the established ritual ways of coping—including, by then, *Kita* itself! Like *Kita*, they promised to bring health, the good life, and children "with hair and nails" through a new ceremony or cult or magical substance (see Kopytoff, 1964). These movements de-

manded no reorganization of existing beliefs; rather, they complemented these beliefs with a yet newer piece of supernatural technology involving individual initiation and an individual rite of passage
(of the most elementary kind in the later movements). Like *Kita*, they
perceived the general social malaise in aggregate terms rather than in
organic terms and they offered solutions through ritual acting at the
individual level. Thus, *Kita* clearly appears to be one of a class of
phenomena—namely, a succession of revitalization movements which,
historically, swept through the Suku and neighboring areas and each
of which either vanished or became institutionalized into a cult with
more modest pretensions. *Kita*, then, becomes understandable as a
residue of such a process—a residue that survived as an institutionalized cult for half a century or more.

Wallace (1956:267) has, of course, suggested that many religions
are probably institutionalized and routinized descendants of totalistic
revitalization movements. The implication is that they become more
moderate in their claims and that their functional range is reduced.
One may add to this that the kind of theory that the revitalization
movement espouses should have an effect on its subsequent fate. Thus,
one can see how a totalistic, transcendental theory can lead to a religion. If, however, the attempt at revitalization adopts from the beginning a mechanistic and instrumental theory and the idiom of an initiation cult, as did *Kita*, then its routinized and chastened descendant
becomes, appropriately, not a religion but a cult—one of routine rather
than dramatic revitalization, that can easily coexist with other cults
which have their own specialized instrumental claims.

Such revitalization cults are, functionally, over and above other
institutions of coping. Organizationally, however, they exist side by
side with them. But even when routinized, their claims continue to
echo their original promise of total revitalization. In this, there need
not be a contradiction. Thus, in Protestant Christianity, we find routinized yet revivalistic institutions—such as Billy Graham's Crusade—
that combat religious entropy by using the ritual of authentic revolutionary revivalism; but in this instance, they do it at the express
invitation of the established churches, in the same way that a *Kita* expert is invited to complement the everyday institutions of coping. Instead of overthrowing the system—as a totalistic revitalizaton movement does—a revitalization cult claims to act as a rectifier, a kind of
gyroscope within the system. I said, "claims to act." But the claim

may or may not be justified. I would suggest that the difference between claim and reality may, in some measure, account for the process of proliferation of cults in Africa.

Anthropologists have often viewed religion as an institutionalized complex that compensates for the inevitable imperfections of everyday life and for the normal failures of coping with life that all men experience. Revitalization movements have been seen in much the same way, although as an eruptive rather than institutionalized response to the inadequacies of coping, not least the inadequacies of established religion. Interestingly, *Kita* combines both these functions. If we consider the Suku complex of everyday coping—involving elders, ancestors, witches, and medicines—to constitute what anthropologists have called religion, we can see *Kita* then as an institution compensating, at the next functional level, for the inevitable imperfections of this everyday religious coping. To use Bohannan's terminology, *Kita* is thus "extra-processual" at the functional level of everyday religious practice. Yet, this function of *Kita* was formally recognized by the Suku, making it a processually "normal" institution at a higher functional level.

This is, however, a static rendition of the position of *Kita* in Suku religion. Over the several decades of its existence, the position of *Kita* shifts. As it failed to live up to its promise, other revitalization cults came in, taking upon themselves to achieve what *Kita* failed to do. Thus, by the 1930s *Kita* was performed less and less often, and by the 1940s it had vanished. In a sense, *Kita* could only move in two directions. One road—the one it took—was to oblivion, for with the attrition of its higher-level function as the rectifier of the religious system it was beginning to lose its very reason for being. The other direction would have been to redefine its functions somehow, to become yet another specialized cult among others by renouncing its original grandiose claims and settling for something more modest. This road was in fact taken by some later revitalization movements which, in time, shrank into purveying trivial antiwitchcraft medicines. It is thus conceivable that *Kita* might have become transformed into a relatively stable cult of modest pretensions.

The existence of functionally "compensatory" institutions, such as *Kita*, raises some questions about the widespread anthropological tendency to explain (or should we say explain away?) esoteric religious institutions by dwelling on what they "do" and "achieve." Thus, reli-

gious esoterica is said to persist because it compensates for the inadequacies of secular institutions. But in straining to demonstrate the
utility of many an existing religion, we have perhaps made it out to
be too successful—more successful, at any rate, than it may appear to
be to its own practitioners. We have glossed over the many things it
promises to do and does not do—because, in the end, it cannot. This
inevitable failure by a religion that promises empirical results to pass
the empirical test can be handled by its adherents in at least two ways.
One is to obfuscate the testing itself by extraneous interfering factors
and by closed systems of reasoning that will explain any empirical
outcome. This is the adaptation that anthropologists have stressed ever
since Frazer, and this stress has been particularly consonant with functionalist analyses of presumably stable religious systems. The other
adaptation by the adherents of such a religion is more dynamic, however: it is to suffer its failures in full awareness of them until they become too hard to bear and then devise a new religious solution, with
all its potential failings. *Kita*, together with other Suku revitalization
movements, represents this kind of response. A cultural predilection
for this response sets into motion a continuous process that generates
ever new esoteric cults. Each of them promises to do what its predecessors had proved they could not do, and, like them, each fails and
either vanishes or becomes routinized into a humbler cult. This process, it seems to me, can suggest some of the forces that underlie the
singular religious dynamism and cult proliferation that characterize so
many African societies.

   The long-term process I have described departs in significant
ways from the long-term process governing revitalization movements
as developed by Wallace (1956; 1966). In the latter, widely spaced-
out revolutionary leaps occur, bringing profound changes in cognition
and, in effect, producing new religions. The process I have described
is more measured, more continuous, and more superficial in its effects
—a kind of endless one-step-forward-and-one-step-back movement.
This does not give birth to new religions; instead, it creates ever new
cults that join in the procession of preceding cults. Why, we may ask,
this difference? I have already suggested that the pragmatic orientation of Suku religion has something to do with it. The point bears
some elaboraton, not least because it impinges on Durkheimian notions of religion.

Revitalization in Non-Durkheimian Religion

The picture I have presented of Suku religion is that of a stubborn but none too successful attempt to cope with life's uncertainties, punctuated by outbursts of creativity that lead to preordained failure. Suku religion is, above all, pragmatic in orientation, in the sense that its dominant concerns are health, wealth, and social and political well-being—all matters in which success is empirically testable. In this, Suku religion is like many other traditional African religions that are primarily concerned with what Horton (1971) has aptly described as this-worldly "explanation-prediction-control." If we insist on seeing it as "proto" anything, it is protoscientific and technological rather than, let us say, protophilosophical or theological.

In addition to orientation, there is also the matter of social scope. In Suku religion, the scope is parochial. The focus is overwhelmingly on the prosperity of the corporate matrilineage and threats to it and, beyond that, on the intimate circle of kinship-regulated relationships. It is only within such narrow confines that Suku religion approaches Durkheim's (1912) notion of religion as an overarching institution holding society together and perpetuating it over time. But beyond these confines, in relation to the society at large, Durkheim's notion does not hold. Suku religion is not "above" the society, knitting it together, but very much "in" it—an instrument of all its segments, divisions, conflicts, and contradictions.

Kita, however, is exceptional. Like the circumcision ceremony, it is a community-wide ritual, transcending the matrilineage even while focusing on the individual as the object of its action. The ideology underlying *Kita*—that of the inevitable entropy of the social order—is, in fact, very Durkheimian. Here again, we encounter in Suku folk sociology a perception that we ordinarily think of as a prerogative of the social scientist. One can thus see *Kita* as an attempt to break out of the parochialism of the core of Suku religion by expanding the scope of its concern to society as a whole. However, when it comes to means for achieving this goal, the Suku fall back upon their established technological repertoire of medicines and rituals; and when the lineage is removed from these, what remains is the individual novice. *Kita* tries to revitalize society, but its ritual instruments do not let it deal with society; instead, they upgrade the state of individuals, one

by one. This is as far, it seems, as *Kita* has traveled on the Durkheimian road to religion, and later revitalization movements among the
Suku have gone no further. All this gives the long-term dynamics of
revitalization among the Suku the particular cast I have described.

If Horton (1964; 1967; 1971) is correct (as I think he is), this pragmatic orientation is characteristic of African religions in general when
their scope is parochial, that is, focused on the narrow social group.
Not all "traditional" or parochial religions need have this orientation,
to be sure, as witness aboriginal Australian or South American religions. Moreover, a pragmatic orientation usually exists at the parochial
level of the great transcendental religions, as seen in the local peasant
practices within Christianity or Islam, or in the local Vedic cults
within Hinduism. The combination of pragmatism and parochialism,
which concerns use here, may be contrasted with religions, such as
Hinduism, Christianity, or Islam, that are nonparochial and also transcendental and whose theology is in the purview of literate specialists
who are its guardians and spokesmen. At this theological level, such
transcendental religions are indeed above and beyond everyday pragmatic concerns. What model they advance for this world is the model
of how things ought to be—not, as pragmatic religions do, of how
things are. A transcendental religion insulates itself from empirical
testing by avoiding empirical claims, by proclaiming its indifference
to mundane matters, or by subordinating these matters to higher and
unfathomable goals. Famines, plagues, and disasters become grist for
its theological mills, often strengthening its persuasiveness rather than
undermining its credibility, as they do with pragmatic religions. By
standing above local interests, a transcendental religion can also become an instrument of integration of large and lasting political entities.

It is to these transcendental religions, it seems to me, that Durkheim's model of religion as social integrator is most appropriate. In
this model, the usefulness of religion—its function, as some would prefer to say it—lies in giving society its morale, that is, its moral self-
assurance rather than its pragmatic confidence. Historically, this has
been the role of religion in societies that anthropology has generally
neglected—the non-"tribal," literate, complex, stratified, often plural-
istic, but nonindustrial societies of premodern Europe, the Near East,
Southern and Eastern Asia, perhaps Central America.

Concerned with the anomie of modern secular society, as exemplified by France of the Third Republic, Durkheim looked back to this

kind of social-religious configuration in order to understand what it was that modern society seemed to have lost. The assumption behind this was scarcely original—the idea that Christianity and the Church had provided a kind of social glue to premodern Europe was a widespread nineteenth-century notion, whatever its historical truth. And the centrality of religion to the integration of any society had been stressed before Durkheim by both Tocqueville (1840) and Fustel de Coulanges (1861). In his search for a functional equivalent of religion that would reintegrate his conflict-ridden country, Durkheim sought to find the essence of religion in general. And, like other nineteenth-century evolutionists, he sought the essential meaning of it in its origins —and origins, in those days, were to be found among Australian aborigines as the quintessential and irreducible "primitive" society (Durkheim, 1912/1965:1). Alas for anthropological theory, the Australian ethnographic material could be made to support the thesis (as African materials, for example, would not have). Thus, Durkheim did not confront a thoroughly pragmatic religion, and his extension of religion from premodern large-scale societies to the "primitive" world was handed down to structural-functional social anthropology. But given the prevalence of pragmatic religions, that is precisely where the wholesale extension of the thesis should not have been made. The functional stability of transcendental religion should not have been imposed on pragmatic religion, whose concerns are quite different and quite un-Durkheimian.

The revitalization processes in the two kinds of religions we are considering here—the pragmatic and the transcendental—necessarily differ. If a transcendental religion becomes established as a central integrating institution in a society, it becomes socially and politically entrenched. In such a setting, a revitalization movement must offer an appropriately profound reorganization of thought, a reorganization that inevitably spills over into the organization of society at large. At the same time, the ideology of such a revitalization movement, being transcendental rather than pragmatic, can be radically discontinuous with the established ideology. This combination of revolutionary ideology with wide functional scope means that the revitalization movement— if it is at all successful, which it is usually not—can result in a new religion. It is such movements that conform most readily with the revitalization process as originally defined by Wallace.

By contrast, a pragmatic religion submits itself—by self-definition

—to empirical testing. It is therefore perpetually vulnerable in its details to the everyday batterings of reality, in the same way that technological science is vulnerable to them. And like it, pragmatic religion becomes a never-ending quest for new ways of coping which, in the long run, are doomed to prove themselves inadequate—in the case of technology because of new problems, in the case of pragmatic religion because both of new problems and its obfuscations of reality. But this openness to new methods revitalizes the religious paradigm and, as we have seen with *Kita*, can help to maintain it. It is only when the entire paradigm comes to be perceived by its adherents as inadequate that a revitalization movement of a fundamental and totalistic kind is apt to arise. In modern Africa, this has meant the rise of new churches —in effect, new religions (which may, however, be of the pragmatic kind). But most of the time, I submit, African religions have tended to remain within the given pragmatic paradigm. Thus, they have tended to generate transient cults that often began with high pretensions—as new scientific theories are also apt to do—but ended, if they survived at all, by reducing their claims and joining in the array of existing cults.

NOTES

I did fieldwork among the Suku, 1957 to 1959, under the auspices of the Program of African Studies. Northwestern University, and under a grant from the Ford Foundation. I also wish to acknowledge a stimulating discussion of some of the issues raised here with Dr. Sandra Barnes, who read an early version of this paper.

BIBLIOGRAPHY

Beir, L. de. 1975. *Les Bayaka de M'Nene N'toombo Lenge-lenge*. Collectanea Instituti Anthropos no. 5. St. Augustin: Anthropos Institut.
Benedict. Ruth. 1923. "The Concept of the Guardian Spirit in North America." *Memoirs, American Anthropological Association* no. 29. Washington, D.C.: American Anthropological Association.
Bittremieux. L. 1936. "La Société Secrète des Bakhimba au Mayombe." *Memoires, Institut Royal Colonial Belge*. Bruxelles: Institut Royal Colonial Belge.
Bohannan, Paul. 1958. "Extra-Processual Events in Tiv Political Institutions." *American Anthropologist* 60:1-12.

Chapple, Eliot D., and Coon, Carleton S. 1942. *Principles of Anthropology*. New York: Holt.

Durkheim, Emile. 1912. *The Elementary Forms of Religious Life*. Translated by J. W. Swain. New York: Macmillan, 1915.

Fernandez, James. 1974. "The Mission of Metaphor in Expressive Culture." *Current Anthropology* 15:119–45.

Fortes, Meyer. 1962. "Ritual and Office in Tribal Society." In *Essays on the Ritual of Social Relations*, edited by Max Gluckman, pp. 53–88. Manchester: University of Manchester Press.

Fustel de Coulanges, N. D. 1864. *The Ancient City*. Garden City, N.Y.: Doubleday, 1956.

Gluckman, Max. 1962. "Les Rites de Passage." In *Essays on the Ritual of Social Relations*, edited by Max Gluckman, pp. 1–52.

——. ed. 1962. *Essays on the Ritual of Social Relations*. Manchester: University of Manchester Press.

Hallowell, A. Irving. 1955. "The Self and Its Behavioral Environment." In *Culture and Experience*, pp. 75–110. Philadelphia: University of Pennsylvania Press.

Horton, Robin. 1964. "Ritual Man in Africa." *Africa* 34:85–104.

——. 1967. "African Traditional Thought and Western Science." *Africa* 37:50–71; 155–87.

——. 1971. "African Conversion." *Africa* 41:85–108.

Kopytoff, Igor. 1964. "Classifications of Religious Movements: Analytical and Synthetic." In *Symposium of New Approaches to the Study of Religion*, edited by June Helm. Proceedings, American Ethnological Society, 1964, pp. 77–90.

——. 1965. "The Suku of Southwestern Congo." In *Peoples of Africa*, edited by James L. Gibbs, Jr., pp. 441–78. New York: Holt, Rinehart and Winston.

——. 1977. "Matrilineality, Residence, and Residential Zones." *American Ethnologist* 4:539–58.

Lamal, F. 1949. "Essai d'étude démographique d'une population du Kwango." *Memoires, Institut Royal Colonial Belge*. Bruxelles: Institut Royal Colonial Belge.

Laman, Karl. 1962. "The Kongo." Vol. 3. *Studia Ethnographica Upsaliensia* 12. Stockholm: Upsala University.

Langer, Suzanne K. 1942. *Philosophy in a New Key*. 3rd ed., 1967. Cambridge: Harvard University Press.

Plancquaert, M. 1930. *Les sociétés secrètes chez les Bayaka*. Louvain: J. Kuyl-Otto.

Spier, Leslie. 1921. "The Sun Dance of the Plains Indians: Its Development and Diffusion." *Anthropological Papers, American Museum of Natural History*, vol. 16, no. 7, pp. 451–527.

Tocqueville, Alexis de. 1840. *Democracy in America*. New York: Century Co. 1898. Vol. 2.

Turner, Victor W. 1962. "Three Symbols of *Passage* in Ndembu Circumcision Ritual: An Interpretation." In *Essays on the Ritual of Social Relations*, edited by Max Gluckman, pp. 124–73.

——. 1969. *The Ritual Process*. Penguin ed., 1974. London: Penguin Books.

Van Gennep, Arnold. 1909. *The Rites of Passage.* Chicago: University of Chicago Press, 1960.

Van Wing, J. 1920. *De Geheime Sekte van 't Kimpasi.* Bruxelles: Goemaere.

———. 1935. *Etudes Bakongo, II: Religion et Magie.* Bruxelles: Falkfils.

Wallace, Anthony F. C. 1956. "Revitalization Movements." *American Anthropologist* 58:264–81.

———. 1966. *Religion: An Anthropological View.* New York: Random House.

Normal and Revolutionary Divination

A Kuhnian Approach to African Traditional Thought

by Dan F. Bauer and John Hinnant

The historian of science Thomas Kuhn (1962; 1970) has made a distinction in examining Western science between two modes of thought which he calls "normal science" and "revolutionary science." The distinction he makes may be usefully applied to systems of traditional thought in Africa. For Kuhn, the person working within an established scientific tradition is a normal scientist. The scientist breaking with an established tradition and producing a potentially new paradigm for a new tradition is practicing revolutionary science.[1]

In this paper we argue for the utility of making a similar distinction within the thought processes of people usually labeled "traditional." We argue that there are "normal" and "revolutionary" diviners, and that many of the characteristics Kuhn draws for the mode of inquiry as well as the social organization of normal and revolutionary scientists are found among these two types of diviners. The ethnographic settings in which this discussion will take place are the divinatory practices of the Tigray of highland Ethiopia and the Guji Oromo of southern Ethiopia.

Kuhn argues that under most circumstances scientists work under a set scientific tradition, or a "paradigm," through which they "see" the phenomena under study. The paradigm dictates permissible techniques and canons of proof, and sets forth a probable range of outcomes before an experiment has begun. Kuhn draws an analogy between normal science and puzzle solving. The experiment is of a known type, and it is known to have a solution. The normal scientist does not question the theory under which he is working. He accepts it as given. What he is testing in experiments are the hypotheses it generates. He is testing whether the phenomena before him are like one rather than another of the successful experiments with which he is familiar, or he is adding precision to an expected outcome.

By contrast, a scientific revolution may take place when these phenomena are perceived in a new way. For example, combustion was once perceived as the consumption (or subtraction) of phlogiston in a substance leaving a pure, phlogiston-free substance behind. After the "discovery" of oxygen, combustion was seen as the combination (or addition) of oxygen with (or to) another substance to produce, not the pure substance, but an oxidized version of that substance. The normal scientist sees the world within his discipline's paradigm; the revolutionary scientist sees it in a new way. It becomes a different "reality."

The normal scientist legitimizes his research by pointing to the use of the standard procedures of his discipline. The revolutionary scientist is recognized for personal inspiration, as with Einstein's special "gift." It is *his* insight. The new perception is often reported to have come during sleep or while the researcher was doing some non-related activity. The normal scientist is usually trained within the discipline in which he works, in terms of the concepts he accepts on authority. The revolutionary scientist often has been trained in one field and later switches to work in another. In other words, he tends to possess dual cognitive apparatus.

Kuhn sees scientific progress as involving alternating periods of normal and revolutionary scientific inquiry. Most of the time that a paradigm in the sense of an accepted scientific "world view" is firmly in place, scientists discover the expected solutions to the puzzles before them. Any anomalies which may occur are put aside or written off as "bad research" or as "equipment failures." The theory remains intact. Kuhn sees the impetus for paradigm change as coming from the accumulation of bothersome anomalies leading to dissatisfaction with the accepted paradigm. The stage is now set for revolutionary research. However, scientists do not readily abandon an old paradigm without another which promises to answer the anomalies plus most of the questions already answered by the old paradigm. During a period of revolution many competing "theories" are put forward and intellectual chaos threatens. Kuhn quotes Albert Einstein as saying, "It is as if the ground had been pulled out from under one, with no firm foundation to be seen anywhere upon which one could build" (1970: 83).

The scientist who has perceived the new order of things may attract a following, but often also the condemnation of those who do not "see it his way," many of whom remain committed to the old paradigm for the remainder of their careers. For the rest a new paradigm (world view) emerges.

This brief and somewhat simplified account of Thomas Kuhn's view of science will provide the setting for our discussion of divination. The inspiration for this paper came from Robin Horton's interesting and influential essay, "African Traditional Thought and Western Science" (1967). Horton's analysis is directed primarily at understanding the behavior of diviners. Two of his points are particularly significant. He notes that divination is personal (it deals with the problems of individuals), while Western science is nonpersonal (it deals with universals). This point conforms with our own analysis. The second point Horton makes, contrasting African traditional thought with Western science, is more controversial: that is his contention that traditional thought is "closed," allowing for no alternatives, while scientific thought is "open," always seeking alternatives. Kuhn's analysis of scientific thought suggests that it fluctuates in its "openness" over time and that the type of scientific enterprise the practioner finds himself in affects the openness of his mode of thought and inquiry. Our analysis suggests that this is true of divination as well. There are "normal" and "revolutionary" diviners with varying degrees of commitment to a received paradigm, and the relationship between these types of divination is related to the kinds of anomalies the paradigms confront.

The two ethnographic cases pose different problems with respect to the relationship of anomalies and paradigms and the relationship among competing paradigms. The Tigray case will show a stable relationship among competing paradigms, while in the Guji case one paradigm is apparently being supplanted by another. The analysis of divination in these two societies indicates an even greater similarity between science and traditional thought than Horton has assumed.

Another manner in which science and divination differ is that natural science paradigms are relevant to a limited number of situations, while the diviner's paradigms have a much wider range including, or impinging upon, the contexts of everyday life. The social implications of paradigm acceptance and rejection are of central interest to us in this essay.

The two kinds of diviners (normal and revolutionary) as general

types are well documented in the anthropological literature. The Azande diviner (Evans-Pritchard, 1937) uses oracular evidence in making his choices among hypotheses and legitimatizes his findings on the
grounds that the procedures he is using are the established ones, that
they are in effect the standardized laboratory procedures of his branch
of normal divination/science. He defends his findings (and established
theory) against attack, as Horton noted, by pointing to the impossibility of controlling all of the conditions necessary to insure accuracy,
just as Kuhn notes that findings which do not fit the established paradigm of normal scientists are attributed to equipment failures (or by
others to the practitioner's faulty technique), but not to a failure of
the theory itself. Scientists working within an established paradigm
are, Kuhn notes, reluctant to abandon their paradigm. Their failure
invites intellectual chaos and loss of hard-gained professional creden-
tials.

The revolutionary diviner is also well represented in anthropological literature. The leaders of such cults as the Tiv "beef" movement
(Bohannon, 1958) or the various Melanesian cargo movements are
revolutionary diviners (Burridge, 1969). Their ideas and findings are
legitimatized on the grounds of their being either "new" or "foreign."
Their ideas are gained through what might best be labeled "inspiration" and "intuition." Their procedures are never "old," "established"
ones, at least at the ideological level, though they may be permuta-
tions of old ones. The adherents of the new paradigm are those who
have found the old theory wanting, as Kuhn says of the period when
revolutionary science is taking place, an awareness of anomalies in the
established paradigm has taken place for those who abandon it and
begin research under the new paradigm. The rise of such cult movements has often been related to what might be termed paradigm failures.

The life histories of revolutionary scientists and revolutionary diviners also show parallels. Kuhn notes that revolutionary scientists tend
to have worked in another tradition (perhaps physics) before taking
up the one in which they become revolutionaries (say, chemistry).
Travel or exposure to mission school seems to be associated with revolutionary diviners. This is not simply acculturation. They are not
bringing back "customs." What is significant is that as a result of
their experience they tend to be the possessors of dual sets of categorical apparatuses. Revolutionary scientists and revolutionary diviners

find their public receptions mixed, they are lauded by some, often the nonestablished, and debunked as frauds by others.

The ethnographic portion of this paper is devoted to the examination of divination in two societies, each of which has competing divination paradigms within it. The Tigray of northern Ethiopia are part of the same dominant semitic, Christian agricultural tradition as the Amhara. The Guji are part of the large group of peoples called Oromo who were incorporated into Ethiopia by conquest during the last century and are in transition from a herding to an agricultural form of adaptation. Their contrasting relationships with the Ethiopian state are reflected in the relationships between competing divination paradigms within each society.[2]

The next two sections of the paper are devoted to an examination of Tigray diviners as practioners of "normal" divination and of Tigray spirit mediums as "revolutionary" diviners. This is followed by an examination of Guji spirit possession cults as successful revolutionary movements (both as systems of thought and as political movements).

The Tigray *Deftera* as "Normal Diviner"

Tigray diviners, *deftera*, deal with an established Tigray paradigm of the causes of affliction and share many of the characteristics Kuhn ascribes to normal scientists. The cosmological system under which they work is that shared by most Tigray. Most affliction is regarded as being caused by human action, but not necessarily with personal malicious intent. The major causes of illnesses and other misfortunes are sorcery, witchcraft, and excessive pride. Spirits as causes of misfortune involve some ambiguity, as we shall see.

Deftera are involved as practitioners in both diagnosis and healing. Diagnosis involves a choice among alternative causes, using the analysis of symptoms and the administration of tests. For example, a person who is bewitched displays certain characteristic behavior which is regarded as being hyenalike. The symptoms are recognizable to the trained eye. A frequently used test involves the interpretation of smoke from especially prepared incense.

Deftera also prescribe preventions and cures. Talismans and amulets are common preventatives, their efficacy deriving from the quality of the formulas used in their preparation. Cures are of three types: purification, curse removal, and transference. All three are accomplished through symbolic means. Purification to remove "medicines" (*medīhanīt*) is done by using pure substances such as holy water. A curse may be removed by confronting the person or group responsible and forcing its removal. Transference is the more interesting of the three in terms of its implications for the Tigray cosmology. This is the means of removing "natural" afflictions.

Healing of natural afflictions can be accomplished only by transferring the illness to someone else. Affliction is in a sense the complementary analogue of Foster's "limited good."[3] There is a finite and constant amount in circulation. If one is to gain relief, he must give it to someone else.

Transference is accomplished so as to keep the donor and the recipient anonymous. One, of course, does not wish to cause ill to befall a friend, yet one wishes to receive relief. Medicines are used to take the essence of the illness from the victim and place it in a vehicle which will transmit it to the new victim. The "illness" might be placed inside a desirable food such as a chicken or a quantity of spiced beans and placed along a trail where a passerby may step over it, contract the illness, and thus insure the recovery of the original victim. Beer cans thrown out of a truck by American military personnel were perceived as the cause of the death of seven children who died of measles. As an informant put it, "no one could throw out such valuables without reason." A spontaneously aborted fetus contaminates all women of the community, who then must band together and physically throw the fetus across the parish boundary, where it will contaminate the next community unless it too transfers the contamination. Eventually, being thrown into the sea will end its power to contaminate.

The *deftera* work within a paradigm based on a theoretical postulate that affliction in one way or another is usually caused by other humans, either because they wish to harm enemies or because they wish to achieve relief from affliction themselves. Like normal scientists, *deftera* are regarded as effective because they have special knowledge, knowledge which they have gained through learning mostly from other *deftera*. Knowledge of the Bible gained from studying to become deacons and priests may be applied in special formulas to prevent, cause, cure, and transfer affliction. Formulas generally are learned from studying with another *deftera*. A particular power is thought to be derived from his knowledge. A powerful diviner knows more powerful formulas and/or numerically more formulas than does a less powerful one. He has no special gifts other than how to learn or be a good diagnostician.

Deftera are not necessarily moral. Their knowledge, like that of a scientist, makes them powerful; it does not make them good. Some provide "medicines" which the purchaser uses to harm others. These *deftera* are perceived in much the same way as the misguided scientist is presented on children's television in America.

The position occupied by *deftera* is illustrated by the case of a man Bauer knew during fieldwork. This *deftera* was not only a diviner but the leading Bible teacher (*mergita*) and leader of liturgical music for the church. He sold numerous potions with high reputations for efficacy. One day an enemy's house burned down for no apparent cause, while the *deftera* was known to have been some distance away in his own house. It was thought that he had done it through selected readings of Biblical passages. He first denied it but later is said to have admitted it. Though this display of power enhanced his reputation, one need not assume the admission to have been coldly calculated. It seems quite possible that one who frequently used powerful formulas might suspect that an accidental juxtaposition might have been responsible for unforeseen powerful effects.[4] He reconciled with his enemy and retained his high position within the community.

Two other cases illustrate something of the manner in which diviners' findings are validated. Reisa Debrī Melles inherited wealth and displayed it to excess, riding his horse to his door rather than dismounting at the center of the village and walking his horse to the house as is expected of properly humble men. When rinderpest killed most of his herd he hired a well-known *deftera*. Melles suspected the cause to be the use of medicines by jealous relatives or neighbors. The *deftera* using standard, as it were, "laboratory techniques" (incense smoke reading, in this case) determined the case to have been one of "excessive pride" (*mu'*), concepts paralleling the Greek notions of hubris and resulting nemesis (*mesqa*). Melles denied the validity of the diviner's findings but did not hire a second diviner. The community accepts the *deftera's* "findings" and rejects Melles's "contentions."

In another case, Bellay Redda suffered the loss of several head of cattle. A *deftera* confirmed his suspicion of sorcery on the part of one of his "poor" and therefore jealous sisters. Again, the diviner normatively using only "laboratory" (divining) techniques based upon theory developed a finding which conformed to the community's suspicions which were based upon a common sense analysis of social relations. A diviner's skills would no doubt fall into disrepute should the theory-based finding fail too often to conform.

In short, the *deftera* is much like a normal scientist in that he works from an established paradigm and chooses among alternatives which are known to exist. Choosing hubris (*mu'*) over sorcery is like choosing a solution from chemistry rather than physics. His findings are legitimatized as coming from "standard practice" and being the same as another diviner with similar knowledge would find. The divination of Tigray spirit mediums offers a sharp contrast, both in terms of the mode of legitimation of their determinations and in the nature of the paradigm under which they operate.

The Tigray Spirit Medium as "Revolutionary Diviner"

A belief which is shared by many Tigray, but not by all, is that most affliction is the result of possession by spirits.[5] There are a wide variety of possession spirits with a great deal of regional variation. They are usually lumped under the term *zar*, though some spirits contrast with *zar* in its narrowest sense.[6]

A *zar* manifests itself as illness, "odd" hehavior, and in most cases as a highly stylized form of dance accompanied by trance. Only a specialist has the ability to deal with it. *Zar* affliction is not randomly distributed. It affects many women and very few men. A possessed woman's *zar* may be brought under control. Once controlled it allows a woman to go about her business on a day-to-day basis only manifesting itself as trance accompanied by dance on expected occasions. It, therefore, is no longer dangerous. Possession in males becomes a key identity defining most of his day-to-day behavior. Possessed men do their hair in buttered thin braids and wear many rings on their fingers. They usually give up farming and beg door to door.

A person who believes himself or herself to be possessed can only be treated after a spirit medium discovers what the spirit wants. Under proper ritual circumstances the *zar* will speak through the medium. When its demands are met, the affliction subsides.

Typically, a woman's *zar* wishes the woman's husband to provide her with something, usually a luxury. At the time of fieldwork most zar wished to have their physical habitations decorated with elaborately embroidered dresses studded with silver buttons. Men's zar typically wanted silver rings for the fingers of the men they inhabited. Some demands were more idiosyncratic. One rather pretty, but erratic, woman in the village whose priest husband was devoted to her was possessed with awesome frequency. A delegation came to Bauer to say that her zar demanded a ride in a Land Rover to a village some ten miles distant where the woman's sister lived. Two weeks later the delegation came a second time with the news that the zar demanded a return trip.[7]

Husbands, indeed men in general, normally take the position that zar do not exist. This is also the position of the church. Men usually state that spirit mediums are charlatans and that women fake trances to get their husbands to give them things. The possession of one's own wife tends to be regarded as a case of mistaken diagnosis. The problem is really one of "normal affliction" which the woman mistakenly regards as possession. The husband will press her to see a deftara. Should the affliction persist after treatment by normal means, relatives will demand that the husband pay the expense of a spirit ritual.[8]

The reluctant husband is then likely to find that he must incur further expense to fulfill the demands of the spirit. This demand for zar treatment on the part of the priests' wives is a special problem because it puts them in the difficult position of having to choose between being a good husband and being a good priest.

For instance, a widow who regarded herself as possessed was never cured though she herself paid to meet some of the zar's demands. An informant attributed her problem to the idea that zar could only really be satisfied by the actions of her husband.

A number of functional interpretations can be placed upon Tigray spirit possession. Zar possession gives women a greater command over household resources as well as providing a mechanism for redressing husband-wife relations (see note 7). In its formation of a "community of suffering," to use Turner's expressive words, (1957:xxi) zar provides a complement to the political community in which men play a more direct role. However interesting, functional interpretations are not our main concern here. Our major concern is with the systems of thought represented by the practices of deftera and the spirit mediums as systems of thought.

The paradigm under which spirit mediums work contrasts with that of *deftera* in several ways. Spirit possession implies the existence of entities which do not exist in the realm of *deftera*. The logic of spirit possession is different as well. Normal affliction is generally the result of rational acts of other men and is, therefore, subject to a degree of predictability. Spirits come from outside human society and are capricious. Similarly, the spirit medium's abilities are unique. Her abilities are not just like those of another diviner with similar training but are the result of the peculiar qualities of the individual spirit which has possessed her.

One of the major features of spirit possession that emerges from this discussion is that, in contrast to normal divination, it is nonestablished; in other words, in contrast to the established normal science-like paradigm of the *deftera*, it is like an emerging revolutionary paradigm. Some of these qualities of being nonestablished can better be seen in the examination of another Ethiopian society, the Guji Jam Jam Oromo, dealt with in the next section of the paper.

Here we see spirit possession not only providing a kind of alternative community and conceptual system to that established in society, but also being used to create new social rules for the participants. It is, in a social as well as conceptual manner, "revolutionary."

Revolutionary Communities among the Guji

The Guji Oromo of southern Ethiopia have undergone a paradigm shift during this century from a cosmology appropriate to an independent society of warlike cattle herders to one that acknowledges the greater power of forces outside their geographical borders. The cosmology is articulated through two closely related terms, *woyyu* and *kayyo*, which follow a nature/culture dichotomy.[9] *Woyyu* is a power, dimly perceived, that lies outside the orderly realm of society. This "unrestrained power" is associate with lightning, two species of poisonous snakes, and the conflicting relations among affines. *Woyyu* is unrestrained potency. It is epitomized by the great *kallu*, the high priest of all Guji whose most distant ancestor descended from the sky. Congruent with the power he represents, the high priest lives in his own small territory and may not enter the rest of Guji.

Kayyo, "controlled potency," is the power of *woyyu*, "natural potency," brought into society and made to serve the needs of humanity by permitting peace, health, and procreativity of both people and cattle. "Controlled potency" is epitomized by a small number of priests and law givers called *abba gada*.[10] Each *abba gada*, gada "chief," is responsible for the peace and abundance of one of the eight phratry divisions of Guji (each consisting of several closely related clans and their associated territory). Each *abba gada* serves an eight-year term of office, which begins after he has ingested frankincense (*kumbi*) obtained from the high priest by one of his predecessors. During the *abba gada's* first year in office, he visits a number of shrines where he infuses the good *kayyo* he obtains through the high priest's frankincense. He then proclaims the law for his eight years of office. In the past he also appointed the war leaders who would be responsible for defense and warfare against the enemy societies surrounding Guji.

The reign of each successive *abba gada* is seen as a separate epoch. The taking of office of each new *abba gada* signals the beginning of a new period of time and the leaving of office is accompanied by the symbolic termination of all human affairs and time itself. After the retiring *abba gada* has ended his time as priest (by revisiting the shrines and removing his *kayyo*), he visits the high priest and submits to a critical review of his term of office, and then exchanges a large number of his phratry's cattle for a new supply of frankincense. In this system, time is circular, human affairs and the motive force of procreativity are renewed through an endless succession of eight-year periods.

The ultimate source of *woyyu* and *kayyo* is the high god *waka*. Waka is the creator of all living things and the designer of the law (*sara*) by which people maintain an orderly, peaceful society. The offices of high priest and *abba gada* were specifically created by Waka (as is explained in myth). These two types of priests maintain their powers through prayer and animal sacrifice to Waka.

On the local level, each individual can achieve good *kayyo* by following the laws of society and living at peace (*nagea*) with others. In addition, senior men can supplicate directly for good *kayyo* by animal sacrifice and prayer. Should an individual experience misfortune, should he fail to have many children or many cattle, or should there be disease in his family, he will assume his *kayyo* is bad and will undertake redressive action. In this cosmological paradigm, the forces that cause—or prevent—the good life are directly controllable by human action. God is just, he always rewards virtue with good *kayyo*. Ultimately, he always punishes miscreants. Guji religion contains no concept of an afterlife (or a soul), and rewards and punishments are meted out here on earth exclusively.

There are three types of spirits that are lesser refractions of Waka.[11] These are the god of the household shrine (Waka Boro), the god of lightning (Waka Shabola), and the god of birds (Waka Sinbirra). All of these spirits are under the influence of certain patrilineages. Guji *waka* spirits can cause people to go into trance, becoming in effect unconscious "vessels" for the spirit. While in trance, the possessed person acquires the mannerisms and speech patterns associated with the particular spirit. Members of the patrilineages that have hereditary influence over Guji *waka* spirits are not necessarily possessed by them. Rather, the lineage members can send the spirits to afflict others who have offended them.[12] People thus afflicted will become ill, have recurrent dreams of the spirit "owner," or will begin to be violently possessed. Such uncontrolled trance states are considered highly dangerous to the physical and mental well-being of the afflicted. Such people will seek out the spirit owner and become reconciled (*arrarsa*, "reconciliation") with him or her. This is intended to bring an end to random possession and physical affliction.

Those spirit owners whose Guji *waka* spirits have afflicted others will periodically hold a ceremony (*taro waka*) at which the spirit of the afflicted is summoned and is "fed." (All types of Guji spirits come to earth to eat food provided by the possessed.) Failure to attend this ceremony will cause the afflicted to again become ill. *Taro waka* ceremonies are held twice a year and, in addition, on those occasions when a possessed person is seriously ill. The symbolism of *taro waka* rituals is closely similar to that for the ceremonies determining potency (*kayyo*).

Divination in this cultural paradigm is in the hands of men who have built up a reputation as being generally knowledgeable in law and ritual of all types, who are *kalbi*, "calm, intelligent, settled in their ways," and who are able to reconcile those involved in disputes. Typically, this type of diviner will be approached by someone who has serious illness in his famiy or herds or who is troubled by chronic quarreling with others, or who has certain repetitive dreams. The diviner will take a life history of the individual inquiring also about immediate living kinsmen and his recent ancestors. The attempt here is to discover whether anyone in the lineage has quarreled with a spirit owner or whether anyone has failed to make periodic sacrifices to the creator god. All affliction is seen as failure to be reconciled with God or other humans.

Settlement of disputes and sacrifice will restore good "potency" (*kayyo*) if spirits are not involved. If Guji *waka* spirits are involved the afflicted person is sent to a spirit owner who seems to have wished the spirit on the afflicted. If a specific determination by a diviner does not ultimately end the affliction, another ritual solution will be proposed by the same or another diviner. Each diviner knows the full set of options available, and in each divination attempts to examine all of the subtle clues of the case to determine which solution is required. The afflicted person may ultimately lose faith in the diviner if the cure is not forthcoming, but he doesn't lose faith in divination.

This cultural paradigm, and especially its expression in the *gada* system, has become increasingly vulnerable during the last century. Ironically, it is because of the concept of *kayyo* (controlled potency) itself that the conceptual system has been challenged. At the end of the last century the Ethiopian Emperor, Menelik II, greatly increased the territories of the Ethiopian Empire through military conquest. One of the peoples conquered was the Guji. Previously the Guji had been successful warriors who had expanded their territory at the expense of the neighboring Borana. The Guji shrines, where the *abba gadas* sacrifice, are said to be the sites of successful battles. Success in battle was one of the key proofs of the good *kayyo* of the *abba gadas* and their appointed battle leaders. When Ethiopian forces conquered the Guji, blame was, and continues to be, placed on the *abba gadas*, just as they were blamed for drought and disease (which also occurred during this period). The Ethiopian government, aware that *abba gadas* were types of political leaders, saw to it that they were shorn of their power and that they were passed over when local administrators were appointed. In a short while, the *abba gadas* were reduced to the status of priests whose powers were suspect and whose influence on secular affairs was practically nil.

The *abba gadas* stood at the apex of the gada system. With the universal failure of the *abba gadas* to solve Guji problems, discontent with the *gada* system slowly began to grow. During the twentieth century the Guji people witnessed many changes in their lives; changes about which they had little or no say. Garrisons were established by the Ethiopian government in several locations and these gradually evolved into towns with the usual collection of merchants' markets and national courts. It was primarily through the courts that the Ethiopian state exploited the Guji and transformed their society. The courts had the responsibility for administering the national law and for collecting the newly imposed land tax from recalcitrant indigenes. It was through the courts using a northern language that northern Ethiopians applied northern concepts of land tenure against a herding people.

Another aspect of northern Ethiopian domination that has affected the Guji is the government schools. Many of the northern Ethiopian enclave towns in Guji have primary or junior secondary schools. These are attended primarily by the children of townspeople, but increasingly Guji students are completing at least an elementary education. Guji parents often feel ambivalent about their children attending school, fearing that they will learn alien ways but also aware that the students may learn how to cope more effectively with the dominant culture.

Domination did not increase gradually but came in stages. In 1936 invading Italians took over control, only to be removed five years later by northern Ethiopians. During this period communications improved greatly, bringing the Guji into contact with hitherto unknown peoples. Regular truck and bus service was instituted, and at least part of the vast Guji territory was in contact with the rest of the nation.

It was only during or shortly after the Italian period that a new cultural paradigm made its initial appearance in Guji. The new paradigm took the form of a new type of spirit trance called *ayanna*. Interviews with several of the first people to be possessed by *ayanna* spirits reveal that they all were outside Guji when first possessed.

At this time, *ayanna* trance was already present among the Sidamo to the north of Guji and among the closely related Arsi Oromo to the east. The first Guji converts either had been under the influence of a famous woman spirit group leader in Sidamo, or had stayed some time at the tomb of the Muslim saint, Shaek Husain, in Arsi. When the first converts returned to Guji, their *ayanna* spirit gradually "recruited" others by attacking them. The first "converts," who still make pilgrimages to Sidamo or Arsi, through time developed organized spirit groups from those who were attacked by their spirits. It is the nature of *ayanna* spirits, and the structure of the spirit groups, that constitutes the new paradigm.

These new spirits are actually of three types: the talking *ayanna* spirits, the wild animal *jini*, and the greatly feared *shatana*. Each category is a stranger in its own way. The concept of *shatana*, which is new to Guji religion, comes from the world religions of the peoples surrounding Guji. *Jini* are from the realm of nature which is understood to be the place of disorder and danger. *Ayanna* spirits are either Sidamo, Muslim, Arsi or in a few cases, Amhara. None is indigenous Guji.[13]

Ayanna spirits are acquired in the same manner as Guji *waka* spirits. A spirit settles on a new "vessel" when that person has somehow offended a person already possessed. Indicators of possession are also the same. Chronic illness or disputiveness, random possession, or specific types of dreams will cause the afflicted to consult with a diviner. The traditional diviner will usually try other solutions before suggesting *ayanna* possession.

The reason for reluctance to assign *ayanna* as a cause is that it is a demanding, expensive burden that a person must carry throughout the rest of his life, and it removes the individual from the realm of the traditional diviner.

If the traditional diviner does find *ayanna* possession, the afflicted person visits the leadership of an *ayanna* spirit group, consisting of a person who is possessed by many spirits and a nonpossessed intermediary. The possessed leader is usually a woman (*kallitti*) and only rarely is a man (*kallicha*). The intermediary, called "father of law" (*abba sara*), is a senior man who is knowledgeable about the law and ritual practices of *ayanna* worship. He presents problems of all types to specific spirits that are known to be able to handle them. There are different spirits for adjudication, curing disease, and predicting the future. In fact, the number of spirits is limitless.[14] The "father of law" may even have to translate his requests into other languages and then translate the response. In practice, the "father of law" plays a key role in all pronouncements made by the spirit and in the settlement of any breach of law by members of the group.

In consultation with these spirit group leaders the sufferer will make a contract with the spirit agreeing to attend all meetings of the group and to "feed" the spirit at the meetings held twice each week. If this neophyte has an *ayanna*, it will eventually identify itself. A spirit passes from "childhood" to "adulthood" as it is fed (that is, as the neophyte continues to attend ceremonies). The adult spirit is useful to its host and the group in general, and is highly respected. A possessed person with an adult spirit that is known to be effective can start her own branch group in a new locality. She will still be dependent upon her original leader but will also acquire a following of her own. This process replicated the original formation of *ayanna* groups in Guji by the first "spirit mediums" (*kallittis*).

The group includes three categories of persons in addition to the spirit medium and father of law. The *wokil* are a group of nonpossessed men (kinsmen of the possessed) who prepare the food, provide the music, and help control the unrestrained gyrations of the possessed. Among these officiants is the "advocate" who presents cases to the leaders on behalf of the possesed or anyone else seeking help. The possessed followers of the group are called *tamari* (from the Amharic word for student, *tamerti*). Finally, there is another group of kinsmen of the possessed who do not act as officiants but nevertheless attend meetings. They are called *jama*. They constitute the largest numerical segment of the group. It is believed that kinsmen are particularly vulnerable to spirit attack and so they attend the group and follow its rules in order to keep from being possessed.

Regulations for *ayanna* possession groups tend to be uniform. All members of a group must avoid quarreling with each other and assist one another in agricultural labor and any other activity requiring group effort. All members are required to attend each ceremony of the group and contribute food and labor to the rituals. This does not include paying the medium in whose house the ceremony is held. In fact, the medium does not gain directly from her position, nor does the father of law. If members follow all the rules it is believed that they will live forever. If rules are broken, the medium's spirits hear the case and assign punishments. Should any member of the group suffer misfortune of any sort it is assumed that the rules of the group have been broken and the medium is consulted during the regular twice weekly meetings. Often the "offense" is a delict of seemingly no importance; but yet an entire spirit meeting may be devoted to it. If anyone who is not a member of the group offends or somehow wrongs a member of the group, it is believed that that person will become possessed by the member's spirit. In fact, this is the means of recruitment to the group. Even accidental offences cause spirits to settle on the unwitting transgressor.[15]

The nature of the paradigm shift that has been occasioned by *ayanna* possession becomes apparent through the operation of the group. At each meeting, three or more spirits are summoned by the music appropriate for calling them. As each spirit is summoned, the medium becomes possessed by it, as do all possessed members (*ta-mari*) who are "caught" by that particular *ayanna*. Cases (disputes, disease, or whatever) are brought to the "father of law" by the advocate. The former then presents the matter to the medium's spirit which will use its special powers to seek out an appropriate answer and present it to the father of law. Often cases are continued from meeting to meeting. If a member of the group has committed some offense against the law of the *ayanna*, an outrageous punishment or fine will be imposed. It must then be bargained down to something reasonable.[16] Occasionally the orderly succession of spirits will be interrupted when a spirit "appears" uninvited and makes its demands known. Generally something unpredictable happens at each ceremony since unpredictability is a basic attribute of spirits.[17]

Space does not permit a full elaboration of the activities of spirit groups. However, a few contrasts can be drawn between the type of "revolutionary divination" that occurs in *ayanna* possession versus traditional divination. First, divination in these groups never leads individuals to seek solutions outside the group. Traditional divination leads to all manners of possible solutions, including *ayanna* possession. The paradigm of the *ayanna* group is all encompassing, but it is not deliberately set against other Guji belief systems in the sense of people being denied the right to consult them. Rather, the spirit paradigm is made sufficient to serve the needs of the group's members no matter what the nature of the problem.

Second, there is a sharp contrast between Guji *waka* spirit groups and *ayanna* groups. Guji *waka* groups meet twice yearly to celebrate the big and the little rains. Possibly there will be one or two other meetings to help a neophyte come to terms with a spirit. The group centers around someone with hereditary "ownership" of the spirit, a person who is not possessed in most cases. By contrast *ayanna* group membership puts a great demand on the possessed and his or her kinsmen. Meetings are held twice weekly, and all must contribute to the cost of the ceremony. The office of medium is not hereditary, but rather the consequence of the wish of a spirit. Members of Guji *waka* groups may live at great distances from each other and not see one another for months at a time. Members of the *ayanna* groups are compelled to involve themselves in all group activities of other members, just as if they were all kinsmen. People who join a particular *ayanna* group gradually move their houses to the same area (near the medium) and intermarry more frequently than would other types of Guji neighbors. *Ayanna* groups become, in effect, small societies within the larger Guji social realm. Members do not abandon ties to their kinsmen, rather they add another more demanding dimension to the realm of social responsibilities.

Conceptually the two types of spirit possession are also distinct. Guji *waka* spirits are refractions of the traditional cosmology. While they have reference to cosmological powers outside the realm of society, they are not the product of other human societies. They are not strangers. People describe them as "peaceful," "humble," "kind." *Ayanna* spirits are considered to be always dangerous, even after a possessed person has made peace with them. The *ayanna* spirits and spirit groups are, it would seem, symbolic transformations of the forces outside Guji that are its most effective enemies, both traditional and recent. This is especially clear in the case of the Ethiopian state. The spirit group meetings are a transformation of the proceedings of the national courts that have been instrumental in exploiting the Guji. The possessed are "students," and go through a "learning" process as their spirit finds its voice and special powers. What the students finally learn is how to benefit from the alien power of the *ayanna*. The ritual of *ayanna* cults is constantly evolving. New spirits appear unpredictably, and reveal new powers that can affect people's destiny. *Ayanna* cosmology is "open" relative to Guji *waka*, the form and ritual of which are set and predictable. *Ayanna* cults took form when the Guji were already at the mercy of the state, and the state was always making new and unexpected demands. The idiom "to eat" is used to refer to exploitation by representatives of the state, and to the actions of spirits as well. *Waka* spirits come infrequently; *ayanna* spirits eat all the time.

The two cosmological paradigms are kept strictly separate on ritual occasions. *Ayanna* should never be mentioned during traditional *gada* ceremonies which relate to the *waka* cosmology. Neither may Guji *waka* and *ayanna* spirits appear at each other's rituals. In one instance when a medium did go into *ayanna* trance at a *taro waka* ceremony, she was immediately brought out of possession, and the ceremony was considered to be ruined.

On the level of belief, there are three divisions of commitment. Many people continue to hold the *gada* rite of passage ceremonies but also believe in *ayanna* spirits. Others are disillusioned with *gada* and belong to *ayanna* groups. It seems in fact that the *gada* system is steadily losing adherents. At the last investiture ceremony for the new *abba gadas*, many young men challenged the *gada* system as a meaningful part of Guji culture. This challenge was a concerted effort to end the expensive years-long series of rituals and was still being discussed much later at the time of fieldwork. There is a belief that the *gada* system and its basic underlying cosmology failed to prevent the conquest of Guji or the exploitation that followed.

On the other hand, many older people are extremely skeptical about *ayanna* cults, and accusations of fraud perpetrated by unscrupulous group leaders abound. It is said that the leaders invented *ayanna* spirits for their own gain and are duping gullible people.[18]

Guji *waka* spirits are not a topic of debate. For most people they are simply irrelevant. There are very few groups devoted to Guji *waka*, and these are of very small membership. Informants in these groups claimed that in the past membership was much greater, but that "now everyone went to *ayanna* groups."

The final outcome of the paradigm shift in Guji cosmology will probably be similar to what has occurred in other Oromo societies further north in Ethiopia. These societies, all of which had *gada* systems, have now only the memory of a few of the *gada* ranks, but all have very active *ayanna* cult groups. Ultimately the *gada* paradigm has been unable to encompass the overwhelming changes that have occurred when Oromo societies were taken into the state.

Conclusions

In Kuhn's view, scientific revolutions occur because the prevailing paradigm has become increasingly unsatisfactory. This dissatisfaction derives from an increasing awareness that crucial questions are not being answered. From Kuhn's perspective this awareness is generated by an accumulation of persistent, bothersome anomalies. These anomalies take the form of expectations based upon the paradigms which do not come true. Laudan suggests that this sets the stage for a new level of puzzle solving in which the anomalies are the focus of attention (1977:37).[19] For Kuhn a new paradigm must promise to account for the anomalies as well as most of what was already known.

In examining the cosmological issue of the Tigray and Guji we see old paradigms under attack, but with different effects. In Tigray there is an apparent stable relationship between the prevailing paradigm of the *deftera* and that of the medium (*zar*). Among the Guji, *ayanna* appears to be supplanting *waka* and the related *gada* system as a focus of cosmological attention.

The difference seems to lie in the nature and bothersomeness of the anomalies confronting the established paradigms in each case. The established paradigm of the Tigray makes sense to most people most of the time. At a day to day level, the causes of misfortune found by the *deftera* make sense. Misfortune may not be predictable, but it is explainable. For the chronically ill, however, this is not enough, and they tend to seek *zar* as a solution. For many women and some failed males the anomaly is of a different order. It may be explainable, but the explanation is unacceptable. Being poor is the result of God's disfavor. One's plight is in a sense one's own fault because one has displeased God. If atonement fails, *zar* promises a way out. Women are in the peculiar position of having nearly identical jural rights as men but normally having to depend upon men for their household's political representation and political security. *Zar* places them within an alternate political community and gives them greater control over household resources through the expression of the demands made by spirits.[20] For most people the established paradigm remains adequate and useful.

Among the Guji, the situation is quite different. The Guji paradigm shift is not a total transformation any more than scientific paradigm shifts are total. Just as these shifts do not challenge science itself, so the Guji shift does not challenge divination itself, or the belief that people can influence their destiny. Even though *kayyo* is not mentioned in *ayanna* contexts, the approach to evaluating one's well-being and the causes of misfortune are similar. To break the rules of social order (whether derived from *waka* or from the *ayanna* spirits) is to court all manner of bad fortune. Also much of the mundane symbolism of the two paradigms is the same in ritual.

The *waka* paradigm, however, fails at a much more fundamental level. If *waka* is powerful and misfortune derives from failure to follow the rules, then the delicts must be persistent and collective if the *gada/waka* cosmology is to explain their collective and persistent subjugation to the northern Ethiopians. The anomaly is not restricted to a few individuals or to a segment of the population part of the time, as it is for the Tigray. It is persistent and bothersome for all. The alternative is to reject *waka*'s omnipotence and accept a cosmology which accords more with the new political reality. The paradigms we are speaking of here go beyond thought (or thought about a restricted area of reality as is the case with scientific disciplines). These paradigms involve the social order. Acceptance of the *zar* cosmology affects a woman's relations with her husband. Acceptance of *ayanna* creates a radically new social order for the Guji involved. *Ayanna* participants, the possessed and nonpossessed alike, find themselves with new interpersonal social relations governed by structural rules appropriate to agricultural pursuits, replacing traditional structural rules derived from and appropriate to a herding economy.

At the level of theory this analysis suggests that certain revisions may need to be made in our understanding of the nature of traditional systems of thought. S. B. Barnes (1969) and John Skorupski (1976) have suggested that Horton overestimated the openness of scientific thinking. This analysis suggests that he overestimated the closedness of traditional thinking as well. In both, Tigray and Guji individuals are aware of alternatives. Some alternatives are not thought to be incompatible, as with the Tigray choice between excessive pride and sorcery as possible causes of affliction. Other alternatives are incommensurate with one another. Though there are exceptions, those who are committed to Tigray traditional divination generally reject *zar* as nonexistent and spirit mediums as fakes. Similarly, Guji regard *waka* and *ayanna* as incompatible. To accept *ayanna* is to regard *waka* cults as irrelevant and ineffective.

It might be objected that neither society discussed here is "traditional." Guji society is obviously disrupted by external forces, both political and ecological—forces which indeed are the sources of the old cosmology's anomalies. However, the Tigray material suggests that competing paradigms may exist without the presence of significant disruption of the reality to which a paradigm addresses itself. While *zar* is regarded as "foreign" and crosscuts ethnic and national boundaries ranging from Egypt to Somalia, it antedates such potentially disruptive forces as the Italian invasion. Further, Tigray ecology has undergone no such modifications as are found in Guji. Tigray paradigms are in chronic competition and seem to reflect chronic contradictions within Tigray society. A cosmology emphasizing God's blessing on the successful is acceptable to those rising or even standing still; it is less acceptable to society's "losers." Similarly, an emphasis on individualism is acceptable except when a woman is expected to subordinate herself to the demands of the household collectivity. The cognitive importance of anomalies is not the same for all members of Tigray society.

Normal diviners articulate an accepted cosmology for the Tigray in a stable relationship with "revolutionary" *zar* mediums who manipulate and define an alternative cosmology for the disaffected. Guji revolutionary spirit mediums are creating a new conceptual scheme as well as a new social structure for a people whose traditional beliefs can no longer work in an "inverted world."

NOTES

The Tigray material is a by-product of an economically oriented fieldwork project carried out by Dan Bauer in the Inderta region of Tigray province, Ethiopia, between December 1968 and July 1970. It was supported by a predoctoral research grant from the National Institute of Mental Health.

The Guji material was collected by John Hinnant in Sidamo Province 1968–71 and was supported by a predoctoral research grant from the National Science Foundation. We would like to thank Ivan Karp, Larry Taylor, Howard Schneiderman, and Emmanuel Jacquart for commenting upon earlier drafts of this paper.

1. S. B. Barnes (1968) has made an important use of Kuhn's concept in a critique of Horton's (1967) characterization of Western science. His summarization of Kuhn's position is very effective and except in minor ways, one in which we are in accord. This relieves us somewhat of the requirement of making a more extensive summary of Kuhn's argument here. Barnes' criticism is primarily aimed at Horton's characterization of Western science, which Barnes sees as much more closed than does Horton. His major contribution is in demonstrating that while science as an institution may involve alternatives and be capable of rapid change, scientists for the most part do not. Our objective here is aimed at the other half of Horton's comparisons. In this analysis we are more concerned with traditional thought than with science.

2. For a fuller description of the Tigray see Bauer (1973; 1977). For Guji ethnography see Hinnant (1978).

3. George Foster has noted that a number of cultures take as a premise that value or "good" is finite, and that one community member's good fortune must entail some degree of reduction in the fortune of others, a kind of "'fixed pie" model of the universe (1965).

4. The potential sincerity of witchcraft confessions has been noted by Mary Douglas (1970:xxxiv).

5. Possession by some categories of spirits is part of the traditional cosmology (*s̄eytana*, "satans"). Their presence requires exorcism.

6. In Inderta *qolle* is a large category subsuming the geographically more wide-spread set of spirits referred to as *zar*.

7. The effect of spirit possession in redefining a wife's rights has been noted by Lewis (1966; 1971) and by Harris (1957). For other accounts of *zar* possession see Messing (1958), and Hamer and Hamer (1966).

8. The "relatives" include men who, in spite of professed skepticism in other contexts, demand *zar* treatments as a part of a husband's duties to protect his wife from disease when other means fail.

9. The concepts of *woyyu* and *kayyo* are too complex to be effectively glossed, therefore the Guji terms accompany a variety of glosses in the text.

10. The office of *abbu gada* is generated by the *gada* system, a form of generation grading that superficially resembles age grade organization. The various ranks provide all men with a hierarchically arranged sequence of roles, in a form of priesthood. Complex rite of passage ceremonies mark the transition from grade to grade. *Gada* ritual also provides ceremonies for supplication to divinity.

11. Guji *waka* spirits are said to all be Waka (god), and at the same time are viewed as three separate forces, each less powerful than the creator god, Waka.

12. Because such people have the spirit sanctions available to them, they are often selected as elders (*jarsa biyya*, "old men of the country") who settle local disputes of all types. Without spirit sanction, elders have no power to punish (see Knutsson, 1967 for a detailed discussion of "final sanction" in spirit groups).

13. Space does not permit a discussion of *jini* or *shatana* beyond noting that neither develops a personality and the ability to speak, and that both are usually exorcised during a special ritual of a spirit group.

14. During fieldwork this became apparent when an attempt was made to collect a complete list of *ayanna* spirit names. At one ceremony a new spirit possessed a member of the group. When it identified itself it turned out to be a spirit that had never been heard of before.

15. One woman became possessed when she accidentally exchanged her milk container for the medium's at the local market.

16. In one instance a fine of one hundred cattle was reduced to twenty coffee beans after several hours of pleading with the *ayanna*.

17. However, the justice of the *ayanna* is exact and fair. If a possessed person prays to the *ayanna* to attack someone without just cause, the possessed person will be punished by being given a *shatana*, and the intended victim will be safe.

18. When this type of skepticism was mentioned to a medium during an interview she said: "If *ayanna* worship does not work to solve problems, let everyone leave it."

19. Laudan, speaking of anomalies, says "within the history of science . . . it is not so much *how many* anomalies a theory generates that count(s), but rather *how cognitively important* those particular anomalies are," (1977: 37). This interpretation accords better with the material in this essay than does Kuhn's interpretation.

20. For a similar interpretation see I. M. Lewis (1966).

BIBLIOGRAPHY

Barnes, S. B. 1968. "Paradigms, Scientific and Social." *Man* (1):94–102.

Bauer, Dan F. 1973. "Land, Leadership and Legitimacy among the Inderta Tigray of Ethiopia." Ph.D. dissertation, University of Rochester.

————. 1977. *Household and Society in Ethiopia*. East Lansing, Mich.: African Studies Center, Michigan State University.

Bohannon, Paul. 1958. "'Extra-Processual Events in Tiv Political Institutions." *American Anthropologist* 60 (1):1–12.

Burridge, Kenelm. 1969. *New Heaven, New Earth: A Study of Millinerian Activities*. New York: Schocken.

Douglas, Mary, ed. 1970. "Introduction" to *Witchcraft Confessions and Accusations* (ASA 9). London: Tavistock.

Evans-Pritchard, Edward Evan. 1937. *Witchcraft, Oracles and Magic among the Azande*. Oxford: Clarendon Press.

Foster, George. 1965. "Peasant Society and the Image of Limited Good." *American Anthropologist* 67(2):293–315.

Hamer, J., and Hamer, I. 1966. "Spirit Possession and Its Sociopsychological Implications among the Sidamo of Southwest Ethiopia." *Ethnology* 5:392–408.

Harris, Grace. 1957. "Possession Hysteria in a Kenyan Tribe." *American Anthropologist* 59(6):1046–66.

Hinnant, John. 1979. "The Gada System of the Guji of Southern Ethiopia." Ph.D. dissertation, University of Chicago.

Horton, Robin. 1967. "'African Traditional Thought and Western Science." Part 1, *Africa* 37(1):50–71; part 2, *Africa* 37(2):155–87.

Knutsson, Karl Eric. 1967. *Authority and Change: A Study of the Kallu Institution among the Macha Galla of Ethiopia*. Göteborg: Etnografiska Museet.

Kuhn, Thomas. 1962. *The Structure of Scientific Revolutions*. 1st ed. Chicago: University of Chicago Press. Expanded ed., 1970.

Laudan, Larry. 1977. *Progress and Its Problems*. Berkeley: University of California Press.

Lewis, I. M. 1966. "'Spirit Possession and Deprivation Cults." *Man* 1:307–39.

————. 1971. *Ecstatic Religion*. London: Penguin.

Messing, Simon. 1958. "Group Therapy and Social Status in the Zar Cult of Ethiopia." *American Anthropologist* 60:1120–27.

Skorupski, John. 1976. *Symbol and Theory*. London: Cambridge University Press.

Turner, Victor. 1957. *Schism and Continuity in an African Society*. Manchester: Manchester University Press.

Social Change
and the History of Misfortune
among the Bashu of Eastern Zaïre

by Randall M. Packard

One of the thorniest problems in the study of social change is understanding the process by which ideas and systems of thought change through time. This problem is particularly apparent in the study of witchcraft. It has long been recognized that witchcraft beliefs have an historical dimension, in that they emerge, undergo changes, and decline with the passage of time. Yet, neither anthropologists and social historians studying the sociology of witchcraft beliefs, nor intellectual and cultural historians examining witchcraft beliefs from the perspective of the history of ideas, have provided a satisfactory explanation for how and why these developments occur.

Anthropologists and social historians, following Evans-Pritchard's classic study of Zande witchcraft, have stressed the importance of social organization and ecology in shaping the development of ideas and practices associated with witchcraft. Thus, Wilson (1951) and Nadel (1952) argued that differences in the concepts of misfortune found in a number of African societies could be traced to differences in their social and economic organization, thereby implying that changes in a society's social structures were likely to produce changes in its perceptions of misfortune. From a somewhat different perspective the studies of Marwick (1952), Middleton (1963), Mitchell (1956), and others, on the social dynamics of witchcraft accusations, have indicated that changing social and economic relations within a society can affect the distribution and timing of witchcraft accusations. A similar argument is found in the historical studies of Thomas (1970) and MacFarlane (1970) concerning English witchcraft, as well as in Boyer and Nissenbaum's recent study of witchcraft trials in Salem. Finally, studies of witchcraft eradication movements in colonial Africa have demonstrated how social and economic changes brought on by colonial rule stimulated the adoption or development of new ideas and practices concerning the eradication of witches (Richards, 1935; Marwick, 1950; Bohannan, 1958; Willis, 1968, 1970; Vansina, 1971, 1973; Ardener, 1971).

While these studies clearly demonstrate the role of social and economic forces in shaping ideas and practices associated with witchcraft, their explanatory value is limited by their inability fully to explain why, in the face of social change, people adopt one set of ideas as opposed to another. Why, for example, in Willis' study of anti-witchcraft cults among the Fipa of southern Tanzania, did the Fipa adopt the ideas and practices of the Kamcape movement, rather than those of the Watchtower movement which was also present in Ufipa and, like Kamcape, advocated the eradication of witches? Why did the people of Salem village in Massachusetts turn to a belief in witches to give expression to tensions created by social and economic forces which emerged at the end of the seventeenth century, rather than to religious revivalism as did the people of Northampton forty years later? Why in the present study did the Bashu of eastern Zaïre respond to an increase in male-female tensions during the colonial period by developing a new belief in female witches, rather than by expanding the existing category of sorcerer to include women? These questions suggest that we need to go beyond defining the social and economic conditons under which new concepts of misfortune develop if we are to fully understand the evolution of witchcraft beliefs.

Intellectual and cultural historians studying witchcraft in Europe and America (Trevor-Roper, 1956; Monter, 1976; Midelfort, 1972; Demos, 1970; Hansen, 1968; Fox, 1968) have taken a different approach to the study of conceptual change, relating the rise and decline of witchcraft beliefs to the wider world view of the societies in which they occur. These studies suggest how existing perceptions of the world help to shape the development of witchcraft beliefs.[1] They thus contribute to our understanding of why concepts of misfortune take on the particular form which they do, and suggest how we might answer the questions raised by the sociological approach. On the other hand, these studies tend to isolate the ideas they examine from the social context within which they exist. They consequently describe patterns of cognitive change without taking account of the social and economic determinants of change. For example, Trevor-Roper makes a valuable contribution to our understanding of the process by which concepts of misfortune changed in Europe by showing that the decline of

European witchcraft was hastened with the development of a more unitary and mechanistic view of the universe which undermined the old duality of God and Satan upon which European witchcraft beliefs were based. Yet his explanation is limited by his failure fully to explain what was happening in European society at this time to generate this new world view and encourage its acceptance.

Both sociological and cultural approaches to witchcraft have contributed to our understanding of the process by which ideas and concepts change over time. Yet neither approach has successfully incorporated the other's insights, and thus neither has provided a completely satisfying explanation of this process. If we are fully to understand how and why concepts of misfortune change, we need to integrate the concern of anthropologists and social historians for defining the social determinants of witchcraft beliefs, with the concern of intellectual and cultural historians for defining the cultural environment out of which witchcraft beliefs emerge. More specifically, we need to examine the social forces which affect a society's ideas about misfortune within the context of that society's wider conception of itself and the world in which it exists. For to understand the impact of these forces we need to examine how the members of a society perceive them, how they translate them in terms of their own system of thought, and relate them to their wider view of the world. It is, I suggest, through this act of translation, the interpretation of experience in terms of actors' perceptions of their world, that new ideas and concepts about misfortune are formulated.

A few studies have moved in this direction. Thus Bohannan (1958) shows that the adoption of antiwitchcraft cults by the Tiv of northern Nigeria resulted from their interpretation of political changes introduced by the British in terms of preexisting ideas about political power and misfortune. Bohannan argues that the Tiv viewed witchcraft as a corruption of political power. Whenever a person became too powerful he would be attacked as a witch, or more accurately, for using his power, *tsav*, for destructive purposes. When the British imposed chiefs on the segmentary Tiv, the Tiv interpreted this change in terms of their existing ideas about witchcraft and political authority and readily adopted antiwitchcraft cults as a means of reducing the new chiefs' authority. Bohannan's study thus suggests that preexisting ideas about power and authority served as a screen through which the Tiv interpreted social change and responded to it.

Hartwig's study of the evolution of sorcery beliefs among the Kerebe of Tanzania during the nineteenth century takes a similar approach (1972). Hartwig suggests that Kerebe ideas about sorcery evolved during the nineteenth century as a result of the interaction of previous concepts of kingship, with social and economic changes introduced by the expansion of trade. The Kerebe maintained that when kingship was strong the king was responsible for all misfortune as well as all good. When the kingship weakened, however, the power to do harm devolved to individuals, resulting in the emergence of sorcery. Thus the expansion of long-distance trade into Kerebe during the middle years of the nineteenth century resulted in the proliferation of sorcery accusations, for the trade disrupted the kingdom and weakened the kingship, which, from a Kerebe viewpoint, allowed individuals to cause misfortune, i.e., to become sorcerers.

Ardener's study of witchcraft and sorcery among the Bakweri of the Cameroons takes us further in this direction by suggesting a more concise model for explaining how new ideas emerge from the interaction of ideology and experience. Ardener suggests that Bakweri cosmology served as a "template" from which new concepts of misfortune emerged in response to social and economic changes during the colonial period.

> I have used the idea of a template to express the persistence of certain themes in belief, from which 'replication' occurs . . . when other elements in the social and physical environment combine to permit this, the realien, the circumstantial details of the 'content' through which the replicated element is expressed may be different on every occassion—assembled, it may be by that unconscious process of bricolage to which Lévi-Strauss has directed our attention . . . (Ardener, 1971:156).

For Ardener changing ideas about witches and sorcerers among the Bakweri were the product of successive reorderings of a basic symbolic structure in the face of social and economic change, each reordering being an attempt to adjust perceptions of reality to fit the changing needs of Bakweri society.

These previous studies provide a starting point for the present examination of the history of misfortune among the Bashu. The present study differs from these studies, however, in two fundamental ways. First, unlike the studies of Ardener and Hartwig, and to a lesser de-

gree Bohannan, it attempts to clearly define the structures of symbolic
logic from which new concepts of misfortune emerged during the
colonial period, and thus to demonstrate in a more precise manner the
ways in which social change interacted with existing ideas to produce
new concepts of misfortune. Second, the present study rejects the
assumption of diachronic continuity or repetition implicit in Bohannan's reduction of a variety of diverse antiwitchcraft movements to a
single repetitive process, which he calls "extra-processual events" and
in Ardener's use of the template analogy:

> The analogy I wish to bring out is that the molecules that replicate
> do so because their structures are logically limited in such a way
> that the chemical reactions they can take part in compel the same
> end: the replication of the original structures (1971:159).

Bashu material suggests that while the process of interpretation
results in a constant realignment of symbolic elements to fit changing
perceptions of reality, these readjustments do not simply represent
more of the same. It is not, as Ardener puts it, a question of *plus ça
change, c'est plus la meme chose*. Rather, the symbolic logic itself is
changed by the process of interpretation, ultimately giving away to a
new logic, a new view of society and the world. This change is what
Mary Douglas defines as "conversion":

> We should try to think of cosmology as a set of categories that are
> in use . . . spare parts can be fitted, and readjustments made with-
> out much trouble. Occasionally a major overhaul is necessary to
> bring the obsolete set of views into focus with new times and new
> company. This is conversion . . .
>
> Most of the time the readjustments are made so smoothly that one
> is hardly aware of the shifts in angle until they have developed an
> obvious disharmony between the past and the present. Then a grad-
> ual conversion that has slowly been taking place has to be recog-
> nized (1973:179).

The present study argues that such a symbolic transformation or
conversion is occurring among the Bashu and that Ardener's template
model needs to be modified to allow for long-term conceptual change
which represents something new, and not just a rehashing of previous
concepts.

Bashu Concepts of Misfortune on the Eve of Colonial Rule

The Bashu occupy the Mitumba Mountains to the northwest of Lake Amin (Edward) in which is now the Kivu region of eastern Zaïre. They are a section of a larger linguistic and social group known as the Banande in Zaïre, and as the Bakonjo in neighboring Uganda. Like their Nande and Konjo relations, the Bashu are primarily mountain cultivators growing crops of eleusine plantain bananas, beans, and cassava along the slopes of the Mitumbas. They also keep chickens, goats, sheep, and occasional cattle. Coffee cultivation accounts for the main source of cash income today, though in the higher altitudes wheat is also grown commercially. Politically the Bashu are divided into several related chiefdoms, each of which is ruled by a family of chiefs who claim to be descended from a common ancestor. Today the Bashu chiefdoms form an administrative district or "collectivity" which is under the authority of a *Grand Chef*, an official created by the Belgians (who occupied the region in 1923) and later incorporated into the present administrative system of Zaïre.

Bashu concepts of misfortune at the beginning of the twentieth century reflected in large measure the nature of their social environment. Bashu society at this time was fragmented socially along lines of descent and geographically by the ridges and valleys which dominate the Bashu landscape. While social disruption and famine brought on by drought and the expansion of the east African ivory trade into the western rift valley at the end of the nineteenth century stimulated the creation of certain overriding ritual and quasi-political relationships, it also increased political insecurity, and in doing so reinforced local patterns of interaction. The wider ritual and political leadership which emerged at this time provided little in the way of an effective defense against the military forces which threatened a man and his family. Thus the Bashu turned inwards to their kinsmen and neighbors for protection.[2]

The primary unit of interaction during this period was the localized agnatic lineage (*nda*), whose members jointly occupied all, or part, of a ridge, their contiguous homesteads dispersed and separated by banana plantations and other gardens. Members of other *nda* might reside within this lineage neighborhood (*omuyi*), but formed a social minority whose interests were subordinate to those of the dominant lineage from whom they had received land.

While the world of the lineage neighborhood was by no means isolated, being connected to other similar units by agnatic, affinal, ritual, and economic ties, it was the primary focus of daily social interaction. Adjacent neighborhoods were separated from one another by stretches of uncleared land, a river, or valley; relations between them, while varying greatly in quality, were marked by occasional feuding. Thus tensions which arose between members of different neighborhoods could find expression in overt forms of conflict.

Tensions within the neighborhood, arising over competition for the position of lineage head, or from the violation of kinship values, were more difficult to resolve, for the lineage head (*mukulu*) had little authority to resolve disputes unilaterally. It was therefore up to the conflicting parties to settle their differences with the aid and advice of the other members of the *nda*, or maternal kin. This, however, was not always possible, and thus tensions were often chronic. Unresolved tensions within the lineage neighborhood appear to have provided the impetus for most accusations arising from the onset of misfortune. Thus the lineage neighborhood was the primary locus for vectors of misfortune among the Bashu.

The Bashu claim that prior to the colonial period individual misfortune in the form of death, mysterious ailments, sickness, crop failure, and loss of livestock, resulted from one of three major causes:[3]

1. The dissatisfaction of one's ancestors caused by a lack of respect, or by a violation of norms of kinship behavior, especially with regards to other members of the *nda*.

2. The presence in the household of women who had been possessed by certain malevolent spirits of the bush.

3. The actions of sorcerers (*avaloyi*), men who employed special medicine and familiars, as well as curses, to attack people close to them, primarily within the lineage neighborhood, who they envied or held a grudge against.

On the surface these three concepts of misfortune appear to be separate and unrelated phenomena. However, when placed within the wider context of Bashu cosmological ideas about the homestead and bush—culture and nature—they become part of a coherent definition of the source and cause of misfortune.

For the Bashu the homestead (*eka*) and bush (*ekisoki*) were separate and conflicting worlds. The world of the bush was an extremely dangerous place associated with disorder, wild animals, ritual pollution, and malevolent spirits. The homestead, on the other hand, was associated with order, domestic animals, ritual purity, and benevolent spirits. This opposition occurred in a number of different ritual contexts.

All substances, activities, and beings which were viewed as ritually dangerous including the medicines of healers, rainstones, ironmaking, and people who had become polluted, had to be kept in the bush, and away from the homestead, lest by their presence they cause misfortune to befall the homestead. Similarly, spirits which were potentially dangerous to the homestead dwelt in the bush. Lusenge and Nydoka, who curtailed social reproduction by causing women to be sterile or caused the death of children and thus threatened the continued existence of the homestead, were spirits of the bush. The spirits of ancestors who were not accorded proper burial rites were also said to dwell in the bush and to "whistle through the mountains like the wind," causing harm to anyone they met. The spirits of ancestors who had been properly buried, on the other hand, lived within the homestead and could be called upon for assistance.

Certain spirits which inhabited the bush were also called upon from time to time to assist the people of the homestead. Kalisya, the protector of animals, Mulemberi, the protector of children, and Muhima, who protected the village, were but a few of these. However, invocations to these spirits, unlike those to the ancestors, could not be made within the homestead, for despite the potential good that these spirits could bring, they were viewed as creatures of the bush and had to be kept away from the homestead itself. Sacrifices to these spirits were, therefore, performed in the banana plantation which surrounded the homestead. The banana plantation (*mboko*) was a liminal area between the *eka* and the *ekisoki* and thus an appropriate place for communication between these two worlds.

Placed within this wider cosmological framework, the various ideas about possible sources of misfortune described above can be seen as part of a coherent definition of misfortune: misfortune resulted from the intrusion of the world of the bush into the world of the homestead.[4] The sorcerer harmed his victim by bringing his medicines from the bush into the homestead, burying them in the victim's doorway, or hiding them in the roof of his victim's hut. Women brought

misfortune by being trapped by spirits of the bush and bringing them
into the homestead. The position of ancestors in this definition is at
first glance unclear, since ancestors dwell in the home and were normally benevolent. Yet ancestors could withdraw their support and by
doing so allow the forces of the bush to penetrate the homestead.
This becomes clearer when we examine the actions which were seen
as bringing on misfortune.

Informants often condemn the use of sorcery. However, the way
in which the cases of sorcery are disguised reflects an ambivalent attitude toward the victim. Thus in cases in which a man was said to
have ensorcelled his own son, a rare event, informants often commented that a man would only attack a son if the son no longer cared
for his father's needs. Similarly, in cases where a man was attacked by
his own brother, the victim was often said to have been a wealthy
person who refused to share his wealth. These statements about the
motivations behind the use of sorcery are in fact statements about the
violation of kinship and its consequences. A son was supposed to care
for his father when he grew old, brothers were expected to share
their wealth. Thus, it was the failure to follow norms of behavior
which brought on misfortune in the form of sorcery. More precisely,
such actions were said to "break the homestead" (*eritul'eka*). The verb
eritula means to break in the sense of breaking open, exposing the inside to the outside world. It is used in other contexts to describe the
action involved in cutting open a fruit, opening an envelope, or breaking into a house. Thus, to say that a man who refused to support his
aging father had broken the homestead, *mw'atul'eka*, signified that he
had broken it open and exposed it to the outside, which in terms of
Bashu cosmology implied that his actions had exposed the homestead
to the forces of the "bush," and specifically to the force or sorcery
(*ovuloyi*). The idea that certain actions expose the homestead to forces
of the bush and thus cause misfortune is even more clearly seen in
the roles of women and spirits of the bush as vectors of misfortune.

Women were in a sense liminal figures in Bashu cosmology, for
while they were part of the homestead they had strong associations
with the world of the bush. This association gave them influence over
the behavior of certain wild animals and storms. For example, when
a buffalo wandered up into the mountains from the plains, the men of
the mountains would form a hunting band and go after it. At such
times the wife of the hunt leader would stand naked on a hill over-

looking the place where the buffalo was found and cry, *uli nyama y'omukali*, "you are an animal of women." This was said to make the buffalo tame and easy to kill. Through a similar invocation women could deter a violent storm. In this way a woman's influence over the forces of the bush protected the homestead.

Yet while women had influence over the forces of the bush, and thus could protect the homestead, they were at the same time susceptible to these forces and were, therefore, a potential threat to the homestead. Because of this susceptibility women were restricted in the world of the homestead lest their natural affinity with the world of the Bush would cause misfortune. Their daily lives were controlled by regulations related to sexual behavior, childbirth, work activities, and diet. For example, women were prohibited from eating certain foods such as crickets, rats, chickens, and eggs. These foods are all associated in some way with the world of the bush. Crickets and rats are found in the bush. Chickens, while animals of the homestead, often run around in the bush, and, if not carefully watched, will lay their eggs in the bush. Bashu stories about the origin of the chicken describe the chicken as a creature of the bush who was brought into the homestead. This association with the Bush in part explains why chickens were used in sacrifices to those spirits of the Bush which could aid the homestead, as well as why raw eggs were left in the small hut constructed for Muhima, the bush spirit which protected the village. Women were, therefore, prevented from eating these foods to prevent their associations with the bush from outweighing their responsibility to the homestead. This reasoning will become clearer when we look at Bashu explanations about the emergence of female witches.[5]

Yet women could not be totally domesticated. Thus, their association with the Bush could not be eliminated. Consequently, a number of other sanctions existed which prevented women from weakening or polluting the world of the homestead and men. For example, a wife could not touch her husband's spear, for by doing so she would cause her husband to become weak. They were not allowed to cut the bananas used for making beer or participate in the brewing of beer lest their influence make it go bad. Women were not allowed near the site where iron was being smelted lest the process break down. The potential pollution caused by the presence of women in these activities also explains why men who had had sexual intercourse within the previous day were prohibited from participation in these activities. In these and other ways the potential pollution caused by women in the homestead was controlled.

In this context it is worth noting that the woman who helped the hunters kill a buffalo was described as being naked. This image suggests that it was by removing her clothes—the symbols of culture, the homestead, and female domestication—that a woman reestablished her full association with the world of the bush, and thus her influence over it. While this transformation allowed a woman to influence certain forces of the bush, it also made her more susceptible to these forces. While all women were vulnerable to possession by forces of the bush, it was women who had violated or disregarded the restrictions of the homestead, and thus "broken the homestead," who were most likely to be possessed and bring on misfortune. Thus, as in sorcery, misfortune was brought on by a violation of the moral order which held the homestead together and separated it from the world of the bush.

Having examined the concept of "breaking the homestead" as it applied to sorcery and spirits of the bush, it is now possible to see how misfortune caused by the ancestors fits into the wider definition of misfortune as an invasion of the homestead by forces of the bush. For the Bashu the ancestors and the living ideally formed a single community. The ancestors dwelled within the homestead rather than in the bush. They were, in the words of one informant, "always with us. They walked with us and worked with us." Ancestors maintained their interest in the homestead and their presence and concern were seen as essential to its continued well-being. Conversely their separation or absence from the homestead allowed misfortune to befall it, or more precisely the forces of the bush to invade it.

The relationship between the separation of the living and the dead, and the invasion of the homestead by forces of the bush was reflected in the ideas and practices associated with the death of an individual. When a man died, his spirit (*kirimu*) passed out of the homestead into the banana plantation which surrounded it. The banana plantation was a liminal area between the homestead and the bush, and the deceased's *kirimu* was thus in limbo between these two worlds. Funeral rites were designed to reintegrate the deceased into the world of the homestead. If the rites were not performed, or performed improperly, the deceased's spirit would pass into the bush and become a malevolent spirit, separated from the homestead and antithetical to it. Until the deceased's spirit was reintegrated into the homestead, it was separated from it, leaving the homestead open to the forces of the bush. This vulnerability was symbolized by the mourning observances in which normal patterns of social behavior were broken or reversed: the homestead was not swept, gardens went unattended and were choked with weeds, people of the homestead neither bathed nor cut their hair. In essence, the world of the homestead became like the world of the bush. The completion of the funeral rites, marked by the head-shaving ceremony, reintegrated the spirit of the deceased into the homestead and reestablished the relationship between the living and the dead and thus the division between the homestead and the bush as indicated by the resumption of normal social behavior.

For the Bashu, therefore, the temporary separation of the living and the dead at the moment of death "broke the homestead" and resulted in its invasion by the forces of the bush. In a similar fashion, actions which offended an ancestor could cause him to, in effect, turn his back on his descendants, to separate himself from the world of the homestead, and by doing so allow the forces of the bush to invade it. Thus actions which offended an ancestor, like those which invoked sorcery or increased a woman's susceptibility to the forces of the bush, were said to "break the homestead," and by doing so bring on misfortune.[6]

Colonial Rule and Social Change

Bashu concepts of misfortune on the eve of colonial rule were a product of the localized world of Bashu social relations which existed at that time. Notions of inside and outside and of bush and homestead expressed in these concepts were appropriate to a world in which the primary focus of social interaction and security was the lineage neighborhood, and in which social relations outside the neighorhood were marked by potential violence. Similarly, the localization of vectors of misfortune within the lineage neighborhood was appropriate to a world in which social tensions within the neighborhood were pervasive but insoluble through overt action, while tensions outside the neighborhood could be resolved openly.

In the changed social and economic environment of the colonial

world, however, the scale of social interaction expanded, social relationships changed, and new tensions emerged. As a result, Bashu concepts of misfortune, as they had existed before colonialism, became
increasingly inadequate for the interpretation of new social experiences, and new concepts emerged. While there is evidence that some
of these concepts were borrowed from neighboring peoples, their development can best be understood when viewed as an outgrowth of
existing cosmological ideas about homestead and bush. These ideas
provided the structural elements out of which new concepts of misfortune developed.

By the time I arrived among the Bashu in the early 1970s, the
localized world of the lineage neighborhood, and the social relations
which were a part of it, had largely disappeared. Gone were the separate homesteads surrounded by banana plantations dotting the slopes
of the Mitumbas. In their place were consolidated villages, composed
of several lineage neighborhoods, the huts of which were placed close
to one another in parallel rows separated by a wide path. This change
in settlement pattern stimulated the rise of new ideas about sorcery.

The Belgians initiated the consolidated village policy in 1932 to
facilitate their administration of the Bashu region. While the dispersed
settlement pattern was only one of the difficulties facing Belgian administrators among the Bashu, it was one of the more tangible obsta-
cles and thus one which could apparently be remedied with little difficulty. In actual practice, however, village consolidation was not
easily achieved. The Bashu resisted resettlement, often taking the first
opportunity to return to their homesteads. The Belgians eventually
had to use force to drive some groups into the villages.[7]

There were several reasons why the Bashu objected to living in
the new villages. First, it meant, in many cases, living away from their
gardens, which made them more difficult to protect and farm. A
greater obstacle, however, was the Bashu fear that people were more
likely to die in the villages. There was in fact some basis for this fear.
Consolidated villages had been established earlier in the Semliki Valley in a similar attempt to facilitate local administration. This initial
experiment ended tragically, for the consolidated villages hastened the
spread of sleeping sickness which broke out in the valley in 1905. The
new villages became loci of infection and whole communities were
wiped out.[8] Many of the Bashu who were living in and near the plains
were placed in these villages and died. Knowledge of this experience

no doubt helped shape the Bashu response to the creation of similar villages in the mountains. Moreover, once the villages were established they served as a catalyst for the spread of other diseases which affected the Bashu during the colonial period, especially bubonic plague.[9]

The Bashu initially explained the misfortunes which occurred within the consolidated villages in terms of the existing idiom of misfortune, i.e., there were many deaths in the new villages because there was more sorcery there. When asked why there was more sorcery in the consolidated villages than in the lineage neighborhood, several informants responded that, "every lineage has its sorcerers, thus when several lineages live together in a single village, there will be many sorcerers there as well." When I suggested that this should not cause a problem since sorcerers normally only attack their close kin, I was told that when the sorcerers moved into the village they got to know other people and began to attack them as well. Moreover, the Bashu claim that even within the *nda* the activities of sorcerers increased. In other words, within the consolidated villages, sorcerers expanded their sphere of activities to include new categories of kinsmen and strangers. The creation of consolidated villages, therefore, altered Bashu ideas about potential sources of misfortune by expanding the definition of potential victims of sorcery. To understand why this expansion occurred we must first examine the social forces operating within the world of the consolidated village and thus the social context within which Bashu concepts of misfortune evolved. We then can examine how the Bashu themselves perceive these changes and responded to them.

New social tensions accompanied the creation of consolidated villages among the Bashu. These tensions initially emerged because it was difficult to accommodate conflicting norms of behavior within the village world. As noted above, relations between members of a lineage neighborhood were qualitatively different from relations between members of different neighborhoods. In the village this boundary between insiders and outsiders was eliminated and conflicts arose over the ambiguity of dealing with outsiders who were now insiders. These tensions were only partially responsive to overt settlement through the administrative structures of the new villages, because these structures were ineffective. The Belgians appointed a village chief, or *kapita*, chosen normally from the numerically dominant lineage to administer

the affairs of the village. The legitimacy of this man's authority, however, was frequently questioned, especially by members of other lineages within the village. His ability to resolve tensions which arose
between lineages was, therefore, limited. On the other hand, the recourse to violence as a form of settlement was deterred by the threat
of government intervention as well as by a desire to maintain village
peace. Thus the tensions which arose between members of formerly
separate neighborhoods were difficult to resolve.

Other conflicts arose in the consolidated villages between the
members of a single *nda* as a result of the introduction of new values
and ways of perceiving the world which conflicted with existing val
ues and perceptions. This is clearest in the field of economic relations.

The colonial period substantially altered the Bashu economy. The
Belgians introduced new cash crops such as coffee, soy beans, wheat,
and tea. They also created new markets for more traditional crops,
particularly less perishable items such as beans and cassava which
were purchased for shipment to the less productive mining areas to
the west and north, where they were used to feed mine workers. The
Belgians also introduced new agricultural techniques such as terracing
to prevent soil erosion and increase productivity. Outside of the agricultural sector, the Bashu economy was altered by the establishment
of mines and European-run plantations throughout the Kivu region.
Both industries recruited heavily for labor among the Bashu. By 1945,
34 percent of the Bashu male population worked outside of the Bashu
region.[10]

As will be shown below, these changes had important consequences for Bashu social organization. Most directly, however, they
provided new opportunities for individuals to accumulate wealth and
thus for an increase in economic disparity within Bashu society. It was
not, however, just the new opportunities for individual wealth which
created these disparities. It was also the growing unwillingness of
individuals to sacrifice their new wealth for the sake of traditional
values which encouraged the redistribution of wealth. This change in
attitude resulted in part from the introduction by the Belgians of new
imported goods such as bicycles, tools, clothes, and furniture, which
were attractive to the Bashu and which required cash payments. But
it was also encouraged by the introduction of new social values spread
by the Christian churches and mission schools and sanctioned by the
subtle ideology of colonialism which associated Westernization with

upward social mobility in the colonial world. To be successful, one not only had to be educated, which cost money, but also had to assimilate Western modes of dress, behavior, and acquisitiveness. This ideology encouraged resistance to traditional values of economic redistribution and provided an alternative social ethic which justified individual advancement. The conflict between this new ethic and the former values of reciprocity created tensions between successful men who earned wealth outside the traditional economy and their kinsmen who were less successful but wanted a share of that wealth.

One could go on and point to other areas of Bashu life where new Western values came into conflict with more traditional values. What is important, however, is that these conflicts not only increased tensions within relationships which were already prone to conflict, such as that between brothers, but also within relations which had been relatively free from conflict, such as those between a man and his sister or between a man and his son.

Life in the consolidated village was therefore marked by an increase in social conflicts which were difficult to resolve. These conflicts ultimately found expression in accusations of sorcery. Yet it was not, as some anthropologists assume, the conflicts themselves which produced the accusations. The Bashu do not automatically translate social tensions into accusations of sorcery. Rather, the Bashu turned to sorcery as an explanation for misfortune because within the context of their own world view, the social changes occurring in their society increased the likelihood of sorcery.

For the Bashu the creation of consolidated villages opened the world of the homestead—the moral universe of the lineage neighborhood—to the outside world, to the influx of strangers and more distant kin, some of whom were sorcerers. To make matters worse, the Belgians discouraged families from leaving the villages once they had been established, thus reversing the process by which accusations of sorcery had in the past been followed by lineage segmentation, separating sorcerer and victim. They also prohibited the application of the fire ordeal used to detect sorcerers, along with the punishment of sorcerers. The Bashu, therefore, came to view the consolidated village as a place where the forces of the bush, in the form of sorcery, were permitted to mingle with the world of the homestead, resulting in an increase of misfortune and death.[11]

At the same time, the collapse of traditional values of reciprocity between men within the homestead weakened the social strictures which maintained its integrity, and further increased the possibility of sorcery among its members. Thus one occasionally hears people comment that a person who has adopted a Western lifestyle and social ethic, turning his back on his kinsmen, is "breaking the homestead," and inviting ensorcellment. It was thus the interpretation or perception of the social forces which created conflict, in terms of existing ideas about nature, culture, and misfortune, rather than a simple conversion of social tensions to sorcery accusations, which gave birth to new accusations of sorcery and an expanded definition of who a sorcerer was likely to attack. Put another way, the application of existing ideas about misfortune to a new social experience had the feedback effect of altering the existing ideas.

Women, Social Change and the Rise of *Avambakali*

The evolution of Bashu concepts of misfortune did not end with the extension of the definition of potential victims of sorcery. A new source of misfortune in the form of female witches, called *avambakali* (sing. *mumbakali*), emerged during the middle years of the colonial period in response to the changing relationship between men and women in Bashu society.

Avambakali are women whose spirits leave their bodies at night and join the spirits of other women in a witches' coven. These women then attack their victims, predominantly men. *Avambakali* are said to eat their victims in the sense of consuming their victim's *kirimu*, or life force. The imagery used to describe this eating, however, implies corporeal rather than metaphorical consumption. Thus, for example, *avambakali* are said to take their victims to streams which they can stop with special medicine and then boil the bodies of their victims in the stilled water. *Avambakali* are taught the skills of being an *avambakali* by the spirit of a woman who is already an *mumbakali*. Thus, witchcraft is not hereditary. Finally, *avambakali* do not attack their victims at random or out of jealousy or envy, but act out of anger and vengeance.

Victims of *avambakali* occasionally die from the attack. More frequently they succumb to a malingering ailment or strange behavior involving involuntary actions, inability to function normally, to speak, walk, or hear. In such cases the diagnosis of an *avambakali* attack is frequently made by the victim himself, or perhaps more accurately, by the witch who attacked him. For it is often the voice of the witch which speaks through the victim stating the reason why she has attacked him. Such an event is taken as sufficient proof of a woman's guilt and justification for the application of a painful exorcism in which the accused witch is made to swallow a medicine which causes severe cramping and vomiting. Among the particles thrown up by the victim are often fleshlike substances which were said to be evidence of her cannibalistic activities. The exorcism is not seen as a permanent cure, and it is said that the woman can again become involved in such activities if her spirit is drawn out by another *avambakali*.

While there is some evidence that the concept of *avambakali* was borrowed from the neighborhing Bapakombe people of the Ituri forest, its emergence among the Bashu can best be understood by examining the social conditions under which it evolved and Bashu perceptions of those conditions.[12] To understand the social context within which the belief in *avambakali* emerged, we must examine the impact of colonial rule on the role of women in and on the relationship between men and women.

For Bashu women the advent of colonial rule initially meant an increase in labor. While the introduction of cash crops, new markets, and agricultural techniques meant increased opportunities for men to accumulate wealth, they meant more work for Bashu women. For women provide most of the agricultural labor in Bashu society. Men clear the land, but women plant, weed, and harvest the crops. The increase in labor demands resulting from agricultural innovations is most clearly seen in the history of cassava production. The Bashu claim that cassava was known to them before the Belgians arrived, but was only cultivated by those few Bashu who lived close to the plains where the warmer and drier climate was more suitable for its production. Eleusine and plantain bananas were the primary sources of starch for the inhabitants of the higher mountains. The Belgians, however, encouraged the Bashu to grow more cassava because as a tuber plant, it was less susceptible to the vagaries of weather than eleusine, and thus provided a more stable food crop which could be produced cheaply and transported to other regions, particularly the mining areas, with minimal spoilage. While much of the early cassava was grown for marketing and export, the Bashu gradually acquired a taste for it and began consuming it in place of eleusine. Today, cassava has become the primary starch in the Bashu diet.

While cassava require less weeding than eleusine, it is in other ways more time consuming and labor intensive. To begin with, cassava grows best at lower altitudes, thus the gardens of those Bashu living in the higher mountains were often several kilometers from their homes, whereas the eleusine gardens were normally much closer. Cassava cultivation, therefore, required more traveling time. Moreover, because the gardens were located in the warmer region of the mountains, and thus were harder to work during the heat of the day, people either had to leave home an hour or more before dawn in order to descend to the fields, work them, and return before the sun got too hot, or, alternatively, leave later and rest during the heat of the day, an option which meant spending more time away from home. Harvesting cassava was also more difficult because of both the distance it had to be carried and the terrain over which one had to pass. Finally, the preparation of cassava took more time than the preparation of eleusine, for cassava has to be soaked and pealed and dried before it can be pounded in to flour.

The addition of cash crops such as coffee, which required considerable attention and was grown alongside food crops rather than in place of them, further increased labor demands. So too did regulations requiring the Bashu to terrace their lands, since the upkeep of the terracing became the work of women.

Outside the agricultural sector the labor demands placed on women were increased by other Belgian policies. For example, the decision to replace traditional beehive-style thatched huts with new mud and wattle huts involved an increase in female labor requirements. For while thatching was the exclusive responsibility of Bashu men, the construction and repair of mud walls became the responsibility of Bashu women.[13]

Finally, the workload of women was further increased by the extensive recruitment for male labor which occurred among the Bashu. The removal of a large segment of the male population from the work force meant that jobs which had formely been performed by Bashu men now had to be performed by women. For example, women were now required to clear fields, thatch roofs, and even cut bananas for making beer, all tasks which were traditionally reserved for men. Moreover, women increasingly had to act as household heads and make day to day decisions which had formely been made by their husbands. These changes not only represented an increase in labor demands, they also represented a breakdown of the traditional division between men and women in Bashu society, a division which supported male domination.

By the end of the Second World War this breakdown was accelerated by the spread of Christianity. Both the Protestant and Catholic churches became increasingly critical of certain social restrictions placed on women. They were particularly concerned with the food restrictions which Bashu men saw as preventing women from disregarding their responsibility to the homestead in favor of their association with the bush, but which the Church saw as withholding many sources of protein from that segment of the population which had the greatest need for them. Both churches also condemned the practice of polygamy, though their protests were only partially effective. Where the message was headed, however, it gave individual wives greater status in the home, though often at the cost of increased demands on their labor. More recently, both churches have initiated educational programs for women, teaching them about health, hygiene, and nutrition, as well as certain crafts. While none of these changes by themselves greatly affected the role of women, their accumulative effect was one of gradual liberation and a movement toward equality with men.

Despite these changes women remained in a subordinant position, a fact which was manifested in male control over the rewards gained from female labor. It was Bashu men, not women, who decided how surplus income would be spent, a situation which became increasingly frustrating for Bashu women as they became more aware of the imported goods introduced during the colonial period: clothes, jewelry, shoes, utensils, bottled beer. Women, no less than men, were affected by the pressure to Westernize, and responded accordingly. Only, unlike men, they had little control over the income needed to achieve this goal. Thus, Bashu women during the middle and later years of the colonial period found themselves performing increasing amounts of labor, but having little control over the resultant rewards. Moreover, in other ways, their relationship with men was changing as they slowly began encroaching on the world of men, adopting male roles out of necessity and thus reducing male/female distinctions.

In other words the colonial period created a situation of alienated labor combined with rising female consciousness. This ultimately led to increased demands on the part of Bashu women for a greater share in determining the distribution of income as well as for other elements of social equality. Obviously not all Bashu women were affected by these trends in the same way. It is also evident that women were not marching through the villages demanding equal pay for equal work. But here and there, in small ways, demanding money for beer, entering the men's club house, showing a greater readiness to leave their husbands, women began asserting their claim to increased status in Bashu society.

From Bashu testimonies as well as from data collected by Fr. Bergmans (1971) about a similar phenomenon among the neighboring Nande groups, it appears that the belief in *avambakali* emerged among the Bushu sometime during the 1940s and has steadily gained acceptance ever since. The emergence of this concept thus parelleled the social and economic developments described above, and, from a sociological point of view, can be seen as a product of these changes.

This conclusion does not arise solely from the concurrence of changes in concepts and social change, but also from an examination of the cases of misfortune ascribed to the attacks of *avambakali*.[14] In the majority of these cases the victims were men who prior to being attacked had had some type of conflict with the women accused of attacking them. In the few cases where women were the victims, the attack could be connected to a conflict between the accused witch and a male relation of the victim. Finally, in nearly all of the cases the conflict in question revolved around the accused women's attempt to assert her claim to economic or social rights. For example, in one case a woman was said to have visited her father and asked him for five *makuta* to buy some beer. Her father refused to give her the money and she went away, only to return the next day and make the same request. Again her father refused. That night the father said that his daughter visited him in his dream and again asked for money and again he refused. The next day he was found under a tree in the bush incoherent and in a stupor. The people of the village ascribed the condition to his daughter's witchcraft.

In a second case, in which a woman was the victim, the victim had recently married a man who prior to the marriage had been involved sexually with another women who was accused of attacking the victim. The man had evidently promised to marry the accused

woman in order to gain sexual favors from her. Having done so he
refused to marry her. The accused woman then denounced the man
publicly for his deceit and then, according to the victim's relatives,
attacked the man's new wife in order to get revenge.

In these and other cases the accused women were persons who
previous to the onset of misfortune had attempted to assert their positions in society. Women accused of witchcraft were thus individuals
who represented the changing role of women in Bashu society, and
their alleged attacks may be indications of rising female consciousness and assertiveness. Conversely, the accusations of witchcraft
may be seen as a means by which Bashu men attempted to repress
this assertiveness and reassert their own dominance by punishing wom-
en who became too demanding. This repression could not be achieved
by direct punishment, for such behavior would be viewed as unjusti-
fied, and in cases involving affinal or agnatic relations, could bring on
legal or extralegal retribution by the punished woman's kinsmen. At
the same time, existing concepts of misfortune were largely ineffective
in dealing with this problem. While women could be seen as indirect
vectors of misfortune in that they could be possessed by spirits of the
bush, these spirits did not directly attack men. Moreover, women possessed by spirits of the bush were involuntary vectors of misfortune
and thus not wholly responsible for the mishap they caused. Consequently, the treatment applied to such women was less punitive than
remedial, and certainly did not serve as a strong sanction against future possession. The concept of *avambakali* on the other hand provided
a much more effective reponse to the problem of female insubordina-
tion. It was a concept which allowed for direct female attacks on men;
which ascribed conscious intent on the part of women engaged in such
attacks; and which, therefore, justified the application of more strin-
gent sanctions in the form of a painful exorcism procedure.

It is thus possible to see the concept of *avambakali* as evolving
out of the needs of men for an effective means of reasserting their
dominant position in Bashu society. I do not mean to imply that this
was necessarily a conscious strategy on the part of Bashu men. The
evidence in fact suggests that it was not. To begin with the form in
which the accusations are normally presented suggests that the *avambakali* phenomenon contains elements of peripheral spirit possession
as defined by Lewis and others. It may thus represent, at one level, an
unconscious reaction to social oppression, a momentary rebellion, de-

signed to "help the interests of the weak and downtrodden who have
otherwise few effective means to press their claims for attention and
respect" (Lewis, 1971:32). It should be noted that as the role of wom-
en expanded, that of men receded. Their position of dominance in the
homestead was crumbling and they found themselves increasingly under the influence of external forces—colonial officials, new local authorities, European employers—over which they had little control. By
appearing to be possessed by some external force, by behaving in
strange ways, victims of *avambakali* drew attention to themselves and
their psychological plight. At the same time they were relieved of any
responsibility for their actions. In this context, it is perhaps not coincidental that the rise of *avambakali* possession was paralleled by the
introduction, or resurgence, of male circumcision ceremonies and secret
societies which stressed male sexuality and dominance.[15]

The fact that male possession resulted in the accusation of a specific woman does not undercut the unconscious quality of the phenomenon, for the spirirts of the possessed often speak through their
hosts. What distinguishes *avambakali* possession from other types of
peripheral spirit possession is not the possession itelf, but its treatment.
Rather than cure or cleanse the victim as is done in most cases of possession, the Bashu attack the source of the affliction directly, treating
the woman whose spirit has possessed the victim. Thus, *avambakali*
possession serves two purposes. It is both a direct assertion of identity
and an indirect attact on oppressors. This suggests that we need to
revise Lewis's hypothesis that witchcraft accusations and possession
are separate strategies operating in different social contexts (1971:33).
For here, both strategies are combined in a single context.

The unconscious character of *avambakali* belief is further indicated by its continued existence. Today the belief in *avambakali* is
pervasive among the Bashu. Yet it no longer serves as a mechanism for
controlling the behavior of women, for pressure from Church and
state against the application of exorcism procedures have largely eliminated the sanction which applied to women accused of being *avambakali*. Consequently, women have little to fear from being accused.
In fact they are able to employ the belief in *avambakali* to advance
their own position, for Bashu men are reluctant to refuse a woman's
demands lest she be an *avambakali* and attack them. Thus, ironically,
a concept of misfortune which may have initially reinforced male
dominance is now operating in a way which reasserts the position of

women. If the belief in *avambakali* was part of a conscious male strategy, one would expect that the belief would have been dropped once
it was no longer effective. Whereas, in fact, it has become, if anything,
stronger and more pervasive. We must, therefore, assume that the
concept of *avambakali* emerged independently of conscious male intent.

While the above discussion suggests that the belief in *avambakali*
emerged in response to the creation of new social tensions between
men and women, it does not by itself explain why the Bashu responded
by developing a belief in *avambakali*. From an external viewpoint it
would appear that they might just as easily have expanded their definition of sorcerers to include women. This would have served the same
sociological function allowing men to punish women while explaining
their own failures. Moreover, in terms of conceptual innovation, the
expansion of sorcery would seem to be a more economical response.
To understand why Bashu men turned to female witches rather than
female sorcerers one must examine how they interpreted their changing relationships with women.

Bashu men generally explain the emergence of *avambakali* in
terms of their cosmological ideas concerning the role of women in
Bashu society: "Formerly women were prohibited from eating rats,
eggs, crickets, and chickens. Now they eat all of these things and have
begun to eat the flesh of men." This explanation evolves logically
out of previous ideas about women and misfortune. Women are potential sources of misfortune because of their innate association with the
forces of the bush. They are thus controlled in the homestead lest
their natural instincts emerge and create misfortune. Women who
violate the regulations become susceptible to possession by spirits of
the bush and thus to becoming vectors of misfortune within the homestead. Women who totally reject the strictures of the homestead become creatures of the bush whose activities are antithetical to the interests of the homestead and men. They become *avambakali*. For the
Bashu, therefore, the changing role of women represented a breakdown
in the social restrictions which controlled female associations with the
bush, and a gradual increase in these associations. The concept of
avambakali was thus a logical extension, or restatement, of existing
ideas about women and misfortune within the changed social environment of the colonial period.

The concept of a female sorcerer, on the other hand, was antithetical to existing ideas. Sorcerers were always men and were defined in terms of male characteristics. A sorcerer was in control of his actions. He chose to become a sorcerer by actively seeking out the knowledge and objects needed to be a sorcerer. His attacks often required complex strategies in order to place his medicines in the victim's hut or path. Women, on the other hand, were not viewed in these terms. They were emotional creatures, subject to possession and irrational behavior. They could not control themselves but had to be controlled. The Bashu concept of woman therefore clashed with the concept of sorcerer and worked against the extension of the latter to include the former.

Conclusion

In the preceding discussion I have tried to examine both how and why Bashu concepts of misfortune changed during the colonial period and, in doing so, contribute to our wider understanding of the relationship between social change and the development of ideas. By placing Bashu concepts of misfortune within the wider framework of Bashu cosmology it has been possible to show how the application of existing ideas about misfortune to new social situations had the feedback effect of altering the original ideas and producing new concepts.

In the long run, moreover, it is possible to see that this process of interpretation has begun to alter the former polarity of nature and culture, and that a new conception of society and the world is slowly emerging. If one steps back for a moment and looks at the general development of Bashu concepts of misfortune during the colonial period within the context of their initial conceptual model of misfortune, it is possible to see that for the Bashu world the last fifty years, including the postcolonial period, have been marked by a steady encroachment into the homestead of the forces of the bush. The social strictures and boundaries which once kept these two worlds apart have been steadily eroded. Sorcerers have increased in number and attack anyone. Women have rejected their responsibilities to the homestead in favor of their associations with the world of the bush. The world of the homestead has become like the world of the bush, a place of increasing chaos and disorder. The ultimate manifestation of this change is seen in the emergence of a new element in the concept of *avambakali*. Today when you talk to Bashu men about *avambakali*, they will tell you with a combination of horror and dispair that men are becoming *avambakali*, first as assistants then as full-fledged witches. This development has profound implications, for it indicates that a breakdown in the basic dichotomy between homestead and bush is in the process of occurring. When men act like creatures of the bush, the division between homestead and bush can no longer be maintained without a considerable loss in self-esteem and a heightened sense of conceptual incongruity on the part of Bashu men. We must therefore ask whether the duality between homestead and bush must not eventually give way to a new ordering of social experience, an ordering which will take the new values and patterns of behavior which are causing disruption and transpose them into the realm of the socially acceptable, an ordering which will, in effect, convert deviancy to normality. It may be that the existing polarity will be retained but that the definition of the opposing elements will be altered in accordance with contemporary social realities.

On the other hand, if we look at seventeenth-century Europe we see that the old duality of God and Satan which ordered the sixteenth century world view and was at the heart of European witchcraft beliefs broke down and was replaced by one which saw the universe as more unified and mechanical, arising from neoplatonism as redefined by men such as Descartes and Bacon. Thus, it is possible that the duality of bush and homestead may also give way to a new model of reality. Whatever happens, the new formulation must be seen as a major restructuring of the old symbolic order and not simply as a restatement or rehashing of old symbols.

NOTES

1. Anthropologists Lienhardt (1951) and Winter (1963) have taken a similar approach to witchcraft beliefs among the Dinka and Amba respectively, relating specific beliefs about witches to the wider cosmological ideas of each society. They do not, however, deal with the evolution of witchcraft beliefs.

2. Research among the Bashu was carried out between 1974 and 1975 with a grant from the Fulbright-Hays Fellowship Program and the University of Wisconsin-Madison.

3. Reconstructing historical systems of thought in the absence of extensive written records is admittedly a difficult task. While Feierman

(1972) and Cohen (1977) have used physical evidence in the form of palace remains to reconstruct former political ideas, no such evidence exists for concepts of misfortune. Similarly, Ehret (1977) has recently shown how linguistic evidence can be used to reconstruct former patterns of culture and cultural knoweldge. This type of analysis, however, is more applicable to material culture than to non-material culture, and can only be used for reconstructing general cultural patterns in the more distant past. We are therefore forced to rely primarily on information acquired from informants about their past conceptions of the world, supplemented with a few references from early administrative and missionary records. Oral information must obviously be used with care, for it may easily be contaminated with ideas derived from contemporary experience, a problem which increases as one moves backwards in time. While acknowledging the existence of these methodological problems, it may be argued that the information presented by Bashu informants on their former ideas about misfortune is less apt to have been contaminated by subsequent experience, because of the relatively late establishment of Belgian colonial rule among the Bashu. The Bashu were independent of Belgian control until 1923, and major social changes resulting from colonial rule did not begin until the 1930s. The social and cultural conditions described in this section therefore existed within the living memory of many of my informants. It might also be argued that the ideas about misfortune discussed here are consistent with the social conditions which existed among the Bashu on the eve on colonial rule, and which can be documented with written records. They are, on the other hand, inconsistent with contemporary social conditions, and therefore cannot easily be attributed to contemporary conditions. It is thus probable that they reflect an earlier system of thought.

    4. Jackson has suggested that witchcraft among the Kuranko of Sierra Leone is defined as "an invasion of *domestic or village* space by wild and uncontrollable powers, generally associated with animals and the bush" (1975:395).

    5. My understanding of the place of women in Bashu cosmology was greatly enhanced by my reading of Ivan and Patricia Karp's analyses of spirit possession of women among the Iteso of western Kenya (1972; 1978). I. Karp has suggested that the identification of Bashu women with Buffalo and the prohibition against their eating chickens and rats may be based on the fact that these animals, like women, occupy a liminal position in Bashu cosmology. Thus both chickens and rats move between the bush and the homestead, while buffalo may fall between the categories of cattle (domestic animals) and wild animals (personal communication).

    6. This view of the ancestors contrasts with that described by Evans-Pritchard (1956), Karp and Karp (1978), in which ritual activity directed towards the spirits of ancestors is designed to maintain or reestablish the separation between ancestors and living, and in which misfortune caused by ancestors is seen as resulting from the interference of ancestors in the world of the living. For the Bashu, ancestors are more like elders, and the term used to describe them is the same as that used for elders, *avakulu* or *avasekulu*. The concept of ancestors as elders has been discussed elsewhere by Kopytoff (1971) and Brain (1973).

    7. While village consolidation was ordered in 1932 it did not get un-

derway until 1933. The difficulties arising from the policy are a recurring theme in the administrative reports during this period. "Rapport Mensuel aôut 1934," Territoire Wanande-Nord; Conseil des Chefs Bashu 22 Juillet 1936 (Archives de Beni), A.I.M.O. Rapport, Kivu District 1945 in de Ryck collection, Memorial Library, University of Wisconsin-Madison). The policy was complicated by the simultaneous evacuation of the Semliki Valley on account of sleeping sickness. Thus, much of the movement away from the villages was caused by people from the plains and lower foothills trying to return to their home region.

8. See John Ford, 1971, p. 176 for a discussion of the relationship between the Belgian village policy and the outbreak of sleeping sickness in the Semliki Valley.

9. Bubonic plague was, and is, a recurrent problem in the Bashu region. The southern half of the Bashu region was in fact under quarantine for several months during the course of my research. See: A.I.M.O. Rapport, Kivu District 1941, for reference to earlier incidents.

10. A.I.M.O. Rapport, Kivu District, 1945. 34.4 percent of the male population was registered as working outside the "milieu coutumiere" in that year. This was up from 32.50 percent in 1944 and was regarded with some concern by Belgian administrators.

11. The problem of sorcerers and witches in concentrated villages evidently led Africans in southern Tanzania to elect witches by secret ballot as part of the Ujamaa village scheme. The elected witches were then given their own village which permitted the remainder of the population to feel more at ease in their new social surroundings (comment made by T. O. Ranger, citing Marcia Wright at SSRC Conference on Cultural Transformations, Elkridge, Maryland 15 January 1978).

12. The evidence for borrowing comes from three sources: Bashu statements that the *avambakali* came from the forest; the fact that the term *avambakali* is a cognate of the Bapakombe term for a similar concept, *momba/bamba*, the Bashu having added the suffix -*kali* to designate woman since among the Bapakombe *bamba* can be men or women; and the wider distribution of the concept, which suggests a western origin. There are, however, several reasons for questioning the significance of this evidence. First, Bashu claims that *avambakali* came from the forest may simply reflect the symbolic association of *avambakali* with the bush. Second, the linguistic relationship between the Bapakombe and Bashu terms may reflect the parallel existence of a common term which is very old, going back to proto-Bantu (see Ardener 1971:145) and thus may not be a product of recent borrowing. Finally, the existence of similar ideas about witches throughout much of central Africa and beyond Africa in Europe and America—the association with wild animals, nighttime activities, the predominance of female witches, the idea of witches' covens, and elements of cannibalism—undercuts the distributional argument. Yet, even if we assume that contact with the Bapakombe was initially responsible for the introduction of this new concept of misfortune, we must also assume that in borrowing the new concept, the Bashu transformed it so that it coincided with existing ideas and symbols. Thus whether the concept was borrowed or formed independently, its emergence among the Bashu involved a rearrangement of symbols to create a new concept.

13. This was not an arbitrary decision. Women were given the responsibility for mudding walls because the task was seen as a logical extension of their former task of mudding the floor of the hut. In other words, following the line of analysis presented in this paper, the definition of women, rather than men, as wall mudders resulted from the application of existing categories of labor, mudding and thatching, to a new social experience: the mud and wattle hut.

14. These cases were collected during my fieldwork in Zaïre from informants and local court records at Vutengera, the administrative headquarters for the Bashu collectivity.

15. Circumcision rituals may have existed for a long time among the Bashu and simply enjoyed a resurgence during the colonial period. The evidence suggests, however, that the association of circumcision with a secret society known as *omukumo* which provided its members with protection against certain misfortunes, including, according to some, *avambakali* attacks, and with the ability easily to dominate women, is a recent innovation. See Bergmans, 1971:28–35, for a detailed description of *mukumo* among the Banande.

BIBLIOGRAPHY

Ardener, E. 1971. "Witchcraft, Economics and the Continuity of Belief." In *Witchcraft, Confessions and Accusations*, edited by Mary Douglas. London: Tavistock Publications.

Bergmans, L. 1971. *Les Wanande: Croyances et Pratiques Traditionelles.* Butembo: Editions A.B.B.

Bohannan, P. 1958. "Extra-Processual Events in Tiv Political Institutions." *American Anthropologist* 60 (1):1–12.

Boyer, Paul, and Nissenbaum, P. 1972. *Salem Possessed.* Cambridge: Harvard University Press.

Brain, James L. 1973. "Ancestors as Elders: some further thoughts." *Africa* 43 (1):122–33.

Cohen, David W. 1977. *Womunafu's Bunafu.* Princeton: Princeton University Press.

Demos, John. 1970. "Underlying Themes in the Witchcraft of Seventeenth Century New England." *American Historical Review* 75:358–72.

Douglas, Mary. 1973. *Natural Symbols.* New York: Penguin.

Ehret, C. 1977. "'Transformations of Vocabulary of Culture as a Guide to Cutural Transformations." Paper presented at SSRC Conference on Cultural Transformations in Africa, Elkridge, Maryland, 12 January 1978.

Evans-Pritchard, E. E. 1937. *Witchcraft, Oracles and Magic Among the Azande.* London: Oxford University Press.

———. 1956. *Nuer Religion.* London: Oxford University Press.

Feierman, Steven. 1972. "Concepts of Sovereignty among the Shambaa and their Relation to Political Action." Ph.D. dissertation, Oxford University.

Fernandez, J. W. 1977. "The Maintenance of Culture." Paper presented to SSRC Conference on Cultural Transformations, Elkridge, Maryland, 12 January 1978.

Ford, John. 1971. *The Role of Trypanosomiasis in African Ecology*. London: Oxford University Press.

Fox, Sanford. 1968. *Science and Justice*. Baltimore: Johns Hopkins University Press.

Hansen, C. 1968. *Witchcraft at Salem*. New York: George Braziller.

Hartwig, Gerald. 1972. "Long Distance Trade and the Evolution of Sorcery among the Kerebe." *International Journal of African Historical Studies* 4:505–25.

Heusch, Luc de. 1966. *Rwanda et la civilisation interlacustrine*. Brussels: Institut de Sociologie de l'Université Libre de Bruxelles.

Jackson, M. 1975. "Structure and Event: Witchcraft Confession among the Kuranko." *Man* n.s. 10 (3):287–303.

Karp, Ivan, and Karp, Patricia. 1972. "The Ambiguous Woman: Dual Symbolic Classification and the Ritual Role of Women Among the Southern Iteso." Paper presented at the American Anthropological Association Meetings, Toronto, November 1972.

———. 1978. "Living with the Spirits of the Dead." In *African Therapeutic Systems*, edited by D. M. Warren et al. Crossroads Press, for the African Studies Association.

Kopytoff, Igor. 1971. "Ancestors as Elders in Africa." *Africa* 41(2):129–41.

Lewis, I. M. 1971. *Ecstatic Religion*. London: Penguin.

Lienhardt, G. 1951. "Some Notions of Witchcraft among the Dinka." *Africa* 21 (4):303–318.

MacFarlane, A. 1970. *Witchcraft in Tudor and Stuart England*. London: Routledge and Kegan Paul.

Marwick, M. 1950. "Another Modern Anti-Witchcraft Movement in Central East Africa." *Africa* 20 (2):100–12.

———. 1952. "The Social Context of Chewa Witch Beliefs." *Africa* 22 (2):120–35; (3):215–33.

Middleton, John, and Winter, Edward, eds. 1963. *Witchcraft and Sorcery in East Africa*. London: Routledge and Kegan Paul.

Midelfort, H. C. E. 1972. *Witch Hunting in Southwest Germany*. Palo Alto: Stanford University Press.

Mitchell, Clyde. 1956. *The Yao Village: a Study in the Social Structure of a Nyasaland Tribe*. Manchester: Manchester University Press.

Monter, William. 1976. *Witchcraft in France and Switzerland*. Ithaca, N.Y.: Cornell University Press.

Nadel, S. F. 1952. "Witchcraft in Four African Societies." *American Anthropologist* 54:18–29.

Packard, R. M. 1976. "The Politics of Ritual Control among the Bashu of Eastern Zaire during the Nineteenth Century." Ph.D. dissertation, University of Wisconsin-Madison.

Richards, A. 1935. "A Modern Movement of Witchfinders." *Africa* 8 (4): 448–61.

Thomas, Keith. 1971. *Religion and the Decline of Magic: Studies in Popular Beliefs in Sixteenth and Seventeenth Century England*. London: Weidenfeld and Nicolson.

Trevor-Roper, H. R. 1956. *The European Witch-Craze of the Sixteenth and Seventeenth Centuries and other Essays.* New York: Harper and Row.

Vasina, Jan. 1971. "Les Mouvements religieux kuba (Kasai) à l'époque Coloniale." *Etudes d'Histoire Africaine* 2:155–87.

———. 1973. "Lukoshi/Lupambula: Histoire d'un culte religieux dans les regions du Kasai et du Kwango (1920–1970)." *Etudes d'Histoire Africaine* 5:51–97.

Willis, R. G. 1968. "Kamcape: an anti-witchcraft movement in southwest Tanzania." *Africa* 38 (1):1–15.

———. 1970. "Instant Millennium." In *Witchcraft, Confessions and Accusations*, edited by Mary Douglas. London: Routledge and Kegan Paul.

Wilson, Monica. 1951. "'Witchbeliefs and Social Structure." *American Journal of Sociology* 56:307–13.

Winter, Edward. 1963. "The Enemy Within." In *Witchcraft and Sorcery in East Africa*, edited by John Middleton and Edward Winter. London: Routledge and Kegan Paul.

The Village
and the Cattle Camp
Aspects of Atuot Religion

by John W. Burton

Paraphrasing Needham's (1975) masterly brief on polythetic classification Douglas writes that it "defines classes by a combination of characteristics, not requiring any of the defining features to be present in all members of a class. Each included member only needs to show a majority of features in the class" (1978:15).[1] Had social anthropologists employed this method of analysis earlier, perhaps in the study of religion, the enormous attention given to defining pure types, such as sacred/profane, magic/religion, or myth/ritual, might have been better directed. Among its values, Douglas adds, is that polythetic classification "does away with sharp dichotomies" (15).

Instead, a majority of monographs inspired by structural-functionalism in preceding decades delimit water-tight compartments of social behavior, and conclude with chapters on "traditional religion," implying among other things, that the phenomena of religion could be so unambiguously encoded. Further, the peculiarities of a religion were most often "explained" by reference to features of social organization, rather than with regard to their own internal logic. Examples in the African context include studies of ancestrally oriented cosmologies, analyses of state ritual and divine authority, as well as witchcraft beliefs. A more limited number of monographs convey an understanding of varieties of religious expressions and experience in a traditional society, and hence only few convey the importance of religion as a social fact. Among these, Lienhardt's (1961) study appears exemplary. Indeed, the book might be considered to be an illustration of a Dinka polythetic mode. The Dinka concept of divinity "is comprehended in and through natural experience, and not merely as a theoretical force producing the order of the world from without" (158). Likewise, Deng (1973:50) observes, "Divinity in the sense of God is not limited to any particular feature of human experience, but embraces all aspects of life. God is therefore a unification of infinite diversities."[2]

The present essay is an attempt to understand varieties in religious experience of the Atuot of the Southern Sudan, and more specifically, the distinctions they make between religious expressions in the village setting in contrast to religious behavior associated with cattle camps.[3] Forms of rituals and types of spiritual powers in each settlement pattern are notably different, even though both reflect basic facets of "Atuot religion." Socially and culturally the Atuot share strong affinities with the better known Nuer and Dinka, thus offering a well-defined field for comparative study, though emphasis is given here more toward the Nuer. This approach is to some degree arbitrary since the Atuot language is most like that of the Nuer, while their economic adaptation to the local environment resembles more closely the Dinka pattern of transhumance.

I intend the phrase "varieties of religious experience" to refer to the forms and manifestations of spiritual powers known to individuals and the manner in which these can be understood by an observer in viewing manifest differences in rituals and the degree of social participation they involve. Some of those who have read *Nuer Religion* may share a sympathy with the ethnographer's contention that all lesser forms of the Divine God *Kwoth* stem from non-Nuer, Dinka, or Sudanic influences upon the peculiar form and expression of Nuer monotheism. Evans-Pritchard spent most of his ten and a half months in Nuerland living in dry season cattle camps, and as far as the published work indicates, he never resided in a wet season village. Primarily for this reason—the context of ethnographic description—I believe his discussion of Nuer religion in general overemphasizes certain notions to the exclusion of others.[4] I am most certain, at any rate, that this would definitely have been the result with a similar experience among the Atuot.

Like the Nuer, Atuot move with their cattle seasonally between dry season cattle camps and slightly more elevated land during the rainy season, where horticulture rather than pastoralism is the essential economic activity. In the course of fieldwork among the Atuot, I had ample time to spend in each of these types of settlements. The differences which Atuot recognize between spiritual powers in each settlement pattern offer the substantive data of this paper. I do not mean to assert that in this regard Atuot religion and ritual is necessarily similar to that to be found among the Nuer (although this may be more or less the case in western Nuerland than in the areas east of the Nile where Evans-Pritchard carried out most of his studies). Instead, the material may be interpreted to intimate that Evans-Pritchard gave special emphasis to the divine and ubiquitous qualities of *Kwoth* to the neglect of lesser powers, which at least among the Atuot, assume greater importance in the village setting.

Prefacing the analysis of some aspects of Atuot religion it is worthwhile to briefly summarize the information regarding Nuer "earthly powers." Evans-Pritchard (1956:95) suggested that spirits of the below or ground spirits (*kuth piny*) could be labeled as a class "totemic spirits" and writes that in considering "diviners, leeches, owners of nature sprites and owners of fetishes we are on the periphery of the conception of Spirit, where it becomes more and more embedded in the psychical and material." Among the phenomena classified by Nuer as earthly spirits Evans-Pritchard argues that the majority of them "may be considered to be of foreign origin" and to have been fairly recently introduced into Nuerland. One could argue that empirically it would certainly prove a complex if not impossible task to document these innovations. It would appear that Evans-Pritchard classifies them as being "totemic" because each has some sort of physical manifestation. Yet he further asserts that "totemism" is foreign to the Nuer. This is plausible if the Nuer learned of totemism through intermarriage with the Dinka, more precisely, when a Nuer woman was married by a Dinka man. A general feature of these spirits is that they are considered to be "amoral" in their action. "They are acquired in the first instance by purchase . . . for private ends and personal aggrandizement."

But one wonders, did the Nuer *really* only learn of immortality through intermarriage with the Dinka? The central tenet of Nuer religion would seem to contradict the observation, for Evans-Pritchard suggested that to be in the right with God, it was necessary to be in the right with one's fellows. Concluding the chapter of "spirits of the below," primarily an account of Nuer "totemism," he writes "I mention them chiefly for the reason that their rarity and unimportance are

NILOTIC PEOPLES OF THE SOUTHERN SUDAN

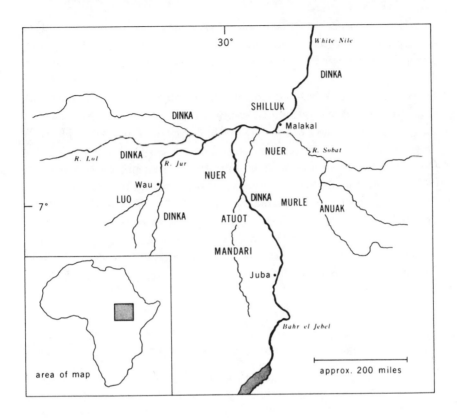

highly indicative of the orientation of Nuer thought, which is always toward spirit" (1956:104).

Howell (1953; see also Crazzolara, 1953:71–89) offers a rather contradictory estimation of the Nuer perception of earthly spirits. Even though Howell never claimed to be an authority on the topic of Nuer religion, his account is important and valuable, for it is clearly based on a more diversified experience in different areas of Nuerland. Evans-Pritchard offered one translation of the Nuer phrase *kuth piny* as "talking medicines." I am more inclined to agree with Howell's statement that the "power" or "spirit" of the earth is preferable since "although they are often associated with material objects . . . it is the spirit within them which is important and such spirits are often found in animals and natural phenomena as well" (85). Within this class are spirits known as *kulangi*[5] including powers said to be of Nuer origin (*kolang*) and those thought to have come from the Dinka, called *goagh*, a term which is certainly cognate with the Atuot and Dinka *jok* (compare Burton, 1978A, n.d.). Howell concludes his brief article by writing:

> I believe the Nuer regard these spirits in three ways. First, as possessed or possessing certain individuals who may use them in diagnosing the cause of illness and for curing it. The *gwan kolang* [possessors of these powers] will demand fees for these services. Second, they may be regarded as free agents which attack people and cause illness without any ill-will on the part of the owner. Finally, the *gwan kolang* may direct the spirit against his enemies in the form of witchcraft . . . but I do not think that this is a common feature of the belief (1953:88).

We have little information about where Nuer believe these powers are especially active, though I hope to show through a comparison with some Atuot data that this is most likely the village setting.

Cosmology and Ecology

The analysis will be facilitated by a brief overview of Atuot environment and economy. Their country lies on the average sixty miles west of the Nile and today exists within the administrative boundaries of Lakes Province, named for the many shallow water-filled depressions which dot the land. Topographically and with regard to soil types the area is well suited to both pastoralism and horticulture. The numerous small streams which traverse the countryside provide abundant quantities of fish, which along with millet, is a staple food. Wet season villages (*cieng*) and cattle camps (*wuic*; sing. *wei*) are located on the ironstone plateau which forms the southern perimeter of the swampland of the Upper Nile basin, and falls between the macro-ecological zones of open and forested savannah to the north, and tropical forest to the south. Atuot divide the twelve months or moons of the ecological year into the season of rains (*deker*, derived from the verb *kaai*, "to mature," hence the season when crops are harvested) and the season of dryness, *mai*, a common Nilotic root meaning "to fish."

The months are named after events experienced during their duration. For example, *abothnon* translates as "the period of hunger," *biildito* as "the time of big durra (millet)," *admuong* as "the time of being together (in dry season cattle camps)."

One referent of the word *cieng* can connote "home" and by logical extension, "village," though wet season settements do not form clusters of huts or homesteads as is implied by the common English meaning of the term. Instead, the typical village consists of widely dispersed settlements often covering miles of territory. Human population densities in these areas are estimated to average eight to ten persons per square mile. In its most common Atuot usage the term *cieng* refers either to the homestead of one individual family or to a much wider geographical area within which seasonal cultivation is practiced. A different word is employed to denote a single hut (*ɣot*). I think in a general sort of way we seem to assume that a village is the primordial fully social arrangement and that the physical existence of clustered habitations imbues social relationships with a measure of permanence. The Nilotic word *cieng* is thus most often glossed with the words "village" or "home". Concurrently, the settlements within which herds of cattle are tethered have been labeled "camps," inferring a different quality in the social relationships found among its human inhabitants. A camp seems necessarily temporary when contrasted to the notion of permanence implicit in the word "village". At the same time, the latter term suggests a degree of population density (see, for example, Granet, 1922; Mauss, 1906). For a number of reasons these translations are inappropriate in Atuot, perhaps most importantly because they

THE ECOLOGICAL YEAR (*ruon*)

	JAN (*hor*)	FEB (*kon*)	MAR (*nyith*)	APR (*kuol*)	MAY (*akoidit*)	JUNE (*akoi tot*)	JULY (*admuong*)	AUG (*alathbor*)	SEPT (*abothnon*)	OCT (*bildito*)	NOV (*biiltoto*)	DEC (*lal*)
season	dry season (*mai*)									season of rains (*deker*)		
camp	dry season camp (*wuic*) (cattle camps in the *toic*)						wet season camp (*wuic*) (cattle camps in the forest)					
settlement	most people in the camp						settlement in villages (*cieng*)					
density	period of greatest social density						period of greatest dispersal					
activity	fishing					first cultivation	second cultivation	hungry months			burning grass	
											harvest	
winds	hot winds from the north							cool winds from the south				
	pastoralism											

consider their wet season cattle camps to be permanent settlements. Areas which are cultivated lose their fertility over longer and shorter intervals and hence vary in location over the years. Atuot ox songs often include reference to the quantity and softness of burnt cow dung ash (*apuo*) found underneath the shelter of one's family in a camp, suggesting and at the same time boasting of a long and prosperous period of residence in the same camp. Most importantly, the typical wet season cattle camp included as many as three hundred individuals, all living within the circular confines of an area with a diameter of about one hundred yards. One observes a remarkably higher population in the cattle camps in contrast to village areas, and, after a period of residence, a greater "moral density" as well. It would perhaps make better sense to speak of cultivation camps and cattle villages.

The divergence in settlement pattern is paralleled by a sexual division of labor. The cultivation of millet (primarily *Sorghum vulgare*) and a variety of additional crops is solely the work of women, whose task it is also to transform the raw goods into edible foods. A husband's only responsibility in this regard is to clear a forested area for planting and later building a hut for each of his wives. In a polygynous household, each wife also has her own garden, very often located as much as a mile distant from that of her cowife. Atuot women told me "It was done like that so that people will have respect between themselves," the word *thek*, respect, meaning in this context, acknowledging one's individuality, status, and independence.[6] Each homestead is surrounded by the woman's garden and is often bordered by a tract of open savannah forest (*gok*) separating it from the next cultivation and hut. The physical dispersion of people in the village corresponds with an equally nebulous moral density. The economic and symbolic world of women is that of the village, an observation made by Atuot when discussing the more general domains of the sexes. The phrase *cek ce tei cieng* can be translated as "the women are [remain] in the village." In terms of subsistence, each homestead is a self-sufficient entity.

After the millet stalks reach their matured height of ten to twelve feet in early November, each hut becomes quite isolated from the next in the most obvious physical manner and is thus a setting that affords considerable privacy (see Lienhardt, 1951; 1970). In the cattle camps, living conditions are as different as might be considering the local environmental possibilities. Cattle camps offer little measure for privacy, even while men living together in a camp maintain a strong sense of respect for each other. Herding cattle—the very reason for the existence of cattle camps—requires collective and cooperative labor. Ox songs often refer to one or another cattle camp as "a place where there is no confusion." Among other things this reflects the ethic that men ought to remain peaceably among themselves in the camp, speaking their words openly (quite often with a delicate hint of purpose) in the continual effort toward maintaining a consensus. By contrast, the village invites hostility since in their view covert privacy suggests plotting, jealousy, and ignorance of the true intentions of others. One song includes the lines,

> Oh, to remain alone is a bad thing
> The settlement of the marriage of a girl,
> Is a thing made with the words of elders
> It is made in the camp of the people of words
> I ignore the words of women
> This is why we remain together peaceably.

The things of cattle, Atuot say, are the things of men (*kuai ɣok era luoi cou*). The relationship of man and beast has an obvious and immediate economic import, since a group of agnates shares rights in the use and distribution of a herd. Men are also in absolute control over the food they consider to be the "sweetest of all," milk. Following his initiation into adulthood a young man is given an ox by his father from which he derives his ox-name. When he later composes songs to praise the beauty of his beast a man refers to himself metaphorically as the animal of the same name (see Burton, 1978; Lienhardt, 1963; Deng, 1973). There exists therefore an obvious dualism in the economic and symbolic spheres of Atuot life. In Atuot cosmology women are associated with a private world, the village setting and agriculture, while men figure in a conceptual class that combines a public world, cattle camps, and pastoralism.[7] During sacrifices made in a village setting invocations are punctuated by rubbing handfulls of millet flour (*tiaar*) across the back of the animal. In the cattle camps, ashes of burnt dung are used for the same purpose. In a number of interesting ways women are also associated with goats. The marital status of a woman is marked especially by her possession of a triangular-shaped shirt fashioned from the treated hide of a goat. The psychic character of women is also likened to the behavior of goats, animals that are conceptually "hot," unpredictable, and subject to outbursts of rage. The "cool hearts of men" figure them as reasoned in behavior, predictable, and forthright. One friend said, "Men stay together like a herd of cattle. Women are like goats because when they are married they disappear into the forests like goats," another way of suggesting that through marriage, they become members of different patrilineal groups. One older woman, respected for both her wit and demeanor, offered a similar comment by suggesting I couldn't be too clever *at all* if I wasn't able to see for myself that cattle and goats behaved in markedly different ways. At least on this account, the collective representation is not simply a reflection of male dominance. It is this association involving women, goats, the village setting, a "heated" ritual status, and leaving one group to join another, which has relevance for understanding some aspects of Atuot religion.

A final comment can be made before continuing in order to draw into relief the social rather than purely ideological parameters of the material under consideration. Very often men apportion a number of cattle to kin living in different camps. Apart from the practical effect this has in protecting cattle from disease and raids, it serves to perpetuate the ethic of cooperation among their owners. A personal anecdote bears this out. When I acquired an ox I took it to be tethered in the camp of my fictive grandfather's sister's son. When he later learned of this, my fictive paternal uncle brought a cow calf from his camp, to be tethered next to my ox, an indication of the good relations which held between us as kin. In contrast, each wife of a polygynous union demands the independence of her own hut as well as her own garden. If she is a successful cultivator the credit is none but her own. Should her cowife fail at the same task, tension inevitably develops between them (see also Lienhardt, 1951). Likewise, at least in men's eyes, if one party fails to make good its promise of a number of bridewealth cattle, the problem is traced to women. Those who agree to live together in a cattle camp are the same individuals who unite to tend and defend the herds (compare Baxter, 1972). Coexistent with these diverse economic pursuits and the associated disparities in population density is a marked difference in social and moral values which constrain behavior in villages and cattle camps. With a hint of romance, Deng notes "the profound difference between the jubilant air of the cattle camp and the subdued atmosphere of the home" (1972:

85). Reciprocity and cooperation are central for the persistence of cattle camps while individual labor and residential isolation characterizes
the world of villages. I hope to demonstrate how these factors are reflected in Atuot religious practice and belief.

Divinity and Powers

The most essential feature of Atuot religion is the acceptance of
the existence of God the Creator (*Decau*), a being whom alone is
imagined to have the puissance of creation (the word is derived from
the verb *cak*, "to bring into existence something which did not exist
before"). The phrase *Decau guar*, "Creator my father," connotes in
Atuot the paternal interests God is thought to have in the well-being
of the people he created. In comparing themselves to the magnitude
and omnipotence of this supreme Divinity—most often in hymns sung
in the course of sacrifices—Atuot speak of themselves metaphorically
as "God's ants," tiny black creatures who inhabit the larger world of
God's creation. Though this concept of God assumes his omnipresence
he is in another sense distant from the world of human beings, and
Atuot interpret his presence more often through lesser powers which
partake of divinity in varying degrees. These "refractions" or what
they take to be manifestations of divinity are broadly classified into
two imbricated classes on the basis of hierarchy and analogy (see
Needham, 1978:19), those directly associated with "the above," in one
way closer to God, and those of the "below," which are more immediately involved in the social world of human affairs. The single term
jok (pl. *jao*) subsumes both categores, however, offering one indication of a polythetic mode of classification in Atuot cosmology. Any single translation of the word *jok* is in some ways unsatisfactory though
its most frequent referent approaches the meaning of the English
words "power," "divinity," or "spiritual agent." I have adopted the
phrase "power (of God)" to convey the Atuot meaning. The concept
jok is idiomatic in Atuot religion to the same degree that a bovine
idiom communicates information about social relationships.

The powers of the above or "heavenly powers" (*jao nhial*) are often referred to collectively as *gaat Decau*, "sons of the Creator." These
are sometimes spoken of as being the first powers that God created
because, I surmise, they are thought to be most directly under his control. Following the same analogy with kinship, the heavenly powers

are inherited patrilineally. The most important of these, *col wic, kulang, kwoth,* and *ring* are mediums of rain, lightning, twin birth, and the essence of corporeal existence. The other category of powers is called *jao piny,* powers of the earth or powers of the below. These are believed to have become more numerous within living memory (compare Buxton, 1973) and are often said to have originated among the Nuer, the Dinka, or the Jur Beli and Sophi. They include *mathiang gook, thong alal, makao, mabier, agok, arop, payenya, mangok, abiel,* and *koro.* These powers are often said to travel in pairs, typically with a "wife." Bernard Jenny, who was carrying out anthropological studies among the Jur Beli and Sophi while I was in Atuot land, kindly offered me the chance to record the names of powers known by these people. About half of them were recognized by Atuot diviners and the remainder thought to have been Dinka. Were I to follow the logic of Evans-Pritchard in his analysis of Nuer earthly powers and state that Atuot "say these are of Dinka origin," I believe it would give the image that there is a veritable "*kula* ring" of spiritual powers in the Nilotic Sudan. I think it is more appropriate to state that they are "foreign" only to the degree that physical illness, with which they are associated, is itself unpredictable.

Rather than being solely inherited by males, earthly powers can be bought and sold by men and women. Without exception, powers of the below are manifested in physical symptoms of illness, such as tuberculosis, forms of dysentery, meningitis, and a variety of other maladies common in environments of this latitude. In a general sense the heavenly powers are positively evaluated since they benefit the lives of all human beings, while earthly powers have only malignant associations. Each of the earthly powers has in turn a number of medicines associated with it, such as varieties of roots and tubers.

The symbolic attributes of persons credited with the control of each type of power exhibit a similar disparity. As indicated, a man cannot buy the power to call rain (often referred to by its ox name *awumkuai*). Rather, it is maintained that God chooses particular individuals to fill their psychic and physical selves with the power. Such a man is spoken of as *gwan kwoth,* a "possessor" or "father" of the spiritual power associated with rain. The individual who incorporates the power of "life" or "flesh," *ring,* is referred to as *gwan riang.* Both in turn are commonly called *gwan nhial,* "possessor of a spiritual power of God." In the same manner they figure in Atuot cosmology as creators and genitors of life by analogy with God's creative power. The *gwan nhial* is possessed by the power and at the same time has a measure of control over it. The category of people who own and communicate with earthly powers are known as *tiit* (sing. *tiet*), a term, I believe, that is derived from the noun *teet*, "hand." God chooses individuals to become possessed by heavenly powers. The decision to become a *tiet* is made by individuals for personal reasons, very often after they have been afflicted by one or another power and later regained health.

Those who are versed in such matters explain that in the course of an exorcism the *tiet* is able to actually see the power within the human body, sometimes in the form of a cat, a monkey, or a spear. One woman explained,

> It was God who put something into the eyes of human beings so they could not see the powers. And then he gave us *tiit* who see them. The people of *jok* see *jok* but the man of *ring* does not see *ring*. He is given *ring* by God. When a person has a big trouble he will go to a man of *ring* who will make things work in his favor by just saying his word. A *tiet* sees a power and sucks it out. The man of *ring* only says his word and it is done. When there is a great suffering among many people the man of *ring* will sacrifice a cow for God.

The text might be better understood after relating a commonly known myth that accounts for the origin of the powers. One point can be mentioned first in regard to the analysis attempted here. The initial dispersion of powers among human beings shares an analogical identity with the manner in which women are "dispersed" among different social groups through the institution of marriage. The text just cited demonstrates clearly enough how Atuot perceive that heavenly powers affect the lives of all people, whereas earthly powers are involved in the affairs of particular individuals.

> People were created long ago by *Decau. Jok* was a different son, and all the people who are now in the world were different sons. They were all in one cattle camp and each had their own side. One time the people went to fish and they caught the fish that belonged to *abiel* [one of the earthly powers] and *abiel* was angry and went up to God and said to him, "The people you have created and gave the fishing spear to have become very strong. They have caught our

fish." God listened and said that later in the day he would send a great wind that would be filled with dust. He told the powers that this would blind the eyes of the people and allow the powers to go along with their own things and catch their fish. [The myth at this point reveals that the events transpired in a dry season fishing or cattle camp. During the months of January to March dry dusty winds blow throughout the day, and it is at this time when people are most likely to suffer attacks of meningitis.] He told all the powers to go hide in the ground. A dog [also called in Atuot *jok*] happened to be nearby and overheard the conversation between God and the power *abiel*. It ran off quickly and unnoticed to the camp of the people and told them what it had learned. He told the people that later in the day when the dusty wind came they should cover their eyes or else they would be made blind. When people heard this they became angry with the dog and kicked it and said "you dog—you go off with your lies. When did you speak to God?!!"

In the meanwhile the powers had gone off to fish and when they returned to the camp the dusty wind began to blow, so they hid themselves in the ground. The people in the camp sat around and expected nothing out of the ordinary. The wind blew up quickly and the dog buried its head in the ground. When the wind had passed the dog could see that all the people had become blind. Then *abiel* went to fish and put some of his catch in the fire to roast. People smelled the food and said among themselves "where is this smell of fish coming from?" *Abiel* then took up its fishing spear and thrust it into the left side of a man. The man fell to the ground and blood streamed from his mouth. The people were astonished and said "where is this death coming from?" Then God saw that the people were suffering and he said I will catch one man [the text reads here *be dom e ɣen nuer me kel*; the verb *dom* refers to the act of catching or grabbing an object] and he will have this power. I will open the eyes of that man and when he goes *abiel* will remain in him to help the lives of people. In the evening *abiel* returned with more fish and put them in the fire, realizing that he could not be seen by the people. He called for the other powers and they shared the fish. Each one then went off to live with a different family. This is how the powers came to us and why the dog that covered its eyes can still see the powers at night.

Some versions of the myth conclude with the suggestion that *ring*, the "oldest" and hence senior of all powers, later argued with *abiel* and insulted it for acting so violently toward human beings and decided in consequence that it would have nothing to do with the powers of the earth (compare Howell, 1953:86–87).

Having indicated a number of the more important ideational distinctions between types of powers, I would like to suggest further that each category might be further distinguished on the basis of being active and passive in nature. The powers of the above enter the lives of human beings regardless of personal involvement or choice. Their human mediums are chosen by them. Conversely, in their possession of one or another earthly powers, individuals actively employ these in response to their hatreds and jealousies by seeking spiritual vengeance through the medium of powers (see also Santandrea, 1977:576–609). This is not a matter of surmise about unconscious motivations, for Atuot are quick to point out that physical symptoms of illness have their etiology in the actions of some other individual, who has either bought a power to inflict harm or called for the services of a *tiet* to realize the same end. Another way of explicating the classifiration "artive/passive" is to note that the power *ring* is characterized as being "lame and old; but even though it travels slowly, its work is always done. Powers of the earth are hot. When you become suddenly ill for no reason, then you know it is a *jok*." The most important ritual of Atuot religious belief, blood sacrifice, differs in praxis and intention in accordance with whether the rite is a direct petition to God, or is mediated by one of the earthly powers. In the former situation the ideal victim is a cow, and in the latter a goat is most often the prescribed animal. Goats, like the misfortune brought by an earthly power, are conceptually hot and dangerous. The heavenly powers are "cool" for they image the genesis and sustenance of life.

Contexts of Sacrifice

In their interpretation of the uncertainties dictating life, death, well-being, and misfortune, Atuot confront existential dilemmas whose ultimate source they believe to be God. From this perspective Atuot religion can be understood as a passive response to what they speak of as "the words and deeds of the Creator" (*ruac Decau*). Moral values on the other hand are a means of constraining the prescribed responsibilities of one person to fellow members of society. Spiritual vengeance through the manipulation of earthly powers is one important means employed in the social world to redress moral wrongs. In other words, self-assertiveness rather than complacency is the norm in the secular world (see also Burton, 1978). One friend, an individual who was widely recognized for his curing powers, suggested that the powers of the earth were like "the policemen of God" as a means of explaining that if a man or woman is morally in the right, God will condont the use of an earthly power to recompense the fault (compare Evans-Pritchard, 1956; Lienhardt, 1961). Collective sacrifices of cattle are made to God in order to ask for life. Individual sacrifices of goats are intended to result in misfortune or death.

These observations can be evaluated by comparing different types of sacrifice. Due to the obvious limitation of space, the following accounts have been greatly abbreviated.

The first sacrifice described was performed in a village called Burtiit in the Luac section of Atuotland. The family concerned had recently bought a cow from the Ceic Dinka, who were said to be dissatisfied with the price received. As a result, those involved interpreted this to mean that the Ceic had sent a power (later diagnosed as *mangok*) "on the back of the cow." The power had "caught" a woman of about fifty and caused her to suffer severe stomach cramps. She had been lying in bed for the past five days unable to move or eat. A *tiet* was consulted and told the family that the power on the back of the cow was demanding the sacrifice of a goat. When the *tiet*, named Ijuong, saw the power, he knew it was *mangok* "because it had blood streaming down its face." Preparations for the sacrifice had begun three days earlier, and I had attended the seances late at night, when close relatives of the woman had made *bull jao*, "a dance for the power" in order that the *jok* would be entertained and cajoled out of the woman's body. On this, the fourth evening of the ceremony, I arrived while Ijuong was walking by himself around the homestead singing, in the process pouring small libations of water at the edge of the yard, into the fire, and across the doorway of the hut. Ijuong later told me he had done this so that his own power, *mathiang gook*, would enter his body and speak, giving him strength to perform the exorcism. Of the seven songs he sang, two are offered here.

I.
It is the powers that always burn people
It is the powers that turn their heads around
A man who is greedy —
A man who overlooks me —
I will agree to the fight

I will cut the throat of the chief [i.e., if there is a power that ignores the presence of the *tiet* his own power will overcome it. Greed and self-assertiveness figure here as the reason a power has come.]
So the people will fear for their lives

II.
I went off into the grass
I do not want the confusion of the words [i.e., he intends to put an end to the anger between people caused by "the confusion of their words."]
The words of the ants are confused
I wonder along in the grass of Jel [At this point Ijuong readies himself for his work. He has called his *jok* to "wake up" inside him.]

After a short while about twenty people had gathered around the fire outside the woman's hut, who was then carried from her bed and laid on the ground with her head resting on her sister's lap. As Ijuong sang he often spit onto his rattle and smeared the saliva across her neck and chest. About an hour after he had first begun to sing, the people gathered sang the choruses of songs he introduced. One song leads almost immediately into the next, accompanied by a steady clapping rhythm.

I.
The prostitute is causing the troubles [insulting the power]
The mother of Acinbaai sits with her legs open
Their daughter has a rotten vagina
The whore stumbles through the forest
Like a dog looking for a husband [i.e. a bitch in heat]

II.
Acol is the father of my power
The people have gathered before me
Mayom said the shafts of the spears have been broken
Mayen [an ox-color] do not break the shafts
The spears we use to fight in the pastures
So it becomes ours forever
I am troubled with the lives of people
You, my father, son of Nyong
Help with the lives

III.
Abuk, my mother, I am left like an orphan
I carry the hatred of others [In Nilotic mythology Abuk is often said to be the first woman. The *tiet* sings that he is left like an or-

phan implying that it is his task to look after his own life, in this
case, the life of the sick woman.]
I am a man left out —
My head spins around with life
The head of a man moves like branches in the wind
Abuk, you come with the lives

IV.
My grandfathers, you help the land
A spirit has fallen in the evening
Where did the spirit fall
It has fallen into these lives
You children of Abuk, you help yourselves
We are going to argue [bargain with the power]
The people of long ago fought for this land
I am hated by all the people
My stomach turns inside
Go and bring life into the hut
This is a cow [a goat] for blood [to bring life]
I pray to God like a monkey
I am troubled with the things of the ants
I do not want the annoyance of people
The bad things that come to God's ants

Ijuong now spent more time close to the woman, shaking the rattle in time with the singing and pausing to massage her body with it,
giving special attention to her neck and lower back. In retrospect,
these acts seemed oriented toward a later stage in the sacrifice when
he sucked at the same places to draw away the "badness" of the illness. Followed by four older men, Ijuong led a goat around the perimeter of the homestead three times, and as they walked, the men sang
the choruses to these songs.

I.
I am praying for the lives of everyone
I pray for the lives of people
I pray for the lives of Atuot
I pray for the lives of Nuer
I pray for the lives of Rek [a Dinka section]
I pray for the lives of Agar [another Dinka section]

II.
If there is no one here,
If the owner of the hut is away
The words of the *tiet* are away

The words of a great man are absent
There is no need for lives
Who is to do it if I do not come?
No man can come in my place
My father, my God
Give me strength in my heart
Strength to take away the hatreds
Make mine a strong heart for the work
My mother Abuk, wash my heart
To take away the hatreds of these people

III.
Separate and untie the hatred of witches
I am overcome by a great thing
I hear the word of a power and I come
Disperse these hatreds of people
My father *awumkuai*, make the thunder again
Scatter the hatred of witches
I find a man helpless in his life
This is a man known to everyone
This is a man struck down

Unless there is a large enough gathering to sing the songs of the powers Atuot expect that little can be done to heal the afflicted person. Indeed, it is a fundamental social obligation to demonstrate one's concern for a kinsman by being present in such a situation, since failure to participate may lead others to suggest one is guilty of witchcraft (*apeth*) or simply longing for the things that properly belong to someone else. In this, the curing ceremony is not just the work of the *tiet* but is a collective enterprise among a circumscribed group of kin.

Soon after these songs were finished Ijuong sat close to the woman and began to shake violently, a sign that he was in communication with "powers." Possession would not be an entirely accurate description, for his *jok* is within him at all times. Instead the power now became an active agent within him while he served as a mouthpiece for the power thought to be inside the woman. He rose quickly and called for a chicken to be brought from inside the hut. Ijuong then stopped shaking as suddenly as he had begun to and stood above the woman so that her outstretched legs lay on the ground beneath his. He held the chicken in his right hand, spat on it a number of times "to invoke his *jok* onto it" and then drew it around the woman's head and body whispering "you God, see the life given to you. Take the cow for the woman." The same act was repeated for the woman's two sisters, her husband, and small child. The chicken was then set on the ground, and oddly enough, sat without moving in front of her. The next moment the singing resumed. The woman's younger sister shrieked and began rising up and down on her knees in double time to the rhythm of singing and clapping. With each movement she emitted a deep, guttural growling sound, which when I first heard it, I thought to be a dog. In the meanwhile Ijuong had stood up and began running back and forth between the woman and the edge of the homestead, carrying his rattle and a spear in his right hand. This continued for about fifteen minutes at which point the sister stood up, and as though solidly hit on the back with a heavy club, screeched once more and fell limp to the ground. Ijuong began hopping and dancing on one foot nearly on top of the woman, and then back to the tethered goat. The violence of his movements in such close quarters made the presence of his *jok* seem all the more obvious. He later told me that his power animated his movements in order to force *mangok* to leave the woman. He said also that the reason why the other woman had become possessed was because his power "was speaking so quickly it had to seek another person to speak through as well." It was a moment, he said, "when there were so many powers rushing in."

Ijuong sat momentarily to regain his calm and then began slowly undressing, at the same time crawling toward the woman on his hands and knees, quite like an animal stalking prey. Just as he was about to touch her, he began shaking once more and dipped his head to bring his head against the woman's stomach. He then lunged toward her chest and began to "suck out the power" while she was held secure by her family. Then Ijuong jumped to his feet and ran off to the edge of the yard to spit out the "badness." This was repeated a number of times, concentrating in turn on her lower back, shoulders and neck. The woman's sister shouted loudly that the song must be sung louder to draw out the *jok*, and in the middle of her remonstration, Ijuong recoiled from her body and screamed as he shook violently, then, suddenly, became rigid and corpselike, falling on top of the woman. Two men rose to carry him to the edge of the homtstead and returned to the woman's side without the *tiet*.

Ijuong later told me something others had emphasized before: when the *jok* comes out of the person and enters the *tiet* it burns like fire. About ten minutes later he returned to the gathering, and the singing ceased for the first time in more than two hours. He placed his mouth quite delicately against the woman's neck and taking a hold of his rattle once more, rubbed this against her body in the same places where he had sucked at before. Following this, the goat was untethered and led to where the woman lay prostrate. Its head was brought up against hers while Ijuong drew his left hand across her head from the back toward the forehead, and then onto the head and back of the goat. This was done in order to "put the power on the back of the goat." Looking rather exhausted (more than five hours had passed since the first songs were sung) Ijuong turned toward the people around the fire and said, "the work of exorcism is finished, the badness has gone" (*teet e ce thu, tuiny ce wei*). The goat was then held to the ground, its throat severed by Ijuong and its flesh butchered. The blood was collected in a small calabash and placed inside the hut next to the carcass in order that "*mangok* could sit on the animal and drink its blood," that is, take the life it had been given. It was now two o'clock in the morning, seven hours since the last series of ritual in the exorcism had begun. The immolation of the animal appeared to me to be rather anticlimactic in relation to the rest of the evening's activities (see also Lienhardt, 1961:236; Evans-Pritchard, 1956:215).

Early the next morning a mince was prepared from the internal organs, those which Atuot speak of as carrying on the life of human beings and animals. About half the mixture was placed above the doorway of the woman's hut and the remainder placed next to the fire to be consumed later. I was told that on occasion, when she later resumed her normal routine of preparing food, she would place small bits of food above the door "for *mangok* to eat and so it could see that the family was respecting it." Toward mid-morning Ijuong severed the head from the chicken by the doorway of the hut. Instead of running about the yard aimlessly, the typical and expected behavior of a fowl in this condition, it hobbled directly toward the stake where the goat had been tethered and sacrificed the night before, and fell dead upon it. Understandably, this was interpreted as further evidence that the exorcism had been successful. Later in the day the woman shared the mince of internal organs with her husband and sister. For his work in making *teet* Ijuong was given two Sudanese pounds (about U.S. $4.00), the hide of the goat, one hip, and a leg. The remaining flesh (except for the heart and lungs which were pilfered by my dog) was prepared for people who happened to be around the homestead. About

a month later a forked-branch shrine (*jath jao*; lit. "tree of the *jok*")
was erected on the west side of the hut so that *mangok* would remain
within the homestead to protect them.

Ijuong commented on the sacrifice saying "this is the way it always
is with *jok*. The *jok* comes to claim its property. The *tiet* sees the
reason it comes. If a cow is stolen, the *tiet* sees the *jok* keeping the
cow. The power says 'this is mine, I am coming for this and that.' "

The second sacrifice I want briefly to describe took place in a
cattle camp called Wunarok, where I had been living for a number
of days. Early one morning fifteen cows were collected from the fifteen
hundred or so in the camp and tethered together outside the thorn
and scrub brush fence around the camp. One white cow was tethered
alone to the west of the other animals and on the ground by its side
a bundle of green leaves had been set afire, producing whisps of ashen
smoke. These cows were described to be *nake Nhial*, suffering through
an act of God. The general complaint seemed to be that they were
listless and had not been producing much milk. As I approached the
gathering a senior man, who later officiated at the sacrifice, was walking among the cows, aspersing their backs with milk by dipping a
handful of the grass called *mayar* into a calabash and then onto the
animals. A white ram had been brought from the camp and tethered
next to the single cow. A procession of seven younger men followed in
back of the older man as he led the ram around the perimeter of the
cattle three times, singing what Atuot call *dit Nhial*, songs of God or
hymns. After this, the ram was retethered beside the cow. The invocations made over its back, punctuated in this case with burnt cow
dung ash, included the petition, "God, you see this sickness and take
it away. There is no reason for this sickness of cattle."[8]

A number of other songs were sung while the ram was lifted by
its legs by the elder man, who pressed the back of the animal as it was
held upside down against the back of the white cow. This act was
repeated three times and then the ram was held aloft "for God to see."
Following this, the ram was held in the air above the man's head as he
stood facing the east and the light of early morning. Then the ram
was held to the ground on its back between the cattle peg and the
cow, while the older man slit its throat, drawing his spear through the
abdomen and ending at the hip joint. A calabash was placed under its
neck to collect the flowing blood. The carcass was then severed completely in two, resulting in "left" and "right" halves. The former was

carried off into the bush for it was this half that had absorbed the badness of the disease, while the right half was later cooked and eaten. The heart and lungs had been cut out of the chest cavity and placed on the ground next to the calabash filled with blood. The elder man then took the same bundle of *mayar* grass to asperse the backs of the cattle with the blood of the sacrificial ram. Symbolically, the life of the ram as contained in its blood was transferred to the sickly animals. Lastly, the same act was performed over the back of the single cow while he looked aloft and said, "You God, you see this cow and let the camp remain with sleep (i.e., not be troubled by illness or dissease). This life is yours and it is yours to bring or take away."

It has been noted that goats and earthly powers are alike in that they are conceptually hot, while *ring*, a heavenly power with the strongest association with corporeal existence and divinity, is conceptually cool. Atuot say that in their sacrifices "God (and equally often *ring*) wants a sheep, but *jok* always wants the flesh of goats." The Atuot phrase *amel Decau* readily translates as "lamb of God," as this sacrifice demonstrates. Further, sheep, like the power *ring*, are "slow but determined."

These cattle were kept secluded from the rest of the herd while grazing that day, but were retethered inside the camp when they returned in the evening.

Summary Comments

Communication with a heavenly power involves sacrifices with a collective intent, for the powers that are addressed affect the lives of all people. In this, sacrifice is its own end since it assumes a moral unity (see Lienhardt, 1961:251). Atuot assert unequivocally that if a person is struck down by lightning or if there is drought or excessive flooding it has been God's doing. If a person falls ill and later dies from what we call amoebic dysentery, and what they associate with an earthly power, they seek out the human source that sent a *jok*.

I admit most honestly that this may be a deficiency in my own data, even though I attended many ceremonies involving exorcism of earthly powers, but in all the cases which I observed or otherwise learned of, the victim "caught" by the power was a woman or a young child. However, I believe this is an accurate account since Atuot say that "powers come into the village. It is only God that comes to the cattle camp." The same phrase was repeated when I asked if it was a *jok* that had caused the cattle to suffer ill health. One of the texts states that people are "blind" to the powers. In the village setting one cannot "see the ways of others" since people live separately and privately. Earthly powers are thought to be active at night, when it is often most difficult to see beyond the dim illumination of the homestead fire. As indicated, the villages themselves are located in forested areas, where the roots and tubers for medicines are also found. The common theme in stories which account for the origin of different powers is that they were come upon "in the forest," a notion with two distinct but related components. The forest symbolizes separation from human beings generally, and more specifically, separation from one's own kin, those one depends upon in the course of daily life. That is, the forest is the home of earthly powers, a world hidden from people. *Tiit* find powers in the forest because they can see them. This notion is expressed most clearly in song:

> The bitter medicine that kills a man
> Where was the medicine found
> It is amidst the grass
> I brought the power to help the lives of people
> *Mathiang gook* has spoiled the land of Nuer
> *Mathiang gook* has spoiled the land of Jaang [Dinka]
> The strong power of Jur
> I dig up the medicine of the power
> I work for the power until I am exhausted
> I brought the power from Atim Akuei
> And I slept away with it.

The last line suggests remaining away in the forest to learn the ways of the power. The image of blindness also involves the notion that in the hours of darkness, the earthly powers attack their victims, causing people to "remain without sleep." Concurrently, people are said to be prone to such maladies at night. As a result, sacrifices for earthly powers are performed at night when these are thought to be most active, and hence, liable to human control. Sacrifices in which God is directly petitioned are normally performed in the early hours of morning, a time when the light of a new day symbolizes the creative and life-giving attributes of God. In the same manner of thinking, Atuot say that human beings die during the daytime, while witches die at night.

Nearly every homestead has on its west side some distance from the doorway of the hut a forked-branch shrine which is thought of as the home of the earthly power which the family owns. Atuot consider it essential to own one or a number of powers in order to protect themselves from the potential evil intentions of others, or for directing their own toward the same end. As I suggested, those most endangered are women and children, whose social and economic roles are symbolized by the homestead. Sitting one afternoon in a cattle camp I asked a friend why there were no shrines there.

> There are no shrines of *jok* in the camp like those in the village. The powers do not come to the camp. Here, it is only God. A peg is made like all the other pegs for tethering cows and it is driven into the ground. This is a cow that God has chosen and that peg is used to tether the cow. When another cow first gives milk we make clarified butter and put it on the head of the cow to give it to God.

That is, the animal thus dedicated becomes a "cow of God."[9]

If one definition of religion was to equate its ideas and rituals with an "ideology of community" (see, e.g., Wilson, 1973) this would be most evident among the Atuot in the setting of the cattle camp. The measure of control which men can assert over experience by religious action is closely associated with the strongly corporate nature of existence in the cattle camp. In a very different manner, earthly powers are used in evidence of independence and self-help. Writing generally on the topic of primitive religion, Lienhardt suggests, "The relative lack of centralized coercive secular power in primitive cultures leaves to the gods the important sanctions for correct behavior . . . When the relations between kin form the fabric of local community this idea of the retributive justice of the gods is a powerful sanction for approved behavior," an observation which is fully in accord with the data discussed in this paper (1974:1042). From another perspective one could state that one difference in religious experience between villages and cattle camps is based on the degree of individual as opposed to collective participation and intent, a point analogous to that which Mauss (1972) posited between magical and religious ritual. These vary not so much in structure or purpose as in "the circumstances in which these rites occur" (24). A woman offered an illustration of the difference between powers of the above and earthly powers by reference to a checkered tablecloth in my hut. As she pointed to the individual squares of color she said "these are like the many powers, and they are scattered among the people. The piece of cloth is like the heavenly powers of God because it covers everything."

It still remains to offer an interpretation of why women and children are most subject to vengeful retribution, though I am unable to give any single, satisfactory rationale. But I presume that this is in some way a reflection of other social institutions. Evans-Pritchard writes that "the curses of an unrelated man can do you no harm" (1937:108). In theory, were it possible to live with no social contact whatsoever, the occasion for vengeance would never arise. One of the primary means by which Atuot society exists through time is in the exchange of women between different patrilineal groups in marriage. Temporary barrenness is often ascribed to a condition dependent upon the power of God to give and take away life. Yet at the more immediate level of face to face relationships, spiritual vengeance which may result in barrenness is commonly viewed as a consequence of neglecting to make good one's promises in transferring a number of bridewealth cattle. In this situation a moral sin is redressed and sanctioned by religious ideology. The earthly powers, as was noted, become the "policemen of God." The woman who was taken as a bride is made to suffer from her own maternal kin, in their effort to seek retribution from the family that did not complete the bridewealth.

Stated differently, women are where the cattle are not: by agreeing to a marriage it is implicit that an equivalence of exchange has been reached. Lienhardt similarly observes for the Dinka, "when two families have a marriage between them, each has provided the means for the continuation of the other" (1961:129). On her part, the bride is expected to bear many healthy children, and should she fail in this task or leave her husband, spiritual vengeance once again offers a sanctioned recourse. This offers a further reason why I prefer to characterize earthly powers as "active agents." Diviners function in a sense as ad hoc rural sociologists, for if in the course of ritual they find little wrong in the affairs involving kin and affines, the source of suffering will more likely be attributed to the will of God rather than the ill will of another human being. Hence, little benefit could be expected from directing a *jok* against an individual outside one's social world since there exists no basis upon which a breach of moral expectations could be ascertained. A man with the power *ring* is embued with the ability to curse an unknown enemy as well as promote life, for like the power of God, this spirit transcends the narrow confines of domestic relationships. Cattle are instead "wandering shrines" of heavenly powers, while earthly powers are tethered to the shrines of their owners in village homesteads.[10]

Sacrifices petitioned to God are made in response to "the things of God" which Atuot recognize to be beyond their control. This is what I intend to be understood in characterizing the greater powers as passive agents. As the origin myth suggests, the earthly powers long ago went off to live scattered among people in different families and homesteads. Through the institution of marriage women effectively do the same. Atuot cosmology relates women with the village setting and the sacrifice of goats. Atuot religion can in this way be understood as "this-worldly" in orientation with regard to the active agents of earthly powers. At a different level, apparent especially in cattle camps, religious orientation is decidedly "other-worldly" as it involves powers which enter into the welfare of human beings quite apart from their own choice.

In conclusion it is observed that a fundamental member of the polythetic class "Atuot religion" is blood sacrifice, which differs according to intent and purpose in villages and cattle camps.[11] Both forms are basic, common, and essential aspects of Atuot belief, for to neglect a discussion of one, would result in the misrepresentation of the other.

NOTES

An abbreviated draft of this essay was read for a colloquium in the Department of Sociology and Anthropology at the University of New Hampshire, Durham. I am grateful to the members of that department for the opportunity to air some of these ideas as well as for their suggestions regarding the data and its interpretation.

1. Polythetic classification in one sense approximates the Oxford English Dictionary definition of "idiom," being "a peculiarity of phraseology . . . having meaning not deducible from those of the separate words" and "a characteristic mode of expression." In pastoral Nilotic cosmology one analogic mode classifies cows and cucumbers as members of a class "things to be sacrificed." Each can be a transmutation of the other. Regardless of

the victim—a sheep, goat, chicken, bull, or lump of tobacco—the situation of sacrifice defines it as "cow."

2. In another sense one might characterize Lienhardt's study as a philosophical exposition on the Dinka concept of "experiencing self."

3. The Atuot are a group of Nilotic-speaking pastoralists estimated to number 35,000, living in eastern Lakes Province of the Southern Sudan. Called Atuot by their Nuer and Dinka neighbors, their own term for self-reference is *Reel*, the founding ancestor of these peoples. Field research in Atuotland (October 1976 to November 1977) was made possible through grants provided by the Social Science Research Council and the Wenner-Gren Foundation for Anthropological Research, whose assistance is gratefully acknowledged. To date, published sources on the Atuot are limited to Burton, 1977, 1978A, 1978B, 1978C.

4. I should like to stress the fact that I do not intend to deny or question the brilliance of his work on the Nuer. Evans-Pritchard's account of Nuer religion simply is more structurally oriented and hence would not necessarily include the type of data which I have selected for discussion here. Indeed, as Lienhardt (1974) asks, who else could have done all he was able to under the circumstances. Compare Crazzolara (1953:215–20) who suggests that nearly every Nuer homestead possesses a "spirit of the below."

5. The Atuot word *kulang* denotes an important "power of the above," as mentioned below. This congruence of terminology between Atuot and Nuer suggests a number of ethnological problems, which are discussed in part elsewhere (Burton, n.d.A.).

6. As in the Nuer and Dinka languages, the Atuot term *thek* is polysemic, connoting among other things, a man's ox, "taboo," avoidance, and "totem" (see Burton, n.d.B).

7. At one level of analysis it could be demonstrated how Atuot cosmology involves the familiar binary mode of moral and symbolic classification, while clearly, "religious experience" is considerably and consistently more complex.

8. Compare Almagor, "Dassanetch say that a man does not grow grass for his own but that God provides it for all cattle" (1978:50).

9. Lienhardt phrases this relationship for the Dinka more elegantly than I am able. "Dedicated beasts are intended only for future sacrifice to the divinities to which they are dedicated. It is so strongly believed that to part with such dedicated animals will bring sickness and misfortune that it is not considered equitable for a creditor to seize a dedicated beast from his debtor, no matter how pressing his needs. He would be held responsible for subsequent sickness or death in the debtor's family if he did so, and public opinion would certainly be against him" (1961:133).

10. Faron records for the Mapuche a notion similar to that which characterizes this distinction in Atuot religion. "While it is to *nenechen* that final appeal is made, for only he is able to control minor gods, the closest ties between men and the supernatural exist between the Mapuche and the regional gods and godesses" (1964:53). In Atuot one would simply replace the last phrase with "powers of the earth."

11. Sacrifice involves the exchange of animate life for human well-being. All sacrifices have of course also their social implications, among these, the meting of the animal's flesh. Evans-Pritchard writes, "though

men [one feels constrained to add *women* as well] eat the carcass, and
any man may partake of the flesh, their eating of it, however important socially this festival side of sacrifice may be, it is not a sacramental meal,
but an ordinary commensal act of family and kin, which, moreover, falls
outside the sacrificial rites" (1956:274). Certainly this is true for the Atuot
as well.

BIBLIOGRAPHY

Almagor, U. 1978. *Pastoral Partners: Affinity and Bond Partnership among
the Dassenetch of Southwest Ethiopia.* Manchester: Manchester University Press.
Baxter, P. T. W. 1972. "Absence Makes the Heart Grow Fonder: Some
Suggestions Why Witchcraft Accusations are Rare among East African Pastoralists." In *The Allocation of Responsibility,* edited by M.
Gluckman. Manchester: Manchester University Press.
Burton, J. W. 1977. "The Peoples Called Atuot." *Sudan Now* 12:42–44.
———. 1978A. "Living with the Dead: Aspects of the Afterlife in Nuer
and Dinka Cosmology." *Anthropos* 73:141–60.
———. 1978B. "Ghost Marriage and the Cattle Trade among the Atuot of
the Southern Sudan." *Africa* 48:398–405.
———. 1978C. "Ghosts, Ancestors and Individuals among the Atuot of
Southern Sudan." *Man* 13:600–17.
———. 1978. "God's Ants: A Study of Atuot Religion." Ph.D. dissertation,
S.U.N.Y. at Stony Brook.
———. n.d.A. "The Wave is My Mother's Husband: A Picatorial Theme
in Pastoral Nilotic Ethnology." Unpublished.
———. n.d.B. "Atuot Totemism." *Journal of Religion in Africa,* forthcom-
ing.
Buxton, J. 1973. *Religion and Healing in Mandari.* Oxford: Clarendon Press.
Crazzolara, J. P. 1953. *Zur Gesellschaft und Religion der Nuer.* Wien:
Studia Institut Anthropos.
Deng, F. M. 1972. *The Dinka of the Sudan.* New York: Holt, Rinehart and
Winston.
———. 1973. *The Dinka and Their Songs.* Oxford: Clarendon Press.
Douglas, M. 1978. *Cultural Bias.* London: Royal Anthropological Institute.
Evans-Pritchard, E. E. 1937. *Witchcraft, Oracles and Magic among the
Azande.* Oxford: Clarendon Press.
———. 1956. *Nuer Religion.* Oxford: Clarendon Press.
Faron, L. C. 1964. *Hawks of the Sun: Mapuche Morality and its Ritual
Attributes.* Pittsburgh: University of Pittsburgh Press.
Granet, M. 1922. (1975). *The Religion of the Chinese People.* Translated
by M. Freedman. Oxford: Basil Blackwell.
Howell, P. P. 1953. "Some Observations on 'Earthly Spirits' among the
Nuer." *Man* 60:85–88.
Lienhardt, R. G. 1951. "Some Notions of Witchcraft among the Dinka."
Africa 21:303–18.

————. 1961. *Divinity and Experience: The Religion of the Dinka*. Oxford: Clarendon Press.

————. 1963. "Dinka Representations of the Relations Between the Sexes." In *Studies in Kinship and Marriage*, edited by I. Shapera. London: R.A.I.

————. 1970. "The Situation of Death: An Aspect of Anuak Philosophy." In *Witchcraft Confessions and Accusations*, edited by M. Douglas. London: Tavistock.

————. 1974. "Primitive Religion." *Encyclopedia Britannica*. Vol. 14:1040–47. Chicago: Encyclopedia Britannica.

————. 1974A. "E-P: A Personal View." *Man* 9:299–305.

Mauss, M. 1906. "Essai sur les Variations Saisonnières des Societés Eskimos." *L'Année Sociologique* (1904–06):39–132.

————. 1972. *A General Theory of Magic*. Translated by R. Brain. London: Routledge and Kegan Paul.

Needham, R. 1975. "Polythetic Classification: Convergence and Consequences." *Man* n.s. 10:349–69.

————. 1978. *Essential Perplexities*. Oxford: Clarendon Press.

Santandrea, S. 1977. "Jur-Luo Texts and Comments: The Family." *Anthropos* 72:557–609.

Wilson, B. 1973. *Magic and the Millennium*. London: Heinemann.

SECTION IV. *Comparisons*

African Religions
Types and Generalizations

by Wyatt MacGaffey

In recent decades, anthropologists studying the religions of Africa in particular have developed a number of apparently technical concepts on which they seek to base generalizations and comparisons more accurate than those associated in nineteenth-century anthropology with such terms as "fetishism" and "animism." The low productivity of the enterprise can be traced to the pseudoempirical character of the new concepts: as definitions they appear to segregate distinct types of phenomena for comparison and explanation, but they are not accompanied by criteria enabling the observer to tell whether the phenomena are in fact present. To make my dissatisfaction clear I will discuss probably the best known pair of concepts, which is also important for my own argument, to be developed later.

It has become conventional in anthropology dealing with Africa to distinguish between witchcraft and sorcery. People writing new monographs feel that they have to observe this convention, even if they are writing in French, which lacks suitable words. The distinction is borrowed from the Azande, described for us by Evans-Pritchard, who think that a witch has an innate, mystical power to harm others; this power may operate without his knowledge, although the witch is able to cool his witchcraft, by a prescribed ritual, when his attention is drawn to the fact. On the other hand, a sorcerer is one who deliberately uses a quasi-technical device, external to himself. This distinction I shall call the distinction of means, mystical versus technical. It is important to the Azande because it differentiates two kinds of accusations and two likely outcomes for the accused: witches, after performing the cooling exercise, are left off, but sorcerers are punished (Evans-Pritchard, 1937).[1]

Now in fact the anthropologist is unable to ascertain, by means under his own control, that anyone is either a witch or a sorcerer. To determine the presence of the phenomenon he must observe that the concept exists, distinct from other concepts, and that it is applied as a label to some apt individual by an approved social process. If the people in question do not distinguish witchcraft from sorcery it makes no sense for the anthropologist to do so by attempting to sort into Zande categories the diverse and conflicting statements he may hear about how witches are supposed to operate.

The same kind of criticism is applicable to other contrasted terms such as spirit possession and spirit mediumship, ancestors and shades, spirit possession and soul loss.[2] None of these pairs is related to any of the available bodies of theory in social science by which we might be able to comprehend its nature and occurrence. As Augé says about "sorcery," monographs that deal with it are based on an implicit scheme taken for granted; their descriptions and analyses illustrate an absent theory. Then there emerges a contradiction between the supposed unity of the phenomenon described and the variety of functions attributed to it (Augé, 1975:85). In the many instances of beliefs that confound the anthropologist's categories it becomes necessary to invent new ones of the same ad hoc and pseudoempirical kind, a process classically described as butterfly collecting (Leach, 1961:2–3).

An alternative approach rests on the recognition that the ethnographer's primary material is social action, including verbal utterances in which are implicit on the one hand the philosophical and cosmological assumptions of the actors and, on the other, the political and economic constraints under which they act. History is the record of successive compromises between these sets of factors (Fortes, 1970).[3]

Social action is cooperative, and presupposes cues between the actors which identify the play to be performed. The decision as to which play is performed involves choice and is essentially political. For that reason, the conceptual distinction between one standardized behavior sequence, or play, and another is likely to be much clearer than the conceptual consensus about the content and meaning of any particular play or its performance. Herein lies the usefulness to the anthropologist of the disinction the Azande make between witchcraft and sorcery; it is a question of which script to follow, rather than whether X in fact did what sorcerers are supposed to do, or even whether all are agreed what it is that sorcerers do, or whether witchcraft is hereditary, and so on.

Looking again at the Azande, we find that the set that includes witch and sorcerer is incomplete without witchdoctor and magician, who are also distinguished from each other by the criterion of means. Like the witch, the witchdoctor is endowed with *mangu* or witchcraft substance, whereas sorcerer and magician rely on external devices. The difference between witch and sorcerer, on the one hand, and witchdoctor and magician, on the other, is a function of another criterion, that of legitimacy, a difference between bad and good.

The four roles in the set are thus differentiated by two intersecting criteria, the distinctions of means and legitimacy. This is the structure of the set of roles, which is a set of normative prescriptions for social action. This abstract set of relationships, of differences, is the proper object of anthropological study, rather than "witchcraft" or "sorcery" conceived as empirical realities.

The set of dealers in the occult recognized by the BaKongo of western Zaïre is entirely different. The elements of the set are listed by Buakasa, although without displaying their structure. Occult power is called *kindoki*, and four kinds are recognized, belonging to the chief, diviner, magician, and witch. The structure of the set becomes evident to the anthropologist in the discriminatory comments people make to influence his judgment, or the similar remarks that healers make in order to define themselves in the eyes of their clients. The BaKongo distinguish private from public ends, and destructive from productive effects, that is, powers of life or death. Chiefs and witches kill, diviners supposedly use their powers in the public interest, whereas witches and magicians are egotistical.[4]

It is important to note that these definitions are functions of normative judgments, not descriptions of real behavior. A diviner becomes a diviner because he is consulted as such, although his clients put the relationship the other way around. An example of the kind of verbal discrimination one encounters in the field was provided in an interview with a magician, published in the Kinshasa press in 1973. The man said, "In principle, a good healer does not kill. He should think of healing. Hence the longstanding discord between *nganga-buka*, 'sorciers guérisseurs,' and *ndoki*, 'sorciers maléfiques.'" He went on to say, "I am sometimes accused of asking excessively high prices." Most of what is known as healing in contemporary Kongo consists of little besides the claim by one wishing to be known as a healer that healing has taken place, and acceptance of that claim by others in accordance with the distinctions of ends and effects.

It follows from what has been said that BaKongo make no distinction between "witchcraft" and "sorcery." They are aware of both kinds of means as components of *kindoki*, but attach no significance to the difference. It also follows, in a formal sense, that the minimal definition of Zande "witchcraft" is "a mystical power used illegitimately," whereas the minimal definition of Kongo witchcraft is, "destructive power used for personal ends." The use of English expressions such as "witchcraft" and "magic" tends to conceal the fact that the Zande and Kongo concepts to which they are applied have nothing in common. Cross-cultural search for social and psychological correlates to these expressions is absurd, since their application has to do with English rather than African culture. In brief, there is no such thing as witchcraft, except presumably in English-speaking cultures.

It may be objected that what any two different peoples say about antisocial occultists is similar enough that we can use the word witchcraft with reasonable assurance that we will understand each other. In both instances, let us suppose, witches fly about at night, have red eyes, and appear upsidedown in photographs. The trouble is that any two phenomena can be shown to have attributes in common, if the lists of attributes are made long enough. Proceeding on the basis of haphazardly selected attributes, we group heterogeneous phenomena in the same class, and perhaps exclude others that belong there. The total description of any single element is impossible, since different informants give somewhat different accounts of it. The analogy with phonemics is obvious. Sets of religious commissions may be thought of as forms in contrasting distribution; in Kongo the common environment is the concept *mbevo*, the individual afflicted by chief and witch, healed by priest and magician.[5]

Pouillon has compared Zande, Ndembu, and North African religious role sets. In the Zande material he notes the presence of "sorcerer" and "magician" as two kinds of "technician," and that the former is also classed with the "witch" as malevolent, but he omits "witchdoctors" from his analysis on the curious ground that the Azande have little respect for them (Pouillon, 1969:88–89)! Evans-Pritchard says, however, "A clever witchdoctor is an important person," and "Magicians have no great prestige" (1937:251, 428).

The principle of comparative work, that only sets of elements can be compared and not elements in isolation, has long been accepted in kinship studies; nobody now studies the avunculate without reference to the kinship system to which mother's brother belongs. It is not generally accepted in the anthropological study of religion, although Dumézil has made it the foundation of his studies of the Indo-European triad of divinities, a role-set roughly comparable to the religious commissions of Bantu speakers (Dumézil, 1971–74; Littleton, 1966; Leach, 1961).

Types

Identification of the Kongo set of religious commissions permits various interesting departures, of which I will mention only the fact that it brings order to the other world as well, the land of the dead. Verbal labels for and descriptions of the several classes of the dead are largely interchangeable; attempts to classify the spirits according to purely verbal statements by informants lead to no clearly defined concepts. The various spiritual beings are most clearly distinguished by their roles, that is, by the activity pattern imposed on people by their perceived relationship to one or another class; so, an ancestor is an ancestor because he is addressed by his descendants. As Weber said, "[The] abstract conception becomes really secure only through the continuing activity of a 'cult' dedicated to one and the same god— through the god's connection with a continuing association of men, a community for which he has special significance as the enduring god" (Weber, 1963:10). Vansina, who is very skeptical about the notion of religious "systems," writes of the Tio:

> What then had informants in common? Basic notions as to who the sorts of spirits were and what they were responsible for in terms of situations and rituals. For the rituals were held in common, ritual action presupposed some common acceptance of the presence of other worldly spirits and they were named in it. Therefore all held this too in common. But once they went beyond this, everyone was free to believe what he wanted to. The Tio had no sacred books, no dogma, no catechism, no compulsion to believe the same things as long as they participated fully in the same rituals (Vansina, 1973A: 227).

This comment refers simultaneously to the impossibility of defining a nonliterate religion as a system of ideas, and the possibility of defining it as a system of behavior. In Kongo, as among the Tio, the four classes of the dead, corresponding to the ritual congregations of the living, are ancestors, ghosts, local or "nature" spirits, and charms. Ritual thus produces order in the domain of myth.

It is curious how often in looking for a "system of ideas," equivalent to a theology, ethnographers assume that it would take the form of a hierarchy of spirits fitted into a chain of command leading up to God. Yakö spirits, according to Forde (1964:212), fall into "conceptually independent and operationally unintegrated" categories, which he lists in a hierarchy from the Creator to the ghosts of the recently dead (compare Willis, 1968). This is of course the model of a centralized religion appropriate to a centralized state, and reminds us of the corresponding and equally sterile preoccupation of political anthropologists with centralization, the emergence of "the" state, and the like. In political studies, Forde was one who pointed out the inadequacy of the centralized-acephalous dichotomy, which does not fit the Yakö. Neither does the model of a spiritual hierarchy. It could well be that in the study of a particular religion the concept of a high god, though present, might be inessential or residual, the *least* important concept upon which to focus.

In Kongo, "God" was the paradigmatic spirit, Nzambi Mpungu, "the highest *nzambi*"; the lowest was, in appropriate context, any living person. The intervening hierarchy of spiritual entities of increasingly general, that is, decreasingly particularistic significance, varied in time and place with the degree of social hierarchization among the living. When political and economic conditions did not permit the evolution of a hierarchy of increasingly more inclusive ritual congregations, the hierarchy of spirits of which BaKongo were conscious was correspondingly impoverished.

The perception of structures of difference provides us with endogenous categories in which to discuss historical change and variation within and between particular societies. For example, a Kongo elder, referring to modern rather than nineteenth-century holders of occult power, lists them differently from Buakasa, since his list substitutes Christian prophets for diviners.[6] The common normative function of diviners and prophets as healers in the public interest provides a formal framework in which to evaluate the important differences between them. This approach to religious change can be taken back in Kongo history to the sixteenth century.

For synchronic comparison, an example of a similar structure is provided by the Bolia group of western Mongo in Zaïre, who recognize four types of living agents of the power called *iloki*, obtained from spirits through the mediation of ancestors. These agents are the political chief, the earth chief, the witch, and the magician. The cultural content of the set is very similar to Kongo, as is Bolia social structure (Van Everbroeck, 1961). Much further afield, among the Tonga of Zambia, described by Colson (1962), the cultural similarities are not quite so marked, but the role set is the same. From Colson's work we also learn the important lesson that the terms used for rainmaker, for example, are not constant from one part of the country to another. Linguistic analysis, that is to say, is no substitute for sociological analysis. Colson also shows how in recent times the functions of local priest have been partly taken over by prophets, whose local affiliations are less marked, although they too, like the priests, speak for communal spirits called *basangu*. In other words, the persistence of the category and function does not mean that the cultic content is fixed. I make this remark to refute the mistaken criticism that structures and history are somehow incompatible.

Tonga "local," "rain," or "earth" shrines are associated with spirits called *basangu*, originating from first settlers and believed to have power only in their own localities. Prophets were not so confined, though they too spoke for and were possessed by *basangu*, and were themselves called *basangu* and sometimes "lords of the rain." Tonga identify *basangu* with the *mhondoro* spirits of the MaShona, but in some areas *basangu* means "evil spirits" (Colson, 1977; 1962:216 note). *Basangu,* as rain spirits, "cannot be invoked as agents of individual ends. [They] concern themselves only about public matters" (1977: 124).

Tonga elders are thought to owe their survival to protective witchcraft, and are described as *basikulowanyina*, "those who bewitch one another." Colson translates *mulozi* as "sorcerer," because a *mulozi* used medicines and therefore seems closer to Zande "sorcerer" than Zande "witch." "The line between having powerful medicines for protection and using these medicines against others is believed to be exceedingly thin." Divination performed by *munganga* is "a private consultation on behalf of an individual," whereas witchfinding is a public service for which the client is the community (see also Colson, 1966). *Basangu* are supposed to be different from *mizimu*, "ancestors," but the essential difference lies in cult practice: those of the dead who might be *basangu* in another context are "ancestors" when they are addressed by kin groups (1962:92–93).

The religious roles do not include modern "chiefs," who are government appointees. The complete set is:

	Public	*Private*
Death	elders	"sorcerer"
	(*basikulomanyina*)	(*mulozi*)
Life	a. rain priest	herbalist-diviner
	(*musangu*)	(*munganga*)
	b. prophet	
	c. witchfinder	
	(*usondo*)	

On the basis of specified criteria, I have grouped the religions of the Kongo, Bolia, and Tonga as exhibiting the same structure. Another and radically different structure characterizes the religion of the Yakö of southeastern Nigeria. When Forde wrote of the "supernatural economy" of the Yakö, he referred to the choices available in a limited inventory:

> In the formulation and the selection of ritual action, the Yakö of Umor appear to be guided less by a sense of the logical implication of particular dogmas or of need to establish intellectually coherent relations among them, and more by the opportunities that they severally afford to allocate among specific supernatural agencies means for the achievement of particular ends of groups and persons. In other words: the various supernatural entities which have come to be established as objects of Yakö thought and ritual action are handled as a series of alternative and complementary, but at the same time largely dissociable, means for obtaining material and social benefits and for averting threats to these. Thus ritual activities seen as a whole take on something of the character of an economic system (1964:213).

The choices available include one between "witch" and "sorcerer" founded on a distinction of means like that employed by the Azande.

As is often the case, however, it is necessary to distinguish between available roles and those that are in fact filled in the course of social action. Though the Yakö believe that sorcerers exist, and react to certain deaths in terms of the belief, no one is accused of sorcery, so in fact the role is vacant. As a matter of social practice, the religious activities of the Yakö center on matriclan shrines and diviners, both associated with life-giving powers, and on witches and fetishes, associated with destructive powers. Sorcery is misuse of fetishes. In addition to the criterion of effects, a criterion of means is operative: witches and diviners both employ an internal, mystical capacity, whereas fetishes and shrines are external, "technical" devices.

There were two main classes of fetish objects, serving as a means of access to spiritual forces. The *ase*, owned by the matriclans, were regarded as sentient and sympathetic beings capable of conferring benefits on the matriclans and the whole village, promoting fertility, harmony, protection, and the destruction of witches and sorcerers. Thus in the *ase* "generalized productive capacities had been mystically segregated," whereas *ndet* cults involved negative sanctions against any who threatened the social order (267). Adepts of the main *ndet* cults were recruited from local or patrilineal groups, but other *ndet* cults were owned by individuals. Anyone wishing to protect himself against theft could evoke an *edet* to inflict on the thief a disease it controlled. The custodians of the corporate *ndet* had to swear they would not misuse them (sorcery). "*Ndet* were not thought of as primarily beneficent for any benefit individually obtained from an *edet* was usually that of withdrawal of the disability it was believed to control. To this extent *ndet* were completely antithetical to the *ase*, which were believed to confer health, fertility, prosperity, and peace" (278).

Witchcraft was generally believed to be inherited in the matriline, but it could also be acquired, either unwittingly or as an unintended unintended effect of *edet* medicine. Diviners partook of the omniscience of Obasi (God), and could "see"; they were initiated after a possession attack into a guild whose head was associated with the *ase* priests in the council of leaders (*Yabot*). The spirit world toward which cult activity was oriented is populated by Obasi, the creator; the ghosts of the recently dead; a multitude of punitive spirits (*ndet*); and the tutelary spirits of the matriclans (*ase*).

The set of cults described by Forde can be summarized as follows:

	Mystical	*Technical*
Death	witches (*Yatana*)	fetishes (*ndet*)
		a. public
		b. private
		i. legitimate
		ii. illegitimate (sorcery)
Life	diviners (*yabunga*)	matriclan spirits (*ase*)

This system is relatively complex, as befits the greater complexity of Yakö social organization, which includes more kinds of corporation than does Kongo. It also shows, below the level of primary categorization, two additional principles articulating hierarchically rather than orthogonally with the others. One of the primary distinctions is shared with the Zande set, the other with the Kongo:

Zande: distinctions of means and legitimacy
Kongo: distinctions of ends and effects
Yakö: distinctions of means and effects

To these we may add the Nyakyusa and Safwa of Tanzania, who employ distinctions of means and ends (Harwood, 1970).

Generalizations

With respect to the systems outlined above, the most conservative view would hold that each was unique, thereby denying the possibility of analytical comparison. In a less conservative perspective, culturally and structurally similar sets such as Nyakyusa and Safwa (neighbors) or Kongo and Tonga (distant but culturally related) could be regarded as being alike. I do not view them as having "the same religion," but as having "religions of the same type" if, like the Azande of Sudan and the Kuranko of Sierra Leone, they showed structural similarity with cultural difference. In the assessment of cultural similarity, language, myth, visual symbolism, historical connection, and the like will be essential factors.

An objection to this implicit definition of "a religion" may come from those who equate a religion with an orthodoxy. Orthodoxies are only possible, however, in literate traditions, and even there, as in Christianity, for the scholar to define his subject in terms of an orthodoxy is to allow himself to be coopted by the politics of the situation he studies. The poverty of this approach has long been evident in work that seeks to distinguish "true" from "syncretic" examples of Christianity or Islam in Africa.

Classification permits systematic rather than random comparison. If we can identify, shall we say, the Bolia and the Tonga as having the same religion, their beliefs and practices are rescued from the vast, mysterious bin of so-called primitive religion, and we can begin to discuss their origins and compare the development of local trends. Since the Kongo set or type contrasts sharply with others such as the Yakö or Azande, yet is found through most of Bantu-speaking Africa, it is presumably not a simple response to local social, political, or economic factors nor a product of any short-term history. Since the Nyakyusa are also Bantu-speaking, the set is not merely a product of language; indeed we have already noticed that linguistic analysis alone is not a good guide to conceptual systems. The Kongo or Bantu set also occurs in the lower Ivory Coast and may be general in the forest zone of West Africa.[7]

In the sets mentioned in this paper, the distinction of means (technical/mystical), effects (death/life), ends (public/private) and legitimacy (good/bad) are distributed as follows (other variables may appear in other sets):

Distinction	Means	Effects	Ends	Legitimacy
1. Kongo		+	+	
Bolia		+	+	
Tonga		+	+	
Alladian		+	+	
2. Zande	+			+
Lugbara	+			+
Kuranko	+			+
3. Nyakyusa	+		+	
Safwa	+		+	
4. Yakö	+	+		

Besides the comparison of whole sets, a still less conservative position would assume the cross-cultural identity of constituent variables, such as the distinction of means, and seek sociological or other correlates. This relatively rash undertaking has in fact been standard procedure among anthropologists who have seen no difficulty in the assumption that the distinction of means is "the same" wherever it is encountered, even to the point of identifying it among peoples who themselves do not recognize it. Middleton and Winter find that "most . . . reports of African societies mention beliefs in both witchcraft and sorcery" (1963:8), but this generalization is highly unreliable. When Gray says, for example, "The Wambugwe distinguish linguistically between 'witchcraft' and 'sorcery,'" he really means that they distinguish between *osave* and *wanga* in much the same way that the Ba-Kongo distinguish between *kindoki* and *kinganga*, and not "witchcraft" and "sorcery" as defined by the editors of the collection to which he is contributing (Middleton and Winter, 1963:143).

Exploring the sociological conditions of the distinction of means, Middleton and Winter have suggested that congruence exists between the use of witchcraft beliefs and ascriptive social relationships, on the one hand, and on the other, between achieved or voluntary relationships and reliance on sorcery beliefs for accusations. Since not only wrongdoers but, among the Azande, witchdoctors and magicians are distinguished by the means they supposedly employ, the question becomes a broader one, but with some adjustment the hypothesis holds. The distinction of means is really a question of claimed or disclaimed responsibility. The witch is allowed to disclaim responsibility by cooling his witchcraft, which takes the blame, so to speak. The witchdoctor, on the other hand, seeks in the name of his *mangu* an authority that the society does not routinely allot to him. The sorcerer, according to the theory of technical means, is not allowed to disclaim responsibility. Magic, on the other hand, is a special power claimed as of right by the occupants of ascribed, categorical statuses: "Owners of medicines are usually old or middle-aged men. . . . Youths, like women, ought not to practice magic, which is the privilege and concern of their elders." Nevertheless, youths acquire medicines for youthful pursuits, and women for feminine pursuits (Evans-Pritchard, 1937:428). Access to oracles, and the relative authority of oracles, follows the same hierarchy. In other words, approved technical means characterize and are intended to maintain ascribed status distinctions;

disapproved "mystical" (intrinsic) means characterize the misuse of these same social responsibilities. Approved mystical means characterize certain marginal "achieved" statuses; sorcery accusations are a way to pin inescapable blame on similarly nonincorporated figures.

The Zande functions, arranged in accordance with normative conceptions, are:

Legitimacy		*Good*	*Bad*
means:	Technical	magic, oracles	sorcerers
	Mystical	witchdoctor	witch

Arranged in accordance with "responsibility claims":

responsibility:		Praise	Blame
status:	Achieved	witchdoctor	sorcery
	Ascribed	magic oracles	witchcraft

This analysis also works for the Safwa (Harwood, 1970), the Kuranko (Jackson, 1975), the Yakö, and the Lugbara. For the Kuranko of Sierra Leone (no cultural continuity with any other society mentioned here), Jackson says "Turner challenges the analytical usefulness of the Zande distinction but for Kuranko society the distinction is apposite and the native terminology supports it" (407, note 7). Witches are supposed to possess *suwa'ye*, "witchcraft," as are the masters of witch-finding cults. Medicines (*besekoli*), quite different from witchcraft, are private or collective. The set of functions is:

		Good	*Bad*
means:	Technical	medicines a. collective b. private	sorcery
	Mystical	witchfinder	witch

Witch and witchfinder have it in common that they are associated with "wild" or intrusive bush spirits and animals. Medicines, on the other hand, especially the men's medical associations, are explicitly devoted to maintaining male prerogatives against women: "The Master of the Kome cult said, 'The work of the cults is to maintain the distance between men and women' " (Jackson, 1977:220). Jackson says, "The exclusiveness of the cults confirms the major social category distinctions" (221), and in this sense they are functionally similar to Zande oracles; both are hierarchically arranged, as a set of powers attributed to corporate categories. As with the Azande, the cult system and the secular system of chiefship are thought of as being entirely separate.

Though the hypothesis in its modified form applies satisfactorily to a certain range of data, its terms require closer examination. "Ascription" and "achievement" are value-laden expressions difficult to apply in practice. What Middleton and Winter have in mind as the principal empirical example of their generalization is the harmonic social regime, in which "unilineal kinship principles [ascriptive] are employed in the formation of local residential groups larger than the domestic household" (1963:12). In this situation, witchcraft accusations are to be expected. Sorcery accusations are to be expected in the negatively defined category of societies in which unilineal principles are not so used, and a person's rights and obligations to his neighbors result from his choosing to live with them (achievement). Thus what is at issue is the relationship between locality and descent, which in turn expresses the relationship between the spatial extension of society as a productive system and its reproduction from generation to generation. As Jackson says, with respect to the Kuranko,

> The lineal (or vertical) dimension of Kuranko social structure is a reflection of growth and change through time. . . . The complementary principles of social organization which are variously called lineage/locality, kinship/residence, ancestors/Earth, descent/territoriality, can be abstractly and heuristically polarized as a distinction between temporal and spatial modes of structuring. Descent essentially defines modes of relationship between predecessors and successors; by contrast, the sociospatial dimension can be viewed in terms of modes of relationship between consociates and contemporaries (1977:24).

Since both locality and succession are socially determined and never "given," it is necessary to look beneath these modes of structuring for the processes that maintain them, which vary with the mode of production. [8]

Religious Values and Relations of Production

According to Rey, the relation of reproduction (Jackson's "vertical dimension") is the factor that distinguishes one mode of production from another. In any mode there exists, in the system of relations of production, a dominant relation which determines the others, because it fundamentally distributes the means of production and the places in the production process. "This is both the scene and the object of the class struggle." The nature of the fundamental relation itself is determined by the nature of the separation between the particular units of production in the mode in question; in all modes of production there are mechanisms to create and maintain this separation. Separation, as of local groups, descent groups or nation states, can be abolished by conquest, but is conserved by exchange between the units, since exchange presupposes separation (Rey, 1975B:516).[9]

Within each mode, the totality of intergenerational links governing the relations between labor and material resources, including patrifiliation, matrifiliation, succession, inheritance, distinctions of class and estate, slavery and pawnship, as they occur, must be regarded as elements of the system of social reproduction, offering alternative norms and legitimations of equivalent value and urgency.[10] Where, as in the lineage mode of production, descent is the fundamental relation, it is ascriptive only to the extent that relations of production and exchange are routinely reproduced; in practice, even routine requires political activity to maintain it, and anthropologists are now aware how open genealogy is to manipulation. In chiefdoms such as occur among the Kuranko and Azande, the reproduction of local units, which include many clans of diverse origins, is a matter of patronage relations that are much more obviously political, though they also take routine, quasi-ascriptive forms expressed in terms of locality and descent."[11]

The practice of exchange between politically constituted units only becomes institutionalized, according to the further development of Rey's thesis (1975B:517), when one part of the society denies on its own account the separation between units; that is, it organizes itself as a class, whose function is to manage the fundamental, reproductive distribution of persons between the separated units. Chiefs, elders, and capitalists represent themselves as competing on behalf of their dependents, yet their exchange agreements reinforce their collective control. Rey has argued that "class conflict" exists even in unstratified societies in which, in principle, young men (cadets) eventually all become elders themselves (Rey, 1975A). More recently it has been pointed out that the category of dependents includes women, whose productive labor and reproductive capacity are the principal scarce resources in most African societies; yet women generally remain permanent cadets (Molyneux, 1977).

In sum, therefore, "in a class society" (meaning all societies known to history except some hunters and gatherers) the functions of exchange are: 1) reproduction of the elements of the work process, 2) reproduction of the separation between units, 3) reproduction of the unity of the dominant class under the appearance of division and hostility (Rey, 1975B:518). In the African societies we have been discussing, hostility has two dimensions: 1) between chiefs or elders as heads of competing groups, 2) between elders and their (male) cadets who aspire to become elders by participating autonomously in exchange (as by arranging their own marriages or those of their own dependents, or by obtaining titles and the like). The latter form of hostility presupposes the common interest of elders and cadets in the subordination of most women and all men (such as slaves) who are categorized as permanent cadets.

The ethnography of the Azande, Lugbara, and Kuranko, all of whom share what appears to be the same set of religious values, does not permit us to say whether they represent the same mode of production, although the similarities are striking and the integration of religious and political values appears to be the same. In all instances, the political control exercised by chiefs or elders is linked with the highest order of cultic procedure: princes' oracles, in the case of the Azande, which alone can sanction military decisions and the equivalent of capital accusations; for the Kuranko, the medicine associations, especially the Kome cult, which provides ritual defenses for the boundaries of chiefdoms and other local units against enemies, witches, and dangerous bush spirits; for the Lugbara, the complex of shrines and oracles through which male elders contact their ancestors. In all instances, with or without the presence of "chiefs," political and local units are conceptually fused; their populations are largely recruited by clientage in a context of warfare, land shortage, poverty, and other hardships; and the presence of a difference between "insiders" and "outsiders" is associated explicity with a distinction of means. All of these societies lack the bilateral features and alliance strategies characteristic of Bantu systems.

The economic structure of Kongo can be specified more precisely, in the language of "modes of production," since Rey developed the concept of the lineage mode of production after fieldwork among the BaKunyi, a northern Kongo group (Dupré and Rey, 1978). Production and exchange of subsistence goods were carried on in lineally heterogeneous local groups. Membership in such groups was governed by marriage, descent, and their variations, including several degrees of slavery, which limited the choice of places of residence and work open to individuals. Adult women were expected to marry and live with their husbands. Freeborn male members of a matrilineal clan lived on its land or on the land of another clan to which they were related as a result of marital alliances contracted in previous generations. For slaves, male and female, the range of possibilities was much narrower than for the freeborn. Exchanges, including marriage, between the occupants of different statuses were mediated by gifts of subsistence goods, mostly foodstuffs, in the production of which the labor of women predominated.

The ascription of free or slave status was not automatic, and the word "ascriptive," as applied to descent, can be misleading. Slavery in Kongo meant not forced labor but interrupted pedigree, brought about by such means as capture, slave trading, witchcraft accusation, or judicial award. These activities, closely linked to continental and Atlantic trade, were reserved to men. Exchanges in this sphere, including ritual fees and fines, local transfers of slaves, and access to chiefly and other title, were mediated by prestige goods, obtained in trade. This is the sphere of the "fundamental distribution," whose outcome, for individuals, was their allocation to free or slave status in this or that clan (MacGaffey, 1977A). This segregation of functions (routine economic production and politically controlled social reproduction) is ritually celebrated in the distinction of effects, production vs. destruction.

In most Bantu-speaking societies, and also I think rather generally in the forest zone of West Africa, chiefs and witches are identified, in principle, by the power to kill.[12] Conversely, priests and magicians are healers, although the concerns of priests in particular are more extensive than healing. Those who exercise the power of life in the public interest commonly attract a cluster of English labels, none of them entirely satisfactory, such as earth priest, priest of nature spirits, rainmaker, public diviner, and prophet. It is clear that they represent the concerns of local communities, occupying land as productive units. Their business includes rain and the management of fertility and disease. This is the business primarily of women. It includes ironworking, a male occupation, because smiths produce necessary tools. The power of death, on the other hand, exercised by chiefs and elders, primarily corresponds to the concerns of men and their activities in criminal justice, war, hunting, and trade, including trade in slaves. The segregation of these activities is clearly symbolized by the BaTonga, among whom prophets wear dark colors associated with rain clouds. Colson says, "Red beads or anything red in color is taboo during consultation because red symbolizes blood. An appropriate gift is a hoe blade, symbol of cultivation (and of femaleness). Spears and axes, symbols of maleness and the hunt and war, do not appear to be used as gifts to either prophets or local shrines" (1977:126).

"Class struggle," if that is what it is to be called, is explicit among both the BaKongo and the Yakö, and related in both instances to the distinction of effects, between destructive powers associated with masculine interests and benevolent powers associated with feminine interests. Yakö ideology, like that of other descent-based societies, emphasized the solidarity of clansmen in competition with members of other clans, and the common interests of men in politico-jural affairs. So doing, it tended to disguise the marked stratification of rich and poor. Of *ndet* fetishes, Forde says that some were held by associations of elders. The Leopard Spirit (Ekpe Edet) of the Korta association "was as negative as those of [the matrilineal shrines] were positive, for its powers were held to be essentially punitive" (1964:267). It sanctioned mainly "settlements appertaining to hotly disputed claims to land and inheritance of goods, as well as restrictions on external trading and other movement following inter-village quarrels." Another Leopard Spirit cult, Okengka, drew its members from the leaders of all the wards, and settled disputes: "The rights of property of members and others were protected by such judgments" (268).

On the other hand, the younger men also owned a Leopard Spirit, Ngkpe:

> Members and others for a fee could obtain its protection for their goods and also its sanction for claims in disptues over debts and, in particular, marital rights over women.
>
> *Control of women* . . . was often given as a reason for the large membership of Ngkpe. . . . It was also said by some elders to be *misused against them* by ambitious and envious young men. Its supposed activities were frowned on for their unregulated and destructive character by the village priests and ward leaders, who were in turn accused by the young men of past injustices (Forde, 1964:277, emphasis added).

Whereas the punitive and patrilineal *ndet* expressed the distinctive function of men in controlling resources in land and people, the matrilineal spirits were primarily responsible for the well-being of the village as a whole, for the fertility of crops and women, and for protection against fire and witchcraft. Forde describes "a clearly expressed conception of village welfare. . . . The hopes for material well-being and social harmony had clustered around a central concern for the fertility of women . . . conceived as passing from mother to daughter (265). Material well-being was a function of the importance of female labor, as well as of childbearing; without a wife, a man did not farm or produce palm oil for sale. Purchases of slave girls were motivated by this need (89). The Yakö also practiced "adoption" extensively; it included both the purchase of foreign children and the voluntary incorporation of sisters' sons into their mother's brother's patrilineage, and does not contrast sharply with the "slavery" of western Bantu societies.

In the Yakö instance, the opposition between the death-dealing forces associated with male control of social reproduction and the life-giving forces associated with women and cultivation is combined with a distinction of means between the technical resources of dominant, "insider" men and the mystical resources of "stranger" women and marginal diviners. In Kuranko, Azande, and Lugbara, too, the insider occupants of "ascribed" statuses are male, their perpetuation of their control over women, or at least of the illusion of such control, is a major preoccupation, and the occult resources available to them are "technical." In all these instances, the local group consists of the members and adherents of an autonomous corporation said to own a discrete territory, whether that corporation be a lineage or a chiefly dynasty; the religious expression of locality is in terms of "mystical" powers, whether approved or disapproved.

In Kongo, as in most Bantu societies, the distinction of means is lacking. The difference may be related to the system of government, which only superficially resembles a series of discrete sovereignties. Kongo government was constituted not by the members of a lineage or dynasty, but by a necessary relationship between fathers and children, in such a way that no clan head or chief could so much as worship his ancestors or bury his predecessor without the participation of children and grandchildren from other clans, whether they lived locally or not. Chiefship, in fact, can be regarded as a supplementary rather than a basic feature of Kongo government, which consists essentially of a nonterritorial network of patrifilial links between matrilineal nodes. The identity of corporate descent groups is defined by the intersection of particular patrilateral relations, rather then by its apical ancestor or its founding warlord (MacGaffey, 1970B:212–14, 229–36).

In such a system it is impossible to categorize people as "strangers," unless they are slaves, or to delimit domains by frontier zones, as among the Azande. Local identities are established by reference to natural features, the haunts of local spirits, not by refence to political dominion. This, defined more positively, is the system referred to by Middleton and Winter as one in which unilineal principles are not used in the formation of local groups and in which "sorcery" accusations arc to be expected—but the type example they give of "sorcery" is Nyoro *burogi*, equivalent to Kongo *kindoki*. Kongo "witchcraft" accusations have no local dimension, are not restricted to women. As the negative aspect of political relations, they pervade the society; the occult powers of elders and chiefs are simply the approved or legitimate (because "public") aspect of the same relations. The ideological attribution of violence to chiefs does not mean that they were in fact always violent; it is at least partly a metaphorical statement of their capacity, as a function of institutionalized processes, to transform social identities and group relations and boundaries, modifying what would otherwise be the routine recruitment of local, productive units.

The similarities between the BaKunyi and certain peoples of southern Ivory Coast, notably the Alladian, have been remarked by

M. Augé, who has independently analyzed the connection between the economic structure and the ideology of powers (Augé, 1975:195–233). Among the Alladian, the compound, uniting fathers and their classificatory sons, is the unit of production. Father helps to provide son with a wife and contributes profit from the son's labor to a matrilineage treasury on which the son has no claim. Son has no close economic links with his own matrilineage until he becomes an elder, although his elders may decide to pawn him. The lineage controls the circulation of prestige goods, which in Alladian, as in Kongo, are the medium of exchange for the fundamental resources. The prestige sphere, which Augé calls the sphere of circulation, accumulation, and exploitation, is organized socially as a system of matrilineages; ideologically, it is a sphere of violence. The subsistence sphere, founded on production and reciprocity, is organized socially by patrifilial co-residence; ideologically, it is a sphere of benevolence, fertility, and protection. These qualities are attributed to two kinds of spirit, lineal and local (*génie de trône, de cour*).

The Nyakyusa are among the exceptions to the prevalence of Kongo-like religious commissions among Bantu-speakers. The set is:

	Public	*Private*
Mystical	defenders	witches
	abamanga	*abalosi*
Technical	medicines	sorcery
	imikota	*ubutege*

Wilson's analysis of this set clearly relates it to the unusual structure of Nyakyusa local groups, in which "defenders" uphold morality against "witches." "Medicines," on the other hand, consecrate lineal statuses, including offices. Sorcery is not locally bounded, and kinsmen are supposed to use it against each other, not witchcraft. Wilson has also compared Nyakyusa "witchcraft" with Pondo "witchcraft." In the terms used here, these two beliefs are formally distinct, since the Nyakyusa recognize a distinction of means and the Pondo do not. Pondo "witchcraft" is associated, in Wilson's analysis, with their marriage rules (Wilson, 1951; 1963:125–26). The present argument formalizes and extends Wilson's observations.[13]

Conclusion

By nonintuitive and replicable procedures, I have shown how certain African religions, some of them widely separated in space, belong to the same or different types. Four types have been identified, those of Kongo, Zande, Nyakyusa, and Yakö. The classification prepares the way for an analytical exploration of sociological conditions and historical evolution, elaborated without reference to any such ambiguous concepts as ancestor worship or animism. It is gratifying rather than surprising to find that such classifications as emerge from the use of this method confirm, on the whole, both intuitive evaluations and the known distributions of language and culture.

In the latter part of this paper I have considered the sociological origin of religious distinctions one by one, for greater ease of presentation, and have explored certain hypotheses relating such distinctions to both political and economic structures. In fact, the interdependence, or systematic covariation of the lateral (economic) and vertical (political) dimensions (the functions of production and social reproduction) indicates that the corresponding religious values are interdependent, and that we should not seek the sociological correlates of any one of them, such as the distinction of means, as though it were an isolable trait. The organizing concept is that of the mode of production, of which a set of religious commissions is one institutional level.

It is futile to reify an abstraction we call religion and then ask what its relations are to other abstractions we call government or economy. At best, such questions belong to the theoretical study of social systems. Religion may be a set of representations of the social structure, but it is certainly also a part of social relations as they are lived. In associating religion with economy, Forde was intent on showing that spirits are not merely symbols of society, nor responses to intrinsically awesome or mysterious natural forces; they are associated with individual and collective ends, that is, with real concerns and anxieties. Realization of religious roles, for whatever reason, presupposes certain political and economic conditions, since no matter what beliefs are current, no priest or witchfinder can set up in business as such unless the public needs his services and is able to support him. (Included among the political conditions bearing upon the audience must be the policies and forces of the ruling class or colonial regime, if any.) Religion is an intrinsic element of social reality, neither an influence on it nor a reflection of it. To treat it as an independent set of symbols, values, and beliefs impinging on people's real lives in some way is to trivialize it.

Modes of production include economic and political as well as religious institutions, but they cannot be reduced to single technological factors such as ironworking or pastoralism. The critical factor in differentiating them is the reproductive relation, itself a political-economic complex. Middleton and Winter, in their reference to harmonic regimes as giving rise to "witchcraft" accusations, and to the "contractual" relations between authorities and their subordinates in "centralized states," where "sorcery" is to be expected, point obliquely to this dominant relation, as does Augé when he relates the dysharmonic regime (matrilineal, patrilocal) to the distinction of effects.

In all cases, however, it is necessary to look behind the social forms to the processes that generate them. "Contractual" relations in conquest states are no more voluntary than is wage labor under capitalism. Unilineal descent is a product, not a prime factor; the patrilineages of the Lugbara and Swazi reproduce themselves by different processes. In the lineage mode of production, descent groups may be matrilineal, patrilineal, or replaced by varying froms and degrees of bilaterality; the critical feature is not unilineal descent per se but filiation manipulated by alliance (MacGaffey, 1977A; Augé, 1975:chapter 2; A. Kuper, 1978). The significance of alliance, in the present context, is that it is a system of direct control of military force, land, or another necessary resource. It is the particular interaction of exchange and succession that characterizes a mode of production, and which may be grasped on the ideological level as a particular set of religious values.

Although I have included in this study widely separated societies from several different cultural traditions, I have not drawn any examples from North Africa, Ethiopia, or the Nilotic-speaking areas. I believe this kind of analysis is useful in these other areas, and outside Africa, and would also apply to Christianity and Islam as manifested historically in particular societies. These explorations are of course tentative, especially with regard to the characteristics and discreteness of modes of production.

NOTES

This is a revision of a paper read at the annual meeting of the African Studies Association in Baltimore, November 1978. I am indebted to Ivan Karp, Marcia Wright, Harriet Whitehead and especially Ben C. Ray for their useful comments.

1. It is interesting that the devout pseudoempiricist attributes the "vital" distinction between witchcraft and sorcery to Evans-Pritchard himself; for example, Marwick (1965:69), although the Cewa in question do not make the vital distinction. Douglas (1967:72) says Evans-Pritchard vigorously disavowed the intention of foisting a terminological straight jacket on future generations. The inventor of the straight jacket seems to have been Max Gluckman (1944; 1956). Turner (1964), deploring taxonomy, indulges his distaste for all structures; the choice between taxonomy and dynamics is forced.

2. Firth (1959); Beattie and Middleton (1969); de Heusch (1962). "In practice we find empirically that while these explanations may coexist in some cultures, or in some contexts of trance in a particular society, other people, if they even explicitly draw this logical inference, do not trouble to stress it" (Lewis, 1971:46, 51).

3. "Constraint" is to be understood here cybernetically, not mechanically; the system, and our explanation of it, are (as Bateson puts it) "negative" (Bateson, 1972:399). "Un même système de correspondances renverrait d'une part à l'appareil psychique de l'individu, d'autre à l'organisation économique de la société" (Augé, 1975:195).

4. Buakasa refers to the Ndibu area of central Kongo, of which he is a native. He says the four kinds of *ndoki* (usually translated "witch") are: 1) the initiated clan head, who should use his powers to safeguard the followers whom he may in fact illegitimately "eat," like a witch; 2) *ngang'a ngombo*, "diviner"; 3) *ngang'a n'kisi*, "operator of charms"; 4) "*ndoki privés*" (Buakasa, 1968:163; MacGaffey, 1970A). Elsewhere Buakasa asserts that there are two kinds of *kindoki* resembling Zande witchcraft and sorcery. Once made, however, this distinction disappears from his study. Moreover, in asserting that the only difference between Kongo and Zande beliefs is that Kongo witches possess no internal witchcraft substance, he cites as the Zande word for the substance (which is, in fact, *mangu*) the term *likundu*, which is the Mongo word cognate with the Kongo (*di-*) *kundu*, "witchcraft substance" (Buakasa, 1973:253–54; compare Masamba, 1976:32).

5. "Concepts are purely differential, defined not positively by their content but negatively by their relations with the other terms of the system. Their most exact characteristic is to be what the others are not" (de Saussure, 1969:162). "The arbitrary or unmotivated character of the sign means that the signifier—in this case, 'witchcraft'—may refer to a wealth of phenomenological states or mental representatives which, in essence, overflow the terminological category which seems to confine and define them. In other words, we should resist any tendency to regard witchcraft as a phenomenon sui generis. We must also allow the possibility that the phenomena which are designated by the term 'witchcraft' in one society may also exist in other societies but go under other names" (Jackson, 1975:388).

6. Kusikila kwa Kilombo, *Lufwa evo kimongi e?*, translated in Janzen and MacGaffey, 1974, no. 13; compare MacGaffey, 1977B. The identification of Kongo religion as a system in four parts is a radical departure from the usual ethnographic account, which lumped together private and public healing cults, and then invented a geographical contrast between "nature spirits" (*bakisi*) in the west and "fetishes" (*minkisi*) in the east. Restoration of the cult of local spirits as a distinct element immediately relates Kongo religion to those of east central Africa, where on the other hand the writers concerned with such cults have usually been too preoccupied with local trees to notice the continental woods, with unfortunate consequences for historiography. For improvements here, see Werbner (1977).

7. The Kongo type is found throughout Bantu-speaking Zaïre (Vansina, 1973B:52, note), and from the Duala of Cameroun (Bureau, 1962) to the Swazi of South Africa (H. Kuper, 1947), including the Tio (Vansina, 1973A), the Luapula peoples (Cunnison, 1959), the Ila (Smith and Dale, 1920), the BaGanda (Mair, 1934), the Shona (Daneel, 1971), and the Thlaping Tswana (Pauw, 1960). See also Augé (1975) for Alladian (Ivory Coast). Benjamin C. Ray has pointed out to me that BaGanda distinguish between mystical and technical means (possession relationship to a spirit; use of *mayembe* devices) and also between the legitimate and illegitimate use of *mayembe*. Similar comments could be made about the BaKongo. The point is that in neither instance do these distinctions serve, as among the Azande, to segregate religious roles.

8. The literature on modes of production in Africa is extensive and irritating. The chief contributors are unable to agree even on the definition of a mode of production, either theoretically or in concrete examples. See Law, 1978; Foster-Carter, 1978; Seddon, 1978; and *Critique of Anthropology*. vol. 3, no. 9/10 (1977), passim. I myself have found the contributions of C. Meillassoux and P. P. Rey most useful.

9. "Reproduction" here means neither human reproduction nor the reproduction of the totality of the conditions of social production, but "allocation of agents to positions within the labor process over time" (Edholm et al., 1977:103–10).

10. Peters' argument on this point, with respect to an entirely different context, is incisive: "There is no such thing as a general primacy with regard to any form. The concept of agnation as the centre of all political problems, disturbed or disrupted by, say, matrilaterality, is as inadequate as saying that the nucleus which pulls all other components into position is matrilaterality, with agnation as a disturbing element. In reality there are numerous components present in all situations . . ." (1967:272; compare Forde, 1963).

11. Despite the traditional anthropological emphasis on descent, the reality of unilineal descent groups in Bantu Africa is often uncertain (MacGaffey, 1972:26–27). A. Kuper has recently demonstrated the merits of alliance theory to illuminate Swazi descent (A. Kuper, 1978). This demonstration could be extended to many societies of Angola and Zaïre (De Sousberghe: 1966; 1967), where descent theory has often been bailed out of its difficulties by generous use of the concept "double descent."

12. On the violence of chiefs see, for the Baganda, Mair, 1934; the Tetela, de Heusch, 1962; the Bini, P. Ben-Amos, 1976:246; the Swazi,

Beidelman, 1966:398; the Shambaa, Feierman, 1974:58–59; the BaLuba, Lucas, 1966–67.

13. The Pondo are a Nguni people, like the Swazi.

BIBLIOGRAPHY

Augé, M. 1975. *Théorie des Pouvoirs et Idéologie: étude de cas en Côte d'Ivoire*. Paris: Hermann.

Bateson, G. 1972. *Steps to an Ecology of Mind*. New York: Ballantine.

Beattie, J., and Middleton, J., eds. 1969. *Spirit Mediumship and Society in Africa*. New York: Africana.

Beidelman, T. O. 1966. "Swazi Royal Ritual." *Africa* 36:373–405.

Ben-Amos, P. 1976. "Men and Animals in Benin Art." *Man* 2:243–52.

Buakasa Tulu kia Mpansu. 1968. "Notes sur le 'kindoki' chez les Kongo." *Cah. des Relig. Africaines* (Kinshasa) 3(2):153–70.

―――. 1973. *L'Impensé du discours*. Kinshasa: Presses Universitaires du Zaire.

Bureau, R. 1962. *Ethno-sociologie religieuse des Duala et apparentés*. Recherches et Etudes Camerounaises no. 7/8. Yaounde: Cameroon University Press.

Colson, E. 1962. *The Plateau Tonga of Northern Rhodesia*. Manchester: Manchester University Press.

―――. 1966. "The Alien Diviner and Local Politics among the Tonga of Zambia." In *Political Anthropology*, edited by M. J. Swartz, V. W. Turner, and A. Tuden. Chicago: Aldine.

―――. 1977. "A Continuing Dialogue: Prophets and Local Shrines among the Tonga of Zambia." In *Regional Cults*, edited by R. Werbner London: Academic Press.

Cunnison, I. 1959. *The Luapula Peoples of Northern Rhodesia*. Manchester: Manchester University Press.

Daneel, M. L. 1971. *Old and New in Southern Shona Independent Churches*. Vol. 1. The Hague: Mouton.

Douglas, M. 1967. "Witch Beliefs in Central Africa." *Africa* 37:72–80.

Dumézil, G. 1971–74. *Mythe et épopée*. 3 vols. Paris: Gallimard.

Dupré, A., and Rey, P. P. 1978. "Reflexions on the Relevance of a Theory of the History of Exchange." In *Relations of Production*, edited by D. Seldon. London: Frank Cass.

Edholm, F., Harris, O., and Young, K. 1977. "Conceptualizing Women." *Critique of Anthropology* 3:101–30.

Evans-Pritchard, E. E. 1937. *Witchcraft, Oracles and Magic among the Azande*. London: Oxford University Press.

Feierman, S. 1974. *The Shambaa Kingdom*. Madison: University of Wisconsin Press.

Firth, R. 1959. "Problems and Assumptions in an Anthropological Study of Religion." *J. Roy. Anthrop. Inst.* 89 (2): 129–48.

Forde, D. 1963. "Unilineal Fact or Fiction." In *Studies in Kinship and Marriage*, edited by I. Shapera. London: Royal Anthropological Institute.

————. 1964. *Yako Studies*. London: Oxford University Press.

Fortes, M. 1970. "Time and Social Structure." In *Time and Social Structure*. London: London University Press.

Foster-Carter, A. 1978. "The Modes of Production Controversy." *New Left Review* 107:47–77.

Gluckman, M. 1944. "The Logic of African Science and Witchcraft." *Human Problems in British Central Africa* 1:61–71.

————. 1956. *Custom and Conflict*. Oxford: Blackwell.

Goody, J. 1976. *Production and Reproduction*. Cambridge: Cambridge University Press.

Harwood, A. 1970. *Witchcraft, Sorcery and Social Categories among the Safwa*. London: Oxford University Press.

de Heusch, L. 1962. "Aspects de la sacralité du pouvoir en Afrique." *Le Pouvoir et le sacré*. Annales du Centre d'Etudes des Religions no. 1. Brussels: Universite Libre de Bruxelles. Institut de Sociologie.

Jackson, M. D. 1975. "Structure and Event: Witchcraft Confession among the Kuranko." *Man* 10(3):387–403.

————. 1977. *The Kuranko*. New York: St. Martin's Press.

Janzen, J. M., and MacGaffey, W. 1974. *An Anthology of Kongo Religion*. Lawrence, Kansas: University of Kansas Press.

Kuper, A. 1978. "Rank and Preferential Marriage in Southern Africa: The Swazi." *Man* 13:567–79.

Kuper, H. 1947. *An African Aristocracy*. London: Oxford University Press.

Law, R. 1978. "In Search of a Marxist Perspective on Precolonial Tropical Africa." *Journal of African History* 10:441–52.

Leach, E. R. 1961. "Rethinking Anthropology." In *Rethinking Anthropology*. London: University of London Press.

Lewis, I. M. 1971. *Ecstatic Religion*. Baltimore: Penguin.

Littleton, C. S. 1966. *The New Comparative Mythology*. Berkeley: University of California Press.

Lucas, S. A. 1966-67. "L'Etat Traditionnel Luba." *Problèmes Sociaux Congolais* 74:83–97; 79:93–116.

MacGaffey, W. 1970A. "The Religious Commissions of the BaKongo." *Man* 5:27-38.

————. 1970B. *Custom and Government in the Lower Congo*. Los Angeles: University of California Press.

————. 1972. "Comparative Analysis of Central African Religions." *Africa* 42(1):21–31.

————. 1977A. "Economic and Social Dimensions of Kongo Slavery." In *Slavery in Africa*, edited by S. Miers and I. Kopytoff. Madison: University of Wisconsin Press.

————. 1977B. "Cultural Roots of Kongo Prophetism." *History of Religions* 17:177–93.

Mair, L. P. 1934. *An African People in the Twentieth Century*. London: Routledge.

Marwick, M. G. 1965. *Sorcery in its Social Setting*. Manchester: Manchester University Press.

Masamba ma Mpolo. 1976. *La Libération des envoûtés*. Yaounde: Editions CLE.

Middleton, J., and Winter, E. H. 1963. *Witchcraft and Sorcery in East Africa*. London: Routledge and Kegan Paul.

Molyneux, M. 1977. "Androcentrism in Marxist anthropology." *Critique of Anthropology* 3(9/10):55–81.

Pauw, B. A. 1960. *Religion in a Tswana Chiefdom*. London: Oxford.

Peters, E. 1967. "Some Structural Aspects of the Feud among the Camel-herding Bedouin of Cyrenaica." *Africa* 37:261–82.

Pouillon, J. 1969. "Malade et médecin: le même et/ou l'autre?" *Nouvelle Revue de Psychanalyse* 1:77–98.

Rey, P. P. 1975A. "The Lineage Mode of Production." *Critique of Anthropology*, no. 3, pp. 27–79.

———. 1975B. "L 'Esclavage lignager chez les tsangui, les punu et les kuni du Congo-Brazzaville." In *L'Esclavage en Afrique précoloniale*, edited by C. Meillassoux. Paris: Maspero.

de Saussure, Ferdinand. 1966. *Course in General Linguistics*. Translated by Wade Baskin. New York: McGraw-Hill.

Seddon, D., ed. 1978. *Relations of Production*. London: Frank Cass.

Smith, E. W., and Dale, A. M. 1920. *The Ila-Speaking Peoples of Northern Rhodesia*. London: Macmillan.

de Sousberghe, L. 1966. L'immutabilité des relations de parenté par alliance dans les sociétés matrilinéaires du Congo ex-Belge. *L'Homme* 6(1):82–94.

———. 1967. "L'Immutabilité de l'alliance dans les sociétés patrilinéaires du Congo." *Anthropos* 62:433–52.

Turner, V. W. 1964. "Witchcraft and Sorcery: Taxonomy versus Dynamics." *Africa* 34:314–24.

Van Everbroeck, N. 1961. *Mbomb' Ipoku, le seigneur à l'abîme*. Archives d'ethnographie 3. Tervuren: Musée Royale de l'Afrique Centrale.

Vansina, J. 1973A. *The Tio Kingdom of the Middle Cong 1880-1892*. London: Oxford University Press.

———. 1973B. "Lukoshi/Lupambula: Histoire d'un culte religieux dans les régions du Kasai et du Kwango (1920-1970)." *Etudes d'Histoire africaine* 5:51–97.

Weber, M. 1963. *Sociology of Religion*. Boston: Beacon.

Werbner, R., ed. 1977. *Regional Cults*. London: Academic Press.

Willis, R. G. 1968. "Changes in Mystical Concepts and Practices among the Fipa." *Ethnology* 7(2):139–57.

Wilson, M. 1951. "Witch Beliefs and Social Structure." *American Journal of Sociology* 56:307–13.

———. 1963. *Good Company*. Boston: Beacon.

CONTRIBUTORS

W. Arens is Associate Professor Anthropology at the State University of New York, Stony Brook.

Dan F. Bauer is Associate Professor of Anthropology at Lafayette College.

T. O. Beidelman is Professor of Anthropology at New York University.

Charles S. Bird is Professor of Anthropology at Indiana University, Bloomington.

John Burton is Assistant Professor of Anthropology at Wheaton College.

James Fernandez is Professor of Anthropology at Princeton University.

John Hinnant is Associate Professor of Anthropology at Michigan State University.

Luc de Heusch is Professor of Anthropology at the Université Libre de Bruxelles.

Ivan Karp is Associate Professor of Anthropology at Indiana University, Bloomington.

Martha B. Kendall is Associate Professor of Anthropology at Indiana University, Bloomington.

Igor Kopytoff is Professor of Anthropology at the University of Pennsylvania.

Wyatt MacGaffey is Professor of Anthropology at Haverford College.

Randall Packard is Assistant Professor of History at Tufts University.

Benjamin Ray is Associate Professor of Religion at the University of Virginia.

James H. Vaughan is Professor of Anthropology at Indiana University, Bloomington.

Index